Globalization, Economy and Society

About the Editor

Dr. Jagdish Chander Mehta is Head of P.G. Department of Sociology at D.A.V College, Sector-10, Chandigarh. He is a member of Post Graduate and Undergraduate Board of Studies in Sociology, Panjab University, Chandigarh. He is gold medalist in M.A. (Sociology) from Punjabi University, Patiala and got his Ph.D Degree in Sociology from Panjab University, Chandigarh.

His areas of specialization are Sociology of Education, Sociology of Development, Family and Gender, Labour and Migration.

He has been teaching Sociology to undergraduate, honours and Post-Graduate students since 2001. He is a member of 'Editorial Board' of refreed Research Journal 'DIVINER-A Research Journal of Humanities and Social Sciences'. As a resource person, he has delivered extension lectures and presented number of papers on diverse themes in national and international level seminars. He has published number of books and research papers in various journals of repute. He has successfully completed two research projects. One project is on 'Smuggling of Migrants from India to Europe particularly U.K' funded by UNODC office, New Delhi and another major project on 'Bonded Labour in Haryana' funded by Department of Labour, Government of Haryana. He has also supervised many students at M. Phil and Ph.D level. He is a member and convener of various administrative committees of the college and university. Besides Academics, various social issues are close to his heart and he has been working extensively in them. He is also the President of 'HEAL SOCIETY' Chandigarh—a voluntary organization registered under 'Society Registration Act, 1860 and worked extensively on various social issues.

Globalization, Economy and Society

Edited by

Dr. Jagdish Chander Mehta
Sn. Assistant Professor & Head,
Department of Sociology
D.A.V. College, Chandigarh

Published in Association with
HEAL SOCIETY, Chandigarh
by
CONCEPT PUBLISHING COMPANY PVT. LTD.
NEW DELHI-110059

ISBN-13 : 978-93-5125-059-3

First Published 2014

Published and Printed by

Concept Since 1974

Concept Publishing Company Pvt. Ltd.
A/15-16, Commercial Block, Mohan Garden
New Delhi-110059 (India)
T: 25351460, 25351794, *F*: 091-11-25357109
E: publishing@conceptpub.com, W: www.conceptpub.com
Editorial Office: H-13, Bali Nagar, New Delhi-110 015, India.

Cataloging in Publication Data—*Courtesy:* D.K. Agencies (P) Ltd. <docinfo@dkagencies.com>

National Seminar on 'Globalization: Socio-Cultural & Economic Concerns in North-West India' (2013 : D.A.V. College, Chandigarh)
Globalization, economy and society / edited by Jagdish Chander Mehta.
p. cm.
Includes bibliographical references and index.
ISBN 9789351250593

1. Globalization—Economic aspects—India—Congresses. 2. Globalization—Social aspects—India—Congresses. 3. Industries—India—Congresses. 4. Agriculture—Economic aspects—India—Congresses. 5. Sustainable development—India—Congresses. I. Mehta, Jagdish Chander. II. Title.

DDC 330.954 23

Preface

This Book is the outcome of the National Seminar on ***'Globalization: Socio-cultural & Economic Concerns in North-West India'*** organized by the Department of Sociology, D.A.V. College, Chandigarh in collaboration with HEAL SOCIETY, Chandigarh. Social Scientists from different parts of the country participated in this Seminar. The Seminar was thought provoking, lively and well attended. After the seminar was over, we received a request from paper presenters and the publisher for publication of the proceedings of the seminar in the form of a book. Then the idea of sharing the deliberations in the seminar with a wider audience got strengthened by publishing the presentations of the seminar into a book. We could not incorporate all the contributions in this book due to variety of reasons. The research papers included in this book have been slightly modified for suiting the publication requirements. The ideas and interpretations are of the authors and we do not necessarily subscribe to it.

In organizing the Seminar, all the faculty members, students and non-teaching staff of the college, provided their valuable time and help. For proof reading, we are thankful to Mrs. Deepti Madan, Mr. Amit Narula, and Ms Ruchika Arora. This event would not have been possible without the support and grant made available by ICSSR, North-West Regional Center, P.U. Chandigarh.

We are also very grateful to all the authors for experiencing pain in the preparation of good quality papers. All the papers collectively are providing a new angle to analyse the Globalisation and its impact on various aspects of Indian society.

My special thanks are due to our respectable Dr. B.C. Josan, Principal, D.A.V. College, Chandigarh who is always kind enough to offer all kind of possible support for academic dialogue and vibrant intellectual pursuits in our college.

Finally, we are thankful to Mr. Ashok Kumar Mittal of Concept Publishing Compnany Pvt. Ltd., New Delhi for publication of this book.

Chandigarh
October, 2013

Jagdish Chander Mehta
Head, P.G. Department of Sociology
D.A.V. College, Chandigarh

Editor's Note

Globalization describes the political, economic, cultural and educational spheres of today. At no time in History has the world been so interconnected and interdependent as it is today in the age of globalization. The problem being faced by the people in different parts of the world may show local forms and manifestations, but very often they have global roots. Naturally, their solutions also require a global approach and global efforts.

Globalization is defined by different people in different ways. It is a complex phenomenon. This process refers to mutual interdependence of the countries of the world, particularly their economic interdependence and freedom to integrate with one another through trade, investments, and capital flows. Globalization has economic, social, political, cultural and several other dimensions and has made tremendous impact across cultures. In fact, this process has changed the world scenario and cultural landscape of our planet. This has rendered the world into a 'global village'.

A unique feature of the current globalization process is the globalization of national policies and policy making mechanism that until recently was determined by the States and people within a country have now increasingly coming under the influence of international agencies and processes or by private corporations and economic and financial players. This has lead to the narrowed ability of governments and people to make choices from options in economic, social and cultural policies. Most developing countries have seen their independent policy-making mechanism capacity being eroded and have to adopt policies influenced by other entities, which may on balance be detrimental to the countries concerned. The developed countries where the major economic players reside, and which also control the process and policies of international economic agencies, are better able to maintain control over their own national policies as well as determine the policies and practices of international institutions and the global system. However, it is also true that the large corporations have taken over a large part of decision-making even in the developed countries, at the expense of the power of the State or political and social leaders.

However, at the end of the day, one has to understand and accept that globalization is the stratagem for the new millennium. Every country, developed and developing, has to accept this and formulate their economics around it. The issues that concerns developing countries are how one can insure greater participation of the weaker economies, in the global process and what needs to be done to ensure that the course of globalization benefits people extensively all over the world.

Societies all over the world are experiencing the globalization of more and more aspects of life, but accompanied by the contradictions of growing inequality within and between countries. The debate on merits of globalization continues, with one side argument is that it raises living standards and the others that it worsens poverty and inequality. Certainly, economic globalization has led to increased wealth for many in some countries. But it also led to shattering economic crisis, collapse in standard of living, widespread societal and ethnic conflicts, social disintegration and greatly increased insecurity for disproportionately large part of the world population.

Globalization and Its Impact on Indian Society

It is the right time to measure the impact of Globalization on the Indian economy and other social services and institutions as more than two decades are over after the introduction of globalization. It has attracted not only a wide range of appreciation, but also strong criticism. The UNDP report 1999 says that Globalization expands the chances and opportunities for some but shrink those chances for others. It generates growth and favours profits. But it misses its goals of equality, poverty eradication and erodes human security (Gupta Chandansen, 2001). The net benefit has not increases rather decreased considerably (Samuel Bowelers, 2001). It has widened the gap between the skilled workers and unskilled workers. But there is some improvement in human development. It has also been argued that globalization has resulted in increased standard of living, decreased death rate and infant mortality rate and a substantial improvement in life expectancy at birth.

Indian society is drastically changing as a result of globalization. "Cultural imperialism has two major goals—one economic and the other political— to capture markets for its cultural commodities and to establish hegemony by shaping popular consciousness... Cultural domination is an integral dimension of any sustained system of global exploitation." There is a systematic cultural penetration and domination of the cultural life of the popular class by the ruling class of the West in order to reorder the values, behaviour, institutions and identity of the oppressed people to conform with the interests of the imperial class.

In new horizons, "Contemporary India and Popular Culture", Samual Manohar (1998) speaks about India's changes very well: Modern India has its stark contrasts and its own share of contradictions. It is the largest democracy alive. It is emerging with its liberalization and market reforms, as one of the dynamic major Asian economies. It is a world leader in several areas—its indigenous-built communication satellites has been successfully launched, it has the best computer software system in the world, its telecommunication technology has successfully reached the remotest rural areas, and it has a strong army. Yet it is one of the poorest countries in the world, with a population expected to touch world's highest with a high illiteracy rate.

But at the same time, we can say that India has embraced a market economy, and as a result it has lead to unequal distribution of income and wealth which in turn leads to unequal distribution of power and hence to the exploitation by those with economic power over those who lack sufficient economic power. This has lead to the over-exploitation of natural resources of India, damages to the environment, pollution, and other such evils.

Thus, under the garb of Globalization, our Indian society is facing a complex pattern of contradictory change. The social-economic life and ecology is diversely influenced by it. Even our future generations are going to be influenced by this process. There is no uniform consensus among the scholars about the impact of globalization on Indian society.

Thus, the present book is the outcome of a collection of selected research papers presented at a National Seminar on *Globalization: Socio-Cultural & Economic Concerns in North-West India* organized by the Department of Sociology, D.A.V. College, Chandigarh on February 8-9, 2013 in the Conference Hall of the College. This seminar was organized in association with Heal Society and S-4 Trust, Chandigarh. About 300 participants that included teachers, educationists, research scholars and students from various colleges and Universities of Punjab, Haryana, Himachal Pradesh, Uttar Pradesh, Delhi and Maharashtra were participated in the Seminar. Resource persons of academic repute were invited from Universities and other institute of Higher Education and Research. About eighty papers were presented in the seminar. The Seminar focused on Globalization and its repercussion on the different aspects of the society.

Dr. B.C. Josan, Principal, D.A.V. College, formally welcomed the distinguished chief guests and speakers on this occasion and congratulate the Department for selecting such an important theme for the seminar. He said, the theme *Globalization: Socio-Cultural and Economic Concerns in North West India* is most suitable according to need of hours. Today, we cannot live in isolation and we are living in a global village. Globalization has increased the connectivity and efficiency of the whole system, upgraded the infrastructure and provided numerous services to mankind. This is one side of the story. Another part of the story breaks our myth and reveals the brutal face of globalization.

The process of globalization has effected dramatic changes in the social, economic and cultural habits of people all over the world. In the era of globalization even the education structure is changing. Globalization has its pros and cons for education. Since accumulation of knowledge is not restricted by distance and national boundaries, the student's community has benefited from globalization. Innovative forms of transnational education—Internet based distance learning, branch campuses, educational "franchising" have greatly expanded opportunities for students to study and learn outside their country of origin. In addition, there is now increasing global competition for the economic potential of education, particularly higher education, as a service export sector.

For the first time in history, large segment of the world's student population truly have access to a "global marketplace" of education. Today's globalization has made the free movement of capital but forbade the free movement of labour, because it suits the interests of ruling classes of the world. Now it is upto the experts to present a rational and balanced version of globalization.

Despite the affinity that is developing between various nations, there is a fear that globalization will suppress the voice of the downtrodden and only multi-national companies will prevail over local industries, thus pushing developing countries towards financial dependency. The only hope lies in developing 'Global Consciousness' where the organizations have a healthy mindset and the benefits are shared equally amongst organizations and the society. He expressed his hope about the successful deliberations of this two day national seminar that will surely be fruitful for researchers, academicians, policy makers and for whole society.

Dr. Jagdish C. Mehta, Head, Department of Sociology, D.A.V. College and Convener of the Seminar while introducing the seminar theme discussed the positive and negative trends of Globalization.

The inaugural morning session started with the scholarly presentation made by the chief guest Dr. Pramod Kumar, Director, Institute for Development and Communications and Chairperson of Punjab Governance Reforms Commission. Dr. Pramod Kumar in his presentation traced the historical development of the Globalization process from the early 19th century which reached its zenith during 1940-70 which is also regarded as the 'Golden Age of Capitalism'. In the present era globalization in form of privatization has been responsible for wage inequalities, poverty, and unemployment in our society. Making a vital observation Dr. Pramod stated that though globalization has been successful in giving freedom of economy from state but on other hand it has made economy a prisoner of the market. He also provided a comparative analysis of the different states with regard to Globalization and the role played by the fallacy in the policy making system. It was indeed enlightening and enriching explanation of globalization.

Prof. S.L. Sharma, an eminent Sociologist and formerly Chairperson, Department of Sociology, Panjab University. Chandigarh in his key note address analyzed the globalization process from dual perspective. The first which was Neo-Liberal perspective takes globalization as a great source of growth and prosperity while the later, which is, called as Socialist blames globalization for creating inequalities and disparities in society. Though rich have become richer but poor have not become poorer unlike the earlier maxim, Prof. Sharma on the basis of some empirical facts and studies stated that how globalization has indeed helped in social and economic upliftment of downtrodden especially SC and ST in state of U.P. in last 20 years. The need of the hour was the strong communication direction through media and networking which can become a strong integrative mechanism to tackle socio-economic inequalities of society.

The process of Globalization involves the integration of different economies of world without creating any barrier and imbalance in flow of goods and services, capital and technology between them. The aim of Globalization is to treat world as a Global village. One can treat it as integration of economies, societies and people as well. For developing countries like India, it can be treated as the engine of growth. But we must analyze the impact of such extreme openness on our economy, society and culture as well. Present piece of work is an effort to assess the impact of Globalization on various socio-economic aspects of life. The article covers the broad spectrum of issues relating to agriculture, banking, industry, trade, human resource development, business and investment, and environment and sustainability, and focused to extract certain conclusions and implications. The book contains 26 articles including key-note address and presidential address. Some of the articles throw light on the economy and social aspects of globalization, and the other focused on the industry, agriculture, and sustainability.

Therefore, the book is divided into three parts. The first part of the book deals with the articles based on the impact of globalization on economy and society in general. The second part of the book focus upon the industry and agriculture, and the third part deals with the issues of sustainability in India emerged due to globalization.

Part I: Globalization, Economy and Society

Surrendra G. Thakur in his paper on *"Impact of Globalization on Socio-Economic and Cultural Aspects of Rural Society"* examines the impact of Globalization through Information technology on socio-economic and cultural aspects of agro-based resort cultivator in rural India. For knowing this, focus was placed on the use of workplace as a resort and the neighbouring women as the labour market. In this study, twenty respondents from whole population have homogeneous character by occupation selected. Qualitative as well as quantitative means mixed method used for collecting data from this agro-based resort cultivator. Constructive sociology as a new theoretical approach is used for this study.

Manoj Sharma in his article titled *'Globalization and Socio-Economic Concerns in India'* has pointed out that Globalization is a multi-dimensional phenomenon that not only touches political, economic, social and cultural spheres of any society but also reshapes the traditional way of studying the "social world and human nature". Globalization is often associated with strengthening of the worldwide social relations and to measure its extensity and impact on a particular society and therefore, it is needed to study separately. Taking this into consideration, the socio-economic challenges before India should be examined.

Amrit Kaur in her paper on '*Impact of Globalization on Socio-Economic Mobility among Scheduled Castes*' focused on the impact of globalization on the bottom of the society that is among scheduled caste people residing in the rural area because globalization can bring change in the upper caste as well as lower caste. The present study attempts to assess the impact of globalization on Socio-economic mobility among the Scheduled Castes in the two villages of Rupnagar (Rural Area, i.e. Dugri and Mugalmagri) District of Punjab in India.

Anju Sharma in her article titled '*Poverty and Inequality in the Globalized Era*' has expressed that Globalization promotes growth and affects its standing also. The world has become a much smaller place over the past two decades due to globalization. Globalization means linking the economy of a country with the economies of the other countries by means of free trade, free mobility of capital and labour, unrestricted flow of goods and services, technology and expertise among different countries of the world. Present study has analyzed the effect of the policy of the globalization on poverty and inequality after examining its various positive and negative effects. In regard to India, after independence, the condition of Indian economy was not very good as the country was struggling to come out from the tag of stagnate economy at that time. India adopted the policy of globalization in July 1991. After that Indian economy has shown tremendous growth rate in approximately all sectors like foreign investment, partial convertibility of Indian rupee, liberal foreign trade policy and reduction in tariffs, export promotion and freedom to repatriate. As a result it becomes successful in grabbing the tag of second fastest growing major economy in the world, but it has also led to shattering economic crisis and creating inequality among people.

Sunanda Sharma in her article titled '*Innovative Human Resource Development in Global Context*' has emphasized upon the need of using innovations to compete cut-throat competition in business. Innovation and Human Resource Development are important to achieve the predetermined goals of the business because these are directly linked with human behaviour and deal with personnel and important element of the directing function of the management. Strategic human resource management is the management of people. An organization has to make strategies related to human resource and use innovation in these strategies for competing globally with similar organizations.

Meenu Gupta in her paper on '*Impact of Globalization on Business and Management Education*' discusses the role and impact of management education in the post-globalization era. Management Education in India is at cross roads. With the dawn of new millennium, while there was phenomenal growth in the number of Business Schools, the benchmarks were also on the rise. The Globalization doesn't seem to have happened just to the Industry but also to Indian Business Schools. In the post-globalization era this scope has increased immensely for global multinational companies as Government of India has also played a very crucial and supportive role in this respect through liberalized policies and legislative structure. Indian Market leaders are going global. But there are certain negative impacts occurred aftermath the globalization impact in India.

Sapna Jain in her paper '*Global Perspectives in Human Resource Management*' identifies the understanding of key areas of human resource management, the global developments, contingencies and key challenges facing human resources management and draw on a range of best practices in HRM. She has discussed a critical understanding of the key social, cultural, political and economic challenges impacting upon the theory and practice of HRM and the role of the HRM practitioner. She examines the HRM policy in different countries and the major international HRM strategies and the ability to explore cross cultural differences in HRM policy and practice.

Amneet Kaur in her paper titled '*Globalization and Indian Economy*' has tried to workout the impact of LPG on Indian economy. Globalization has ushered in a remarkable change in the Indian mindset, as it deviates from the traditional values held since Independence in 1947, such as self-reliance and socialistic policies of economic development, which mainly due to the inward looking restrictive form of governance, resulted in the isolation, overall backwardness and inefficiency of the economy, amongst a host of other problems. India, removing constraints and obstacles to the entry of MNCs in India, allowing Indian companies to enter into foreign collaborations and also encouraging them to set up joint ventures abroad; carrying out massive import liberalization programmes by switching over from quantitative restrictions to tariffs and import duties, therefore, globalization has been identified with the policy reforms of 1991 in India.

Neelam Choudhary and **Ritika Sharma** in their paper on *"Globalization and Foreign Direct Investment – Role in Indian Economy"* attempt to make an analysis of Foreign Direct Investment (FDI) in India and its impact on growth. One of the economic aspects of globalization is the fact that increasing investments in the form of foreign direct investments. In the recent times due to the global recession most of the countries have not been able to pull investments. India has been able to attract better FDIs than the developed countries even during the crisis period also. Especially in the recent years the FDI in India has been following a positive growth rate. Since 1991 the government has focused on liberalization of policies to welcome foreign direct investments. These investments have been a key driver for accelerating the economic growth through technology transfer, employment generation, and improved access to managerial expertise, global capital, product markets and distribution network. FDI in India has enabled to achieve a certain degree of financial stability; growth and development to sustain and compete in the global economy.

Soumita Chakraborty and **Nayanika Singh** in their paper on *"Falling Wage Share in the Manufacturing Sector and Trade Union Movement in India: An Analytical Study"* attempt to provide an empirical relationship between the wage share in the national income and the trade union movement in the organized manufacturing sector in India, spanning from 1992 to 2007. Furthermore, the study attempts to provide an analysis of the significance of the rising strength of the labour theory in context of the manufacturing sector (1992-2007) and the role and relevance of the trade union movement post-enforcement of the New Economic Policy in 1991. They show that in the past few decades, the Indian manufacturing sector witnessed decreasing wage share. The probable explanation to it is that the average wage rates and the average labour productivity have not been able to keep pace with the productivity growth especially in the manufacturing sector. It is observed that in case of the manufacturing sector in India, during the study period (1997-2007), increasing labour productivity outpaced the real average wage per worker thereby forcing the wage share in value added to decline over the period. Trade unions which are considered to be an ardent collective pressure group to deal with the challenging capitalistic demands in India, however, have failed miserably to be able to make their voice heard to fetch themselves lucrative wage deals. This declining bargaining power of the Indian trade unions may be one of the important causes behind the falling wage share in Indian manufacturing sector.

Seepana Prakasam in his paper on *"Impact of Globalization on Quality of Employment in India"* finds out the fact that Globalization paved the way for structural changes which lead to transfer of jobs from formal to informal sector. The maximum number of jobs created during globalization lacks quality, is a big problem to enhance living standards and to achieve inclusive growth. There are increased proportions of workers who do not receive secure wages or social security benefits either from the employers or from the state. The 'jobless growth' and the 'quality jobless growth' have become a specific feature of our economic reforms process. The deteriorating quality of employment as signified by the rising share of casual labour, decreasing share of wage bill against rapidly rising profit share and worsening bargaining capacity of the working class. It is evident that the dream of 'inclusive growth' remains a dream which has given way to quality jobless growth and in fact 'exclusive growth'. Therefore, he suggests that the country should improve total factor productivity by increasing investment in informal sector to augment skill formation so that there will be significant improvement in the earnings of the workers. Strengthen law enforcement agencies to strictly implement labour laws by the employers

Devinder Singh in his article titled *'Globalization and Consumerism: Consequences for Transitional Economies'* has furnished the fact that Globalization has resulted in transforming societal practices and convergence of consumption patterns. Transitional economies or emerging markets like India have established themselves as the drivers of world economic growth, and this has led to increase in disposable income of the consumers. The economic growth coupled with aggressive multinational marketing strategies has led to changes in consumer behaviour.

Part II: Globalization, Industry and Agriculture

Dr. K. Gopal Iyer and **Dr. Jagdish Chander Mehta** in their paper on '*Globalization, Agrarian Crisis and Farmers Suicide*' in India touched the issue of farmers' suicides in India due to agrarian crisis, that is linked with combination of macro liberalization and globalization policies of Central Government for farmers the single most adverse effect has been the combination of low prices and output volatility for cash crops. The new liberal economic reform strategy led to financial liberalization measures, removal of restriction on internal trade in agricultural commodities and liberalization of external trade. The rural people have been left out of the process of globalization or have been marginalized or excluded. Debt burden itself is only a symptom of the wider malaise. The increase in the number of farmer's suicide and its proximate cause is the most dramatic sign of extreme despair and hopelessness. The most extreme manifestation of this crisis is in the suicide by farmers and agricultural labourers, who are typically driven to desperate act by the inability to repay debt incurred in the process of cultivation. The burden has fallen disproportionately on small and marginal farmers and rural labour. The volatility of crop prices has been a major source of income instability and distress for farmers. A substantial part of price volatility has been related to external trade liberalization.

Rajiv Bhatia and **Renu Sharma** in their paper on *'Agrarian Crisis in the Era of Globalization in India'* highlighted the crisis facing by the agricultural sector due to economic reforms period. Free trade has not been free from problems. The decline has resulted in worsening state of welfare of people dependent on agriculture. Globalization and liberalization have increased the commercial proposition of this sector but it is facing a number of challenges with regard to technology, infrastructure, price and competition. There is deceleration of output and acceleration of vulnerability of farmers to poverty. Modernization without moderation has led to a crisis situation in Indian agriculture. This paper is an attempt to trace the problems of agriculture during the reforms period and advocates the urgent need of finding ways and means of resolving the present crisis in order to develop Indian agriculture into a vibrant sector contributing substantially to the growth of Indian economy.

Savita Saini and **Shilpa Gupta** in their article titled *'Globalization and Challenges Before Indian Agriculture'* have examined the challenges before Indian agriculture due to liberalized policies in India. Agricultural sector is the mainstay of the rural Indian economy around which socio-economic privileges and deprivations revolve, and any change in its structure is likely to have a corresponding impact on the existing pattern of social equality. No strategy of economic reform can succeed without sustained and broad based agricultural development, which is critical for raising living standards, alleviating poverty, assuring food security, generating buoyant market for expansion of industry and services, and making substantial contribution to the national economic growth. They have analyzed how economic reforms have affected Agriculture sector in the current scenario and to answer what should be done to improve the agricultural growth.

Sunaina Jain in her article titled *'The Façade of Globalization: Agrarian Crisis in Punjab'* has expressed that Globalization has brought about an unprecedented change in the agricultural economy of Punjab. The present paper also seeks to ascertain the true social, economic, and environmental costs of globalization on the agricultural sector of Punjab and how it failed to deliver the promised returns, through empirical evidence. The green revolution approach has converted the self-sufficient and sustainable agriculture in Punjab into a non-sustainable economy through the increased use of insecticides, pesticides, herbicides, and intensive irrigation. However, the potentials of Green Revolution were soon exhausted after the over-use of chemical inputs and intensive irrigation.These resource- and capital-intensive chemical inputs and mechanization have forced small farmers to incur huge debts, and the failure to pay back loans has compelled many to resort to suicides.

Pramod Bhargava in his paper on '*Globalization: A Boon for Micro, Small and Medium Enterprises In India*' highlighted the positive impact of globalization over small industries on the basis of secondary data collected from RBI and Ministry of Micro and Small, Medium Enterprises. The process of Globalization is an unavoidable fact. It has been bringing the world closer, through the swap over of goods, products, information, jobs, knowledge and culture. But Globalization has also its side effect which creates a stiff competition between MNCs and domestic industries. The small scale sector is a vital constituent of overall industrial sector of the country. As the small scale sector forms a dominant part of Indian industry and contributing to a significant proportion of production, exports and employment so, there is a need to study and analyze the impact of Globalization on Indian Small Scale Industries. This paper focuses on the implication and effect of Globalization on SSIs and analyzes the performance of small scale industries based on number of units, employment, production, investment and exports on post-liberalization.

Harneet Kaur in her article titled *'Small Scale Industry in India under Globalization'* has tried to ascertain the impact of Globalization on small scale industrial sector of India. Small scale industry development has been one of the major planks of India's economic development strategy since independence. Globalization in India is generally taken to mean 'integrating' the economy of the country with the world economy. The real thrust to the globalization process was provided by the new economic policy introduced by the Government of India in July 1991 at the behest of the IMF and the World Bank. Globalization has led to an 'Unequal Competition'—a competition between 'giant MNCs and dwarf Indian enterprises'.

Harneet Kaur in her article titled *'Globalization and the Banking Industry'* has tried to pinpoint the impact of reforms on Banking sector in India. The transformation of the banking sector in India needs to be viewed in light of the overall economic reform process along with rapid changes that have been taking place in the global environment within which banks operate. Indian banking, going forward, is poised for interesting times as it aligns itself with global best practices in terms of sophisticated risk management systems in the form of Basel norms and practices while, at the same time, continues the policy objective of reaching the excluded in the hinterlands of the country and promoting inclusive growth.

Gaurav Vats in his article titled *'Globalisation and its Impact on Retail Sector in India'* has tried to capture the changes in tastes and preferences of customers in context with Globalization. There is increased sophistication in the shopping pattern of customers, which has resulted to the emergence of big retail chains in most metros; mini metros and towns being the next target. Customer taste and preferences are changing leading to radical transformation in life-styles and spending patterns which in turn is giving rise to new business opportunities. Multiple factors influence retailers today. There are global trends, also called megatrends, such as globalization, which have a long-term influence on society. Besides these trends, there are various forces that affect the retail market, such as the power of suppliers, new entrants into the market, or substitutes for particular products or services a retailer offers. Mainly the the study highlighted the retail sector in India in Global scenario.

Manjit Kour in her article titled *'Changing Face of Business Ethics in Globalization'* has commented upon the changing business ethics in era of Globalization. The challenge is to find the right balance between emerging global norms, values, and standards and local cultures, business practices, and community needs. Businesses in emerging market economies face many challenges. We live in an age of innovation, the growth of free markets, and a world economy. New technologies, roles for government, and players on the global scene offer challenging opportunities, demands, and constraints. More peoples and nations are working together to spread freedom and democratic principles; to nurture free markets; to protect individual property rights; and to encourage respect for human rights, the rule of law, and the environment. With Globalization the way people perceive and do business has drastically changed. The present paper is a modest attempt to understand the effect of Globalization on Business Ethics.

Part III: Globalization and Sustainability

Mohinder Kumar Slariya in his paper on *'Globalization Led Clean Development Mechanism Based Developmental Projects: A Threat to Natural Ecological Order'* touched the issue of environment degradation due to hydro-electric project under the Clean Development Mechanism

(CDM) is introduced by US government as flexibility mechanisms under Kyoto Protocol and allows developed countries to meet their emission reduction commitments by promoting clean development in developing countries. As a policy mandate, it aims to design project-based mechanisms to reduce emissions. These reductions are produced and then subtracted against a hypothetical baseline of emissions which are predicted to occur in the absence of a particular CDM project. India as a signatory of this protocol have been registered 2313 projects up to August 2010, out of these, 64 projects are of hydro power generation and Chanju power project of 36 MW is one of the CDM projects in India.

He analysed the comparative analysis between the expected benefits received by the executing agency under CDM and the actual benefits people are expected to receive from Chanju-I Hydro Electric Project. The results revealed that at the initial stage of project, people were happy because of their illiteracy and not knowing the facts, but when respondents have been told about the factual situation they are expected to face, and then their response was altogether different. Because in the stretch of 25 km there are 7 power projects expected to produce 56 MW power, putting lives, livelihood and age-old profession of water milling, and putting environment of this virgin area at stake, are some areas of the concern of present paper.

Sandhya Rohal in her article titled *'Globalization and Corporate Responsibility in Sustainable Development'* has explained that Globalization in the last few decades assumed a prominent position in the area of international trade and contemporary societies worldwide. Globalization has been characterised by the rise of the economic, social and political power of corporations. Globalization has influenced trade all over the world. Companies have looked for new opportunities in doing business outside their home country in recent years and the corporate social responsibility has gained recognition as a new emerging form of governance in business. It is already established in global context, with international references standard set by the United Nations Organisation for economic co-operation and development guidelines and international labour organisation's convention. Corporate social responsibility is now operating as a building loyalty and trust amongst the shareholders, the employees and the customers. Corporate social responsibility applies to a wide variety of company activities, especially in enterprises that operate multi-nationally in different social and environment settings.

Dr. Rajan Bhandari and **Bharti** in their paper on '*Water Resource Management of Kuhls of Kangra: Declining Community Participation*' talked about the community-managed Kuhl irrigation systems in the Kangra Valley of India's Western Himalayas. Importance of the kuhls of Kangra Valley is declining day by day due to decreasing community participation in their maintenance and management. In the era of globalization non-farm employment has resulted decline in agricultural practices and has affected the sense of community participation for water management. Their study has focused on the indigenous way of kuhl's management and community participation, causes for decline in their importance and possible way outs for its restoration. One kuhl of Palampur tehsil (Kangra district) has been selected for opinion based field survey to understand the problem and solution. The paper highlights: (1) sense of strong element of community participation, (2) water uses of kuhls in past, present and future, (3) causes and implications of declining use of kuhls water.

Dr. Sukhwinder Virk and **Ivneet Walia** in their article on '*Globalization: The Imperatives of Energy Law for Sustainable Development touched the Issues of Energy Laws and Sustainability*' has mentioned that many challenges threaten the movement towards sustainable development. The most significant of these objectives include the simultaneous (i) social development and poverty alleviation, and (ii) economic growth, while (iii) protecting the environment. Past and present forms of economic growth have created very uneven distribution of wealth between and within nations, and placed severe strains on the environment, resulting in urban air pollution, regional acidification, and global climate change, to name but a few. Current trends in energy systems development and several of the linkages between these systems and current unsustainable global socio-economic development patterns are discussed here. The main findings is that strong links exist between sustainable development challenges and the energy systems in the world, and that major changes in energy systems are required to achieve sustainability at large.

Arun Sharma and **Madhuri Aggarwal** in their paper on '*Impacts of Globalization and Tourism on People of Himachal State*' highlighted the impacts of globalization on culture and life style of people in Himachal Pradesh by considering the tourism industry as a catalyst for the same. This research is based on qualitative study. Data collection is conducted through in-depth interviews among long and short term travellers as well as among local people of the state. Research questions emphasize on the process of globalization, the role traveller's play in the creation of modified culture and diffusion of existing ones, impacts of globalization on the life styles of locals and community perception towards the same. A hermeneutical approach to data analysis was chosen. After qualitative analysis, paper concludes both positive as well as negative impacts of globalization on culture with suggestions.

We are greatly indebted to the contributors for experiencing pain in preparation of such good quality papers. All the papers collectively are providing a new angle to analyse the impact of Globalization on Indian society, economy and sustainability.

Jagdish Chander Mehta

Contents

PART II
GLOBALIZATION, INDUSTRY AND AGRICULTURE

PART III
GLOBALIZATION AND SUSTAINABILITY

List of Contributors

Aggarwal, Madhuri, Asst. Professor, Rayat Bhara Institute of Hotel Management, Mohali (RBIHM) and Research Scholar Management PTU, E-mail: Sharma.arun84@gmail.com

Bhandari, Rajan, Assistant Professor, Department of Geography, D.A.V College, Chandigarh, E-mail: bhandarirajan77@gmail.com

Bhargava, Pramod, Assistant Professor, Department of Commerce, D.A.V. College, Chandigarh, E-mail: psbhargav@gmail.com

Bharti, Research Scholar, Department of Geography, Panjab University, Chandigarh, E-mail: janjua_bharti@yahoo.co.in

Bhatia, Rajiv, Assistant Professor, Head, Department of Economics, S.A.V.J. College, Ludhiana, E-mail: rajivbhatia76@yahoo.com

Chakraborty, Soumita, Asst. Professor, Department of Economics, D.A.V College, Sector-10, Chandigarh.
E-mail: soumi_29@rediffmail.com.

Choudhary, Neelam, Associate Prof., Department of Economics, Maharshi Dayanand University, Rohtak. E-mail: ritikadavesar@yahoo.com

Gupta, Meenu, Assistant Professor, Dept. of Commerce, GGDSD College, Chandigarh. E-mail: meenubansal_2006@rediffmail.com

Gupta, Shilpa, Assistant Prof., Department of Commerce and Management, D.A.V. College, Chandigarh.
E-mail: shilpa31.mahajan@gmail.com

Iyer, K. Gopal, Prof. of Sociology (Retd.), Panjab University, Chandigarh, E-mail: iyergopal1942@gmail.com

Jain, Sapna, Assistant Prof., Department of Commerce, D.A.V. College, Chandigarh. E-mail: jainsapnachd@gmail.com

Jain, Sunaina, Assistant Professor, MCM, D.A.V. College, Chandigarh, E-mail: jainsunaina14@gmail.com

Kaur, Amneet, Assistant Prof. SGGS College, Sector-26, Chandigarh.
E-mail:amneet_gurjit@yahoo.com

Kaur, Amrit, Assistant Professor, Department of Sociology, Post Graduate Government College for Girls, Sector 42, Chandigarh. E-mail: kauramrit.1234@gmail.com

Kaur, Harneet, Assistant Professor, Department of Commerce Government College for Girls, Sector-11, Chandigarh.

Kour, Harneet, Assistant Prof., Department of Commerce & Management, DAV College, Chandigarh. E-mail: harneetkaur27@gmail.com

Kour, Manjit, Assistant Prof., Department of Commerce, Guru Gobind Singh College for Women, Sector-26, Chandigarh. E-mail: manjuz_99@yahoo.com

Mehta, Jagdish Chander, Sr. Assistant Professor and Head, Department of Sociology, D.A.V College, Chandigarh. E-mail: jagdishdavc@yahoo.co.in

Prakasam, Seepana, Assistant Prof., P.G. Department of Economics, Govt. College for Girls, Sector-11, Chandigarh. E-mail: drsprakasam@gmail.com

Rohal, Sandhya, Assistant Prof., Department of Laws, Panjab University, Chandigarh. E-mail: sandhyarohal@rediffmail.com

Saini, Savita, Assistant Prof., Department of Commerce and Management, D.A.V. College, Chandigarh. E-mail: savu_kwel@yahoo.co.in

Sharma, Anju, Associate Prof., R.G.G.D.C., Shimla. E-mail: anju.sharma1970@yahoo.com

Sharma, Arun, Research Scholar, Travel and Tourism, Central University of Himachal Pradesh, Dharamshala, E-mail: sharma.arun84@gmail.com

Sharma, Manoj, Assistant Prof., Department of Commerce, Himachal Pradesh University Regional Centre, Dharamshala. E-mail: manojhpu@gmail.com

Sharma, Renu, Assistant Prof., P.G. Department of Commerce and Management, K.L.S.D. College, Ludhiana. E-mail: rajivbhatia76@yahoo.com

Sharma, Ritika, Research Scholar, Department of Economics, Maharishi Dayanand University, Rohtak. E-mail: ritikadavesar@yahoo.com

Sharma, Sunanda, Assistant Prof., P.G Department of Commerce, R.S.D. College, Ferozepur City. E-mail: ssunanda82@yahoo.com

Singh, Devinder Pal, Assistant Prof., Punjabi University Regional Centre for IT and Management, Phase-7, Mohali-160059, Punjab, India. E-mail: sidhudps@gmail.com

Singh, Nayanika, Assistant Prof., Department of Psychology, D.A.V College, Sector-10, Chandigarh, E-mail: nanikasingh@gmail.com

Slariya, Mohinder Kumar, Associate Professor, Environmental Sociologist, Government P.G. College, Chamba, HP, India-176310. E-mail: mkslariya@gmail.com

Thakur, Surrendra G., Head, Department of Sociology, Elphinstone College, Mumbai-32 E-mail: surrendrathakur@gmail.com

Vats, Gaurav, Assistant Prof. in Department of Commerce and Management, D.A.V. College, Chandigarh. E-mail: pbvats@gmail.com

Virk, Sukhwinder, Assistant Prof., Rajiv Gandhi National University of Law, Patiala, Punjab. E-mail: ikwalia@gmail.com

Walia, Ivneet, Research Scholar, Rajiv Gandhi National University of Law, Patiala, Punjab E-mail: ikwalia@gmail.com

Key Note Address

Globalisation and Social Transformation in India

S.L. Sharma

Introduction

As an overarching trend of our times, globalisation signifies a transformative force of enormous significance. It represents a force of reorganisation of a global economic order based on advocacy of open-door economic policy between nations. Understandably, it has emerged as a powerful catalyst of economic transformation, particularly in developing nations, entailing significant socio-cultural fallouts. While its importance as a catalyst of economic transformation in developing countries has been widely acknowledged, its role in their socio-cultural transformation has not yet received intense scholarly attention. Therefore, it is time to undertake systematic studies of the socio-cultural impact of globalisation in developing countries. A modest attempt in that direction is being made here with a focus on India, being one of the major beneficiaries of globalisation.

A look at the sociological discourse on globalisation in India reveals that it has been concerned more with the cultural consequences of globalisation than with its social outcomes. This is evident from the writings of Singh (2002) and Dhanagare (2003) among others. The social fallouts of globalisation have received at best a cursory treatment. A question of seminal sociological significance to ask in this regard is: Has globalisation generated a trend of social transformation in India and, if so. what is its direction? This is precisely the question I seek to address in this paper. In order to deal with this question in a systematic manner, I set for myself the following specific tasks: (1) to clarify the concept of globalisation; (2) to problematise the term 'social transformation' and articulate it as a concept; (3) to delineate the socio-cultural fallouts of globalisation in India and (4) to appraise their transformational potential.

Understanding Globalisation

There are many different interpretations of the term 'globalisation', almost as many as its interpreters. This is hardly surprising in view of its multifaceted and dynamic character. However, it leaves a reader highly perplexed about the exact meaning of the term. In order to steer clear of the conceptual mess, I would like to unravel the meaning of globalisation in a systematic manner. An analytical scrutiny of its various definitions reveals two distinguishable conceptions: (1) globalisation as a process of unification of the world brought about by extraordinary advances in ICT and (2) globalisation as a process of unification of the world by means of market integration across nations. A number of scholars have defined globalisation as a spatial and temporal compression of the world accelerated by recent advances in ICT. McLuhan was the first to conceive the idea of the 'global village' in the context of mounting significance of media in uniting the world. Startling advances in cyber technology have enabled mankind to conquer time and space. Accordingly, Robertson has defined globalisation as a process that 'refers both to the compression of the world and the intensification of consciousness of the world as a whole' (1992). Similarly, Giddens interprets globalisation as 'distanciation'. which implies compression of time and space facilitating 'social action at a distance' (1990:64). More pointedly, Waters defines globalisation as 'a process in which the constraints of . geography on social and cultural arrangements recede and people become aware that they are receding' (1995:3). Viewed in this manner, globalisation, for all practical purposes, signifies emergence of a 'networked world', thanks to the rise of the worldwide web and other advances in ICT.

Turning to the other formulation, i.e., globalisation as market integration, the following definition by the International Monetary) Fund (IMF) may be cited as a representative one: 'Globalization is characterized by increases in flows of trade, capital, information as well as mobility of individuals across borders'. Similarly. Friedman and Kaplan (2002) have defined it as 'a process of integration of markets, finance and technology in a way that shrinks the world'. These and such other definitions thus project globalisation as mobilisation of capital, goods and services across borders without many restrictions.

The above delineated two constructs of globalisation obviously differ in their points of emphasis, one stressing the communicative aspect while the other highlighting its economic dimension. Their differences of emphasis apart, the two need not be viewed as rival but as complementary constructs, only that they have to be reconciled in terms of primacy of one over the other. In my view, globalisation is primarily a process of economic reorganisation of the world aided and accelerated as much by stunning advances in ICT as by sponsored liberalisation of domestic economic policies. As a consequence, it also entails informational and cultural flows across borders.

In order to have a proper understanding of globalisation, a few clarifications need to be made. First, that globalisation in its present import is a new development, and not an age-old process. The earlier moves in the direction of effecting global unification such as those undertaken by world explorers, religious missionaries and enterprising traders, followed by colonisation and modernisation, may aptly be viewed as precursors to globalisation. While it is true that globalisation is a cumulative consequence of all these moves, what distinguishes it, however, is the design of late capitalism to launch it as a global project. The idea of globalisation actually gathered momentum following three developments of historic significance in the 1980s. These events include the collapse of the Soviet Union, the demolition of the Berlin Wall and the advent of the worldwide web. While the collapse of the Soviet Union and the demolition of the Berlin Wall signified triumph of capitalism over socialism, the advent of the worldwide web paved the way to a networked world. It is the historic synchronisation of these three developments (hat constructed the specific historical context from which (he notion of globalisation arose.

Second, globalisation is not an innocent process of global unification. Instead, it is a transformative project of global capitalism to recast the world in its own mould. The reasons in support of my contention are: (1) that a call for globalisation came around the 1980s from the global development agencies, including the World Bank and the IMF. They urged the less-developed nations to adopt the Structural Adjustment Programme (SAP) and to open up their markets for integration with the global market; (2) globalisation is commended as a new strategy of development for developing nations, one that is claimed to be more effective than the earlier strategy, which laid stress on capital, technology and expertise; and (3) globalisation is projected as a progressive policy *vis-à-vis* (he policy of protective tariff followed earlier. Developing nations are accordingly advised to do away with restrictions on import and export and follow instead an open-door economic policy. The credibility of these claims apart, there is more to the idea of globalisation than what meets the eye. The fact of the matter is that globalisation is a consequence of the development of productive forces of leading industrialised nations necessitating search for markets in developing nations to sell off their surplus produce (Castro, 1998). It is essentially their need which is why they are the powerful advocates of globalisation. What is more, their pressure on developing nations to abandon the policy of protective tariff is in contradiction of their own past policy of protective tariff, which they themselves had used as a ladder to reach their present level of development, as documented by Chang (2003).

A third point is that globalisation is not a process of free flow of trade, finance and a service across the world, as it is generally projected to be. Instead, it is a hegemonically negotiated process of economic and cultural flows across borders. This is evident from the experience of developing countries, which for most part, have remained largely at the receiving end. Take, for example, the immigration laws of advanced nation, including the USA and Britain. The laws have become more stringent in recent years restricting the entry of people from developing nations. It is the same story with the trade of certain commodities from developing nations. Most important of all, it is evident from the parleys at the ministerial level meeting of the WTO, held earlier at Doha and Concun and more recently at Hong Kong, where leaders of developed nations managed to manipulate reluctant consent of their counterparts from developing nations on the question of phased withdrawal of farm subsidies, in spite of fierce protests from the latter. All this is understandable in view of the absence of a level-playing field between the developed and the developing nations on account of their unequal levels of development.

Finally, globalisation is not a fixed but an evolving reality. Its contours have changed significantly in the last few years. Launched as a hegemonic process of unilateral flow of trade and capital from the developed to the underdeveloped nations in the 1980s, globalisation has now turned into a multilateral flow of investment and services from the developing to the developed world also. This is evident from the inroads made into Europe and America by Chinese and Indian multinationals, besides software professionals in recent years. Furthermore, not limited to economic flows, globalisation has as well accelerated a stream of cultural flows across the world. It has generated a matrix of growing intercultural contact and communication among diverse national cultures, which have been brought face-to-face in the marketplace. Il has thus created a scenario of cultural confluence as much as of economic interdependence.

Defining Social Transformation

Few terms have gained as much currency in contemporary sociological parlance as social transformation. This is evident from its frequent use in prevailing sociological discourses and in recent writings. Its extant usage is understandable in view of the momentous changes taking place in society. However, the use pattern of (he term reveals a tendency towards its indiscriminate use. Often than not, it is used in an interchangeable sense of social change. Its referents range from all kinds of passing changes to profound ones. It has thus become a part of sociological vocabulary but not of sociological dictionary. Unlike other terms, such as social evolution, progress, revolution and development, which figure in sociology texts as distinguishable forms of social change, the term 'social transformation' has yet to acquire a technical connotation. Therefore, there is a need to articulate it as a sociological concept and indicate its *differentia specified.* This is precisely what 1 seek to do here.

The literal meaning of the term 'transformation' is change from one form to another. It connotes a kind of change that transcends the original form of the object to which it is applied. In this sense, it signifies a systemic change rather than an incidental one. The term 'social' refers to a system of social relationships, institutions, identities and values. Thus, taken together, 'social transformation' literally means systemic change in the frame of social relationships, institutions, identities and values. To illustrate this, it is important to distinguish between two types of changes in society: transitory and transformative. In my view, transformative changes are distinguishable from transitory trends in terms-ot three parameters, i.e., their profundity, magnitude and power of persistence. Profundity-wise, they are fundamental; magnitude-wise, they are phenomenal; and persistence-wise, they are relatively irreversible. To elaborate on the first, transformative change is that which represents a fundamental departure from the root, i.e., from the original form of a social unit/system to which it pertains. Take, for instance, the trend of gay marriages. Given the original and the usual idea of marriage as a union of individuals of opposite sexes, a gay marriage represents an instance of social transformation once it gains social acceptability. Moving on to the second distinguishing feature of transformative change, i.e., its phenomenal magnitude, social transformation is not a case of small but of substantial change. Proliferation of civil society. groups, such as social action forums, civil rights unions and social resistance movements in a communal society, provides a telling illustration of this, in that it is indicative of transformation of a communal society into a civil society, Coming to the third parameter, i.e., irreversibility, a transformative change is that which is not likely to revert to its original point of departure. Rise of the new middle class cutting across caste lines in a caste-ridden society is a graphic example of it.

A radical pace of change may as well be considered as a usual, although not a necessary feature of transformative change. Unlike gradual pace of change, as in the case of social evolution, social transformation is marked by a rapid pace of change. This means too tall a change in too short a time. A good example of it is the change in gender relations from a culture of hierarchy to that of equity. Even as radicalness is a usual feature of transformative change, it cannot be regarded as a parameter of social transformation for two reasons. One, that a systemic change does not necessarily take place as a sudden break with the past. There is generally a cumulative background to it. Two, radicality is more a distinctive feature of revolution, which may or may not result # transformation. Therefore, in the interest of conceptual precision social transformation may better be viewed a a case of fundamental, phenomenal and irreversible change in a given social script.

In order to further clarify the notion of social transformation, it may be reiterated that for all practice purposes, it signifies a case of structural chang Structural change connotes a profound change in soc institutions, relational frames, identities and values. decode it, institutional innovations such as a 'live-arrangement as an alternative to conventional marriage; is a clear instance of profound change. In the domair relational frames, a trend of change from asymmetrical to symmetrical relations, as in the case of intercast; relations, is certainly an indicator of structural transformation. In respect of identities, when in-l identities give way to achieved identities, this consul a case of transformative change. In the realm of value change from communitarian to individualistic or authoritarian to emancipatory value system provide telling illustration of social transformation.

A final point to note about the concept of s transformation is that it is a value-neutral category clarification is important in view of the fact that gen the victims of a given system raise a demand for transformation, implying thereby transformation as a change for the better. In my view, social transformation is a fact, not a value. It is not a normative category for two reasons. One. because it stands for all kinds of structural shifts better as well as worse. For example. rise of a consumerist middle class in a society known for its culture of frugal living as a value is as much an instance of a transformative change as emergence of a civil society in a traditionally communal society. Thus, social transformation is about all sorts of structural shifts regardless of their being desirable or otherwise. Two, that treating social transformation as a judgmental construct will render it indistinguishable from such other varieties of social change as progress and development which obviously are value laden.

Socio-Cultural Fallouts of Globalisation

The era of globalisation started in India in 1991 with the introduction of economic reforms comprising the trinity of liberalisation, privatisation and globalisation, popularly known as LPG. While the three are interrelated, each carries its own specific connotation. Liberalisation refers to the policy of liberation of economy from the shackles of state control, marking the end of the era of 'licence-quota-permit raj'. Privatisation stands for the policy of allowing entry of private sectors in all fields of economy, including those earlier monopolised by the state, such as power, transport, oil, gas and so on, leading to the prevailing trend of disinvestment of public sector undertakings (PSUs). Globalisation, as distinct from liberalisation and privatisation, signifies an open-door economic policy for integrating the domestic market with the world market. Among other things, it means allowing foreign multinationals to enter into the Indian market as much as Indian multinationals to go global.

There are three notable points about the onset of globalisation in India. First, unlike many other nations India opted for it more out of her domestic economic compulsions than out of volition. Given its increasing debt burden, fiscal deficit, poor state of balance of payment, high inflation and depletion of foreign reserves, the Indian State was left with no other options, and hence opted for globalisation together with its two other -accomplices, i.e., liberalisation and privatisation. Third, unlike several other nations, including China, which settled for selective globalisation, the Indian State went for it in a relatively big way.

Whatever be the background, globalisation has done a miracle to the Indian economy. It has transformed the economy from a poor, backward and stagnant one to a buoyant, robust and fast-growing one. This is evident from all accounts. The rate of growth has surged from a low 3.5% in the pre-reforms period to a high of 9.2% in 2006-2007. According to the

World Bank Report (2005-2006), India has emerged as the twelfth richest nation of the world in 2005 based on its GDP, which grew at 13.4% in dollars. Little wonder that India earned the enviable distinction of being the 'fastest-growing free-market economy" at the World Economic Forum's Annual Summit at Davos in 2006. Furthermore, according to the Merrill Lynch Capgemini World Wealth Report 2006, the number of dollar millionaires in India grew by 19.3% in 2005, this being the second fastest in the world. The Economic Survey (2006-2007) reveals that India's foreign exchange reserves have reached a record $185.1 billion, which has grown to $276 billion in 2007 *(Tunes of India,* 8 January 2008). This is a far cry from the pre-globalisation era when India had to mortgage its gold reserves for getting foreign exchange. Similarly, the total foreign investment inflows into India have increased from almost zero in 1990 to $20 billion in 2005 and foreign remittances to over $24 billion. India is also now the sixth largest service exporter as well as a top destination for off-shoring according to a survey by A.T. Kearney in 2007. Above all, India became a trillion-dollar economy in April 2007. and thereby joined the elite club of eleven nations with such a distinction. In view of these developments, the assessment of India in the Goldman Sachs BR1C report by Wilson and Purushothaman (2003) as an emerging global economic power, along with Brazil. Russia and China sounds so prophetic. By all accounts. the Indian economy has remained on the move on a fast track. However, it has received a set-back during 2010-2011, as its GDP has come down to nearly 6%, and the Indian rupee is highly devalued today *vis-à-vis* the US dollar. But that is due to the trend of economic downturn worldwide. Happily for us, the fundamentals of the Indian economy arc relatively stronger compared to the European and American countries.

When economy is on the move, especially at this incredible pace society cannot remain unmoved. Globalisation has set in motion a stream of changes in India's socio-cultural panorama as much as in Indian economy. These trends are noticeable in the domains of social stratification, institutions, values and identities. In the realm of social stratification, it has sprung up trends such as the following: widening disparities in the midst of glowing prosperity, rise of the new middle class, marginalisation of peasantry, growing caste polarisation and Dalit assertion. Let us illustrate these before moving on to trends in other domains.

Disparity in The Midst of Prosperity

It is obvious that globalisation has generated an overall climate of prosperity in India. One has only to recall the depressing days of pre-globalisation period in order to appreciate the state of relative prosperity today. Globalisation has, for sure, opened up opportunities for people with some measure "of competence. Such opportunities were not available to them in the pre-globalisation phase. Little wonder that many people of the lower classes have been able to make a grade to the lower middle classes as claimed by Friedman (2005). A similar sentiment is reflected in Gurcharan Das's book 'India Unbounded' (2002). Developments such as these, coupled with the story of the world-class enterprise of Infosys in Bangalore, have led Thomas Friedman, the *New York Tunes* columnist, to contend that the world is flattening, the global economic playing field is getting levelled and that many people in India and China have grown out of poverty, thanks to globalisation (Friedman, 2005:9).

While the above observation of Friedman is valid, it presents only one side of the coin. Globalisation has no doubt enabled a wider population to see the benefits of economic growth, but it has made the rich super-rich, leaving the poor largely unaffected. For the same reason, it has led to the widening and deepening of disparities.

This is evident from almost all the available reports. For example, the rounds of National Sample Survey (NSS) conducted in the mid-1990s point to deepening inequalities. Similarly, a report of the Department of Economic Affairs, UNO, points to rising economic disparities in India in the 1990s. Likewise. India's poverty ratio stands at a disgraceful 28% (Aiyar. 2006). Most important of all, the Gini Coefficient, which is a measure of socioeconomic disparities, has risen for India from 0.37 to 0.42 in 2007. What is more, according to the 'Wealth Report', published by Knight Frank in May 2007, India is on the way to becoming a plutonomy, a society sharply stratified by a super-wealthy top brand at one end and abject poor at the other, as reported in a leading national daily *(Times of India,* 2007).

On top of it, we have abundant observational evidence to see the widening gap between two Indias, which I would like to call a *glittering* India and *littering* India. The glittering India consists of the super-rich, while the littering India consists of the gutter-poor. The glittering India belongs to the super-earners and super-consumers, who enjoy lavish lifestyles, patronise mega malls, five-star hotels, multiplexes and night parties. On the other hand, the littering India belongs to pavement dwellers, rag pickers, scavengers and sweepers, rickshaw pullers. brick kiln workers and undernourished millions. The story of the two Indias may be an old one, but what makes it more distressing in the era of globalisation is an 'almost complete disconnect in-between the 300 million, high flying Indians and the remaining 750 million of their countrymen, many of whom seldom gel two square meals a day' (Malhotra, 2006). At any rate, the littering Inch; remains unincorporated in globalised India. Nothing illustrates the existing scale of disparity in globalising India better than the eloquent title of Loretta Schwartz book, 'Starving in the Shadow of Plenty'.

Rise of the New Middle Class

One of the most visible consequences of globalisation i India is the emergence of a new middle class. It is gettin bigger, richer, younger and spendthrift by the day. Its size has grown to an estimated 300 million, roughly 22%; against 12% elsewhere in the world. The new middle class is different from the traditional middle class in some significant respects that is. in its composition, age group, income level, lifestyle and social outlook. It is composed of company executives, IT specialists, finance and management consultants, media professionals and the neo-rich, including the 'bullock capitalists' from the countryside to use Varma's phrase (2006). In terms of age composition, the new middle class is younger than its traditional counterpart, which is understandable in view he special value of its professional skills which are in demand in the fast-growing knowledge economy in era of globalisation. Not surprisingly, it is lauded by commentators like Varma (1998) for its buoyancy, energy, entrepreneurship and resilience. Its income levels have increased to an amazing high, due to lucrative packages offered by transnational and private corporations. This has consequently enhanced its purchasing power and its spending proclivity. No wonder that the new middle class has emerged as a consumerist class and it is willing to pay to live in style. More than its mode of living, the new middle class differs from the old in terms of its changing mores. Unlike the traditional middle class that distinguished itself by upholding the norms of conventional morality, the new middle class is seen as holding a brief for rethinking conventional morality. Well informed, alert and articulate, the new middle class is getting global in its world view. Progressive on all these counts, it leaves something to be desired in respect of civic sensibility as it glosses over larger public issues of poverty, inequality, corruption and oppression.

Marginalisation of Peasantry

The effects of globalisation are not confined to urban India. They are well noticeable even in the countryside. Gilobalisation has brought the market forces to bear on agriculture in a big way. For the same reason, it has generated trends of corporatisation of agriculture, crop diversification, monoculture. genetically modified crops and above all, creation of Special Economic Zones (SEZs). These trends coupled with the WTO-induced pressure to reduce farm subsidies have produced new dynamics in agrarian structure, different from the one generated earlier by the forces of Modernisation. If the thrust of modernisation was on farm mechanisation together with the use of modem chemical inputs, the stress of globalisation is on marketisation strategies. In effect, globalisation has accelerated a trend of depeasantisation of small and marginal farmers as well as immiseration of agricultural labour driving many of them away to cities. It has as well affected middle peasantry and big farmers in some very insidious ways. Sandwiched between rising costs of agricultural inputs and minimum support price fixed by the state, the middle peasantry has come under the terrible burden of indebtedness. Tills has led to an alarming trend of increasing incidence of farmers' suicides in several states, such as Andhra Pradesh, Karnataka, Maharashtra and Punjab. A number of studies, including those conducted by the author (Kumar and Sharma, 1998; 2006), have brought out the pre-eminent role of globalisation in accelerating this trend. The latest shot has come in the form of the state policy of setting up SEZs, a move prompted by globalisation, which has intensified unrest by fanners and has led to their vigorous protest against the state. Farmers' mobilisation in Singur and Nandigram provides solid evidence of it. While land acquisition by the state for promoting SEZs has caused widespread consternation among farmers in general the trend of large-scale buying of rural land close to cities by dealers and builders to construct malls and multiplexes is a new trend. This has come as a boon to some fanners. By and large, globalisation has led to marginalisation of the rural folk.

Dalit Assertion and Caste Polarisation

Dalit mobilisation is not a new phenomenon. It dates back to the days of Mahatma Jyoti Rao Phule and B.R. Ambedkar. Globalisation has only intensified it and led to a renewed form of Dalit assertion. It has produced such an effect on account of its patronage to privatisation on the one hand, and its stress on disinvestment of the PSUs, on the other. The contraction of the public sector has led to neutralisation of the reserved job opportunities made available to the Scheduled Castes (SCs) and Scheduled

Tribes (STs) in the public sector. Irked by this development, leaders of the SCs and the STs, as well as the youth of these groups have raised a demand for reservations in the private sector. This demand is being stoutly opposed by the leaders of industry and proprietors and managers of the corporate sector, as well as non-SC/ST students. In effect, it has led to further unionization of Dalits on the one hand, and reaction formation among the non-Dalits, on the other. The Dalit intellectuals have now begun to justify their demand for reservations in the private sector on the basis of systematic data rather than in terms of their general apprehensions. The research-based observation by Thorat convincingly illustrates it. He observes: 'After July, 1990, the new measures have led to decline in the employment of the SCs in government services and jobs... Identical trends were observed in employment of SCs in public sector undertakings' (2001:10). The leaders of private corporations are resisting this move by foregrounding the key importance of professional competence for organisational growth in this age of global competition. If Dalit youth are agitated about their shrinking job prospects in the wake of globalisation, non-Dalit professional students are militating against the move of reservation in private sectors as it sets their careers at stake. Be that as it may, the point to note is that globalisation has set the two against each other, and thereby has intensified the phenomenon of caste polarisation.

Impact of Globalisation on Basic Social Institutions

Liberalising Marriage Moves

Turning to the impact of globalisation on basic social institutions, it will be apt to focus on marriage, family and gender. Let us take them one by one. Rise in the age at marriage is a notable consequence of globalisation. The youth today, particularly those drawn into the corporate sector, have begun to accord precedence to career over marriage. This has become a source of anxiety to parents, especially those whose daughters of marriageable age shy away from marriage on account of their preoccupation with their careers. Globalisation of the culture of dating is another remarkable trend that is catching up with youth in the metropolitan centres. This points to a trend of self-assertion by youth in matters of marriage. Equally important is the trend of commercialisation of wedding arrangements, which have been taken over by professional agencies leading to change of venue from homes to hotels and now to farm houses/ marriage gardens.

Globalisation has also set in motion a move towards demerger of sex and marriage. This is evident from the increasing incidence of pre-marital and extra-marital sex, as reported by a number of surveys (Vieira, 1998; Bhandare, 2003; Wadhwa, 2004). This trend is of profound significance in the sense that it runs counter to the domain of marriage, i.e., sex in wedlock only. There is now a tendency of ignoring the pre-marital affairs of the mate, which earlier used to constitute an important consideration in mate selection. As with pre-marital affairs, so with extra-marital alliance: there seems to be growing a measure of tolerance of it as is evident from the emerging idea of 'office spouse'. There is thus a spouse at home and another at office/organisation where one has now to spend a longer time. The office spouse is a colleague of the opposite sex with whom one develops intimacy and shares private matters which one is traditionally supposed to share with one's life partner. Since the work scenario has changed in a manner that it has substantially cut down on one's family time, the couple hardly finds time for sharing and caring. The office spouse is thus a surrogate partner for fulfilling this need. It signifies more of a romantic relationship than essentially a sexual one. The work organisations are reported to be acquiescent about it in the hope that it retains employees for a longer time at the workplace, contributing to organisational growth. This should not be mistaken to mean decline of sexuality in wedlock. On the contrary, globalisation has sparked of a culture of super-sex in the wedlock. As in the boardroom, so in the bedroom, there is a growing passion for being innovative. Super-sex is about getting better, aesthetic, fantastic and creative in sexual pleasure. Yet another development relates to the emergence of weekend unions particularly in cases where the husband and the wife are working for two different organisations located at such a distance that it prevents the two from living together at one place. Most important of all is the rise of live-in-unions. an institutional alternative to marriage. The trend of live-in-unions first appeared in Sweden, from where it has spread to other countries, including India. One result of these developments is that marriage is no longer a taken-for-granted institution. Now efforts need to be made by the spouses to make marriages work. In view of this, it will not be wrong to observe that in many cases conventional marriage is proving inadequate to cope with the new developments.

Changing Familial Relations

The pre-globalisation era witnessed a sociological debate on the disintegrative impact of modernisation on the joint family system. In the present times, it seems that globalisation has led to destabilisation of the nuclear family as well. The increasing incidence of marital discord caused by an excessive demand of the corporate world over family time of its employees is a proof enough of it. It is well known that in the era of globalisation, commitment to career and consumerism has taken precedence over family obligations. This has led to several consequences, including its adverse effects on marital harmony, childcare and care of aged parents. Little wonder that it has given rise to a trend of childless couples by choice and abandoning of aged parents, resulting in shrinking of the size of the family. The trend of decline in the family size is not altogether new. It had stalled in the era of modernisation itself, which paved the way from 'double income single child' (DISC) preference to 'double income no child' (DINC) choice. The rise of globalisation and the resultant growth of careerism have only served to reinforce the ongoing shift from the 'one-child' concept to the 'no-child' preference. What distinguishes it is the new mode of justification. Earlier, it was a consequence of the lure of double income to provide for better parenting; now it is prompted by precedence to professional career over parental role. Although the number of couples opting to stay 'issueless' is quite small, it nevertheless is important enough to indicate that the thought has germinated and is likely to spread. This is no insignificant development in a society, which values parenthood and frowns upon childless couples.

Another remarkable consequence of globalisation is the changing conjugal power relations. Globalisation has generated opportunities for women to enter into high- profile occupations and entrepreneurial positions. This has led to a new kind of power equation between the husband and the wife, with the wife becoming more assertive and the husband getting more accommodative. It has also set in motion a trend of gender role reversal in a few cases. The increasing incidences of husbands participating in household chores as well as wives' active say in decision-making are a testimony of this. The role of parents in socialisation of children is another dimension of family change. Fathers have begun to take on added responsibility in raising children, which has made them more of a friendly figure, unlike the earlier image of a patriarch. Mothers, on the other hand, have begun to assume the role of disciplinarians in their own ways. Both parents seem to be concerned more about the career of children than about their character. For the same reason, they are enrolling their children in reputed schools and in additional skill-building courses with a view to sharpening their intellect and honing their talents. This has put children under pressure to perform.

As such, along with the popular impression that globalisation has led to parental neglect of children, it is also true that it has enhanced parental concern and quality of parenting. It is a different matter though that parental influence in respect of character training is somewhat on the decline. The media has emerged as an alternative agency of socialisation with strong influence on the young generation. Accordingly, peer culture, which is largely shaped by the media, seems to be exerting greater influence over the choices, preferences and value orientations of the youth. The mounting influences of the media, including television, computer and Internet. which are an integral part of globalisation, have also impacted parent-child relations. The traditional paradigm of parental authority and child obedience has begun to yield ground to the emerging pattern of child rights and parental obligations. As a result, what we have is a phenomenon of assertive child and accommodative parents. Today, parents are faced with a dilemma about their cultural obligation to discipline and restrain the, child and the limits set on by the civil obligation to grant freedom of choice to the youth. This is more than just case of generation gap. There are two ways to look at # (1) as a case of generation break, and (2) as a case of generation bridge. It signifies generation break as the 'young generation today has begun to question the rationale of traditional norms in a manner as never done before. Given the exposure of the young generation to global information about cultural diversities and more so about the emerging norms of civil society, the interrogation of traditional norms is almost belligerent. Hence, a case of generation break. Viewed from the other perspective, it represents a case of generation bridge in the sense that the old generation is responding positively to the new situation. It is showing commendable accommodation in putting up with the emerging situation. Both ways of looking at the changing parent-child relations seem to be valid as they touch upon two different but complementary facets of the same reality.

Yet another consequence of globalisation for the family system is the emerging problem of abandoned aged parents. With their increasing concern for career and demanding corporate obligations, young adults find it hard to take care even of their children, let alone their ageing parents. Add to it the prevailing ethos of pragmatism and privacy prompted by globalisation, which is taking a heavy toll on the bonds of affectivity for which the Indian family has been known worldwide. Thus, globalisation has led to the narrowing of the circle of family relations, resulting in many cases of neglect of aged parents. The enormity of this problem can be gauged from the fact that the Indian State has had to come up with the Maintenance and Welfare of Parents and Senior Citizens Act 2007. The purpose of the Act is to make it obligatory for children to care for their aged parents above 60 years of age.

Upsurge of Culture of Consumerism

Globalisation has impacted not only social institutions but also beliefs and values. This is evident from the outbreak of the culture of consumerism, moral ambiguity and declining civility. Let us take them up one by one. Celebration of the culture of consumerism is one of the most visible consequences of globalisation. This is evident from the proliferation of mega malls, marts, multiplexes and magnificent markets. This is also obvious from the emerging brand-conscious lifestyle, tastes, choices and preferences. Above all, this is reflected in the growing mentality of acquisitiveness resulting in possessions far in excess of needs.

The culture of consumerism is not just about consuming more. It actually refers to a 'classy' lifestyle. The distinctive traits of such a lifestyle are concern for brand equity, craze for the latest, proliferation of wants over needs and a tendency of exhibitionism. Brand equity serves as a measure of status. Accordingly, it is patronised as a status symbol. The connection between brand equity and globalisation is clear from the manner in which multinationals and domestic companies invest in the projection of their brand equity for purposes of marketing. Craze for the latest, another element of the culture of consumerism, implies an attitude of discarding the old and adopting the new, i.e., abandoning yesterday's buy in favour of today's fad. This desire for the latest is systematically kept up in the market by continuously coming up with something 'new and different'. It is also sustained by stimulating a desire to stay ahead of others. The third ingredient of the culture of consumerism signifies a crucial distinction between needs and wants. Needs represent necessities, while wants represent luxuries. One may not need what one wants. This, in fact, is often the case and far more so in the era of globalisation. Wants are manufactured desires, generated by advertisements, and patronised by the media. Little wonder that globalisation has led to multiplication of wants over needs and a trend of unabashed consumerism. This development is at variance with the values of our culture, which puts premium on curtailment of needs. Thus, globalisation has moved us from a state of simple living to that of high living and mindless consumerism. It calls for a revision of Descartes' classic dictum 'I think, therefore, 1 am' to 1 consume, therefore, I am', as cited in an editorial of a leading national daily (*Times of India,* February 24, 2007).

Conventional Morality under Interrogation

Morality is a subjective phenomenon. Built or. the notion of human good, it provides a normative framework for judging propriety of conduct pertaining to interpersonal relations, including sex norms. Its defining feature is its stern applicability to self as much as to others. Hence, its primary dictum is: do unto others what you want others to do to you. Derived from this dictum are certain universal values, such as truth, honesty, fidelity, integrity. incorruptibility, non-stealing and selflessness. Beyond such universal values, which are usually incontrovertible, there arc some relative values which are time-space specific. They vary from community to community. Take, for example, kissing in public, dating and courtship. These are viewed as immoral in India, but not so in the West. However, even in India, today there is no more strong indignation of such acts.

Proud of its tradition of morality, the Indian society today abounds in moral ambiguity. There is ample evidence of deviance from moral norms of truth, public probity, integrity, concern for others, pre-marital sex, etc. What is more, there is also emerging a tendency of open defiance of these norms in public. From *deviance* to open *defiance* is a notable trend. Conventional morality is increasingly coming under interrogation, and it is confronted with 'alternative morality'. Globalisation has ushered in a new era of alternative lifestyle (consumerist), alternative sex morality (liberalised) and alternative relational molality (pragmatic). Prompted by a market-driven economy, such a morality is now viewed as 'progressive morality'. Mass media is glamorising it in a big way. Leisure industry is marketing it vigorously. While conventional morality has not yet lost its ground, alternative morality has yet to gain a firm foothold. As of now. the custodians of conventional morality view the present situation as a case of value decadence, while the protagonists of alternative morality look upon it as morality in quest of redefinition. Whatever it is, it certainly points to a state of moral flux, if not of breakdown of moral order.

Civil Values in Disarray

Civil values are different from moral values in that they pertain to the public domain unlike the latter, which relate to the community domain. Public is a political category, while community is a social entity. Accordingly, civil values represent the virtues of public good, such as liberty, equality and secularism, etc., while moral values imply. the idea of human good. As with moral values, so with civil values: globalisation has led to their impairment. This is evident from the disconcerting trend of fundamentalism, recurrent stream of communalism, rampant corruption, criminalisation of politics, falling standards of public conduct: callousness towards, the downtrodden and diminishing concern for environment and ecology. Not generated by globalisation, for sure, but globalisation has certainly led to the aggravation of these trends by giving an upper hand to market over state. profit over people, economy over ecology, inequity over equity, meritocracy over compensatory justice and 'haves' over 'have nots'.

These unwholesome developments have not gone un-resisted. A number of civil and social resistance groups have come up in order to protest against these disconcerting trends. The roles of civil rights unions. environment groups, social forums, anti-corruption organisations and, above all, anti-globalisation movements are some of the instances in point. These are healthy signs, of course, as they point to the rise of the civil society, but these developments are the unintended consequences of globalisation.

Cultural Traditions and Identities under Threat

Globalisation is not just about economic flows; it is also about cultural flows. As a result, it has generated stirring effects on cultural traditions and identities across the globe, particularly in the non-Western parts of the world. Like elsewhere, in India too, there has been a debate about the repercussions of globalisation on cultural traditions and identities. Voicing a popular concern in this regard, D.N. Dhanagare has highlighted the 'pernicious effects' of globalisation on local communities and cultures. In particular, he deplores the role of multinational corporations (MNCs) and media for exerting shattering impact on ethnic traditions and crafts. Without mincing words, he observes local economies are being swallowed gradually, by the global capitalism and traditional cultures are being displaced by the ever-expanding global market and consumer culture (Dhanagare, 2003:23). On the other side, Yogendra Singh (2000:98) contends that globalisation also accelerates the growth of cultural self-consciousness' and cultural identities. Admitting that 'the penetration of external market and capitalist interest may threaten local of regional cultures by new modes of appropriation ant erosion of traditional cultural values', he argues that 'improvement and enlargement of the reach of communication may provide means to people to strengthen cultural identities' (Ibid.: 96). In this sense, he adds: 'the globalisation process, instead of being a threat to such identities, has become a means for their construction' (Ibid.: 97).

For a systematic appraisal of the cultural consequences of globalisation. I find Fukuyama's conceptual phrase of 'globalized production of homogenization' (1992), and Appaburai's 'globalized production of differences' (1996) quite revealing. I would, therefore, like to build upon the same for analysing the Indian situation. For sure, globalisation has resulted in 'globalized production of homogenization". In (he cultural field, this is evident from the upsurge of the following: culture of consumerism. commercialisation and commodification of culture, pop culture and virtual culture. These may be regarded as cultural universals of globalisation. As elsewhere, so in India, the culture of consumerism has made inroads into all local cultures, its greater visibility is in the new middle class. The proliferation of malls, marts and multiplexes, the easy availability of finances, the entry of big players in retail and rural marketing are going to give a further fillip to the culture of consumerism. Its disruptive implications for the traditional cultures in a land known for its value of frugal living are too obvious to require any elaboration. Similarly, the trend of commercialisation of cultural events and activities as also of commodification of cultural symbols cuts across cultural frontiers. This has led to trivialisation of ethnic and local cultures.

The universal spread of media-patronised pop culture is another force of homogenisation. Known for its domination by American themes and concerns, it combines selective elements of British, African and some exotic cultures. McDonaldisation, 'Coea-coiisaiion, Valentinisation and Reggae mesmerisation are some of its prominent markers among many others. Titillating in its appeal, if is known for luring people, especially the youth, away from their cultural roots. More importantly, its polluting effects on classical and folk culture are as much resented in India as in other parts of the world. The emergence of the virtual culture is yet another manifestation of" homogenisation. The virtual culture is a product of the stunning advances in ICT. All productions of electronic media, including films, television programmes and Internet communication are parts of (he stream of cultural productions. The stupendous growth of cultural productions constitutes a distinguishing mark of the age of globalisation. If the era of modernisation was an era of mass-scale material productions, the era of globalisation is an era of mass-scale cultural productions. These cultural productions have generated a virtual culture, which consists of animated signs, manufactured images and make beliefs. Such is the mounting significance of virtual culture in the age of cyber technology that it has acquired an autonomy of its own. For all practical purposes, it is independent of existential culture. Its autonomy can be gauged from (he quality of its role in socialisation of the young generation. Virtual culture indeed has emerged as a powerful agency of socialisation, one that is more powerful in shaping the perceptions, choices and preferences of the youth than existential culture and its agencies like the family and the school. Even as the virtual culture is largely illusory in its content, it is vital in its impact on the young generation. This is so all the world over.

The above-outlined forces of globalised production of homogenisation have led to erosion of certain aspects of local cultures. The invasion of the culture of consumerism has adversely affected traditional lifestyles and tastes. customary practices, sanctity of rituals and even (he normative order. Similarly, commodification of culture has turned local and ethnic cultures into a marketable commodity and thereby robbed them of their symbolic-value. In much the same way, the pop culture has not only marginalised classical and folk culture traditions of arts and aesthetics but also led to their obliteration on account of mixings and blending. Above all. the rise of the virtual culture has served to erode (he very foundations of existential local cultures. For all these reasons, globalisation has in some way created a threatening situation for cultural diversities and distinctions. There is a threat perception in local cultural circles, and it is feared that MNCs-led globalisation is destroying traditional cultures and identities.

However, there is another side of the repercussions of globalisation on traditional cultures. This relates to what *Appadurai* (1996) rails 'globalized production of differences". Paradoxical though it may appear, globalisation has as well triggered off certain trends, which are indicative of upsurge of cultural distinctions and identities. Prominent among them air. enhanced salience of ethnic pride and products, identity assertion by diverse cultural communities. rise of fundamentalism and resurgence of diasporic cultures. Like modernisation, globalisation has resulted in the sharpening of ethnic consciousness as well as craze for tilings ethnic. The upsurge of ethnic consciousness is a case of ethnic backlash against the homogenising forces of globalisation. However the craze for ethnic things, including food art and crafts, is generated by globalisation in order to cash in on them. Advertently or inadvertently, in both the eases, the net result is the upsurge of ethnic pride. Another fallout of globalisation is the trend of identity assertion by diverse culture groups. Faced with the challenge of hegemonic homogenisation thrown up by globalisation, local, regional and national cultures have responded by animated articulation or reinvention of their respective identities. This is evident from the trend of identity assertive celebration of religious festivals and regional fairs, be it Durga Puja in West Bengal, Ganesh Utsava in Maharashtra or Gur Purab processions in Punjab (Sharma, 1990). Such celebrations serve as measures of identity reaffirmation by local and regional cultures. In organising such celebrations, interestingly enough, the local cultural groups enthusiastically use all the new means and resources of globalisation to reiterate their respective cultural identities. Thus, there is as much evidence of appropriation of globalisation by ethnicity as of ethnic entities by globalisation.

Aside from the activisation of ethnicity, globalisation has also precipitated ethnic fundamentalism, especially religious fundamentalism. The spurt in ethno-nationalism and in fundamentalism, both in India and abroad, is its ample proof. Academic indictment of Huntington's thesis of clash of civilization' (1996) notwithstanding/the incidents of 9/11 and its sequels in Iraq and Iran, provide telling illustration of it. Similarly, the recurrent events of terrorist attacks in India bear further testimony to this.

Finally, globalisation has led to the activisation of diasporic cultures. Not a new phenomenon, diasporic cultures have gained salience in the wake of globalisation. This is so partly because of enhanced incidence of "translocation" of cultures and of people due to globalisation and partly because of the emergence of transnational networks between diasporic groups of the same nationality. Globalisation has generated a scenario of face-to-face contact of diverse national cultures in an alien setting. In a situation such as this, every diasporic culture shows a proclivity to retain its identity *vis-a-vis* others. As a matter of fact in such a setting, culture serves as an identity resource for its people to maintain their identity and their integrity. This is reflected abundantly in the diasporic literature. Furthermore, the development of transnational networks between diasporic groups of the same 'homeland' has led to further strengthening of their cultural integrity across nations. This fact has been brought out by recent diasporic research (Bhat, 2005).

At this point, it will be in order to appraise the above alluded to debate about the cultural fallouts of globalisation. Let us take the homogenisation thesis first. On the face of it, the 'homogenisation' thesis seems to be credible in view of the near universal spread of the culture of consumerism, mass-mediated pop culture and virtual culture. However, on closer examination, these trends do not make for convergence of cultures, nor for uniform global culture, or neutralisation of cultural diversities and distinctions. Therefore, the homogenisation thesis is untenable. On the other hand. the thesis of 'globalised production of differences'. although largely valid, is also not wholly true. Notwithstanding the evidence of backlash of ethnic or local cultures, their identity assertion and the salience of diasporic cultures, the fact remains that they are no longer the same authentic cultures as before; they represent reinvented versions, and they have lost some of their integrity under the spell of globalisation. Thus, because of globalised production of differences, globalisation has made a difference to their authentic forms. In view of the substantial evidence of identity consciousness of local. regional and national cultures, the popular threat perception seems to be a case more of panic reaction than rational contention. All the same, a dispassionate look at the situation suggests that traditional cultures are not going to remain the same any longer.

Theoretical Inferences

Having deciphered the trends of change in the Indian socio-cultural panorama under the impact of globalisation, it will be in order to bring out their theoretical implications. To this end, the following three questions are of core sociological significance:

1. Has the structural adjustment of economy led to structural shifts in society?
2. Has the upsurge of global market economy insinuated marginalisation of traditional cultures?
3. Has globalisation ushered in some new trends of socio-cultural transformation, which are different from these unleashed by industrialisation and modernisation?

The theoretical significance of these questions lies in the fact that they address the seminal sociological issue of interrelations in economy, society and culture.

To take up the first question, it is evident from the above analysis that globalisation hats led to a measure of mobilisation in the realm of social institutions and role relationships. In some ways, it has generated structural shifts as well, such as the rise of a new middle class, marginalisation of peasantry and proliferation of civil society groups.

However, it has not been able to make a dent into the basic social structure of the Indian society. It has served in a way to reinforce the caste structure. For sure, the recent caste-based student mobilisations, both of the Dalits and the forward castes, have been precipitated by the impact of globalisation on the policy of reservations. However, these mobilisations are indicative of the power of structural diversities to assert them in the face of globalisation. Similarly, various other social groups have been negotiating with the forces of globalisation, influencing the course of globalisation. Thus, the impact of globalisation on Indian social diversities is not uniform and unilateral. It is indeed dialectical as the socio-cultural diversities have also been impinging on globalisation and influencing its character.

Turning to the impact of globalisation on traditional cultures, it is evident that globalisation has introduced some elements of the global culture in India, such as the culture of consumerism, pop culture and virtual culture. We could see a semblance of culture transformation entailing a threat of annihilation of the identities and distinctions of traditional and local cultures. However, a deeper probe reveals that the traditional and local cultures have not taken it lying down. There is ample evidence of backlash in the form of re-invocation of ethnic pride and reiteration of cultural identities and distinctions. More noticeable is the substantial evidence of traditional cultures usurping the material and communicative resources of globalisation for proclaiming their identities and distinctions. On net balance then, we find considerable evidence of cultural transformation. As such. globalisation provides a site for the contest of economy and culture. As a form of economic reorganisation. globalisation has generated some measure of cultural change in India. At the same time, cultural systems have-also shown a great deal of vibrancy and agility to keep their identities intact in spite of the bulldozing effect of globalisation' The upshot of it all is that like the relationship between globalisation and social structure, the relationship between economic globalisation and culture is also not unilateral, but it is dialectical.

Coming to the third question, it may be observed with some measure of theoretical reflection that globalisation has generated limited socio-cultural transformation. Two points are particularly notable: one relates to the locus of change and the other to its direction. It is well known that the era of industrialisation heralded changes in the forces and relations of production, resulting in the emergence of capitalism and capitalist class structure Unlike that, the era of globalisation is marked by changes in the larger frame of social relations, i.e., in the mode of how people relate to one another beyond the frame of class relations. A discerning mind can see it that in the wake of globalisation, people have begun to relate themselves more in the frame of egalitarian relations than in terms of class relations. Globalisation has opened up opportunities for all to make a grade and be counted on his/her merit. To recall Friedman's phrase, it has led to the emergence of a 'flat world'. This obviously points to a new direction of change - from hierarchical to egalitarian, puritanical to liberal, and oppressive to emancipatory. A recall of the trends of change in the wake of globalisation clearly indicates such a direction. This renders the impact of globalisation distinguishable from that of industrialisation, which patronised a structure of unequal socioeconomic relations.

Undoubtedly, globalisation in its elemental form represents a project of hegemonic homogenisation of the world. Therefore, it is not so much because of its intent that globalisation has turned out to be an emancipatory force. Actually, this is due to the emergence of certain ideological developments which coincided with the course of globalisation, including the movements for gender justice, compensatory justice to the underprivileged, human rights and civil liberties. Many of these trends indeed emerged in the era of modernisation. Globalisation has only served to accelerate them. Thus, globalisation has not produced transformative trends all by itself, or independent of other factors and forces, but has certainly sharpened them in conjunction with several other forces.

REFERENCES

Aiyar S.S.A. (2006). "End of Poverty", *Sunday Times of India*, New Delhi, 17 December.

Appadurai A. (1996). *Modernity at Large: Cultural Discontents of Globalization*, Minneapolis, University of Minnesota Press.

Bhandare N. (2003). "Classified Information', *Hindustan Times*, December 4.

Bhat C. (2005). "Indian Diaspora and Transnational Networks: The Emergence of Global Networking among the Telugus", Presented at the International Seminar on Indian Diaspora, Vallab Vidya Nagar: Sardar Patel University, 4-5 January.

Castro F. (1998). *On Imperialist Globalization*, Leftwood Books, New Delhi.

Chang H.J. (2003). Kicking Away the Ladder: Development History, Anthem. London.

Das G. (2002). *India Unbound: From Independence to the Global Information Age*, Profile Books Ltd., London.

Dhanagare D.N. (2003). "Globalization: Towards an Alternative View", *Sociological Bulletin*, 52(1) March.

Friedman T.L. (2005). *World is Flat: A Brief History of the 21 Century*, Farrar, Strauss and Giroux, New York.

Friedman T. and Kaplan B. (2002). "States of Discord", *Foreign Policy*, March-April, pp. 64-70.

Fukuyama F. (1992). *The End of History and the Last Man*. Free Press, New York.

Giddens A. (1990). *The Consequences of Modernity*, Polity Press, Cambridge.

Huntington S.P. (1996). *The Clash of Civilisation and the Making of World Order*, Simon & Schuster, New York.

Kearney A.T. (2007). "Microsoft Case Studies", http:// www.microsoft.com/ casestudies.

Kumar, Pramod and S.L. Sharma (1998). *Suicides in Rural Punjab*, Institute for Development and Communication.

Lall R.R. (2007). "India's Super Rich are Getting Richer". *Times of India*, Chandigarh, May 10.

Malhotra I. (2006). "India's Economic Paradox. High Growth. Growing Disparities", *The Tribune*, October 20.

Robertson R. (1992). *Globalization: Social Theory and Global Culture*, Sage Publications, London.

Sharma, S.L. (1990). "Salience of Ethnicity in Modernization: Evidence From India", *Sociological Bulletin* 39 (1 & 2), March-September.

Sharma, S.L. (2003). "Globalization and its Socio-Cultural Discontents', in Paramjit S. Judge *et al.* (eds). *Development, Gender and Diaspora: Context of Globalization*, Rawal Publications. Jaipur and New Delhi.

Singh Y. (2000). *Culture Change in India: Identity and Globalization*, Rawal Publications, Jaipur and New Delhi.

Thorat S.D. (2001). "New Economic Policy and its Impact on Employment and Poverty of the Scheduled Castes", presented at the National Seminar on Liberalization, Dalits and the State, Chandigarh: Punjab University, Department of Sociology.

Varma P.K. (1998). *The Great Indian Middle Class*, Viking, New Delhi.

Vieira W.E. (1998). "Changing Marriage Mores", Business World, 22nd July.

Wadhwa S. (2004). "Sex Survey: Fleshed Out". *Outlook*, December 2.

Waters M. (1995). *Globalisation*, Routledge & Kegan Paul. London.

Wilson D. and Roopa P. (2003). "*Dreaming with BRICs: The Path to 2050*", www2.goldmansachs.com/ insight/research/ reports/99.pdf.

PART I
GLOBALIZATION, ECONOMY AND SOCIETY

Chapter 1

Impact of Globalization on Socio-Economic and Cultural Aspects of Rural Society

Surrendra G. Thakur

Historical Background of Globalization

The term globalization refers to the integration of economies of the world through uninhibited trade and financial flows, as also through mutual exchange of technology and knowledge. Ideally, it also contains free inter-country movement of labour. Harris (1993) defines globalization as "the increasing internationalization of the production, distribution and marketing of goods and services."

In context to India, this implies opening up the economy to foreign direct investment by providing facilities to foreign companies to invest in different fields of economic activity in India. It suggest to removing constraints and obstacles to the entry of MNCs in India, allowing Indian companies to enter into foreign collaborations and also encouraging them to set up joint ventures abroad; carrying out massive import liberalization programmes by switching over from quantitative restrictions to tariffs and import duties, therefore, globalization has been identified with the policy reforms of 1991 in India.

As the bright side of Globalization, the rate of growth of the Gross Domestic Product of India has been increased from 5.6 per cent during 1980-90 to seven per cent in the 1993-2001 periods. In the last four years, the annual growth rate of the GDP was impressive at 7.5 per cent (2003-04), 8.5 per cent (2004-05), nine per cent (2005-06) and 9.2 per cent (2006-07). As the Dark Side of Globalization, agriculture has been and still remains the backbone of the Indian economy. It plays a vital role not only in providing food and nutrition to the people, but also in the supply of raw material to industries and to export trade. In 1951, agriculture provided employment to 72 per cent of the population and contributed 59 per cent of the Gross Domestic Product. However, by 2001 the population depending upon agriculture came to 58 per cent, whereas the share of agriculture in the GDP went down drastically to 24 per cent and further to 22 per cent in 2006-07.

This has resulted in a lowering the per capita income of the farmers and increasing the rural indebtedness. In this way, Globalization is best understood, in terms of developing markets, deregulating business activities, privatizing state enterprises, lowering National barriers and expanding world trade and invests all creating a world community.

Impact of Globalization on Socio-Economic and Cultural Aspects of Agro-based Farmer through Information Technological Innovation

India primarily is an agricultural Nation. We Indians, work more, talk more, eat more and grow our own food. The Indian economic system is based on agriculture. The rural areas are still home to 72 per cent of the India's 1.1 billion people. A large number among these are poor and most of the rural poor depend on rain-fed agriculture and fragile forest for their livelihoods. Agriculture and cultivation is dependent on monsoon, and it needs hard work and patience, coordination and cooperation and a joint assimilation of peasants and farm labour. Hence it would not be an exaggeration to entitle peasants and labour the backbone of Indian agriculture.

In today's World of globalization the Information Technology has deeply affected all fields of knowledge and society, including agriculture. In addition, science and IT have proved to be a milestone in agricultural revolution. In this modern scenario, the coexistence of the peasant and farm labourer has undergone a sea change. Yet their combined efforts remain crucial to the health and growth of agriculture. Therefore, today both labour and information technology remain equally important for Indian agriculture.

Information technology (IT) is the use of computers and software to manage information. In some companies, this is referred to as management information services or simply as soft-skill services. The information technology department of a large company would be responsible for storing, protecting, processing and transmitting the information as necessary, and later retrieving information as required. The twenty first century is the age of IT which has affected trade, industry, education, knowledge, science, arts, music, transport, service, philosophy and even individual life, both outwardly as well as internally. In such an age, there has also been an impact on the peasant, farm labour, their roles and interrelationships for their work place and available market place.

The present research paper focuses on agricultural and agro based user resort and the manner in which farmers in these occupations are able to successfully obtain skilled and sufficient labour using IT in this Global era. It also attempts to throw light on socio-economic and cultural aspects of agro-based farmer through IT media in Global Modern World.

It is a present challenge to use and successfully employ appropriate media in socio-economic and cultural aspects of agro-based resort cultivator. If these media are to be used fully well, then there is no alternative to IT. Thus, we can conclude that it is possible to improve the human labour needed for agriculture and to keep it active in relation to occupations using IT. For this purpose, individual contact, group contact, mass contact, audio-visual aids and the combinations of methods are sometimes used individually or in blend. To sum up, it seems impossible to successfully make high gains in any profession without the fruitful use of Globalization through Information Technology.

Work Place and Labour Market Concept in Agro-Based Society

The term 'Work place' refers to a place where formal and informal groups collaborate as a team on employment tasks for short or indefinite period of time. The quality circle movement makes work groups central to the production system, with responsibility to study and resolve production problems. Thus, a farmer fixes upon a particular workplace for his farming and resort business and other such ancillary activities. While deciding upon a 'work place' the farmer has to focus equally on the farming activities as well as the 'resort' business for this purpose. Information Technology assumes extraordinary significance. It is only using IT that the farmer is able to successfully fulfil his responsibilities related to his business because of Globalization.

The term 'Labour market' refers to the market where human effort is made into a commodity which is bought and sold under terms which in law are deemed to constitute a contract. The manpower required spreading out agriculture or any related profession is known as 'labour'. The labour force required in this field needs to be skilled and trained in the agriculture as well as resort sector and be hard working while not required to be highly educated. IT makes it possible to provide information about such labour force and to get access to the same in a short time. As a result, all dealings related to resort are able to meet their entire labour demands in time and grow well.

Globalization is a process, which has affected many areas of human life, one of those being work place and labour market in agriculture as a socio-economic and culture aspects of agro-based resort farmer in rural India.

Objectives and Methodology

I. Objectives

1. To know the availability of household amenities and assets by agro-based resort farmer.
2. To understand the impact of Globalization through IT on the business of agro-based resort farmer.
3. To study the impact of globalization on socio-economic and culture aspects of agro-based farmer in India.

Theoretical Perspective

Constructive sociology a new approach is used for this research paper. Here, Impact of Globalization through IT is provided liberty, integrity, efficiency, new identity and rational control of socio-economic and cultural life of agro-based resort farmer.

II. Research Design

It includes all the strategies or decisions taken to conduct the field study after formulating a research problem.

III. Dimensions or Paradigms of Research

Mixed method (qualitative and quantitative) of social research and in-depth interview method having a set of questions is used as a tool of data collection. In addition, observation method was also used when required.

IV. Sample Design

Universe of the study or Geographical area of the study: The universe of the study is conducted among rural villages located in India.

Sources of Data Collection

The sources used for data collection are primary as well as secondary. The primary sources include peasants only from rural village. The secondary sources include periodicals, research journals, internet, articles etc.

Sample Size

Total population of agro-based resort farmer in this village is forty six. Fifty per cent of the peasant population is twenty respondents selected out of this universal area for research. This population has homogeneous character by occupation as resort business.

Sampling Technique

Simple random method used for selecting respondent for avoiding bias.

Sampling Frame

For random sampling, researcher has collected valid, updated and complete list of village from village Pãnchayat.

Sample Unit

Only agro-based resort farmer are respondents of this research.

Method of Data Collection

Observation and interview schedule used for collecting data.

Tool for Data Collection

Questionnaire and interview guide are (written format instruments) used for data collection.

Tool Design

For preparing tool design operational design, variables and the levels of measurements.

Statistically Analysis

In this design, researcher has to decide where to use correlation test, chi-square test and where to use bar chart, pie chart etc. In this research, researcher used statistically analysis software SPSS.

Discussion

Kothalaj, a village in Akotala block of Ambala district in Haryana has an entirely different look today from what it was fifteen years before. Thanks to the coordinated efforts of the farmers, InfoTech, labour and government, has got at least one 'resort' in each home as an agro based business. Poverty has been totally eradicated so also illiteracy. Each member of community earns ₹ 4000 to 6000 per month from this resort business. What made this sea-change possible? Fifteen years are not much in the histories of Indian village which are prone to remain static frescos in the Indian development firmament. How has Kothalaj been able to present a success story, deviating from the present trend of rural poverty, ill health, illiteracy and unhygienic condition? The answer lies in the one name which is 'Globalization and Information Technology'—Kothalaj village is becoming an importanι destination

Table 1.1: Education of Peasants

Years of Education	*Frequency*	*%*	*Valid %*
4	1	5.0	5.0
7	3	15.0	15.0
10	5	25.0	25.0
12	6	30.0	30.0
15	4	20.0	20.0
17	1	5.0	5.0
Total	20	100.0	100.0

It is seen that the education frequency of the agro-based resort farmer in Kothalaj village. Thirty per cent peasants have completed their Higher Secondary education means 12 years of education. The minimum years of education are 4 and maximum are 17 years of education with the range of 1. Seventy five per cent of the peasants have up to 12 years of education and 25 per cent of the peasants have completed up to 17 years of education. Over all observation is that all farmers from this village are literate people and it is advantage for developing any business like resort.

The data of this research has been collected through peasant's in-depth interview, participatory observation and using interview schedule. Ninety five per cent farmers were found to be engaged in resort as well as farm business in 'Kothalaj' taluka Akotala. Some of them were found to arrange housing and boarding as a resort at their own houses for the tourists. Some of them were totally professional so they have even changed the structure of their own houses to attract the tourists. In spite of lot of efforts, agricultural production has been failure before fifteen years. Consequently, farmers for their livelihood, had chose their agro based tourism as occupation.

Table 1.2: Selection of Agro-based Resort as a Profession—Socio-cultural Change

Causes for selecting resort business	*Frequency*	*%*
Need	9	45.0
Interest	8	40.0
No other option	3	15.0
Total	20	100.0

In this village, each and every farmer has put up the hoardings, banners, advertisements and available service facilities to attract the tourists in front of their houses. Also the farmers have access to mobiles, internet, TV, computer, Laptop and professional website for their agro based resort business. Some of these farmers are associated with HTDC (Haryana Tourism Development Corporation) and connect with tourists directly. In this way, these farmers are able to connect with tourists using individual contact (i.e. mobile), group contact (i.e. e-mail), mass contact (i.e. hoardings or MTDC), audio-video aids like banners and combination of method like mouth advertise, newspapers etc. Agro based resort business is needed by forty five per cent (45%) of peasants and already so many farmers were financially strong they had interest to occupy this type of business. Only fifteen per cent peasants accepted this business because they didn't have any option for survival. The researcher has found one thing in this village is that, these farmers are very possessive and believe in hard work and ready to use different assets for their business as a part of Globalization or Global World, that is why they are succeeded in this business.

Table 1.3: Purposes of Household Amenities and Assets

Purpose of household amenities and assets	*Frequency*	*Per cent*
Calling labour	2	10.0
Advertisement	5	25.0
Marketing facilities	3	15.0
For all facilities	8	40.0
Any others	2	10.0
Total	20	100.0

Labour is the rock stone of this occupation. On permanent basis labour are not available in this village. However, labourers are available on hourly basis like, two hours, four hours or six hours etc. The neighbourhood and the women have an important role as a labour for this occupation. Mobile, internet, television, computer, fax, scan, Laptop, website, hoardings and banner are household amenities and assets used by these farmers for calling labour, for advertisement and accessing all market facilities for their customer because of Global market and Liberalization, privatization. Almost all problems of labour were solved by mutual cooperation of women through mobile and telephone in this village. Much urgency demands and medical facilities are fulfilled as early as possible with the help of IT. Information technology is used for calling labour, for advertisement, for marketing facilities and other necessary need of tourist. Agriculture is very costly and entirely depends on monsoon. Thus, the loss is inevitable many a times. However, the reality is to successfully carry out both these occupations simultaneously for survival. It is possible, only when, you are taking the support of Information Technology for work place as a resort and labour market as neighbourhood women. It means that, Information technology through Globalization plays a role as a catalyst for developing agro based resort business.

Conclusion

In this way the agro-based Resort Farmers of Indian village are found using complete Information Technology globally through mobiles, Internet, e-mail-communication, computers, fax, scan, hoardings, newspapers, even personal blogs and websites of their own and the governmental agencies like HTDC. To follow the profession of resort, originally the geographical structure of this area was responsible, as the overload of water restrained them from growing crops like rice and therefore, they started without option the profession of resort. Today the same profession has become one of the most important professions there. The neighbourhood labour especially women are helping effortlessly to grow this profession with all its fruitful possibilities.

In this way, Globalization has led to specialisation, expansion of the market and finance of scale. It creates free movement of labour. It implies emergence of rich powerful corporations and there is also encouragement to selective immigration of skilled persons.

REFERENCES

Baviskar, Amita. (2010). *In the Belly of the River*. New Delhi: Oxford University Press.

Beteille, Andre. (2010). *Caste, Class and Power*. New Delhi: Oxford University Press.

Rajan, R.V. (2011). 'The Complex Dynamics of Rural Marketing and Communication', *Vidhura* (34-36).

Singh, Yogendra. (2009). *Social stratification and change in India*. New Delhi: Manohar Publishers and Distributors.

Thariyan, Ninan. (2011). 'Media and Advertising Grapple with Constantly Changing Roles', *Vidura* (27-29).

Bender, Peter. (1961). *The Community and Social Change in America*. Baltimore: John Hopkins University Press.

Foster, Janet. (1990). *Crime and Community in the City*. New York: Routledge.

T.K. Velayudham. *Globalization Trend and Issues*.

Globalization and Poverty: Centre for International Economics, Australia.

Globalization and India—Lecture: Prof. Sagar Jain, University of N.Carolina.

V.N. Ray's lecture on 'Repositioning India in the Globalised World'.

A.K. Ojha. (2002). "Globalization and Liberalisation" Prospects of New World Order, *Third Concept—An International Journal of Ideas*, August.

Chapter 2

Globalization and Socio-Economic Concerns in India

Manoj Sharma

Introduction

Present-day globalization has produced many changes in our socio-economy. A society can only be developed when all the amenities are fulfilled or achieved. In India certain issues have been over come and achieved but still since India's Independence in 1947, country is facing several social and economic issues.

Socio-Economic Challenges

Public Health System

In India Public Health System suffers from many problems which includes insufficient funding, shortage of facilities leading to overcrowding and severe shortage of trained health personnel. There is also lack of accountability in the public health delivery mechanisms. These are some of the reasons which have placed India at the lowest rank in the Human Development Index. India, however, holds top position in migration of physicians to developed countries like the UK and the US. According to Planning Commission the country has a shortfall of six lakh doctors, 10 lakh nurses and two lakh dental surgeons. For every 10,000 Indians, there is just one doctor.

Solution

- In every state construction of hospital on the model of AIIMS;
- Opening of hospital with all the modern facilities in the areas of SC/ST;
- Opening of new medical colleges in the public private partnership;
- Increase in medical seats in all the colleges;
- Fill all the medical vacancies especially in the rural areas of the country;
- Motivating the youth to work in rural parts of the country; and
- Free checkup and other facilities at all hospitals.

Population

India suffers from the problem of over-population. The population of India is very high and ranks second in the world, and is expected to be the most populated country by 2040.

Solution

- Special increments to the government employees, if they adopt the small family structure;
- Monthly incentive for the family adopting the small family;
- Advertising and educating about the benefits of small family;
- Advertising and educating about plans launched by the government; and
- To take the regular feedback regarding the implemented programmes by the government.

Unemployment

The problem of unemployment has become a massive. Various problems have caused this problem. There are individual factors like age, vocational unfitness and physical disability. External factors includes economic and technical factors. Other factors like shut down of the sick industries, unplanned and uncontrolled growth of technology is causing havoc on job opportunity. Our educational system has its own irrevocable defects and its contribution to the unemployment is an open truth. Our education does not prepare the minds of young generation to become self-employed on the contrary it makes them dependent on government vacancies which are hard to come.

Solution

- Promotion of concept of entrepreneurship amongst youth of the nation;
- Loans on zero interest to start entrepreneurship;
- Promote village tourism and SSIs;
- Motivating the farmers to cultivate cash crops; and
- Continue with the seed and fertilizer subsidy to the farmers.

Education

Since the Constitution of India was finalized in 1949, education has remained one of the priorities of the Indian government. The first Education Minister Maulana Azad founded a system of education which aimed to provide free education at the primary level. Primary education was made free and compulsory for children from 6 to 14, and child labour was banned. The government introduced incentives to education—for instance, the provision of mid-day meals in schools were introduced and the largest of such initiatives is Sarva Shiksha Abhiyan, which actively promoted "Education for All". The Right of Children to Free and Compulsory Education Act was also imposed in 2009. Despite these initiatives, education continues to persist as an impediment to development.

Issues

- While many schools were built, they had poor infrastructure and inadequate facilities. Schools in the rural areas were especially affected. According to District Information System for Education (DISE) in India, only about 51.5 per cent of all schools in India have boundary walls, 16.65 per cent have computers and 39 per cent have electricity.
- Furthermore, the absence rates of teachers and students were high, while their retainment rates low. The incentives for going to school were not apparent, while punishment for absence was not enforced. Despite the government's decree on compulsory education and the child labour ban, many children were still missing classes to go to work. The government did not interfere even when children missed school.
- Economic and social disparities also plague the fundamentals of

the education system. Rural children are less able to receive education because of greater opportunity costs, and rural children have to work to contribute to the family's income. According to the Annual Status of Education in 2009, the average attendance rate of students in the rural states is about 75 per cent. Though this rate varies significantly, states like Uttar Pradesh and Bihar had more than 40 per cent absentees during a random visit to their schools. In the urban states, more than 90 per cent of the students were present in their schools during a visit.

Solution

- Ensure time bound construction of infrastructure and provide adequate facilities in the schools;
- More focus on technical education right from middle level schooling;
- To make compulsory to every private/convent school to enroll 50 per cent students from the rural and BPL families;
- Proper implementation of all the government policies and proper feedback of them;
- To shut down immediately those universities running from one room; and
- To fill all the teaching and non-teaching posts at all levels of education.

Economic Issues

Poverty

One-third of India's population (roughly equivalent to the entire population of the United States) lives below the poverty line and India is home to one-third of the world's poor people.

Though the high class has gained from recent positive economic developments, India suffers from substantial poverty. According to the World Bank's estimates on poverty, India has 456 million people, 41.6 per cent of its population, living below the new international poverty line of $1.25 (PPP) per day. The World Bank further estimates that 33 per cent of the global poor now reside in India. Moreover, India also has 828 million people or 75.6 per cent of the population living below $2 a day, compared to 72.2 per cent for Sub-Saharan Africa.

Solution

- Construction of special pool of states facing this problem maximum;
- Construction of special homes for the beggars and other such people and involve them in some innovative work;
- Free primary and higher education to all such people;
- Re-looking the policies framed for the upliftment of the poor;
- Involvement of NGOs and also a proper check on their working; and
- Continuous feedback of the programmes implemented by the government.

Wealth Distribution

Wealth distribution in India is fairly uneven, with the top 10 per cent of income groups earning 33 per cent of the income. Despite significant economic progress, one-fourth of the nation's population earns less than the government-specified poverty threshold of $0.40/day. A 2007 report by the state-run National Commission for Enterprises in the Unorganized Sector (NCEUS) found that 25 per cent of Indians or 236 million people, lived on less than 20 rupees per day with most working in "informal labour sector with no job or social security, living in abject poverty."

Solution

- Strict implementation of new Companies Act, which says that some specified companies have to adopt compulsory social responsibilities (Clause 132);
- Government must continue with social reforms and try to provide more employment opportunities for the people leaving BPL.

Water Supply and Sanitation

Most of the population in India for agriculture still dependent on the rain water. In the 21st century we have witnessed many cases of suicide by our farmers because of draught in their area and they are unable to payback their loans either to bank or indigenous bankers.

Further, lack of proper sanitation is a major concern for India. Statistics conducted by UNICEF have shown that only 31 per cent of India's population is using improved sanitation facilities as of 2008.http:/

/en.wikipedia.org/wiki/Socio-economic_issues_in_India-cite_note-unicef-stats-14. It is estimated that one in every ten deaths in India is linked to poor sanitation and hygiene. A lack of adequate sanitation also leads to significant economic losses for the country. A Water and Sanitation Programme (WSP) study of the Economic Impacts of Inadequate Sanitation in India (2010) showed that inadequate sanitation caused India considerable economic losses, equivalent to 6.4 per cent of India's GDP.

Solution

- Proper utilization of available water in the country;
- Every year selecting the 3 to 4 states which are affected the most form draught and Construction of the canals in the strict time manner;
- Advertising and educating the people about the importance of construction of toilets and framing the policies to construct free of cost toilets especially in the rural areas; and
- Introducing some chapters at the school level on the problems of water supply and sanitation.

Corruption

Corruption is widespread in India. In India, corruption takes the form of bribes, evasion of tax and exchange controls, black money etc. Recently country has witnessed biggest ever corruption cases.

Solution

- *"Taking and giving bribe both are crimes"* strict implementation of this rule;
- To advertise the corruption in such a way that this is the kind of disease that will destroy the entire country;
- Concessions to the employees and small business houses if they deposit their taxes in advance as for corporate houses; and
- Motivating the people to declare their black money and formulation of a strong and durable policy to get back the country's money.

Violence

Religious Violence

Constitutionally India is a secular state, but large-scale violence have periodically occurred in India since independence. In recent decades, communal tensions and religion-based politics have become more prominent which will be very dangerous for the nation in future.

Terrorism

The regions which are affected mostly by terrorism are Jammu and Kashmir, Central India (Naxalism) and some parts of northern states. After most acts of terrorism in India, it seems that Pakistan is playing the major role in importing the terrorism to India. Recently, both the US and Afghanistan have accused Pakistan of carrying out terrorist acts in Afghanistan.

Naxalism

Naxalism is an informal name given to communist groups that were born out of the Sino-Soviet split in the Indian communist movement. Ideologically they belong to various trends of Maoism. Initially the movement had its centre in West Bengal. In recent years, they have spread into less developed areas of rural central and eastern India, such as Chattisgarh and Andhra Pradesh.

Caste Related Violence

Over the years, various incidents of violence against *Dalits* have been reported from many parts of India. At the same time, many violent protests by *Dalits*, such as the 2006 *Dalit* protests in Maharashtra, have been reported as well.

Solution

- To impart the compulsory training at school level to deal with the terrorist activities;
- To expose the Pakistan at every international forum;
- Modernization of our security forces;
- To motivate the people to laid down their weapons;
- For the proper harmony in the society, ensuring regular talk between different religious groups and try to constitute a joint forum of them.

Conclusion

The basic idea of this exercise is just to highlight those issues that still we have to address and also to suggest some remedies to the concerned authorities to overcome these challenges.

REFERENCES

Bhandari, Amit and Almas Heshmati, (2005), "Measurement of Globalization and Its Variations Among Countries, Regions and Over Time", IZA Discussion Papers 1578, Institute for the Study of Labour (IZA).

David, Held, Anthony McCrew, David Gold Blat, and Jonathan Perrato, (1999), *Global Transformation: Politics, Economics and Culture*, Stanford University Press.

Global Economic Symposium, (2010), "Democracy and Development", www.global-economicsymposium.org.

Jaffee, David, (1998), *Levels of Socio-Economic Development Theory*, Greenwood Publishing Group.

Robinson, William, (2005), "Globalization, the World System, and Democracy Promotion" in *US Foreign Policy Theory and Society*.

Chapter 3

Impact of Globalization on Socio-Economic Mobility Among Scheduled Castes Residing in Rural Area

Amrit Kaur

Rural communities in India are stratified on the line of caste differentiation and class interests, thereby giving rise to mutual prejudices, suspicion cleavage and factions. Rural society in India is typical in its social and economic life. It has unique characteristics of kinship, greater rigidity of social structure, and also greater homogeneity than the highly advance societies. These characteristic features are undergoing changes as a result of several forces. Globalization, education, industrialization and urbanization, and contact of the people with foreign cultures are a few major forces that have favoured the transformation of the rural society in India. Several measures adopted by the government and also responsible to considerable extent for these changes.

Globalization, industrial and urban impacts have revolutionized the life of the village communities. Urban attractions, scarcity of fertile lands and lack of employment opportunities have forced the villagers to migrate to urban areas in search of urban occupations. Those who work in the urban centre are subjected to urban influence who, in turn have influenced the life and the attitudes of the villagers. They have imitated the urban way of life. There is a change noticed in the dress and the food habits. Many of the urban dishes have found place in these villages. Drinking coffee and tea have become regular items in their daily life. Youth who go to work in the city differ in dress from those who remain in the village doing farm work. The youth particularly in these villages, who are either employed in the factories or who have frequent urban contacts, resist the authoritarian dominance of the father, and have developed a tendency to disregard the traditional occupations. As a result of the impact of these forces mentioned above the values of land and buildings have also increased. The improved economic opportunities have revolutionized the attitudes of the rural people. The use of cosmetics, the use of soap for bath, and the types of dress they wear, in these villages are all the indications of urban and industrial influences.

Globalization and Rural Development

Rural development has emerged as a distinctive field of research and has acquired a central role in theory and practices of development right from the 1950s when it began with a stress on the community development approach: the pursuit if which has been following ever changing Perspectives on development over these years. Accordingly, there have been concomitant changes in policies and approaches to rural development. In fact, concepts of development have provoked compelling questions about pattern, values, methods, action and choices every time there is a change in development perspective. From attempts to answer these questions, the development paradigms are still competing (at an ideological level) and therefore, prone to further change. In the process, the rate of obsolescence of development fashions and ideas accelerates (Chambers, 1993:1) and there have been many 'development fashions' over the years (Haq, 1976). Moreover, the concept of development is no more viewed in terms of only economic analysis. In view of these changing perspectives on development, there has been emerging a sharpened, broadened and holistic concept (Hope, 1984: 64) in each new development paradigm.

Even in the age of globalization, rural development has acquired the central role in international development discourse. This is because there is a shift in development paradigm along with the process of globalization that emphasizes on 'reversals' of the approach, more precisely, 'putting the last first' (Chambers, 1983, 1993). Put otherwise, the new development paradigm that has emerged and is taking shape right from the early 1990s, precisely with the Human Development Report of 1990, lays emphasis on 'enlarging people's choices'. This bottom up approach to development is put into practice within the theoretical and empirical frame of good governance, decentralized and micro-level planning, and for participatory development. Obviously, the context is rural development as policy and practices, and also a process *vis-à-vis* globalization.

Change can be observed in many aspects of rural life in India: in fact changes are the dominant theme in villages. Different forces of modernization created and improved means of communication increase in the scale of economic and social activities and other factors largely ideological in nature have affected Socio-Economic relationships in rural areas. To a certain extent, the availability of goods and services on cash and altered the scale of social interaction in villages. The changing rural scene provides an important area for investigation to social scientists.

Caste System of Rural India

Caste is a powerful organization in rural society. It determines the functions, the status, the rank and the available opportunities as well as the handicaps for an individual. Castes difference determines the difference among individuals. It also determines the domestic and social life, the type of houses and the cultural patterns of the people. It is also noticed that even land ownership in rural society exists on caste lines. Caste has further favoured the social distance, and superior-inferior relations existing in society. Such an institution has also undergone change owing to political and ideological forces. Many of the functions of caste have undergone modification and it is slowly losing its validity. Its role, which used to determine the opportunities available to individuals for material, for cultural self-advancement, has changed. Its monopoly in matter of economic power educational and cultural facilities has disappeared. As a result of these changes, frictions among caste-groups are commonly noticed. They are largely visible in elections. Sometimes, these tensions are also visible in struggle in local organizations for material gains and supremacy of power.

It is further noticed that caste rigidity is gradually breaking down. Restrictions against eating and drinking have been loosened. Slowly, because of the contact of the people with the urban and industrial centres as well as global word, inter-dining and into drinking are spreading from the town into the villages. Any breakdown of the rigidities in this respect is considered revolutionary and serves itself as a source of further changes. Education opportunities have further destroyed many of the traditional caste restrictions. Caste professions have also been changed as a result of market economy and socio-economic transformation which have taken place after independence. The old hierarchy of caste system based on birth, status and ritual hallmarks is being transformed into a new hierarchy. Owing to those changes, castes are new competing with castes. Sometimes, power shifts from some of the upper castes remain low and become weaker in this conflict.

Social Status of Scheduled Caste in Rural Areas

Social status of a person in the society is determined by caste, class, occupation, income etc. In the category of Scheduled Caste there is majority of service provider castes. But these days the social status of a person is determined by the education, wealth and types of Government/ Private Jobs. These days due to reservation, impact of globalization, urbanization and other facilities provided by the Government to the Scheduled Castes are helpful to arise their level of standard of life. When I asked to my respondents that how they feel about their social status in the village and how they were treated by the people of upper castes in the village, most of them answered that they were treated indifferently. Very few of them answered that they were treated badly by the people of upper castes in the village. Thus we concluded that most of the people among the Scheduled Castes were treated indifferently by the people of dominant castes.

Objectives

- To explore the influence of globalization on rural Scheduled Caste people.
- To explore the socio-economic factor's effect due to globalization.

Methodology

The present study attempts to assess the impact of globalization on Socio-Economic mobility among the Scheduled Castes in the two villages of Rupnagar (Rural Area, i.e. Dugri and Mugalmagri) Districts of Punjab in India. Proper care was taken to collect information with the application of both primary and secondary sources. Accordingly, an interview schedule was prepared and questions were framed both open ended and close ended, for the purpose of data collection through primary source. Apart from that, a few secondary sources of data collection like observation of respondents and their family background, informal talks with the family members of the respondents, focused group discussion (FGD) were held for the purpose of getting supplementary information regarding the study.

50 respondents from each village have been taken as a sample size "Snow Ball Sampling Method" was used for collection of data.

Village Profile

The study was carried out in the two villages of Rupnagar District of Punjab. As far as, the demographic profile of the village is concerned, there are about 2998 households in the village. There are *pucca* houses for every family unit in the village. Mostly people are small businessman, e.g. tailor, confectioner shop, vegetable vendors etc. There is one government senior secondary school at the entrance of Dugri village. Apart from that, there are about four places of worship to meet the religious and spiritual requirements of the residents. In Dugri village there is separate Temple and Gurdawara for Scheduled Caste people.

Data Discussion

After collecting the data, the information collected was coded and tabulated on the basis of the responses given by the respondents, in order to generalize the responses of the respondents.

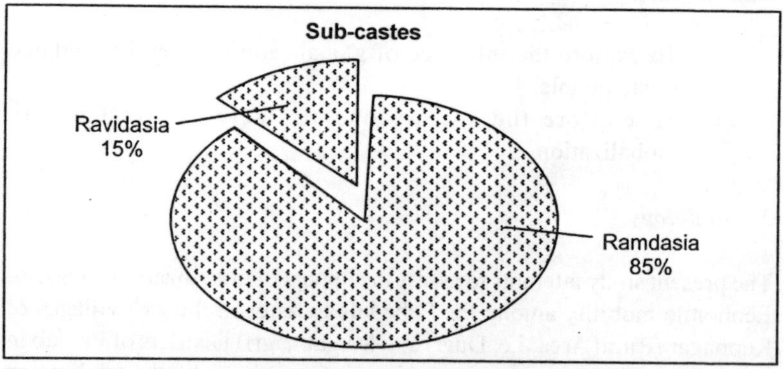

Fig. 3.1: Distribution of the Respondents according to their Sub-Castes

It is important to state that 38 sub-castes have been listed in the Scheduled Caste Category in Punjab. The Sub-Caste distribution of the Sampled Respondents indicated that the major Sub-Castes in the two villages are Ravidasia and Ramdasia. Out of the total Respondents Ramadasia constitutes 85 per cent and Ravidasia constitutes 15 per cent.

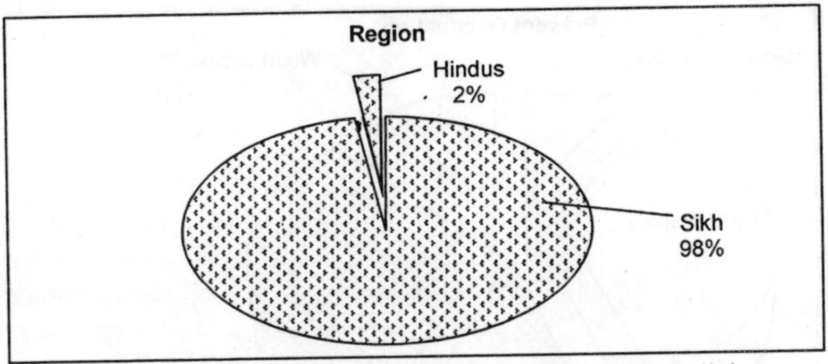

Fig. 3.2: Distribution of the Respondents according to their Religion

The Pie Chart shows that out of the total respondents 98 per cent are Sikhs and 2 per cent are Hindus. Thus we can say that majority of our respondents are of Sikh community in two villages.

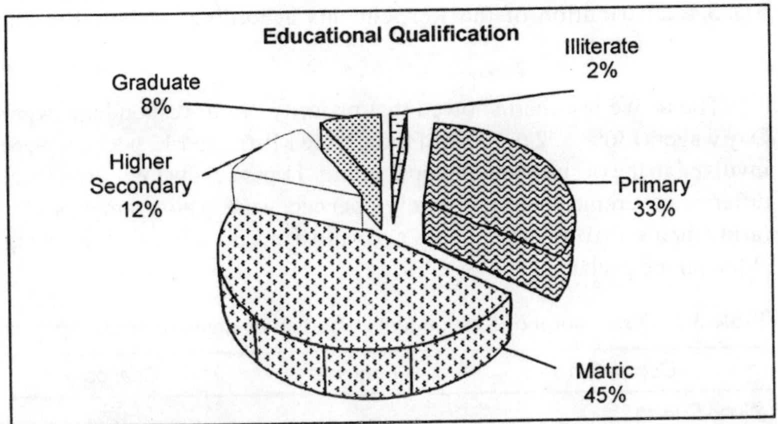

Fig. 3.3: Distribution of the Respondents according to their Educational Qualification

The Pie Chart shows the level of education of the respondents. It shows that 2 per cent respondents were illiterate, 33 per cent respondents were Primary, 12 per cent respondents were Higher secondary and the majority of our respondents (45%) were educated up to Matric level. It also shows the mostly head of families were educated. There is a few numbers of respondents who were well educated, like Graduation, those are only 8 per cent.

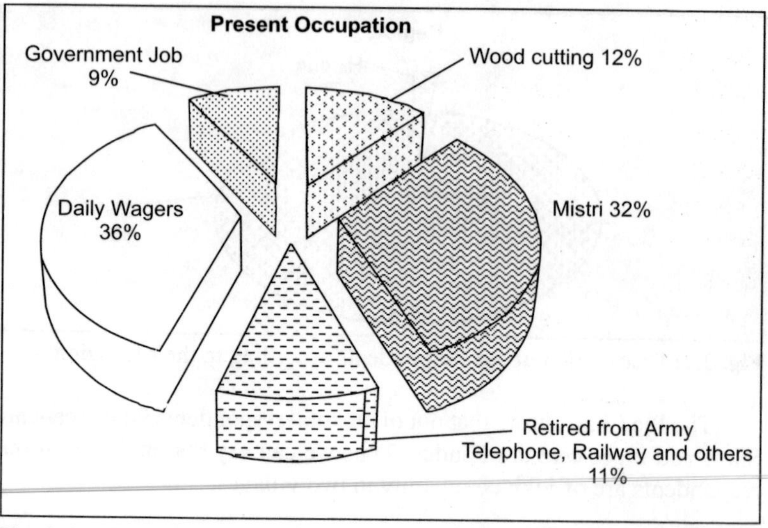

Fig. 3.4: Distribution of the Respondents according to their Present Occupation

The above pie chart showed that majority of our respondents were Day wagers (36%). 32 per cent of them were Mistri, and 12 per cent were involved in the occupation of woodcutting, 11 per cent were retired from different government jobs and hardly 9 per cent were in government sector (army men's, drivers in roadways and railways, and some were working at telephone exchange etc.).

Table 3.1: Distribution of Respondents who had changed their Occupation

Occupation	*Previous*	*Change*
Wood Cutting	3%	12%
Mistri	6%	32%
Retired	6%	11%
Daily Wagers	6%	36%
Government Jobs	3%	9%
Weavers	80%	0%
No change	2%	0%

It is interesting to observe that Ramdasia sub-caste is not following their traditional work named weaving. Majority of them had changed their occupation and adopted the other occupations. Due impact of globalization on their life style they changed their occupations. It was revealed that lack of input in their previous traditional business forced them to change their occupation. There was only 2 per cent of respondents who never changed their occupation.

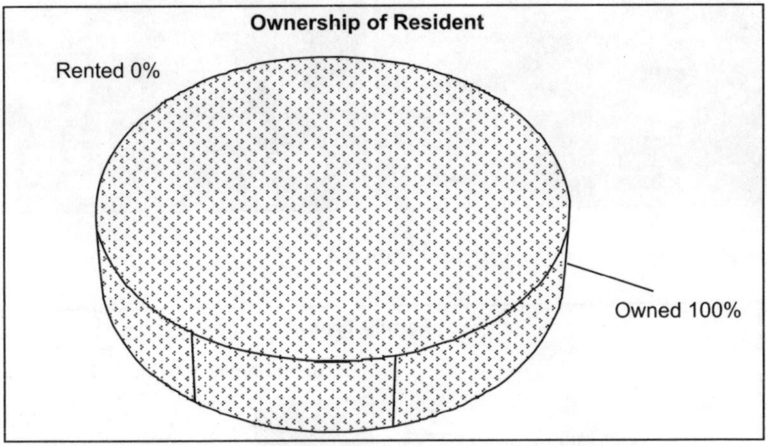

Fig. 3.5: Distribution of the Respondents according to Ownership of Resident

The Pie Chart shows that 100 per cent respondents have their own houses and no single respondent lives in rented home at both villages.

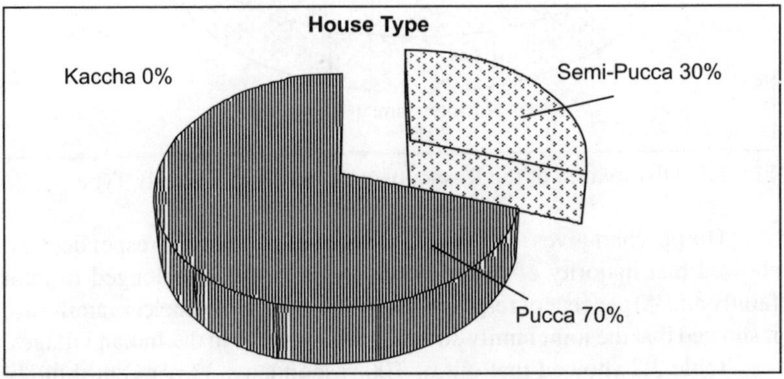

Fig. 3.6: Distribution of the Respondents according to their House Type

Pie chart shows that there was no signal respondent who had kaccha house. Out of 100 Respondents 30 per cent had semi-pucca houses. Apart from the 70 per cent respondents lived in their own pucca houses.

Photo 3.1

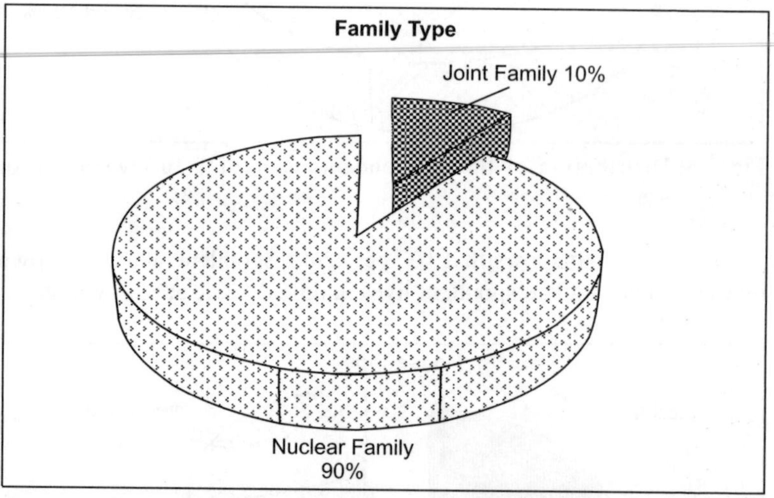

Fig. 3.7: Distribution of the Respondents according to Family Type

The pie chart gives the analysis of type of the family of respondents. It showed that majority of our respondents (10%) were belonged to joint family and 90 per cent of respondents were belonged to nuclear family. So, it showed that the joint family structure still prevails in the Indian villages.

Table 3.2 showed that out of 100 respondents 32 per cent thought that Economy had changed their life, 9 per cent of the respondents felt that education had improved their lives. 16 per cent were reported that the change had come in their lives due to the social contact with other communities, 10 per cent due to media, 14 per cent due to communication, 9 per cent due to transportation and 7 per cent due to awareness.

Table 3.2: Factors Responsible for Change in the Lives of the Respondents

Factors	*Percentage*
Education	11
Social	16
Economic	32
Psychological	10
Communication	14
Media	6
Transportation	8
Awareness	3

Table 3.3 showed that 100 per cent of respondents had television, ceiling fan and table fan, L.P.G., Chulha, mobile phone appliances, 98 per cent of them had refrigerator. 90 per cent had DVD, Telephone and Cycle. 85 per cent of them had room cooler, 68 per cent respondents had motor cycle, 50 per cent had washing machines.

Table 3.3: Distribution according to ownership of Household Assets

Assets	*Percentage*
Cycle	90
Car	5
Telephone	90
Television	100
Refrigerator	98
Celling Fan/Table Fan	100
Room Cooler	85
D.V.D.	90
Washing Machine	50
L.P.G.	100
Chulha	100
Mobile	100
Motor Cycle	68

The Pie Chart shows the Relationship of upper caste people towards Scheduled Castes. When we asked them how they were treated by the people of upper caste in the village. Most of them, i.e. 98 per cent answered that they were treated equal, good and 2 per cent answered that they were treated badly by the people of upper castes in the village.

Photo 3.2

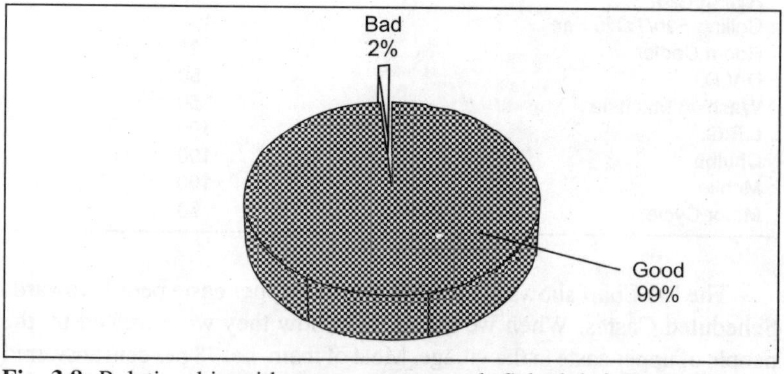

Fig. 3.8: Relationship with upper caste towards Scheduled Castes

Table 3.4: Knowledge about the concept of 'Globalization'

Knowledge about the concept	*Percentage*
Globalization	Nil
Westernization	15
Modernization	85

Above Table shows the knowledge of the respondents about the terms—Globalization, Westernization, Modernization. While analyzing the knowledge of Globalization, we found that out of 100 respondents, none was aware about the term Globalization but 15 per cent respondents know about the term Westernization and 85 per cent respondents were aware of Modernization. Thus we can say that majority of our respondents were not aware of Globalization, because most of them were not highly qualified.

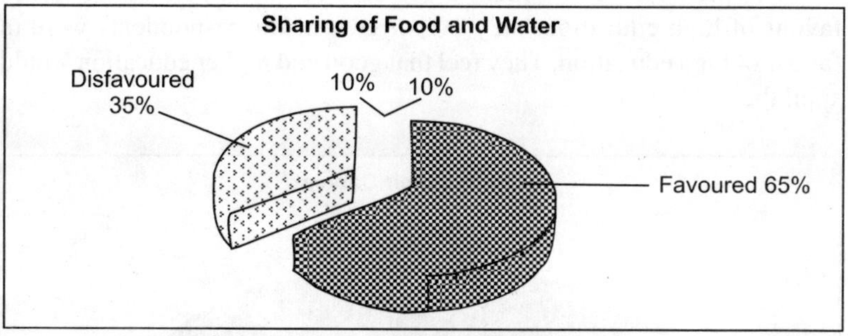

Fig. 3.9: Feelings of Scheduled Castes for taking food and water by Higher Caste people

In the above pie chart 65 per cent respondents out of 100 respondents were felt that the higher caste people were now in favour of taking food or water from Scheduled Castes and 35 per cent respondents were not in favour of taking food or water from them. Thus we can say that due to education and modern occupations the SCs were taking off their traditional unclean occupations, most of the people of upper and middle strata were in favour of taking food or water from the lower caste people. So we concluded that the restriction and bondage of caste system are broken due to the globalization, westernization, modernization, education and availability of legal provisions by Government.

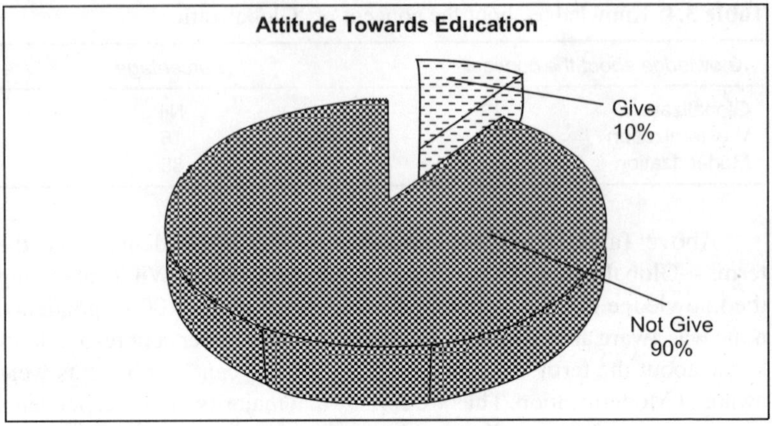

Fig. 3.10: Attitude of respondents towards Education

The pie chart shows that 90 per cent of respondents were not in favour of high education, only 10 per cent of the respondents were in favour of high education. They feel that good and higher education would spoil their children.

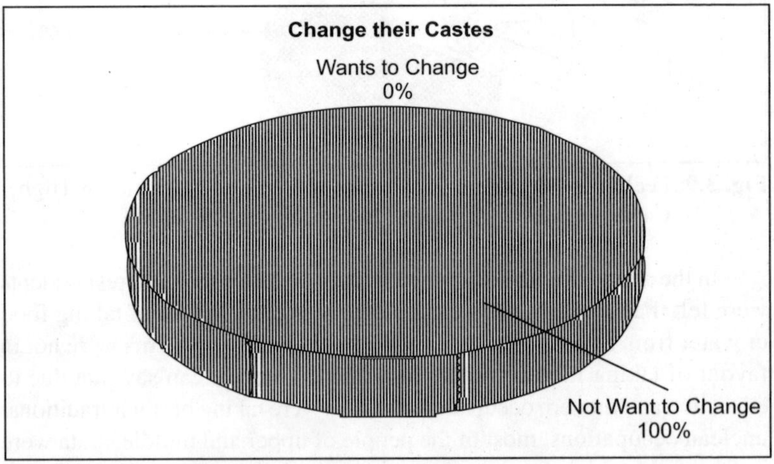

Fig. 3.11: Respondent's views about to change their Caste

The pie chart shows that 100 per cent of respondents in two villages don't want to change their caste. They were happy in their own castes.

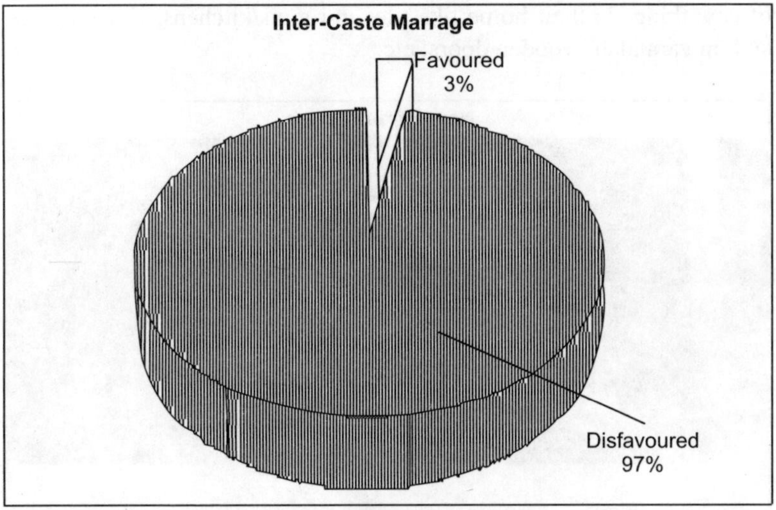

Fig. 3.12: Respondent's views about Inter-Caste Marriage

The pie chart showed that 97 per cent respondents were not in favour of inter-caste marriage but 3 per cent were in favour of inter-caste marriage.

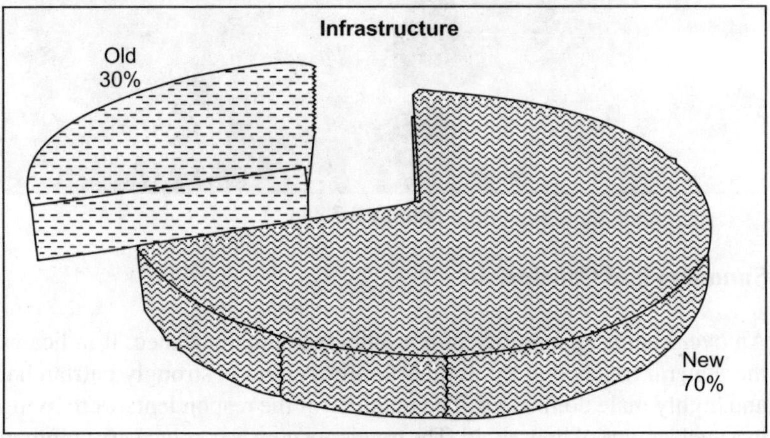

Fig. 3.13: Distribution according to Infrastructure

Pie chart 3.13 showed that 70 per cent of respondents had new infrastructure and 30 per cent had old infrastructure. They had used lots of new things in their home like tiles in rooms/kitchens, chine's ports, sink in varandah, wooden doors, etc.

Photo 3.3

Summary and Conclusions

An overwhelming majority of households are male headed. It indicates the general trends that the Indian family system is strongly patriarchal and highly male dominated. The majority of the respondents were living in a nuclear type of household. The trends are now becoming very common in rural areas too, which was once known for a traditionally joint family system. While studying the occupational patterns of the respondents, it was revealed in this study that the large number of respondents were working on daily wages and very few of them were employed in government/private services. It is interesting to observe that Ramdasia sub-caste is not following their traditional work named weaving. Majority of them had changed their occupation and adopted the other occupations due to global trade. These respondents changed their previous occupation due to heavy loss. They started occupations other than their traditional occupation. It was observed that all of the respondents had their own houses and majority of them resided in *pucca* houses. It was also noticed that they had all kinds of luxury assets in their houses like T.V. telephones, D.V.D., sitting pots, motor vehicles, marbled houses and well-furnished furniture and infrastructure. Education, communications, media, transportation, psychological mind and social contacts with other communities found major factors of changes in the Scheduled Caste people in rural areas. In the end it was also found that majority (90%) of Scheduled Caste people were not in favour of higher education.

The forces of globalization are likely to change the life style and cultural practice of the people, since the world is going to be a global village. The value system of the people is becoming more and more individualistic and materialistic. The association between the life styles and the impact of globalization was examined and found to be statistically significant. It was observed that the respondents with low change in their life styles had perceived high impact of globalization as compared to the respondent with high change in their life styles.

It was found that majority of the respondents did not experience untouchability and most of them said that their relationship with the other castes was good and quite a large number of them had said that their social status was improved during the past few years. Upper caste people started accepting food from lower caste people. Both upper caste and lower caste people participate in social interactions. In spite of all these cordial relations many a times they felt that upper caste behave indifferently with them.

REFERENCES

Ambedkar, B.R. (1948), *The Untouchables: who were they and why they became Untouchables?*, Delhi, Amrit Book Company.

Chambers, Robert (1983), *Rural Development: Putting the Last First*, Longmans.

Chambers, Robert (1993), *Challenging the Professions: Frontiers for Rural Development*, ITDG., London.

Desai, I.P. (1985), Caste, Caste Conflict and Reservation, New Delhi, Ajanta Publications.

Government of Punjab, (2001), *Educational, Social and Economic Programmes for the Upliftment of Scheduled Castes and Backward Classes*, Chandigarh, Department of Welfare of Scheduled Castes and Backward Classes.

Jogdand, P.G., Prashant, P. Bansode, N.G. Meshram, (2008), *Globalization and Social Justice Perspective, Challenges and Praxis*, Rawat Publication, New Delhi.

ul Haq, M., (1976), 'Towards a Just Society' *Development*, Vol. XVIII No. 4, 15th World Conference.

Chapter 4

Poverty and Inequality in the Globalized Era

Anju Sharma

Introduction

Globalization promotes growth and growth reduces poverty. As economic growth is an immense factor behind the improvement of poverty. The world has become a much smaller place over the past two decades due to globalization. Globalization means linking the economy of a country with the economies of the other countries by means of free trade, free mobility of capital and labour, unrestricted flow of goods and services, technology and expertise among different countries of the world. The ultimate aim of globalization is to look in the lead of world as a global village, i.e. to bring different economies of the world closer to each other. Globalization has brought opportunities but the lion's share of every dollar of wealth produced in the world economy goes to wealthy or middle-income countries. Only three cents of every dollar, says the World Bank, goes to the low-income countries that are home to 40 per cent of the world's population. More than 1 billion people live in extreme poverty, as subsisting on less than 1 dollar a day. Yet poverty rates are much lower today than twenty years ago. In the last two decades, the percentage of the developing world living in extreme poverty has been cut in half. While poverty rates were falling, developing countries became increasingly integrated into the world trading system.

India has succeeded in diversifying her trade sources as well as product range. Manufacturing and services have emerged as major trade items of India. Indian trade has increased from $ 86 billion in 2000 to $

812 billion in 2011. India has taken various trade promotion measures both at bilateral and multilateral level of promotion of trade. India is amongst the fast growing underdeveloped nations where the concept of globalization has been initiated in July 1991 through liberalization of the regulatory framework and by encouraging privatization. Globalization has become a major factor behind the high economic growth in the country. The favourable economic conditions have put a positive impact on the overall standard of living of the country. Over the years India has gradually become one of the fastest growing economies in the world. It has become the 4th largest economy in the world in terms of the purchasing power parity (PPP). The per capita income has increased which has improved the standard of living of the masses

Review of Literature

A research of Dr. Abhijit Sen, member of Planning Commission shows that the poverty ratio during 5 years duration (2004-05 to 2009-10) has come down in the country but the absolute number of poors in the country has gone up.

Harrison in his book Globalization and poverty (2009) concluded that the poor will indeed benefits from globalization if the appropriate complementry polices and institutions are in places. He also concluded that globalization has been associated with rising inequality and the poor do not always share in the gains from trade. His findings also states that the poor in countries with an abundance of unskilled labour do not always gain from trade reform. Another is that the poor are more likely to share in the gains from globalization when workers enjoy maximum mobility, especially from contracting economic sectors into expanding sectors (India and Colombia). Gains likewise arise when poor farmers have access to credit and technical know-how (Zambia), when poor farmers have such social safety net as income support (Mexico) and when food aid is well targeted (Ethiopia).

The comprehensive surveys by Winters *et al.* (2004), Goldberg *et al.* (2004), and Ravelling (2004) all knowledge that they can only review the indirect evidence regarding the linkages between globalization and poverty. There have been almost no studies which test for the direct linkages between the two.

Nussbaum (2006) criticized Rawls for his assumption that states are equal in the global economy. She states that we need to acknowledge the fact that the International Economic System, and the activities of multinational corporations, creates severe, disproportionate burdens for poorer nations, which cannot solve their problems by wise internal policies alone. Economic analysis cannot evaluate the philosophical merits of these different responses, but can shed some light on the reasons for the disparity across nations in income levels and the role of globalization in their propagation. A better understanding of the reasons for economic inequality can yield insights into the reasons why some nations prosper over time but others do not, and what can be done about this disparity.

Objectives of the Study

(i) To study the effect of globalization on Indian poverty level.
(ii) To evaluate inequality in comparison with development.
(iii) Suggestion to improve the negative effect of globalization on poverty and inequality.

Methodology

The study is based upon the secondary data collected from different sources; mainly, Economic Survey of India, RBI Bulletin, Reports of National Sample Survey Organization of India etc. The data has been tabulated suitably. The tools of analysis are mainly compound growth, year-wise average decadal growth, ratio and percentage. The results have been accordingly interpreted and on the basis of *analysis* and findings, measures have been suggested.

Result and Discussion

Poverty is one of the main issues, attracting the attention of sociologists and economists. The term 'poverty' has been defined in different societies in a different way but all of them are conditioned by the version of minimum or good life to be obtained in society. For instance the concept of poverty in USA would be significantly different from that in India because the ability to afford a higher living standard is much higher in the United States. Poverty is a relative term. Its definition changes with the economic conditions of the country concerned.

Poverty Line in India

Poverty indicates a condition in which a person fails to maintain a living standard adequate for a comfortable lifestyle. According to National Sample

Survey Organization (NSSO), International Poverty line is defined as per capita consumption expenditure of less than one US dollar per day. In India, consumption expenditure of ₹ 599 per capita per month in urban areas and ₹ 368 per capita per month in rural areas (at 2004 prices) is treated as poverty line. Though India boasts of a high economic growth, it is shameful that there is still large scale poverty in India. Poverty in India can be defined as a situation when a certain section of people are unable to fulfil their basic needs. India has the world's largest number of poor people living in a single country. Out of its total population of more than 1 billion, 350 to 400 million people are living below the poverty line. Nearly 75 per cent of the poor people are in rural areas, most of them are daily wagers, landless labourers and self-employed householders. There are a number of reasons for poverty in India. Poverty in India can be classified into two categories, namely rural poverty and urban poverty.

Some of the basic reasons of rural poverty in India are unequal distribution of income, High population growth, Illiteracy, Large families, Caste system. Problems of Rural Poverty are presence of malnutrition, illiteracy, diseases and long term health problems. Unhygienic living conditions, lack of proper housing, high infant mortality rate, injustice to women and social ill-treatment. The causes of urban poverty in India are improper training, slow job growth, failure of PDS system. Problems of Urban Poverty are restricted access to employment opportunities and income, lack of proper housing facilities, unhygienic environments, no social security schemes, Lack of opportunity to quality health and educational facility.

In spite of 62 years of planning, the problem of poverty is still persisting in the country. It is the most crying economic problem of India. No hardship, no suffering is greater and bitter than the lack of means to satisfy one's basic necessities of life.

Trends of Poverty in the Past and Present Scenario

Table 4.1 shows the position of poverty in India. It clearly reveals that after independence poverty is on the track of declining. In 1973 the poverty ratio was 54.9 per cent and in 2000 it was 26.1 per cent and in 2011 it was 24.8 per cent of the total population.

Table 4.2 shows the International Comparison of population below poverty line on the basis of US $ 1.25 per day criteria. The table shows that in developed countries like UK and USA, the population below the poverty line is less than 1 per cent whereas in India 49.4 per cent of population is living below the poverty line. It is more than a China (28.4%) and Pakistan (35.9%).

Table 4.1: Position of Poverty in India

Period/Year	*Million People Below Poverty Line*	*Population*	*Ratio*
1973-74	321	584.699	54.9
1993-94	320	888.889	36.0
1999-2000	260	996.168	26.1
2011	300	1209.677	24.8

Source: National Sample Survey Organization and Economic Survey of India, various Issues.

Table 4.2: International Comparison of Population Below Poverty Line (Year 2010)

Country	*Percentage of Population below Poverty Line (US $1.25 per day)*
Bangladesh	57.8
India	32.7
Pakistan	35.9
China	28.4
Sri Lanka	16.3
UK	<1
USA	<1
Japan	<1
Germany	<1

Source: World Development Report 2010.

Tendulkar Committee Report on Poverty

Tendulkar Committee was set up in March, 2009 to look into the methodology of estimating poverty in India. This committee was set up because there was widespread criticism that Planning Commission is underestimating the figures of poverty. The calorie criterion adopted by Planning Commission, i.e. 2,400 calories per capita per day in rural areas and 2,100 calories per capita per day in urban areas. As per Planning Commission criterion, the cost of food to attain this calorie level is estimated in rupees and is defined as poverty line.

Tendulkar Committee has moved away from just calorie criterion definition to a broader definition of poverty that also includes expenditure on health, education, and clothing in addition to food. Using this approach, new poverty line for the years shows ₹ 447 per capita per month in rural areas and ₹ 579 per capita per month in urban areas. In daily terms, poverty line has been raised from ₹ 12 to ₹ 15 per capita per day in rural areas and from ₹ 18 per capita per day to ₹ 19 per capita per day in urban areas.

According to this report, in 2011, 41.8 per cent population in rural areas and 25.7 per cent population in urban areas are living below poverty line.

The Global Hunger Index

The Global Hunger Index is a tool adapted and further developed by the International Food Policy Research Institute (IFPRI) to comprehensively measure and track global hunger. The GHI incorporates Ranking of India and neighbouring by three interlinked hunger-related indicators—the proportion of undernourished in the population, the prevalence of underweight in children, and the mortality rate of children.

Table 4.3: Ranking of India and neighbouring Nations in Global Hunger Index-2010

Nation	*Ranking*	*Global Hunger Score*
China	2	5.1
Sri Lanka	37	14.4
Pakistan	57	19.7
Nepal	60	20.3
India	65	22.9
Bangladesh	68	24.0

Source: International Food Policy Research Institute.

The index ranks countries on a 100-point scale with 0 being the best score (no hunger) and 100 being the worst. Values less than 5.0 reflect low hunger, values between 5.0 and 9.9 reflect moderate hunger, values between 10.0 and 19.9 indicate a serious problem, values between 20.0 and 29.9 are alarming, and values of 30.0 or hunger are extremely alarming.

Table 4.3 shows that, the list of 84 nations in China has been placed at 2nd place showing better situation in dealing with hunger in the country. India despite of having robust economic growth indications have been placed at 65th rank in global hunger index which is worse even with the ranks of Sri Lanka (37th), Pakistan (57th) and Nepal (60th). According to IFPRI, India's GHI score was 30.3 in 1990, which fell to 22.6 in 1996. It again rose to 24.2 in 2001 and stood at 22.9 in 2012, almost touching the 1996 level. The GHI aims to raise awareness of regional and country differences in hunger and trigger action to eliminate hunger.

Status of Unemployment

The phenomena of globalization came up with the hope of employment generation but no substantial change has taken place so far. There is a huge disparity in terms of unemployment in the rural and urban areas of the country. The rural region is still lagging behind. The increase in literacy has caused increased unemployment amongst educated youth. The migration of people from the agrarian sector to the industrial and urban regions is also responsible for unemployment. The intensive highly innovative technologies have been introduced which have increased production and have resulted to cut employment avenues. The existing status of unemployment is 9.4 per cent in the country. This is not a good indicator for the economy of the nation where employment generation is the major requirement of human development.

Status of Trade

Trade has a long history. Prerequisite for trade was the surplus production. Initially this surplus production was consumed in the domestic market but with the increase in means of communication and improved methods or production, the surplus production has to be sold in overseas market. The mechanical interpretation in terms of the economic criteria of globalization based upon statistical data, clearly indicates that globalization has proved to a boon india which is considered as the leader and a champion of last economic growth amongst the under developed countries. As an evidence of it the position of foreign trade has indicated that for the last four decades there has been a tremendous growth in the imports and exports. It is pertinent to mention that such growth of imports and exports has been more in the post reforms period in comparison to both of them in the pre-reforms period.

Table 4.4: Position of Foreign Trade in India

(₹ in crores)

Year	*Exports*	*Imports*	*Balance*
1970-71	1535	1634	–99
1980-81	6711	12549	–5838
1990-91	32558	43193	–10635
1991-92	44042	47851	–3809
2000-01	2035571	230873	–27302
2010-11	1157475	1605315	–447840

Source: Economic Survey of India, various issues.

Table 4.4 clearly shows that the compound growth in exports and imports during the two decades of pre-liberalization period was 17.015 per cent and 19.367 per cent respectively against their compound growth in the post-liberalization period of two decades till 2011 recorded as 19.978 per cent and 21.303 per cent respectively.

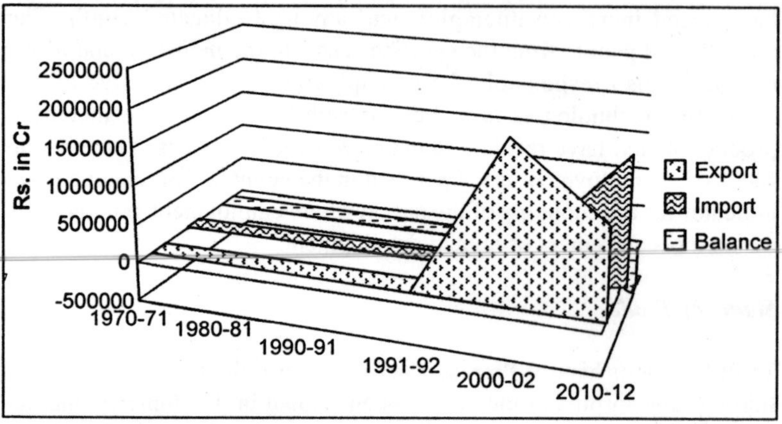

Fig. 4.1: Position of Foreign Trade in India

Fig. 4.1 shows the position of foreign trade in India. However the balance of trade has been found negative in both the periods. Further, the trend of negative balance of trade has increased manifold in the post liberalization period. This shows that the growth in imports is much more, which is not a healthy sign for the economy of the nation. The New Foreign Trade Policy (2009-14) clearly gives the message to double India's exports of goods and services by 2014 and double its share in global trade by 2020.

Inequality

History is likely to judge the progress in the 21st century by one major yardstick, i.e. there a growing equality of opportunity between people and among nations. The disparity in global income has become the focus of much scrutiny, inquiry and debate.

History of Inequality

Inequality has long been a characteristic of the world economy. The differences in the levels of income per capita reflect variations in the growth of income in different regions, and these rates have also varied over time. In 1870, at the beginning of the first modern era of globalization, the world's average per capita GDP was $873. Average income in the richest nations—the U.S., Canada, Australia and New Zealand was $2,419, while income in the poorest African nations was $500, a spread of 5:1. By 1950, at the start of the second era of globalization, income had risen to $9,268 in the same upper-income group but only $890 in the African nations, and the spread had risen to 13:1. By 2003, the corresponding income levels were $28,039 and $1,549, and the spread between the top and the bottom of the international distribution of income stood at 18:1.

Inequality in India

Inequality is a measure of unequal distribution of income (or consumption) among individuals or households. The lower (higher) the number, the more equal (unequal) is the distribution. Inequality in India in comparison to other countries has shown in Table 4.5.

Table 4.5: Ranking of India and neighbouring Nations Gini Index-2010

Nation	*Ranking (Gini Index)*
India	36.8
Brazil	55.0
Turkey	43.2
Thailand	42.5
China	41.5
Indonesia	39.4
Vietnam	37.8
USA	40.8
Singapore	42.5
Hong Kong	43.4
Portugal	38.5

Source: Human Development Report 2009.

Table 4.5 shows that India's Gini index 36.8 was more favourable than that of comparable countries like Brazil (55), Turkey (43.2), Thailand (42.5), China (41.5), Indonesia (39.4), Vietnam (37.8) and even the USA (40.8), Singapore (42.5), Hong Kong (43.4) and Portugal (38.5), which are otherwise ranked very high in human development.

The Inequality in India has been estimated by the National Sample Survey Organization (NSSO) based on household consumer expenditure for 2004-05. The Lorenz ratio for total consumption expenditure was 0.30 for rural India and 0.37 for urban India which indicates that higher relatively inequality in urban areas. In addition to this disparity in consumption of durable goods are much higher than in the consumption of cereals.

Measures Undertaken by the Government to Remove Poverty and Inequality

In year 2009-10, government has targeted to reduce the proportion of people living below poverty line to less than half from the current levels by year 2014. Like—Employment Generation Programmes are Swaranjayanti Gram Swarozgar Yojana, Sampoorna Grameen Rozgar Yojana, National Food for Work Programme, Prime Minister Rozgar Yojana, Swaranjayanti Shahr Rozgar Yojana, Differential Rate of Interest Scheme, Pradhan Mantri Gramodya Yojana, Concessional Loans to Start Cottage Industries. Other programmes for alleviating poverty are Minimum needs programme, Twenty-Point Programme, Annapurna, Shiksha Sahayog, National Social Assistance Programme, National Old Age Pension Scheme, National Family Benefit Scheme, Maternity Benefit Scheme, Janshree Bima Yojana, Antyodya Anna Yojana Aam Admi Bima Yojana, Targeted Public Distribution System, Bharat Nirman, Rashtriya Swasthya Bima Yojana, Indra Awas Yojana and Rajiv Awas Yojana, National Means-cum-Merit Scholarship, Setting-up Unique Identification Authority of India.

Conclusion and Suggestions

The relationship between globalization and poverty is complex in nature. In India, globalization of the economy through liberalization in July 1991 was to strengthen the socio-economic set-up. However, since 2008, the trade recorded more adverse trend, the growth in balance of payments declined, the foreign exchange declined and portfolio investment was recorded negative in the year 2008-09. During the time of recession, the pace of economic growth of India has been registered more than 8 per cent. This has definitely influenced the quality of life and sustainability of the national economy in such a precarious era when the economies of the majority of the nations world-wide, faced economic crisis. However, nearly one-fourth of the population is below poverty line and one-third of the population has the earning of less than $1 a day.

The high GDP growth in India has reduced poverty, but the disparity between the rural and urban regions of the nation, has increased in terms of all human development indicators which is a most serious threat to the socio-economic set-up as more then seventy per cent population of the country belongs to the rural areas where the pace of development is still very low and the concept of globalization is only accessible to the urban and industrial regions and the majority of the regions which come under the rural areas, are not even touched. In regard to global hunger index India's latest score (22.9) has returned to the 1996 level, after showing a minor deterioration between 1996 and 2012. There is a evidence that export growth and incoming foreign investment have reduced poverty everywhere from Mexico to India to Poland. Yet at the same time currency crises can cripple the poor.

Suggestions

Globalization produces both winners and losers among the poors. The relationship depends not just on trade or financial globalization but on the intraction of globalization with the rest of economic environment like invest in human capital, infrastructure, promotion of credit, technical assistance to farmer and improving the poverty situation in India. There is a need to encourage Foreign Direct Investment in first priority.

Globalization needs to be encouraged in terms of positive trend of trade and balance of payments for which, the nation needs to strengthen and make the optimum use of all economic sources for which, the government need to be directed to generate their own sources through exploration of the existing resources to be self-reliant. However to achieve a higher rate of equality and poverty reduction, India will also need to address inequalities in opportunities that impede the poor from participating in the growth process. Keeping in view that our government is a welfare state by properly analyzing various factors globalization will really put a positive impact to improve the poverty situation.

REFERENCES

Economic Survey, (2009-10); Monthly Economic Report April 2010.

Http://www.indiaenvironmentportal.org.in/category/thesaurus/national-sample-survey-organisation-nsso Http://www.rbi.org.in/scripts/BS_viewbulletin.aspx.

K.S. Rana (2012), *International Business and India*, Commonwealth Publishers, Pvt. Ltd., pp. 3-4, Government of India, (1991 to 2008).

Economic Survey, Various Issues, Ministry of Finance, Economic Division, New Delhi.

National Sample Survey Organization (2004-05), Government of India, Department of Economic Analysis, Statistical Wing, New Delhi. Http://indiabudget.gov.in/es2010-11/estat1.pdf.

Planning Commission, (2010), Government of India, SME Clusters in India.

Pratiyogita Darpan (2012), Vol.1 A, Swadeshi Bima Nagar, Agra, p. 315.

RBI, (2011), *Development Research Group on Productivity, Efficiency and Competitiveness*.

Roy Kartik, Chandra and Sidras Jorn (2006). *Institutions, Globalization and Empowerment*, Edward Elgar and Publishing, USA.

S.S. Narta (2011), *Globalization Issues with Reference to India*, Kanishka Publishers, New Delhi, p. 20-21.

Chapter 5

Innovative Human Resource Development in Global Context

Sunanda Sharma

Introduction

In Global context, innovative Human Resource Development is the main key for business development. Strategic human resource management is the management of people. It requires thinking ahead, and planning ways for a company to matching the needs of company and employees for global competitiveness. This can affect, the way things are done at a business site, improving everything from hiring practices and employees training programmes to assessment techniques and discipline. Strategy is an action plan which sets the direction that a company will be taking. It is a decision making choice and would involve consideration for internal strength, weakness and external environment affecting the company. Strategy involves choices that determine the nature and direction of the organization's activities towards the attainment of goals. Innovation in strategic management means finding new ways for improving methods of human resource development. For running business successfully and its diversification, formulation of strategies and its implementation is an essential. An important aspect of strategic human resource management is employee's development. This process begins when a company is recruiting and interviewing prospective employees. In a cut throat competition, a business can be successful if it has a strategic human resource management because it is run by human resource. Using innovation in Human Resource practices is the best way for achieving success and business development in Global context.

Innovation can be defined as idea selection, development and commercialization. Creativity and Innovation are the most important factors in establishing and maintaining a competitive advantage. Logic and linear thinking will remain important, but are no longer sufficient to succeed in a global economy. There are distinct processes that enhance problem identification and idea generation and, similarly, distinct processes that enhance idea selection, development and commercialization. Innovation involves:

- Discover new technologies and process for product development.
- Uncover new applications and markets for existing technologies.
- Identify leading experts and competitors in unfamiliar markets.
- Find potential partners or suppliers.
- Understand potential risks and benefits of new approaches or entering new markets.

An organization has to make strategies related to human resource development for competing globally with similar organizations. Improved interviewing techniques can help to weed out applicants that may not be a good match for the company. Strategic Human Resource Management is an essential tool of business development, because Human Resource is one of the important resource of 5 ms of management, i.e. Man, Material, Machinery, Money and Method. For achieving business objective and development of business, not only efficient, skilled and trained Human Resource is required but their long term tenure is also essential. Various strategies regarding Human Resource are formulated by top level authorities. For making Human Resource Strategies, Human Resource planning is needed.

The need of Human Resource planning is essential for replacement of persons in the organization. A large number of persons are to be replaced in the organization because of retirement, old age, death etc. There will be need of persons for taking up new positions in such contingencies. There will be need to recruit new persons to take up the positions that have left the organization. Wherever, there is a plan to expand or diversify the concern then more persons will be required to take up the new positions. Human Resource planning is essential under these situations. A business works under changing technological environment. There may be a need to train and make them up-to-date with new technology. Human Resource planning helps in meeting the new demands of the organization. Providing specialized on-site training, even if provided by senior members of the company, and offering one-on-one assessment and coaching sessions, can help employees reach peak performance rates

Strategic human resource management is obviously directed at achieving organizational objectives and innovation is used for its development. Whilst it is directed by organizational strategy (which may change depending on whether the organization is expanding activities, developing a new product or reorganizing its activities), strategic human resource management and innovation must be ongoing activities. Management must continuously scan the human resource environment in order to identify developments that can either enhance or threaten its survival.

Human Resource Development Needs Strategic Management

Strategic management may be understood as the process of formulating, implementing and evaluating business strategies to achieve organizational objectives.

Innovative HRD is a set of managerial decisions and actions that determines long term performance of a corporation. It includes environment scanning, strategy formulation, strategy implementation, evaluation and control. The study of strategic management, therefore, emphasizes monitoring and evaluating environment opportunities and threats in the light of corporation's strength and weaknesses. Therefore, strategic management involves four steps as given below:

- Analyses the opportunities and threats or constraints that exists in the external environment.
- Formulate strategies that will match the organization's strength and weakness with the environmental threats and opportunities.
- Implement the strategies.
- Evaluate and control activities to ensure the organizational objectives are achieved.
- Innovative motivation should be done to boost the morale of employees.
- The human resource practitioners should play a vital role in ensuring quality at all levels of the organisation. Quality is achieved through people and in accordance with a basic human resource principle: investment in people as a prerequisite for achieving high quality standards.
- Strategic management is essential for development of human

resource in an organization. Human resource development is a dynamic and evolving field in the world of business. It is the goal of this publication to provide a resource through which HRD practitioners and students can understand the field and grasp its simplicity. It is within that simplicity that an appreciation of the complexity of HRD can be realized.

- Use of more capital intensive methods would result in greater productivity of men necessitating greater motivating and greater human resources approach of management.

Developing Innovative Ways and Human Resource Practices

Managers or leaders must develop innovative ways in Human Resource management so that *successes* can be achieved in business organization. Motivation is an important factor which encourages persons to give their best performance and help in reaching enterprise goals. Motivation is a key element in personnel management. Motivation is psychological phenomenon which generates within an individual. It is an inner-feeling which energizes a person to work more. A person moves to fulfill his unsatisfied needs by conditions his energies. When a manager wants to get more work from his subordinates then he will have to motivate them for improving their performance. Therefore, leaders create an environment within which innovation can flourish:

- Make followers brave so that they can prove themselves by doing new things.
- Be aware of the effect of their words on their people.
- Value diversity and encourage challenges.
- Leaders should not punish people for having a go. They should encourage their followers for new ways.
- Leaders should walk the talk with healthy behaviours.
- Top management should support to innovation and cultivate champions.

Leaders must learn how to create an organizational climate where others apply innovative thinking to solve problems and develop new products and services. It is about growing a culture of innovation, not just hiring a few creative outliers.

Role of Top Level Management in Innovation and Strategic Human Resource Management

Top management must set the context, guide the Human resource process in a participative and fair way. Clearly communicate reasons, expectations and educate employees, defend creative teams from distractions and pressure, appreciate distinctiveness in people and their thinking, welcome 'change' and ask itself what it does to promote the innovation process and how to get rid of these obstacles. However, the role of management is to ensure that innovation is not destructive to the overall health of the company. A culture of innovation has to be cultivated by management through confidence building — giving confidence to an innovative failure — a warm hand that says try harder, and applauding innovation that excels.

Innovation can be facilitated by creating environments that give people space to think and share and providing structures that enable ideas to to captured and explored. Management should play role of facilitators. If the management facilitates the following things their firms would become more innovative.

- Encourage the team to come forward with innovative solutions. and consider the suggestions carefully.
- Make people think of out of the box solutions. Many times logical thinking hinders creative thinking.
- Facilitate support of outside agencies to help in designing the product rather than doing everything from scratch by organization or think of collaborative work with different agencies. It would be cheaper, quicker, and less hassle oriented, and the cost of such developments is easily measurable, which subsequently helps in appropriate costing followed by pricing.
- Encourage team spirit and boost the team to achieve the company's goal. This is the biggest challenge for top management. Select team members with the right frame of mind and ignite the spark in them. The leader has to create a positive atmosphere starting with listening to supporting the team till the end sincerely.
- Wages do provide a source of motivation for employees to perform effectively.
- Each and every innovative effort must be acknowledged and appreciated by the leadership and the reaction should be supportive. The top management needs to go into each initiative

in depth and even if, the suggestion as it is cannot be accepted for implementation, it might be improved upon after further discussions.

Human Resource Planning

Human Resource planning is a critical management function. It provides management with information on resources flow which is used to calculate, among other things, recruitment needs and succession, development plans. There is a need in this new environment for human resource practitioners to take a detailed study of past trends in employment loss and seek to minimise the shock of unexpected shortages of labour, increased and costly surpluses and needless redundancies. When there is a proper human resource plan in place, we will be able to obtain and retain the number of people we need with the skills, expertise and competencies required. This would not have been the case if human resources were properly managed. HRP will also ensure that we develop a well-trained and flexible workforce, thus contributing to the nation's ability to adapt to uncertain and changing environments.

Conclusion

Human Resource management should take a new approach in this new environment brought about by globalization. People should not be seen as a cost to the organization but as a valuable assets. Human resource should be trained and developed to get the best out of them. In global environment, both innovation and strategic human resource practices are essential parts of business organization. These are the two sides of the same coin. Strategy is the long term planning and innovation is inseparable part of it, because change is the law of nature. New methods of performing work, new technologies and techniques take place from time to time. An important aspect of strategic human resource management is employees development by using innovative techniques. In present scenario, innovation is necessity for global competitiveness. This process begins when a company is recruiting and interviewing prospective employees. Ideally HR department and top management work togetherto formulate the company's overall business strategy; that strategy then provides the framework within which HR activities such as recruiting and appraising must be crafted. If it is done successfully, it should result out in the employee competencies and behaviour that in turn should help the business implement its strategies and realize its goals. The human resources management system must be tailored to the demands of business strategy. In order to be successful, the employees should be developed in such a manner that they can be the competitive advantage, for this, the human resource management must be an equal partner in both the formulation and the implementation of the corporate and competitive strategies. In modern context, innovative ways in strategic management should be used to beat the global competition. The days have gone where only leadership was essential for development of the business. In modern context, Leaders of an organization should use new techniques like, strategy, creativity, and innovations in leadership for achieving better results. Top level management should not stick to old rule of thumb. In order to survive, organizations must improve and must innovate.

REFERENCES

Aragon, S.R. and Hatcher, T., (2001), "Ethics and integrity in HRD: Case studies in research and practice", *Advances in Developing Human Resources*.

Donald F. Harvey, (1988), *Strategic Management and Business Policy*, Second Edition, Merrill Publication.

Fred R. Devid, (1995), *Strategic Management*, Third Edition, Prentice Hall.

G.N. McLean, (2001), *Ethical Dilemmas in Conducting International Research*.

Gary Dessler, (1999), *Human Resource Management*, Seventh Edition, New Delhi.

Hartman, L.P.B and Stevenson, (1999), "Exploring the ethics and economics of global labour standards: A challenge to integrated social contact theory", *Business Ethics Quarterly*, Vol. 13 (2003), pp. 193-220.

Kapoor Sangham and Rosy Joshi, (2009), *Business Environment*, Kalyani Publisher, Ludhiana.

Memoria C.B., (1980), *Personnel Management*, Third Edition, Himalaya Publishing House, Bombay.

Pattnayak, Biswajit, (2004), *Human Resource Management*, Prentice Hall of India, Pvt. Ltd., New Delhi.

Pearce and Robinson, (2003), *Strategic Management—Strategies Formulation and Implementation*, New Jercy, Prentice Hall.

Peter Wright, (1996) *Strategic Management—Concept and Cases*, New Jercy, Prentice Hal.

Robert, L. Mathis and John, H., (2000), *Human Resource Management*, South Western Publication Co.

Rosy Joshi and Gupta; Shashi K., (2005), *Human Resource Management and Organization Behaviour*, Kalyani Publisher, New Delhi.
Routlege, (1999), "Strategic Human Resource Management," *The International Journal of Human Resource Management*, Vol. 10, issue 6, U.K.
Sharma, R.K. and Gupta, Shashi K., (2009), *Functional Management*, Fourth Revised Edition, Kalyani Publisher, New Delhi.
Swanson, R.A, (1995), *Human Resource Performance is the Key*.
Sontakki, C.N., (2008), *Strategic Management*, Kalyani Publisher, Ludhiana.
Sontakki, C.N., (2009), *Marketing Management*, Kalyani Publisher, Ludhiana.

Chapter 6

Impact of Globalization on Business and Management Education

Meenu Gupta

Introduction

The principal objective of education has been development of whole individuals. The minimum level of education that was necessary to achieve this goal in the agrarian society, was basic or primary and in the industrial age, secondary. In the present borderless information society, education needs to be able to respond to additional demands of a rapidly globalizing world by raising awareness of environment, peace, cultural and social diversity, increased competitiveness, and the concept of a global village. Such education is to a knowledge or information society what secondary education was to an industrial economy. Education prepares the individual to connect—and live in harmony—with the environment around him. Globalization has changed the size, nature and quality of that environment. The challenge for higher education, therefore, is to reform, create and develop systems that prepare the individual to work in a borderless economy and live in a global society. In other words, our educational institutions need to produce global citizens.

The withdrawal of state from higher education has also been helped by economists, who have had an overly simple way of assessing the return on investments in higher education. The basic problem is that they have measured the return on education exclusively through wage differentials. With reference to someone who has no education, someone who has been to primary school, someone who has completed secondary school, and someone with a university degree, one can ask how much more each earns than the previous. These differences are then compared to the incremental amounts invested in their education to find the return. The results generally suggest that higher education yields a lower return than primary or secondary education—and they have been used to justify the skewing of government budgets and development funds away from higher education institutions.

Research Issues

The article discusses the role and impact of management education in the post globalization era. Management Education in India is at cross roads. With the dawn of new millennium, while there was phenomenal growth in the number of Business Schools, the benchmarks were also on the rise. The rate of return calculations are flawed because they do not take account of the full range of benefits to those who receive higher education. For example, higher education can enhance health, openness, peace, and social development, and at the same time reduce disease, bigotry and blind nationalism, so the private benefits to the individual and to society are not just the direct labour productivity benefits, as the rate of return analysis suggests.

Higher education confers benefits above and beyond enhancing the incomes of those who receive it, and many of these benefits take the form of public goods, such as the contribution of higher education to enterprise, leadership, governance, culture, and participatory democracy, and its potential for lifting the disadvantaged out of poverty. These are all vital building blocks for stronger economies and societies and all routes by which the benefit of investment in higher education multiplies throughout society.

Liberal democracies have traditionally operated on the principle of separation of activities in the social sphere just as they have on the principle of separation of powers in the political sphere. The private sector had been given a relatively free hand in the production and delivery of economic goods while the state concentrated on the provision of healthcare, education and other infrastructure goods, also known as public goods. Globalization has changed all that. The rapid expansion of the influence of the private sector at the global level necessitated a corresponding expansion in their sphere of activities by diversifying into the production and delivery of public goods that had always been within the purview of the state. The takeover was swift and remarkable in the sense that the effort did not meet much resistance.

One of the major consequences of the globalization of education has been commodification and the corporatization of institutions of higher learning. It is said that the for-profit education market in the United States is worth more than $500 billion in revenue for the involved corporates. More than one thousand state schools have been handed over to corporations to be run as businesses. But there is a fundamental problem with the way business models have been applied to the delivery of education and other public goods. Unthinking adoption of the private sector model prevents the development of a meaningful approach to management in the public services in general or to the social services in particular based on their distinctive purposes, conditions and objectives.

Rise of the Globalization Paradigm

Since mid-1980s there has been an explosion of interest in the idea of globalisation. In part this has been shaped by the profound geopolitical shifts that have characterized the world since the early 1970s, by the significant advances in technological and communication processes, and an outcome of the decades of restructuring throughout the 1980s and 90s that put into place neo-liberal policies and programmes. Together, these developments undermined the idea of a cohesive and sequestered national economy and society, and radically altered the nature of the relationship between state, economy,society, nations and their international relationships (Amin and Thrift, 1994; Castells, 1996; Dicken, 1998; Held *et al.*, 1999; Held and McGrew, 2002).

Education has always encouraged and represented openness, inquiry, diversity, research and limitless learning. Corporatization of education would make it elitist—the one provided by corporations for the masses and the poor who cannot afford going to the traditional institutions of learning, and the other for the rich and the affluent.

The delivery of public goods and services is and should remain the primary responsibility of the state. Representative government may not be the ideal or perfect arrangement for governance but it represents the best that is available, and certainly more desirable than the private sector management of public services such as education.

Impact of Economic Reforms on the Market Structure and Performance of Business Sector

India has adopted domestic policies, and institutions that have enabled people to take advantage of global markets and have thus sharply increased the share of trade in their GDP. India has been catching up with the rich ones, our annual growth rates increased from 1 per cent in the 1960s to 5 per cent in the 1990s. Now it is above 8 per cent. Indians saw their wages rises, and the number of people in poverty declined. Government of India is playing a very pivotal role to support competitiveness in Indian business.

Economic reforms were undertaken in the 1990s essentially to instill dynamism in the industrial economy through competition. Competitive forces are expected to take Indian industry out of inertia and place it on a dynamic growth path. In this context, it is important to know how far economic liberalization and globalization has succeeded in changing the market structure so as to allow more competitive free play. Market competition is in turn expected to influence the performance of industry positively. It is proposed to study changes in the market structure for different industries in terms of the number of units, size, structure and ownership patterns in the 1990s as compared with the 1980s, using unit level data for the organized industry. This is to be followed up by a study of the performance of these units/industries in terms of efficiency and productivity.

A related question to be examined is how the new economic environment has influenced the entry and exit of firms, their competitive strategies and their pricing behaviour. Mergers and takeovers have become an important phenomenon of Indian industry after the reforms. There has, however, been very little research on this topic in the Indian context. A study of mergers and takeovers among Indian industrial firms is, therefore, proposed to be undertaken, with a particular focus on how the merger/takeover affected the performance of industrial firms.

New Understanding the Role of Management Education

Management Education in India is at cross-roads. With the dawn of new millennium, while there was phenomenal growth in the number of B-Schools, the benchmarks were also on the rise. The Globalization doesn't seem to have happened just to the Industry but also to Indian B-Schools. The expansion of B-Schools (in Number) doesn't look to be in line with the challenges posed by the globalization of Indian Management Education.

There has been a thickening of multilateral interactions and interconnections in the global governance of education. There are more actors involved in making policy and in delivering programmes in the education sector, aside from the United Nations agencies, donor agencies like DfID, the OECD and more recently the WTO. It includes globalising organisations (such as universities), multi-national firms (such as Microsoft), non-government organisations (such as Oxfam), and regional actors (such as NEPAD, CARICOM, APEC and NAFTA). Nation states are also active on the global stage in promoting their own 'national interests', or the interests of particular fractions of capital, such as in the globalising services sector.

Traditional, time-tested avenues of employment making way for newer opportunities and career paths, and today, most students are faced with a bewildering array of choices of colleges, study subjects, fields of specialization and methodologies. Students are faced with the unenviable task of having to make choices based on popular opinions or trends. Very few, if any, make choices based on potential and real aptitude. This means that finally, most new entrants in the professional field are there because they hope that they are in the right place and not necessarily because that is what they like and are good at doing. Identifying one's own potential and true métier is, therefore, based on experience as well as trial and error. But now, the emergence of such a new dimension has already begun. Companies are feeling the need for global standards to benchmark human resources, and academics are encouraging the use of merit-based candidate selection systems. India's position as a lead contributor to the global IT human resources pool will need to be supported by the adoption of global standards for talent selection.

As more and more well-educated and well-equipped talent emerges, the task of talent selection becomes even more complex. Companies find it increasingly difficult to identify the right candidate for the right job. The onerous task of hiring the best will become more and more difficult; the situation will be exacerbated by the requirement of greater numbers of peoples 'on-the-job'.

Conclusion

Research on the knowledge economy and lifelong learning, particularly as it applies to low-income countries, tends to be prescriptive and normative rather than analytical. Worse than this, while on the one hand the developing countries are being encouraged to think about their education sectors in ways that might enable them to be more globally competitive, on the other hand there is very little sense of what this means in terms of the kinds of knowledge and skills for industries that might contribute to economic growth. What is evident, however, is that for low-income countries to generate an adequate platform for development, there needs to be a significant amount of funding directed to the development, not only of basic education, but to upper secondary and the tertiary sectors where the basis for research and development might be nurtured. This will require investments in these sectors of education, as well as inducements for those working in these sectors to continue to work there in the face of encouragement to pursue opportunities in the north.

In the post globalization era this scope has increased immensely for global multinational companies as Government of India has also played a very crucial and supportive role in this respect through liberalized policies and legislative structure. Indian Market leaders going global. But there are certain negative impacts occurred aftermath the globalization impact in India

In sum, it might be concluded that both technology and access to quality education might well be becoming an even further divide, made more problematic by the way in which knowledge itself is being commodified potentially a higher transaction cost for low income countries.

REFERENCES

AAU (2004) 'Accra Declaration on GATS and Internationalization of Higher Education in Africa', Participants *Declaration, at the Workshop on the Implications of WTO/GATS for Higher Education in Africa,* 27th-29th April, Accra, Ghana: AAU.

Abrahamsen, R. (2000) *Disciplining Democracy: Development Discourse and Good Governance in Africa*, London: Zed Books.

Abu-Ghaida, D. and Klasen, S. (2004) 'The costs of missing the Millennium Development Goal on Gender Equity', *IZA Discussion Paper* 1031.

Adams, J.D. (1989) 'The threat to education from structural adjustment—A realistic response', *IDS Bulletin-Institute of Development Studies,* 20(1): 50-54.

Amin, A. and Thrift, N. (eds) (1994) *Globalisation, Institutions and Regional Development in Europe,* Oxford: Oxford University Press.

Amin, S. (1976) *Unequal Development,* New York: Monthly Review Press.

Arya, P.P. and Chadda, Suresh K., *Quality of Manugement Education*, Deep and Deep Publication Pvt. Limited.

Castells, M. (1996) *The Rise of the Network Society,* London: Blackwell.

Dicken, P. (1998) *Global Shift. Transforming the World Economy,* 3rd. Ed., London: Paul Chapman Publishing Ltd.

Held, D. and McGrew, A. (2002), *Globalisation/Anti-Globalisation,* Oxford: Blackwell.

Held, D., McGrew, A., Goldblatt, D. and Perraton, J. (1999), *Global Transformations: Politics, Economics and Culture,* Cambridge: Polity Press.

Susan Robertson, Mario Novelli, Roger Dale, Leon Tikly, Hillary Dachi, Ndibelema Alphonce (2007), *Globalization, Education and Development: Ideas, Actors and Dynamics*, pp. 68-263.

Chapter 7
Global Perspectives in Human Resource Management

Sapna Jain

The present study identify the understanding of key areas of human resource management, the global developments, contingencies and key challenges facing human resources management and draw on a range of best practices in HRM.

Key Objectives Include

1. Introduction to HR as strategic approach in enhancing skills development within context of organizational change and advancement and societal transformation.
2. A critical understanding of the key social, cultural, political and economic challenges impacting upon the theory and practice of HRM and the role of the HRM practitioner.
3. An introduction to the key policy areas of HR role including culture management.
4. An introduction to the HRM policy in different countries and explore the natural international HRM strategies and the ability to explore cross cultural differences in HRM policy and practice.

Introduction to HRM

Human Resource Management (HRM), is the process of managing people in organizations in a structured manner, different from Personnel Management which is a workforce centred approach, HRM is resource centred. From a macro perspective HRM encompasses the management of people in organizations, i.e. managing people in the form of a collective relationship between management and employees. This approach focuses on the objectives and outcomes of the HRM function.

Green (1999) had criticised HR professionals for not having sufficient awareness of the effects that new HR interventions would have on the organisation, and maintained that in order to provide added value, people professionals needed to provide three things:

- Alignment – pointing people in the right direction.
- Engagement – developing belief and commitment to the organisation's purpose and direction.
- Measurement – providing the data that demonstrate the improved results achieved (Green, 1999).

The **strategic role of Human Resource Management** in a knowledge economy where the difference in the organization is due to human asset require the proper management of this resource by putting in place requisite HRM policies that are in tandem with firm's strategy, structure and controls. HRM policies include the following dimensions:

- Recruitment and Selection,
- Appraisal and Performance Management,
- Workforce diversity, and
- Rewards and Recognition.

Global HRM and Strategic HRM

Contemporary global organisations have workforce diversity due to which these organisations cannot be immune to cultural sensitivities that has necessitated the need of global human resource management. The basic functions of HRM remains the same but the approach to manage the human resources in tandem with global objectives, structure of the organisations remains the same. The state of the national and global economy has a direct impact on all types of organization and will inevitably influence their people practices and strategies. In the simplest of terms, consumer spending power dictates, what goods and services need to be produced, which has an impact on employers' employment decisions and intentions. The CIPD (2009) emphasise the need for HR practitioners to understand the economy and its impact on the labour market. The economy is affected by the interplay of a wide variety of factors including rates of unemployment, the demand for goods and services as reflected by consumer decisions on spending and saving, the costs of importing and exporting goods, and the policies of the political party in power on issues such as inflation.

This makes the following objectives of global HRM imperative as follows:

1. Sensitization of local cultural context without compromising upon the global identity.
2. Generating awareness and respect for cross cultural connectivity between global cultural context and staff of local geographic boundaries.
3. Training upon character, culture commitment and sensitivities of the host country.

Managing Cross Cultural Sensitivity

According to **French (2007)**, 'it is now possible to present a strong case that all managers should possess cross-cultural sensitivity at the level of managing people at work.'

Gert Hofstede's (1980, 1997): Conducted a study of values in the workplace and how these are influenced by culture. Gert Hofstede's model helped in analyzing the workplace culture of different countries on four cultural differentiators. He used the following dimensions are: power distance index, individualism *versus* collectivism, masculinity *versus* femininity, uncertainty avoidance and, later, long-term orientation *versus* short-term orientation. All of these have some effect on how people behave in organisations and will impact on the ways HR managers need to manage people.

Power distance: The extent to which people accept authority structures, i.e. acceptance that it is right for some to make decisions and for others to follow their lead.

Uncertainty avoidance: The extent to which people desire certainty about what to do in various circumstances or about future events. People with high uncertainty avoidance would welcome rules and regulations.

Individualism/Collectivism: The extent to which people's actions are determined with reference to their own individual benefit or benefit of the community.

Masculinity/Femininity: The importance that is placed on material outcomes (masculinity) *versus* the quality of relationships (femininity).

Long-term orientation/short-term orientation: This relates to values associated with a long term orientation such as thrift and perseverance as opposed to values more frequently associated with a short-term orientation such as respect for tradition, fulfilling social obligations and protecting one's face.

To Understand and Critically Review HR Policies in International Organizations and Managing Cross Cultural Issues

HRM's key responsibilities include an ability to understand the interaction between cross-cultural factors and HRM. It acts as a channel in the organization to implement cross-cultural intelligence and encourage cross-cultural communication throughout the organization (Society for Human Resource Management, 2008). In other words, HRM looks after the management and administration of all employment relationships in the organization, consolidating both management and non-management staff (Budhwar & Debrah, 2001).

Range of Best Practices

Cross cultural issues: Policies and procedures will need to take account of cross-cultural issues and if working in a multinational organization there will also need to be decisions made about the way HR policies are implemented within each country. They are likely to have involvement in learning and development initiatives to support this.

Leveraging talent within the global organization: Companies like GSK, IBM, Infosys or Rolls Royce consider their 'employment brand' to be a key asset in the recruitment of talent. The selection of the employee from within the organization is indispensable for foreign assignments as they are properly trained to cope with International assignments. Procter & Gamble, the world's largest consumer products company, promote employees-from-within the organization policy and the belief that the P&G's while selecting from within the assessment of personality is one such major factor. As James Eyring, Dell computer's director of learning and development for Asia, asserts, "You really need not only a set of skills that your company values, but the right approach toward dealing with people in a completely different culture. And often, personality is the key to success" (Silverman, 2006).

Career management: Holding career management discussions with high performers. Rerecruit high potential employees by aligning their interest with organisational interest. Effective succession planning is the need of the hour for successful talent retention.

Benefits Management in an International performance linked fashion: Towers Watson reviewed opportunities to implement a retention bonus programme with a multiyear time horizon for selected high-potential and top-performing employees. Payout would be contingent on business and employee performance, ensuring that the programme effectively pays for itself. merit increases and bonus payouts, reducing payouts to those employees who only partially meet expectations in order to increase the available pool for top performers and high potential employees.

Promoting innovating culture: Another Indian company, Tata Consultancy Services (TCS), is also attempting to spur innovation by empowering its employees to take the initiative in identifying problems or opportunities wherever they may find them. Following the lead of Google, TCS allows employees to devote five hours each week to learning a new skill or pursuing a personal project.

Empowering all employees: Organizations will continue to increase the clarity and transparency with which they communicate to employees about organizational goals in order to further empower their workforce and ensure that employee decisions align with the objectives of top management (Sparrow, *et al.*, 1994: 293-295).

Talent Driven organisation: When Gary Loveman left Harvard Business School to join Harrah's Entertainment, first as its Chief Operating Officer, then as Chief Executive Officer, he adopted innovative strategies to make it the world's largest gaming company. Loveman had definite ideas about how the company's strategy needed to change in order to reach this goal. To move from present to competitive world, efforts were made to expanding the company's "cognitive toolbox" by recruiting employees who would bring new perspectives and new skills to the company. Loveman believed that "the company's collective IQ should increase with every new hire." In other words, Harrah's needed to become a talent-driven organization.

Continuous training culture: As workers become indispensable to organizations because of increased reliance on employee knowledge, it being the only resource that possess this knowledge for business success, the costs of losing employees will increase. This necessitated the provision of training especially the cross-cultural training to their employees for creating cross-cultural awareness; competency development, training need to focus on team synergy, culture of innovation, enhancing risk taking ability and cultural sensitivities, multi-cultural issues, language training and international organization development. It will help in developing sensitivity to cultural norms.

Learning from Others

The global penetration of McDonald, Walmart, PizaHut, KFC is worth appreciating making the world global village. Like in P&G, Howard Starbuck undertook a major strategic shift in response to a sharp downturn in its performance. In 2008, after an eight-year absence, Howard Schultz resumed the role of Chief Executive Officer of Starbucks at a time when the company seemed to have lost its momentum and was struggling to recapture the success that it had long enjoyed. Schultz announced that his top goal was to "restore the distinctive Starbucks experience." But rather than trying to define this himself or depend solely on his management team to come up with all of the answers, he decided to reach out and engage the company's 180,000 employees (known within the company as "partners") as well as its more than 50 million customers.

For identifying talent pool, Procter and Gamble's Talent Development System holds names of 3,000 executives along with details of their backgrounds so as to help identify the right person for the right job.

Maintaining global image as done by companies like GSK, IBM, Infosys or Rolls Royce consider their 'employment brand' to be a key asset in the recruitment of talent.

In March 2008, to promote brainstorming the company launched mystarbucksidea.com. This is a web site modelled after Dell's IdeaStorm, which had been introduced a year earlier. Like the Dell site, mystarbucksidea is an "online community" that invites customers to suggest ideas for new products.

NIIT is a large corporate training firm that is based in India but operates globally. In an attempt to circumvent its traditional hierarchical structure and accelerate innovation, the company supported the creation of a number of employee "clubs" that are focused on initiatives for change. According to NIIT CEO Vijay Thadani, the clubs are loosely structured and "informal" and bring together members from a variety of locations and business functions. They offer participants a chance to experience "the joy of taking on and solving a problem."

Conclusion

Consistent and integrated reward and talent management programmes through global job-levelling programmes create a common framework for managing talent and rewards. For example, by creating career advancement opportunities through frequent job rotations in order to help employees develop effectiveness. Employees and managers together need to have a clear vision of career paths and job levelling.

- Developing global consistency across regions and levels within a programme. Organizations are becoming more globally consistent in how they develop and manage talent and reward programmes. By doing this, organizations are discovering that they can be more successful in the overall effectiveness of these programmes (Tower Watson).
- Increasing commitment and budget for training and development and aligning training with performance appraisal with effective intrinsic and extrinsic rewards (as followed by Infosys promoting professional freedom, innovativeness and opportunities to learn in knowledge workers).
- Focusing on top key performers, critical-skill employees and high potentials, and designing and delivering what is important to them and aligning their interest with organisational objective (i.e. strategic HRM) and also penalising the underperformers and using that pool for value enhancers as followed by McKinsey's.
- Local customization and global standardization—Unique to global HR Information Systems is the balance between global, standardized HR processes and the need for local customization. Although 80 per cent of HR processes are the same around the world (Insight Consulting Partners, 2004) the 20 per cent can paralyze the global HRIS and the organization.

The central tenet of this discussion is that HRD can play a very effective role in organisational well-being by taking account of differing circumstances in foreign firms, but realizing that those differences are not the most significant determinants of what will and will not work in a specific location, HR professionals will then be able to maximize returns both at the subsidiary level and for the global MNC as a whole.

REFERENCES

Budhwar, P.S., and Debrah, Y.A., (2001). *Human Resource Management in Developing Countries*. London: Routledge.

Budhwar, P.S. and Khatri, N. (2001). "Comparative Human Resource Management in Britain and India: An Empirical Study". *The International Journal of Human Resource Management*, forthcoming.

Society for Human Resource Management. (2008). Workplace forecast. Alexandria, VA.

Bhatti, Anant Preet (2006). Cross-cultural issues in HRM. Dissertation, Bachelor of Technology, Punjab Technical University.

Suff, R. (2006). "Managing knowledge workers", *IRS Employment Review*, 861, IRS (www.xperthr.co.uk accessed 22.8.2010).

French, R. (2007). *Cross-cultural Management in Work Organisations*, CIPD.

Green, K. (1999). *Offensive Thinking, People Management*, Vol. 5, No. 8, 27.

Hofstede, G. (1980). *Culture's Consequences: International Differences in Work Related Values*, McGraw-Hill.

Hofstede, G. (1997). Cultures and Organisations: Software of the Mind, revised edition, McGraw-Hill.

Creating a sustainable reward and management programme. Results of the 2010 Global Talent Management and Rewards Study. Retrieved from http://www.worldatwork.org/waw/adimLink?.

Global HR Best Practices: Maximizing Innovation, Effectiveness and Efficiency in HR. A Collection of White Papers, Centre For Advanced Human Resource Studies.

Introducing human resource. Retrieved from http://catalogue.pearsoned.co.uk/assets/hip/gb/hip_gb_pearsonhighered/samplechapter/0273740989.pdf

For a description of Loveman's impact on Harrah's, see Julie Schlosser, "Teacher's Bet," *Fortune Magazine*, March 8, 2004. Available online at http://money.cnn.com/magazines/fortune/fortune_archive/2004/03/08/363688/index.htm.

Richard Adler Rapporteur. Leveraging the Talent-Driven Organization. United States of America, The Aspen Institute.

Praful Anchaliya. Cross-cultural issues. MISL Chapter Retrieved from http://www.slideshare.net/prafful16/cross-cultural-issues-in-hr.

Sparrow, P., Schuler, R., and Jackson, S. (1994). Convergence or divergence: human resource practices and policies for competitive advantage worldwide. *The International Journal of Human Resource Management*, 5(2): 267-299.

Silverman, E. (2006). The global test. Human Resource Executive Online, June 2, 2006. Accessed at: <http://www.hreonline.com/HRE/story, (Managementstudyguide.com). Retrieved from http://www.managementstudyguide.com/global-hrm.htm

Insight Consulting Partners. (2004). Going Global With Your HRIS.http://www.insightcp.com/res_17.htm

Chapter 8

Globalization and Indian Economy

Amneet Kaur

Introduction

Indian economy was in deep crisis in July 1991, when foreign currency reserves had plummeted to almost $1 billion; Inflation had roared to an annual rate of 17 per cent; fiscal deficit was very high and had become unsustainable; foreign investors and NRIs had lost confidence in Indian Economy. Capital was flying out of the country and we were close to defaulting on loans. Along with these bottlenecks at home, many unforeseeable changes swept the economies of nations in Western and Eastern Europe, South East Asia, Latin America and elsewhere, around the same time. These were the economic compulsions at home and abroad that called for a complete overhauling of our economic policies and programmes. The first step towards globalization was taken with the announcement of the devaluation of Indian currency by 18-19 per cent against major currencies in the international foreign exchange market. In fact, this measure was taken in order to resolve the BOP crisis. In order to make the process of globalization smooth, privatization and liberalization policies are moving along as well. Under the privatization scheme, most of the public sector undertakings have been/are being sold to private sector. Allowing Foreign Direct Investment (FDI) across a wide spectrum of industries and encouraging non-debt flows. The Department has put in place a liberal and transparent foreign investment regime where most activities are opened to foreign investment on automatic route without any limit to the extent of foreign ownership. Over the last two decades and based on global trends of trades and investment liberalization the world economy has evolved into highly integrated system. Main features of globalization are as follows:

- **Internationalization of production accompanied by changes in the structure of production:** Technology changes affect the parameters of technology and product flows across countries. Improvements in the transportation network and technology are reducing the costs of transportation while improvements in the information technology have made an increasing volume of information available at all cost to zero costs. Lower transportation cost and communication costs have important implications for the nature of production activities, the flow of knowledge it relies on and the marketing of products that it makes. Reduction of transportation cost and telecommunication cost, for example, raise the intensity of competition and stimulate identification of most economic sites for both manufacturing of products and components as well as their marketing. New technologies have led to another aspect of globalization, i.e. to introduction of flexible production forms. By turning away from vertically integration forms of production which have traditionally been organized in one location and by turning towards specialized production sequences which can be spread across national borders, global production has achieved further geographical dispersion and further extension of its networks. In this way, companies become independent from concrete location, and consequently, the competition for business establishment becomes much more intense than before.
- **Expansion of international trade in goods and services:** The intensified globalization of production is closely interlinked with the second dimension of globalization, i.e. with rapid expansion of international trade of goods and services. International trade data clearly shows the rise in global production networks. In addition to it's inter linkages with the globalization of production, trade in goods and services are important from the globalization point of view for several other reasons. First, it is frequently the primary means of realizing the benefits of globalization.
- **Widening and deepening of international capital flows:** Though the precise definition of globalization is still unavailable.

A few definitions worth viewing, Stephen Gill: defines globalization as the reduction of transaction cost of trans-border movements of capital and goods thus of factors of production and goods. Guy Brainbant: says that the process of globalization not only includes opening up of world trade, development of advanced means of communication, internationalization of financial markets, growing importance of MNCs, population migrations and more generally increased mobility of persons, goods, capital, data and ideas but also infections, diseases and pollution

Globalization and Indian Economy

India opened up the economy in the early nineties following a major crisis that led by a foreign exchange crunch that dragged the economy close to defaulting on loans. The response was a slew of Domestic and External sector policy measures partly prompted by the immediate needs and partly by the demand of the multilateral organizations. The new policy regime radically pushed forward in favour of a more open and market oriented economy. Major measures initiated as a part of the liberalization and globalization strategy in the early nineties included scrapping of the industrial licensing regime, reduction in the number of areas reserved for the public sector, amendment of the Monopolies and the Restrictive Trade Practices Act, start of the privatization programme, reduction in tariff rates and change over to market determined exchange rates. Over the years there has been a steady liberalization of the current account transactions, more and more sectors opened up for foreign direct investments and portfolio investments facilitating entry of foreign investors in telecom, roads, ports, airports, insurance and other major sectors. Fig. 8.1 shows the growth rate of the country.

Globalization and Women Workers in India

The positive effect of globalization is that it has opened up broader communication lines and attracted more companies as well as different organisations into India. This provides opportunities for not only working men but also women who are becoming a part of the workplace. With the new jobs for the women their are opportunities for higher pay, which raises self-confidence and independence. This in turn can promote equality

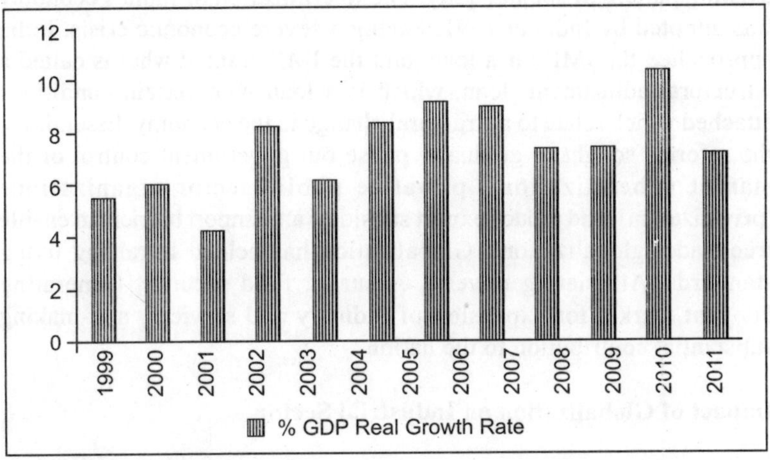

Source: CIA World fact book.
Fig. 8.1: Growth Rate of the Country

between the sexes. Globalization has power to uproot the traditional treatment towards women to afford them an equal stance in the society. Despite the positive effects of globalization through increased employment opportunities for women, globalization has a darker, more sinister side. Out of the total 397 million workers in India, 123.9 million are women and of these women 96 per cent of female workers are in the unorganized sector. Accordingly, although more women are now seeking paid employment, a vast majority of them obtain only poorly paid, unskilled jobs in the informal sector, without any job security or social security. Additionally working women in India are more likely to be subjected to intense exploitation; they are exposed to more and more risks that cause health hazards and are forced to endure greater levels of physical and mental stress. Thus it would appear, that globalization has made many international corporations richer by the billions at the expense of women who are suffering enormously due to this expansion of corporate empires.

Impact of Globalization on Agriculture Sector

Agricultural Sector is the mainstay of the rural Indian economy around which socio-economic privileges and deprivations revolve and any change in its structure is likely to have a corresponding impact on the existing pattern of social equity. The liberalization of India's economy was adopted by India in 1991. Facing a severe economic crisis, India approached the IMF for a loan, and the IMF granted what is called a 'structural adjustment' loan, which is a loan with certain conditions attached which relate to a structural change in the economy. Essentially, the reforms sought to gradually phase out government control of the market (liberalization), privatize public sector organizations (privatization), and reduce export subsidies and import barriers to enable free trade (globalization). Globalization has helped in raising living standards, Alleviating poverty, Assuring food security, Generating buoyant market for expansion of industry and services, and making substantial contribution to the nation.

Impact of Globalization on Industrial Sector

Effects of Globalization on Indian Industry started when the government opened the country's markets to foreign investments in the early 1990s. Globalization of the Indian Industry took place in its various sectors such as steel, pharmaceutical, petroleum, chemical, textile, cement, retail, and BPO. Globalization means the dismantling of trade barriers between nations and the integration of the nations economies through financial flow, trade in goods and services, and corporate investments between nations. Globalization has increased across the world in recent years due to the fast progress that has been made in the field of technology especially in communications and transport. The government of India made changes in its economic policy in 1991, by which it allowed direct foreign investments in the country. The benefits of the effects of globalization in the Indian Industry are that many foreign companies set up industries in India, especially in the pharmaceutical, BPO, petroleum, manufacturing, and chemical sectors and this helped to provide employment to many people in the country. This helped reduce the level of unemployment and poverty in the country. Also the benefit of the Effects of Globalization on Indian Industry are that the foreign companies brought in highly advanced technology with them and this helped to make the Indian Industry more technologically advanced. The negative Effects of Globalization on Indian Industry are that with the coming of technology the number of labour required decreased and this resulted in many people being removed from their jobs. This happened mainly in the pharmaceutical, chemical, manufacturing, and cement industries.

Impact on Financial Sector

Reforms of the financial sector constitute the most important component of India's programme towards economic liberalization. The recent economic liberalization measures have opened the door to foreign competitors to enter into our domestic market. Innovation has now become a must for survival. Financial intermediaries have come out of their traditional approach and they are ready to assume more credit risks. As a consequence, many innovations have taken place in the global financial sectors which have its own impact on the domestic sector also. The emergences of various financial institutions and regulatory bodies have transformed the financial services sector from being a conservative industry to a very dynamic one. In this process this sector is facing a number of challenges. In this changed context, the financial services industry in India has to play a very positive and dynamic role in the years to come by offering many innovative products to suit the varied requirements of the millions of prospective investors spread throughout the country. Reforms of the financial sector constitute the most important component of India's programme towards economic liberalization.

Impact on Export and Import

India's Export and Import in the year 2001-02 was to the extent of ₹ 32,572 and ₹ 38,362 million respectively. Many Indian companies have started becoming respectable players in the International scene. Agriculture exports account for about 13 to 18 per cent of total annual export of the country. In 2000-01 Agricultural products valued at more than US $ 6 million were exported from the country 23 per cent of which was contributed by the marine products alone. Marine products in recent years have emerged as the single largest contributor to the total agricultural export from the country accounting for over one-fifth of the total agricultural exports. Cereals (mostly basmati rice and non-basmati rice), oil seeds, tea and coffee are the other prominent products each of which accounts from nearly 5 to 10 per cent of the country's total agricultural exports.

Conclusion

India is developing into an open-market economy, yet traces of its past autarkic policies remain. Economic liberalization, including industrial deregulation, privatization of state-owned enterprises, and reduced controls on foreign trade and investment, began in the early 1990s and has served to accelerate the country's growth, which has averaged more than 7 per cent per year since 1997. India's diverse economy encompasses traditional village farming, modern agriculture, handicrafts, a wide range of modern industries, and a multitude of services. Slightly more than half of the workforce is in agriculture, but services are the major source of economic growth, accounting for more than half of India's output, with only one-third of its labour force. India has capitalized on its large educated English-speaking population to become a major exporter of information technology services and software workers. In 2010, the Indian economy rebounded robustly from the global financial crisis in large part because of strong domestic demand and growth exceeded 8 per cent year-on-year in real terms. However, India's economic growth in 2011 slowed because of persistently high inflation and interest rates and little progress on economic reforms. High international crude prices have exacerbated the government's fuel subsidy expenditures contributing to a higher fiscal deficit, and a worsening current account deficit. Little economic reform took place in 2011 largely due to corruption scandals that have slowed legislative work. India's medium-term growth outlook is positive due to a young population and corresponding low dependency ratio, healthy savings and investment rates, and increasing integration into the global economy. India has many long-term challenges that it has not yet fully addressed, including widespread poverty, inadequate physical and social infrastructure, limited non-agricultural employment opportunities, scarce access to quality basic and higher education, and accommodating rural-to-urban migration. The implications of globalization for a national economy are many. Globalization has intensified interdependence and competition between economies in the world market. This is reflected in Interdependence in regard to trading in goods and services and in movement of capital. As a result domestic economic developments are not determined entirely by domestic policies and market conditions. Rather, they are influenced by both domestic and international policies and economic conditions. It is thus clear that a globalising economy, while formulating and evaluating its domestic policy cannot afford to ignore the possible actions and reactions of policies and developments in the rest of the world. This constrained the policy option available to the government which implies loss of policy autonomy to some extent, in decision-making at the national level.

REFERENCES

A.K.Ojha, "Globalization and Liberalisation" Prospects of New World Order. *Third Concept - An International Journal of Ideas*, August 2002.

Globalization and Poverty, Centre for International Economics, Australia.

Globalisation: Imperatives, Challenges and the Strategies, p. 39.

Ravi Kastia, *Globalization and India's Business Prospectives* - Lecture.

Sagar Jain, *Globalization and India* - Lecture. University of N.Carolina.

T.K.Velayudham, *Globalization Trend and Issues*, pp. 3, 66.

V.N. Rai, *Repositioning India in the Globalised World*, Lecture.

Chapter 9

Globalization and Foreign Direct Investment

Role in Indian Economy

Neelam Choudhary and *Ritika Sharma*

Introduction

Globalization is the process of international integration arising from the interchange of world views, products, ideas and other aspects of culture. Globalization describes the interplay across cultures of macro-social forces. These forces include religion, politics and economics. Advances in transportation and telecommunications infrastructure, including the rise of the Internet, are major factors in globalization, generating further interdependence of economic and cultural activities. Globalization can erode and universalize the characteristics of a local group. Though several scholars place the origins of globalization in modern times, others trace its history long before the European discovery and voyages to the New World. Some even trace the origins to the third millennium BCE. Since the beginning of the 20th century, the pace of globalization has proceeded at a rapid rate.

The term globalization has been in increasing use since the mid 1980s and especially since the mid 1990s. In 2000, the International Monetary Fund (IMF) identified four basic aspects of globalization: trade and transactions, capital and investment movements, migration and movement of people and the dissemination of knowledge. Further, environmental challenges such as climate change, cross-boundary water and air pollution, and over-fishing of the ocean are linked with globalization. Globalizing processes affect and are affected by business and work organization, economics, socio-cultural resources and the natural environment. Indian economy had experienced major policy changes in early 1990s. The new economic reform, popularly known as, Liberalization, Privatization and Globalization (LPG model) aimed at making the Indian economy as fastest growing economy and globally competitive. The series of reforms undertaken with respect to industrial sector, trade as well as financial sector aimed at making the economy more efficient.

FDI in India

With the onset of reforms to liberalize the Indian economy in July 1991, a new chapter has dawned for India and her billion plus population. This period of economic transition has had a tremendous impact on the overall economic development of almost all major sectors of the economy, and its effects over the last decade can hardly be overlooked. Besides, it also marks the advent of the real integration of the Indian economy into the global economy. This paper focuses on FDI (foreign direct investment) as a vector of Indian globalization. Recently, not only did India become a more frequent destination for FDI, but many Indian firms also started to invest abroad on a very large scale with, stunning takeovers in industrialized countries. The reforms undertaken since 1991 in India have unleashed the potential growth of the economy and stimulated international trade, outsourcing and FDI. Changes have been so many that investors have started to take a fresh look at India. At the same time, some Indian firms have become global players.

This era of reforms has also ushered in a remarkable change in the Indian mindset, as it deviates from the traditional values held since Independence in 1947, such as self reliance and socialistic policies of economic development, which mainly due to the inward looking restrictive form of governance, resulted in the isolation, overall backwardness and inefficiency of the economy, amongst a host of other problems.

Now that India is in the process of restructuring her economy, with aspirations of elevating herself from her present desolate position in the world, the need to speed up her economic development is even more imperative. And having witnessed the positive role that Foreign Direct Investment (FDI) has played in the rapid economic growth of most of the Southeast Asian countries and most notably China, India has embarked on an ambitious plan to emulate the successes of her neighbours to the east and is trying to sell herself as a safe and profitable destination for FDI.

Globalization is the new buzzword that has come to dominate the world since the nineties of the last century with the end of the cold war and the break-up of the former Soviet Union and the global trend towards the rolling ball. The frontiers of the state with increased reliance on the market economy and renewed faith in the private capital and resources, a process of structural adjustment spurred by the studies and influences of the World Bank and other International organizations have started in many of the developing countries. Also Globalization has brought in new opportunities to developing countries. Greater access to developed country markets and technology transfer hold out promise improved productivity and higher living standard. But globalization has also thrown up new challenges like growing inequality across and within nations, volatility in financial market and environmental deteriorations. Another negative aspect of globalization is that a great majority of developing countries remain removed from the process. Till the nineties the process of globalization of the Indian economy was constrained by the barriers to trade and investment. Liberalization of trade, investment and financial flows initiated in the nineties has progressively lowered the barriers to competition and hastened the pace of globalisation.

Foreign direct investment in India has reached 2 per cent of GDP, compared with 0.1 per cent in 1990, and Indian investment in other countries rose sharply in 2006. As the fourth-largest economy in the world in PPP terms, India is a preferred destination for foreign direct investments (FDI) India has strengths in information technology and other significant areas such as auto components, chemicals, apparels, pharmaceuticals, and jewellery. Despite a surge in foreign investments, rigid FDI policies resulted in a significant hindrance. However, due to some positive economic reforms aimed at deregulating the economy and stimulating foreign investment, India has positioned itself as one of the front-runners of the rapidly growing Asia Pacific Region. India has a large pool of skilled managerial and technical expertise. Globalization has altered the economic frameworks of both developed and developing nations in ways that are difficult to comprehend.

The persistent rise in the dispersion of current account balances of the world as a whole, wherein the sum of surpluses match the sum of deficits, has grown substantially since the Second World War. Also the emergence of unregulated global markets appears to have moved towards a more stable and growth oriented economic globe. Economies have been hit one after the other with the fashion and need for market driven capitalist and liberalized economic system has been the urging need. The 90s has also seen the emergence of finance, which apart from the efficiency, product enhancement, and lower cost of transaction has facilitated the crisis frequencies, globalization, and movement of capital lows internationally without much control. India has been ranked at the second place in global foreign direct investments in 2010 and will continue to remain among the top five attractive destinations for international investors during 2010-12 period, according to United Nations Conference on Trade and Development (UNCTAD) in a report on world investment prospects titled, 'World Investment Prospects Survey 2009-2012'. The 2010 survey of the Japan Bank for International Cooperation released in December 2010, conducted among Japanese investors, continues to rank India as the second most promising country for overseas business operations. A report released in February 2010 by Leeds University Business School, commissioned by UK Trade & Investment (UKTI), ranks India among the top three countries where British companies can do better business during 2012-14. According to Ernst and Young's 2010 European Attractiveness Survey, India is ranked as the 4th most attractive foreign direct investment (FDI) destination in 2010.

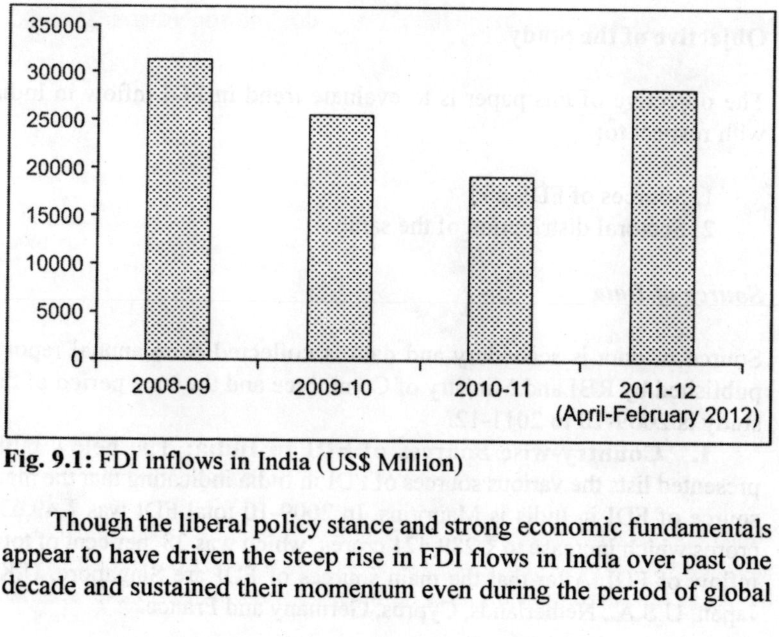

Fig. 9.1: FDI inflows in India (US$ Million)

Though the liberal policy stance and strong economic fundamentals appear to have driven the steep rise in FDI flows in India over past one decade and sustained their momentum even during the period of global economic crisis (2008-09 and 2009-10), FDI inflows to India witnessed significant moderation in 2010-11 while other EMEs in Asia and Latin America received large inflows. This had raised concerns in the wake of widening current account deficit in India beyond the perceived sustainable level of 3.0 per cent of GDP during April-December 2010. This also assumes significance as FDI is generally known to be the most stable component of capital flows needed to finance the current account deficit. Moreover, it adds to investible resources, provides access to advanced technologies, assists in gaining production know-how and promotes exports. A perusal of India's FDI policy *vis-à-vis* other major emerging market economies (EMEs) reveals that though India's approach towards foreign investment has been relatively conservative to begin with, it progressively started catching up with the more liberalized policy stance of other EMEs from the early 1990s onwards, inter alias in terms of wider access to different sectors of the economy, ease of starting business, repatriation of dividend and profits and relaxations regarding norms for owning equity. This progressive liberalization, coupled with considerable improvement in terms of macro-economic fundamentals, reflected in growing size of FDI flows to the country that increased nearly 5 fold during first decade of the present millennium.

Objective of the Study

The objective of this paper is to evaluate trend in FDI inflow in India with respect to:

1. Sources of FDI, and
2. Sectoral distribution of the same.

Source of Data

Source of data is secondary and data is collected from annual reports published by RBI and Ministry of Commerce and the time period of the study is 2009-10 to 2011-12.

1. Country-wise Sources of FDI in India: The below table presented lists the various sources of FDI in India indicating that the main source of FDI in India is Mauritius. In 2009-10 total FDI was ₹ 49,633 crores which increase to ₹ 289,471 crores, which was 38 per cent of total inflow of FDI. After that the main sources of FDI are Singapore, U.K., Japan, U.S.A., Netherlands, Cyprus, Germany and France.

Table 9.1: Share of Top Investing Countries FDI Equity Inflows (Financial years)

Amount Rupees in crores (US$ in millions)

Ranks	*Country*	*2009-10 (April-March)*	*2010-11 (April-March)*	*2011-12 (April-March)*	*Cumulative Inflows (April '00-March, 12)*	*%age to total Inflows (in terms of US $)*
1.	Mauritius	49,633 (10,376)	31,855 (6,987)	46,710 (9,942)	289,471 (64,169)	38
2.	Singapore	11,295 (2,379)	7,730 (1,705)	24,712 (5,257)	77,588 (17,153)	10
3.	U.K.	3,094 (657)	3,434 (755)	45,229 (9,257)	74,661 (15,896)	9
4.	Japan	5,670 (1,183)	7,063 (1,562)	14,089 (2,972)	57,851 (12,313)	7
5.	U.S.A.	9,230 (1,943)	5,353 (1,170)	5,347 (1,115)	47,889 (10,564)	6
6.	Netherlands	4,283 (899)	5,501 (1,213)	6,698 (1,409)	32,325 (7,109)	4
7.	Cyprus	7,728 (1,627)	4,171 (913)	7,722 (1,587)	29,670 (6,400)	4
8.	Germany	2,980 (626)	908 (200)	7,452 (1,622)	20,828 (4,621)	3
9	France	1,437 (303)	3,349 (734)	3,110 (663)	13,378 (2,927)	2
10.	U.A.E.	3,017 (629)	1,569 (341)	1,728 (353)	10,320 (2,243)	1
Total FDI Inflows *		123,120 (25,834)	88,520 (19,427)	173,946 (36,504)	775,006 (170,407)	–

Note: (i) *Includes inflows under NRI Schemes of RBI.

(ii) Cumulative country-wise FDI equity inflows (from April 2000 to March 2012).

(iii) Percentage worked out in US$ terms and FDI inflows received through FIPB/SIA+ RBI's Automatic Route+ acquisition of existing shares only.

Source:

1. RBI's Bulletin May 2012 dt. 10.05.2012 (Table No. 44 — FOREIGN INVESTMENT INFLOWS).
2. **Sectoral share in FDI:** Service sector plays an important role in FDI equity inflow, it was ₹ 19,945 crore (4,176 US$ in millions) and increased to ₹ 145,764 crore (32,351 US$ in millions). So there is remarkable change in FDI equity inflow in service sector. After that telecommunications, construction activities, computer software and hardware, housing and real estate, chemicals, drugs and pharmaceuticals, power, automobile industry, metallurgical industries etc.

Table 9.2: Sectors Attracting Highest FDI Equity Inflows

Amount in ₹ crores (US$ in million)

Ranks	*Sector*	*2009-10 (April-March)*	*2010-11 (April-March)*	*2011-12 (April-March)*	*Cumu-lative Inflows (April '00-March'12)*	*% age to total Inflows (In terms of US$)*
1.	Services Sector (financial and non-financial)	19,945 (4,176)	15,053 (3,296)	24,656 (5,216)	145,764 (32,351)	19%
2.	Telecommunications (radio paging, cellular mobile, basic telephone services)	12,270 (2,539)	7,542 (1,665)	9,012 (1,997)	57,078 (12,552)	7
3.	Construction Activities (including roads and highways)	13,469 (2,852)	4,979 (1,103)	13,672 (2,796)	52,253 (11,433)	7
4.	Computer Software and Hardware	4,127 (872)	3,551 (780)	3,804 (796)	50,118 (11,205)	7
5.	Housing and Real Estate	14,027 (2,935)	5,600 (1,227)	3,443 (731)	49,717 (11,113)	7
6.	Chemicals (other than Fertilizers)	1,726 (366)	1,812 (398)	36,227 (7,252)	47,904 (9,844)	6
7.	Drugs and Pharmaceuticals	1,006 (213)	961 (200)	14,605 (3,232)	42,868 (9,105)	5
8.	Power	6,138 (1,272)	5,796 (1,272)	7,678 (1,652)	33,214 (7,299)	4
9.	Automobile Industry	5,893 (1,236)	5,864 (1,299)	4,347 (923)	30,785 (6,758)	4
10.	Metallurgical Industries	1,999 (420)	5,023 (1,098)	8,348 (1,786)	26,936 (6,041)	4

Note: (i) Cumulative Sector-wise FDI equity inflows (from April 2000 to March, 2012) Annex-B.

(ii) FDI Sectoral data has been revalidated in line with that of RBI, which reflects minor changes in the FDI figures (increase/decrease) as compared to the earlier published sectoral data.

Source: 1. RBI's Bulletin May 2012 dt. 10.05.2012 (Table No. 44 – FOREIGN INVESTMENT INFLOWS).

Findings

1. India is one of the most favourable investment destinations to invest in.
2. Due to open market condition and post-liberalization reforms it is attracting foreign investors.
3. Both UPA and NDA regimes were fruitful for the Indian Economy as there was sharp increment in FDI due to their market friendly policies which attracted the investors.
4. Some sectors of the economies are deprived from the investment

like Defence, Atomic Energy, Retail, Agriculture there some kind of reforms are required in this regard.

5. More liberal policies for the investors like increasing FDI cap, demand and supply based exchange rate and reduction of tariff and decreasing tax attracted most of the investors.
6. The most dominated area attracting FDI is the service sector so this may be a competitive edge for the country.
7. Sectors which are deprived from the FDI are those where large market potential is present but these are ignored by the policy makers and poor infrastructure as well as due to high concentration on priority sectors also contributed to the cause.

Conclusion

From this we have concluded that India is one of the greatest investing destinations for the investors as more and more investors are investing in India. The equity inflow is increasing tremendously due to high GDP India has been the second biggest and fastest growing economy in the world. During the recessionary pressure the GDP continuous to grow because of equity influx, because the exposure of Indian economy for the world Foreign Direct Investment (FDI) as a strategic component of investment is needed by India for its sustained economic growth and development through creation of jobs, expansion of existing manufacturing industries, short and long term project in the field of healthcare, education, research and development (R&D) etc.

After that Government should design the FDI policy such a way where FDI inflow can be utilized as means of enhancing domestic production, savings and exports through the equitable distribution among states by providing much freedom to states, so that they can attract FDI inflows at their own level. FDI can help to raise the output, productivity and export at the sectoral level of the Indian economy. However, it can observed the result of sectoral level output, productivity and export is minimal due to the low flow of FDI into India both at the macro level as well as at the sectoral level. Therefore, for further opening up of the Indian economy, it is advisable to open up the export oriented sectors and higher growth of the economy could be achieved through the growth of these sectors.

REFERENCES

Basu P., Nayak, N.C. and Vani, A., (2007), "Foreign Direct Investment in India: Emerging Horizon", *Indian Economic Review*.

Ministry of Commerce, (2012), Annual Report (2009-2012).

Ministry of Finance, (2012), *Report of the Economic Survey*, Government of India, New Delhi.

RBI's Bulletin, May 2012 dt. 10.05.2012.

Srivastava S., (2003), "What is the true level of FDI flows to India?" *Economic and Political Weekly*.

www.rbi.org.

http://www.investopedia.com

http://www.thehindu.com

Chapter 10

Falling Wage Share in the Manufacturing Sector and Trade Union Movement in India
An Analytical Study

Soumita Chakraborty and *Nayanika Singh*

Introduction

During the past few decades, the manufacturing sector in India has witnessed decreasing wage share. The probable explanation to it is that the average wage rates and the average labour productivity have not been able to keep pace with the productivity growth especially in the manufacturing sector. But, statistics indicate that the rate of decrease has been rapid during the last decade, especially after the implementation of the New Economic Policy in 1991.

The trade unions, however, appear to be the most effective institutions to offer instant relief from exploitation, answering grievances, and labourers' disadvantage, which be done through collective bargaining, strikes and use of other forces in order to alleviate or prevent the exploitation of the workers in the hands of the ruthless capitalists. It is observed that in case of the manufacturing sector in India, during the study period, an increasing labour productivity outpaced the real average wage per worker thereby forcing the wage share in value added to decline over the period. The declining bargaining power of the Indian trade unions may be one of the important causes behind the falling wage share in Indian manufacturing sector. According to Singh and Sharma (1991), a trend of fragmentation of trade unions besides their inability to absorb new workers is the obvious reason behind this decline. Hence, the falling wage share in value added can be explained with the help of the decreasing power of the trade unions in India during the study period.

Hence, the above analysis says that the falling wage share in value-added ratio can be explained with the help of the decreasing power of the trade unions in India during the period under observation, which is reflected in multiplicity of trade unions, i.e. the number of trade unions as well as in the declining average size of the trade unions (Singh, 1984; Sinha, 1994).

The collective bargaining in India remained largely decentralized, i.e. company or unit level bargaining rather than Industry level bargaining. But in some sectors (mostly public sector industries) the industry level bargaining was dominant. However, privatization of public sector transformed the industry level bargaining to company level bargaining. On the other hand, due to drastic infomalization of workforce and downsizing in the industries, the strength and power of the trade unions is heavily reduced. The trade unions mainly represented the interests of formal workers. Increasing number of informal workers in the companies soon transformed the structure of the workforce in such a way that the formal workers became a minority. Moreover, in some sectors like garment, there is almost complete in formalization of the workforce with only a small section of formal worker. It happened in almost all sectors. Due to various reasons informal workers are not able to form their own trade unions, and on the other hand they are not represented by the trade unions of the formal workers. These situations resulted in spurt of individualized bargaining.

High level of informalization of workforce combined with the individualized bargaining actually changed the character of the trade unions in recent times. In relevant sectors and industrial regions, it converted many trade unions (particularly in sector dominated by informal workers) in to legal consultants (pursuing individual cases and charging fees for their services) rather than collective bargaining agents. Declining strength of collective bargaining is also reflected in sharply increasing share of profit and drastically declining wage share (since 2001-02), resulting in depressing purchasing power. Approximately 73 million out of 173 million wage earners throughout India do not receive minimum wages. About 30-40 per cent of these low-paid wage earners belong to poor families (World of Work Report, ILO 2010). On the other hand, the industrialists are not ready to accept trade unions in their factories at any cost. They are unleashing unimaginable repression on workers and trade union leaders when there are efforts to form trade unions in their factories.

Even after the trade unions are formed, managements are not ready to recognize them and therefore deny them space for collective bargaining.

According to the data of Government of India on strikes and lockouts (Indian Labour Statistics 2010), causal factor of 34.8 per cent cases of industrial disputes is recorded as indiscipline. 22 per cent cases of industrial disputes are around demands for wages and allowances (in many cases demanding only minimum wages fixed by the government). Actually these two categories of industrial disputes largely reflect on the sufferings of informal workers and repression unleashed by factory managements on unionization efforts of the workers. Moreover, after the liberalization, man-days lost in the lockouts are far more than the strikes by the workers. This is a consistent trend.

The distribution of national income between social classes is a significant question in political economy. The classical economists see distribution of income the central analysis to economic growth. The share of wages in national income indicates the importance of the working class in the economic structure in general and industry in particular. The proponents of the theory of Rising Strength of Labour (RSL variant) (Broddy & Crotty, 1975: 1978; Glyn and Sutcliffe, 1972; and Weisskopf, 1979) focus on gains by the working class in its struggle with the capitalist class pursuing a line of argument presented by Marx (Marx, Capital, Vol.1, Chapter 25), who originally applied it in explaining cyclical economic downturns in capitalist economies. The RSL variant points out to a fall in the profit share in value added which is a result of rise in wage share. According to the rising strength of labour theory, the capitalist process of accumulation tends to alter the balance of political-economic power between labour and capital, in such a way to enable the working class to increase the wage share in national income. An increase in working class power enables workers to bargain more successfully for higher wages and thereby to increase the rate of growth of money wages as well as real wages. An increase in working class power empowers workers to resist more successfully capitalist's efforts to increase work intensity (measures to increase labour efficiency units per hour of work) and thereby to reduce rate of growth of labour productivity. The rise in unit labour cost, which will sooner or later results from accelerating wages or decelerating productivity, will not be offset by a corresponding increasing in output prices, as a consequence the share of wages will rise.

The present paper attempts to find out the empirical relationship between the wage share in national income (replaced here by value added) and the trade union movement in the organized manufacturing sector in

India during the period 1992-2007, i.e. after the economic reform in 1991. So the objective of this study is to analyze the significance of the rising strength of labour theory in the context of Indian manufacturing sector and the new role and relevance of the trade union movement in India in new economic situation i.e. whether trade unions in India are strong enough to be able to realize the right of collective bargaining.

The last two decades have witnessed a number of changes in the global business environment in the form of redefined national boundaries, the emergence of the World Trade Organization (WTO), the changing world economic order, and so on. The changing pattern of the international division of labour is making its impact on the international labour market, and the bargaining power of trade unions in the capitalist world is capable of turning capitalist societies of wage earners into societies of partner nations (Hong, 1999). It has thus become necessary to study the impact of all these changes on the industrial relations of particular organizations. Keeping this in mind, this study considers the roles of trade unions in India in changing the business environment at a broad level, and specifically focuses on the functioning of plant-level trade unions.

The paper is organized as follows: Data and sources are discussed in Section II. Section III examines the rate of growth of wage share in value added and the real wage rate in both pre and post reform years. Section IV makes an analytical discussion about the relationship between the movement of the wage share in value added ratio and the trade union movement in Indian manufacturing sector during the study period (1992-2007). The next section concludes the entire study.

II

Data

The current study is based on the data provided by Annual Survey of Industries (ASI) spanning over 1992 to 2007 for the organized or registered manufacturing sectors in India. The ASI provides estimates of value added, wages to workers, number of workers, fixed capital, total input etc. Since the industrial data collected from ASI were at current prices, we use the wholesale price indices for the relevant categories as deflators in obtaining the value of output and the value added at constant prices. The stock of fixed and circulating constant capital at constant prices was obtained by deflating the stock of constant capital by the weighted average of the wholesale price indices of the stock of fixed and circulating constant capital. It should be mentioned here that the deflator used for the fixed capital is nothing but the wholesale price indices for machinery and machine tools. For circulating constant capital the weighted average of the wholesale price indices of the intermediate goods used in the production process are used. The average wage per worker is deflated by the cost of living index of an urban industrial worker to get the average real wage per worker. Finally, the year 1981-82 is taken as the base year (1981-82= 00) for the purpose of the study. For the said study, data was collected for a number of trade unions (both registered and submitting returns) the at all India level. The sources of the data included publications from the Labour Bureau, Ministry of Labour, Government of India.

III

The present section attempts to provide a comparative analysis of the growth of wage-share in value added ratio in the manufacturing sector, both in the pre-reform and post-reform periods. Here is an overview of the same:

Growth of Wage-share in Value added Ratio in the Manufacturing Sector, Pre-reform and Post-Reform Period—A Comparative Analysis

From the data available from Indian manufacturing sector it appears that the wage share in value added ratio falls drastically during the post-reform years (1992-2007) as compared to the pre-reform period (1981-91). The data for real wage rate also reveals a similar pattern. The real wage rate increases in both pre-reform and post-reform years. But the rate of increase in post-reform years is lower than the pre-reform period (Table 10.1).

Table 10.1: Annual Rate of Growth (CAGR) of Wage-share in Value Added and Real Wage Rate

	1981-91	*1992-2007*
W/VA	–2.2%	–4.25%
$\hat{W}$	0.96%	0.17%

where, W/VA = wage share in value added

$\hat{W}$ = real wage rate

From the figure 10.1 it is quite evident that the ratio of wage share in the value added, has been diminishing consistently during the period under observation except for some minor fluctuations observed in 1997 and 2000. The labour productivity variable has outpaced the minor increase in the real wage rate during the post-reform years under consideration. The next table (Table 10.1) draws a comparison between the annual growth rate of the wage share in value added ratio and real wage rate of the workers employed in the manufacturing sector during pre- and post-reform years.

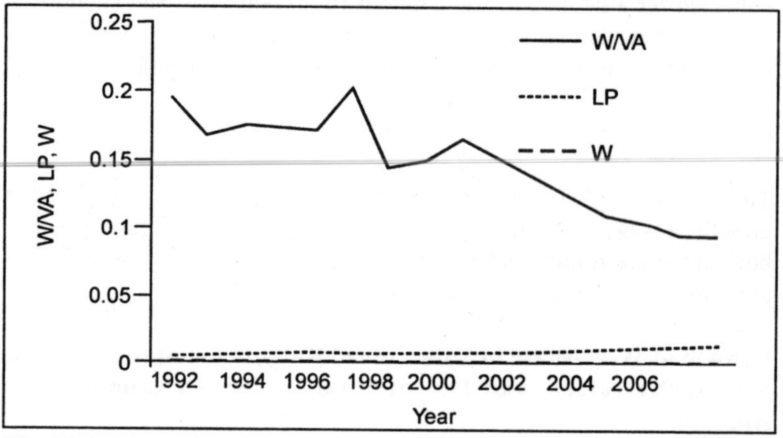

Fig. 10.1: Wages share in value added labour poductivity and real wage rate

The result obtained from the above analysis prompts us to further investigate the significance of the collective bargaining process in the manufacturing sector in India during the post-reform years. So it is essential on the part of this researcher to examine thoroughly the importance of the trade union movement in India during this period especially in the context of falling labour share in the value added.

IV

Role of Trade Unions in Determining Wage-Share: An Analytical Discussion

This section attempts to establish an empirical relationship between the trade union movement and the declining wage share in value added in Indian manufacturing sector during the period of investigation.

The factors which have been considered determination of wages by various wage fixing bodies, employers' associations and trade unions are economic environment, cost of living, workers' budgets, labour productivity and employers' capacity to pay. The weights assigned to them have, however, differed from time to time.

It has been argued that fixation of wages should be made against the background of economic environment of the country and the level of national income. But in the absence of any indicated norms to relate wage levels the application of this factor becomes impracticable. The adoption of employers' capacity to pay factor is likely to widen the wage differentials between industries and may also lead to wage reductions in cases where profit are non-existent or inadequate. This situation would have an adverse impact on wage-structure, workers' incentives and job opportunities. The workers' budget has limited usefulness in connection with the movement of the wage share mainly because of the inherent vagueness in the concept itself (Tewari and Sinha, 1979). Further wages are attached to job rather than to the individual. As such the trade unions never stressed upon this factor, while justifying their claims for higher wages.

So on the basis of the above discussion the factors selected to be the most crucial for wage share determination are cost of living, labour productivity and the impact of trade unions obtained in light of the research conducted by Fonseca (1964), Guha Thakurta (1971), Tewari and Sinha (1979) and Kannan (1994).

The cost of living is taken as an important determinant of the wage share in value added because the adoption of this factor prevents workers' real wages from falling. In principle it requires a 100 per cent neutralization of rises in the cost of living index through payment of dearness allowances. It yields an exactly calculable figure when the problems of base year and proper index to use are overcome. Another important factor whose importance has been emphasized in determining wage share in value added since 1950 is labour productivity (Ross, 1954). Fixation of wage rates on this basis ensures higher wages for higher productivity and provides incentives for further rise in the wage rate raising the wage share in value added. Finally, the trade unions have always been active on the wage front (International Labour Review, ILO, Geneva, January 1968). They have been instrumentai in the upward revision of wages through collective bargaining, strikes etc. on the behalf of the workers. But their role as an independent factor has seldom been recognized. It has, however, been argued that owing to strong trade unions labour enjoyed positive gains in the period of both productivity increments and productivity losses. According to Fonseca (1964), the chief aim of the trade unions is to neutralize the rise in the cost of living. Thus to disregard trade unions would, probably imply undermining their independent role in wage negotiations.

So, on the basis of the foregoing analysis we select cost of living, labour productivity and trade unions (degree of unionization) as variables for operational analysis. Therefore, the wage share in value added is taken to be a function of three variables—the cost of living, labour productivity and degree of unionization for the purpose of our study.

The cost of living is taken as the cost of living index of urban industrial workers and the labour productivity is computed as value added per worker during the period under consideration. Lastly, the degree of unionization is defined as the ratio of membership to average daily employment, which is expressed in percentage terms. Thus, it is measured by the formula:

$$\frac{\text{Union Membership}}{\text{Total Labour Force}} \times 100$$

This is a good measure to analyze the progress of the trade unions in depth, because it does not consider only the new members but also the total membership. The series of the indices of the above variables with 1992 base is given in Table 10.2.

It is evident from Table 10.2 that the wage share in value added ratio shows an almost declining trend in Indian manufacturing sector during the period of investigation. On the contrary, the cost of living index and labour productivity show steady trend to rise. Lastly, the degree of unionization shows a downward movement with minor fluctuations during the period.

In order to measure the effect of the selected variables on the wage share in value added in the manufacturing sector in India, the following linear function has been considered for the purpose of our analysis.

$$Y = a + bX_1 + cX_2 + dX_3$$

Where, *b*, *c*, *d* are the parameters to be estimated and *a* is constant. Here, Y is the index of wage share in value added and X_1, X_2 and X_3 are respectively the indices of cost of living, labour productivity and degree of unionization.

Table 10.2: Indices of Wage-Share in Value Added, Cost of Living, Labour Productivity and Degree of Unionization, 1992-2007

Year	Degree of Unionization	Labour Productivity	Cost of Living	Wage Share in value added
1992	100	100	100	100
1993	54.66	114.0351	106.3291	86.28
1994	68.04	119.2982	117.2996	89.02
1995	99.17	128.0702	129.1139	88.22
1996	87.8	133.3333	140.9283	87.54
1997	112.31	114.0351	151.0549	104.06
1998	86.56402	149.1228	170.8861	73.47044
1999	75.05736	150.8772	178.903	76.62982
2000	59.5179	142.1053	186.0759	84.60257
2001	74.50938	147.3684	193.2489	76.99126
2002	80.00615	161.4035	201.2658	69.45039
2003	78.62278	178.9474	209.2827	63.24679
2004	38.79792	194.7368	216.8776	55.85244
2005	58.4345	205.2632	226.1603	53.09717
2006	62.42993	224.5614	240.0844	49.48483
2007	52.75792	247.3684	255.6962	47.68689

Source: 1. Various issues of Indian Labour Statistics.
2. Various issues of Annual Survey of Industries.

After applying the Ordinary Least Square (OLS) method for estimating parameters the above results have been obtained:–

$$Y = 119.3462 - .00889\,X_1 - 0.34371\,X_2 + 0.1587\,X_3$$
$$(-0.9269) \quad (-3.836)^{**} \quad (1.95)^{*}$$

**t* values are significant at 5 per cent level.
***t* values are significant at both 1 per cent and 5 per cent levels.

$$R^2 = 0.941552 \text{ Adj. } R^2 = 0.92694 \text{ D.W.} = 1.403$$

It is observed from the above result that for one per cent increase in consumer living index (X_1) there would be a fall in the wage share in value added to the extent of 0.089 per cent and that is not significant enough. On the other hand, for one per cent rise in labour productivity (X_2) the wage share in value added decreases significantly by 3.43 per cent during the study period. Lastly, the degree of unionization (X_3) holds a comparatively strong direct relationship with the wage share in value added ratio in Indian manufacturing sector, i.e. as the degree of unionization falls the wage share in value added also falls and *vice-versa*.

For everyone per cent decrease in the degree of unionization the wage share falls by 0.16 per cent. So from the basis of the above results it can be inferred that the increase (decrease) degree of unionization has been the most dominant factor in raising (reducing) the wage share in the manufacturing sector in India during the period under consideration.

Conclusion

The present analysis, therefore, reveals that the working class movement in Indian manufacturing sector was not successful in raising the wage share in value added in the manufacturing sector during the study period. The failure of the trade unions in restoring the interests of the workers (mainly through the process of successful collective bargaining) could not neutralize the increase in the labour productivity as is evident from the negative relationship between the wage share in value added and the labour productivity of the workers in the organized manufacturing sector.

Hence, this result is in contradiction with the argument forwarded by the proponents of Rising Strength of Labour theory (Boddy and Crotty, 1975; Glyn and Suitcliffe, 1972; Weisskopf, 1979), which states that the process of accumulation tends to alter the balance of political-economic power between labour and capital, in such a way as to enable the working class to increase the wage share in national income. But experience of Indian manufacturing sector reveals that the declining wage share in value added can be explained by the inability of the working class to bargain successfully for higher wages. The declining wage share has not resulted in any strong working class movement. So it can be inferred from the above study that the period of liberalization witnessed a accelerated movement of the balance of power in favour of the capitalists.

Acknowledgement

The authors like to acknowledge Prof. Debesh Chakraborty, Department of Economics, Jadavpur University, for his advice to complete the work.

REFERENCES

Ahluwalia, Isher Judge (1985). *Industrial Growth in India—since the Mid-Sixties*, Delhi: Oxford University Press.

Ahluwalia, Isher Judge (1991). *Productivity and Growth in Indian Manufacturing*, Delhi: Oxford University Press.

Arya, P. Prakash (1980). Workers' Involvement in Trade Unions. *Indian Journal of Labour Economics,* Vol. XXIII, No. 3, pp. 115-136.

Bagchi, A.K. (1982). *The Political Economy of Underdevelopment*, Cambridge: Cambridge University Press.

Baran, P.A. and P.M. Sweezy (1966). *Monopoly Capital*, New York: Monthly Review Press.

Bardhan, P. (1984). *The Political Economy of Development in India,* Delhi: Oxford University Press.

Bhattacherjee, Debashish (2000). *Organized Labour and Economic Liberalization*. India: Past, Present and Future, Indian Institute of Management, Calcutta, Joka.

Boddy, R. and Crotty, J. (1975). Class Conflict and Macro Policy: The Political Business Cycle, Review of *Radical Political Economy*, Spring, pp. 1-19.

Booth, Alison (1984). A Public Choice Model of Trade Union Behaviour and Membership. *The Economic Journal*, 94, pp. 883-898.

Datt, Ruddar (1992). Lockouts, Closures and the Role of the State. *Indian Journal of Labour Economics*, Vol. 35, No. 1, pp. 3-22.

Datt, Ruddar (2000). Regional Patterns of Industrial Relations in India: Changing Scenario after Liberalization. *Indian Journal of Labour Economics,* Vol. 43, No. 4, pp. 1062-1098.

Datt, Ruddar (2001). Lockouts in India: A Case Study of West Bengal. *Indian Journal of Labour Economics,* Vol. 44, No. 2, pp. 277-287.

Davanzati, Guglielmo Forges (2002). Wages Fund, High Wages and Social Conflict in a Classical Model of Unemployment Equilibrium, *Review of Radical Political Economics*, Vol. 34, pp. 463-486.

Dhal, Manoranjan and Srivastava, Kailosh, B.L. (2000). Changing Face of Trade Unions in a Liberalised Economy. *Indian Journal of Labour Economics,* Vol. 43, No. 4, pp. 1143-1155.

Fonseca, A.J. (1964). *Wage Determination and Organized Labour in India,* Bombay: Oxford University Press.

Guha Thakurta, S.N. (1971). Wage Determination of Unorganised Labour in Construction Industry, *Economic and Political Weekly*, 16 October, pp. 2211-2215.

Hendricks, Wallace E. and Kahn, Lawrence M. (1991). Efficiency Wages, Monopoly Unions and Efficient Bargaining. *Economic Journal,* Vol. 10, pp. 1949-1162.

Henley, Andrew (1987). Labour's Shares and Profitability Crisis in the US: Recent Experience and Post War Trends. *Cambridge Journal of Economics,* Vol.11, pp. 315-330.

Hussain, Abid (1997). India's Fifty Years of Economic Development- Extract from "India Perspectives", <www.webspawner.com/users/IndustDevelA>.

Kannan, K.P. (1994) Levelling Up or Levelling Down? Labour Institutions and Economic Development in India, 23 July, *Economic and Political Weekly*, pp. 1938-1945.

Laibman, David (1996). Technical Change, Accumulation and the Rate of Profit Revisited. *Review of Radical Political Economics,* Vol. 28, No. 2, pp. 33-53.

Marx, Karl. (1954). *Capital*, Vol. 3, Moscow: Progress Publishers.

Moseley, Fred (1985a). The Rate of Surplus Value in the Postwar US Economy: A Critique of Weisskopf's Estimates, *Cambridge Journal of Economics*, Vol. 9, March, pp. 180-189.

Moseley, Fred (1994a). Unproductive Labour and the Rate of Profit: A Reply to Laibman. *Science and Society,* Vol. 58, pp. 84-92.

Moseley, Fred (1994b). Unproductive Labour and the Causes of Decline in the Rate of Profit: A Reply to Cullenberg's Comment. *Review of Radical Political Economics,* Vol. 26, No. 2, pp. 121-128.

Moseley, Fred and Wolff, Edward N.(ed.) (1994). International Perspectives on Profitability and Accumulation, published by Edward Elgar.

Moseley, Fred (2000). The "New Solution" to the Transformation Problem: A Sympathetic Critique. *Review of Radical Political Economics,* Vol. 32, No. 2, pp. 282-316.

Munley, Frank (1981). Wages, Salaries and the Profit Share: A Reassessment of the Evidence. *Cambridge Journal of Economics,* Vol. 5, pp.159-173.

Nagraj, R. (1989). Growth in Manufacturing since 1980: Some Preliminary Findings, *Economic and Political Weekly*, 1 July, pp.1481-1484.

Nayyar, Deepak (1978). Industrial Development in India: Some Reflection on Growth and Stagnation, *Economic and Political Weekly*, Special Number, pp. 1265-1278.

Norton, Bruce (1991). The Power Axis: Bowles, Gordon and Weisskopf's Theory of Post War U.S. Accumulation. *Social Scientist,* Vol. 19, Nos. 1-2, January-February, pp. 47-78.

Ojha, N.K. (1992). Strikes and Lockouts as Industrial Phenomena. *Indian Journal of Labour Economics,* Vol. 35, No. 4, pp. 392-395.

Pratap, Surendra and Chandra, Navin (2000). Spatial Configurations of Industrial Relations. *Indian Journal of Labour Economics,* Vol. 43, No. 4, pp. 1137-1142.

Ram, G.S. and Ahluwalia, A.S. (2000). Trends in Work Stoppages on Account of Industrial Disputes. *Indian Journal of Labour Economics,* Vol. 43, No. 4, pp. 1099-1112.

Saikh, Anwar M. and Tonak E. Ahmet (1994). *Measuring the Wealth of Nations*, New York: Cambridge University Press.

Samuelson, P. (1971). Understanding the Marxian Notion of Exploitation. *Journal of Economic Literature,* Vol. 9, pp. 399-431.

Sandesara, J.C. (1996). *Industrial Reforms in India: Experience and Prospects*, University of Bombay, Working Paper, May.

Sau, Ranjit (1989). Falling Rate of Profit in India's Industry? *Economic and Political Weekly*, 29 July, pp. 95-99.

Sharma, Richa (1994). Emerging Trends in Indian Trade Unionism. *Indian Journal of Labour Economics,* Vol. 37, No. 4, pp. 781-785.

Shetty, S.L. (1978). Structural Retrogression in the Indian Economy since the Mid-Sixties, *Economic and Political Weekly*, February, Special Supplement, pp.185-244.

Shyam Sundar, K.R. (2000). Regional Patterns of Incidence of Industrial Conflict in India, 1967-75. *Indian Journal of Labour Economics,* Vol. 43, No. 4, pp. 1113-1136.

Singh, R.C. (1984). Indian Trade Unionism: Recent Trends and Emerging Patterns. *Indian Journal of Labour Economics,* Vol. 26, No.4, pp. 459-464.

Singh, Sudama and Sharma, Shyam Sunder Pd. (1994). Some Emerging Trends in Trade Unionism in India. *Indian Journal of Labour Economics,* Vol. 37, No. 4, pp. 750-753.

Sinha, Pravin (1994). Indian Trade Unionism at Cross Road. *Indian Journal of Labour Economics,* Vol. 3, No. 37, pp. 771-779.

Siva Prasad, K. and Yogi, B. Ramachandra (1994). Size, Structure and Changing Role of the Indian Trade Unions. *Indian Journal of Labour Economics,* Vol. 37, No. 4, pp. 765-787.

Subramanium, Alka (1988). Consumption, Trends and Projections up to 2000 A.D: A Study of Paper Industry, *Economic and Political Weekly*, 28 May, pp. M-47–M-52.

Sundaram, S.K.G. (1992). Strikes and Lockouts in India: Past Experience and Future Perspectives. *Indian Journal of Labour Economics,* Vol. 35, No. 4, pp. 369-385.

Sweezy, P.M. (1956). The *Theory of Capitalist Development*, New York: Monthly Review Press.

Chapter 11

Impact of Globalization on Quality of Employment in India

Seepana Prakasam

Introduction

Quality of employment refers to quality of life the job provides or quality of work *per se*. Wages earned in the labour market is the important indicator of the quality of employment because it provides individuals with a source of livelihood. In terms of neo classical theory, wages influence quality of life defined by individual utility, because it enables people to buy market goods and services and enjoy leisure. The maximum number of jobs created during globalization lacks quality, is a big problem to achieve inclusive growth by enhancing living standards. Globalization is a multidimensional process of change in the design of development *via* change in economic structure of the economy. It is multifaceted and each facet may have different effects on economic growth and employment. The growing labour market flexibility and informalization of the economy are the twin problems before the policy makers and academicians to increase the income levels of the vulnerable working poor. The excessive informalization of employment at lower wage rate became an outcome of globalization.

This paper makes an attempt to analyze the issues concerning informalization of the economy and generation of lesser quality of jobs during globalization. This paper is organized into eight sections. Section two deals with the deregulation (Flexibilization) of labour markets. The third section explains magnitude of deprivation. The fourth section emphasized on the contractualization of employment. Section five focused on causalization of employment. The sixth section emphasized on women workers are at receiving end. Section seven is focused on the decent work and the ILO. The last section ended with policy measures and conclusion.

Worried about deteriorating quality of employment in the current labour markets, International Labour Organization (ILO) has set "The World Commission on Social Dimensions of Globalization (WCSDG) to study the social aspects of globalization. The World Commission states in this context: "the current path of globalization must change. Too few share in these benefits; too many have no voice in its design and no influence on its course" (WCSDG, ILO, 2004).

II

The Deregulation (Flexibilization) of Labour Markets

Globalization in developing economies has provided number of challenges and opportunities in shape of increased flexible labour markets, episodes of jobless growth and growing informalization (Heintz, 2006). India, too, has been going through this process of globalization for the last two decades or so. The employment opportunities, no doubt have increased but the share of informal sector in total employment has tremendously increased. Indeed, a significant part of the incremental employment generated during this period is in the unorganized sector. The declining trends in organized sector employment and the corresponding expansion of casualization of employment point towards the worsening conditions of the workers (Kannan and Pillai, 2007).

The structural adjustment caused following changes in the labour market. (1) Marginalization of trade unions, (2) Reduction of permanent work force, (3) Employment of casual, contract or other forms of unprotected labour, (4) Signing of agreement by individual workers bypassing trade unions, and (5) Shifting production facilities to the backward areas where labour is both cheap and ununionised.

Liberalization intensified privatization of public sector, decentralized production through sub contracting, deregulation of labour markets lead to transfer of jobs from formal to informal sector. Labour reforms incorporated into economic reforms have resulted in an abnormal expansion of informal sector in most of the developing nations. The larger segment of the population is working in unorganized sector of the economy, as informal labour (unorganized labour). The composition of employment between formal and informal sectors had changed. Fiscal consolidation policy adopted by the government, reduced formal employment generation capacity of public sector, on the other hand private manufacturing sector in general formal sector in particular adopted labour saving and capital intensive methods of production as a part of strategy to win competitive advantage over others. Liberalization is associated by earning profits which is possible mainly by reducing wage bill in total cost of production is became winning strategy of enterprises. All these factors caused to increase supply of labour in informal sector further imposed pressure on earnings and employment period of the existing labour.

During globalization, wage inequalities are increased between formal and informal jobs because more skilled and highly educated workers are absorbed in formal sector. There are earnings differentials among informal jobs also, i.e. casual, regular, home workers, contract workers and self-employed workers. Liberalization which made easier to import technological equipment and know how by manufacturing sector, further aggravated capital intensive techniques. Employment in informal sector is more flexible, such as casual, contract and temporary forms as a result, the decent work deficit has increased and coverage of social protection to workers has declined, which may endanger our aim to achieve inclusive growth if timely appropriate measures are not undertaken.

Globalization has resulted in making employment of chancy factor, and that too with heavy costs on the petty pockets of common man. Even if one makes it his name is almost nowhere on the muster rolls, he is usually casual or contract labour. Globalization has made the labour force vulnerable and they are always on the firing line. In such a situation it is not usual that they are short changed on over time or denied benefits that are legally theirs.

III

The Magnitude of Deprivation

More than 1000 million people in the world are unemployed, under-employed or working for poverty wages (less than US $1 per day). About 550 million of these are the working poor (ILO, 2003). Less than 10 per cent of the workers in least developed nations are covered by social security (ILO, 2010). Out of about 460 million workers in India, only around 50 to 60 million are covered by some form of social security. India has legal backing only to those employed in the formal sector of the economy, which has been estimated at around 8 per cent of the total workforce. Although there are some state-assisted and/or promoted schemes for social security for workers in the informal sector the coverage has not been more than 6 per cent of the total (NCEUS, 2007).

In India the un-organized sector accounts for 92.8 per cent of the total work force of about 460.22 million (NSSO 66th round). Total employment in India has increased from 397 million to 457.5 in 2004-05 to 460 million 2009-10. Informal employment has increased from 341.3 million to 393.5 million in 2004-05 but declined to 385 million in 2009-10. Whereas formal employment has declined from 35 million to 34.9 million and further declined to 33 million during the same period (Table 11.1). The change in the organized or formal employment has been marginally negative. The entire increase in the employment in the organized sector over this period has been informal in nature, and the terms and conditions of employment are usually precarious.

Table 11.1: Employment (Millions) in Organized and Unorganized Sectors in India (1999-2000 and 2009-10)

Year	*1999-2000 (workers)*			*2004-2005 (workers)*			*2009-2010 (workers)*		
Sector	*Informal*	*Formal*	*Total*	*Informal*	*Formal*	*Total*	*Informal*	*Formal*	*Total*
Informal	341.3	1.4	342.6	393.5	1.4	394.9	385.08	2.26	387.34
	(99.6)	(0.4)	(100.0)	(99.6)	(0.4)	(100.0)	(99.4)	(0.6)	(100.0)
Formal	20.5	33.7	54.1	29.1	33.4	62.6	42.14	30.74	72.88
	(37.8)	(62.2)	(100.0)	(46.6)	(53.4)	(100.0)	(57.8)	(42.2)	(100.0)
Total	361.7	35.0	396.8	422.6	34.9	457.5	427.22	33.00	460.22
	(35.0)	(8.8)	(100.0)	(92.4)	(7.6)	(100.0)	(92.8)	(7.2)	(100.0)

Note: Figures in parenthesis are percentages.
Source: Cited by Santosh Mehrotra *et al.* (EPW).

Table 11.2 indicates that the share of wages in net value added has declined from 30 per cent in 1980 to 10 per cent in 2008. Whereas the share of profits in net value added has increased from 20 per cent in 1980s to 60 per cent in 2008 (Himanshu, 2011).

Table 11.2: Share of Wages and Profit in Net Value Added (1980 to 2008)

Net Value Added	*1980*	*1990*	*2008*
Share of Wages	30	20	10
Share of Profit	20	30	60

Source: Himanshu (2011), "The Work Force Misses the Boat" Live Min.

India's National income and per capita income have been growing very fast, it is in the league of the faster growing economies of the world, still poverty levels are high, because economic growth is not sufficient achieve economic development. Hence this type of quality of growth in India is termed as rootless growth. Table 11.3, shows that in 2004-05, the extremely poor constituted 6.4 per cent, the poor 15.4 per cent, the marginally poor 19.0 per cent and vulnerable 36.0 per cent. All the four categories constituted 77 per cent of total population. During the period between 1993-94 to 2004-05, the marginally poor population has increased from 18.8 per cent to 19.0 per cent, and vulnerable population has increased from 32.4 per cent to 36 per cent on the other hand high income population has increased from 2.7 per cent to 4.0 per cent during the same period. It indicates that economic inequalities are increasing.

Table 11.3: Population in Different Expenditure Classes (%) during 1993-94 to 2004-05

Expenditure class	*1993-94*	*1999-2000*	*2004-05*
Extremely poor	11.5	8.7	6.4(9)
Poor	19.2	17.3	15.4(12)
Marginally poor	18.8	19.9	19.0(15)
Vulnerable	32.4	34.8	36.0(20)
Middle income	15.5	16.7	19.3(37)
High income	2.7	2.6	4.0(93)

Note: Figures in bracket denote average consumer expenditure per capita per day.

Source: Computed from different rounds of NSSO.

Workers depend on informal sector mostly do not have formal legally recognized rights over the property they own. Their lands, buildings business and their assets held in informal sector are dead capital because creditors do not have indisputable proof as to who owns them. Therefore, their properties are not acceptable as collateral for creditors, so the economy is denied major source of credit and infrastructural facilities. Transaction costs of entering into formal sector (long procedure, bribes, time consumption, fees, red tapism), encourages to prefer and join the informal sector (Siddhartha and Mitra, 2005). The problem of poverty and vulnerability and its close association with the unorganized workers status is a systemic problem. However, it should be noted that the incidence of unorganized work status is higher among lower social status groups than the higher social status groups.

Greater competition pressures forces, formal sector firms to outsource labour and production to the informal sector and workers who lost their jobs in import substituting industries are also forced to join in informal sector. Shift of Labour from formal to informal, the demand and supply forces caused reduction in wages and increase in wage inequalities between the sectors. Firms are responded for hiring more temporary or contract workers who are outside the purview of job security regulations, and free from labour market institutions (Ramaswamy, 2008). Social dumping, i.e. exports of goods produced under the substandard labour conditions from developing to developed nations and the danger of race to bottom resulting from the competition between producers from developed and developing nations to lower labour costs by reducing labour standards has increased.

IV

Contractualization of Employment

Table 11.4 indicates that from the year 1995-96 to 2003-04 the number of contract workers increased from around 9 lakh to 15 lakh. The percentage of workers employed through contractor has increased from 13 per cent to 24.5 per cent, and employed as contract workers directly has increased from 15 per cent to 32.5 per cent. Whereas the proportion of contract workers to total workers in the country has increased from 14.1 per cent to 23.30 per cent during the same period. There is inverse relationship between the intensity of contract employment and quality of that employment.

Table 11.4: Contractual workers employed *via* contractor and direct contract by workers (1995-96 to 2003-04)

Year	*Number of employed contract workers*	*Employed via contractor (%)*	*Direct contract by workers (%)*	*Contract workers to total workers (%)*
1995-96	9,04,715	13.17	15.16	14.1
1996-97	10,58,870	16.58	19.88	—
1999-2000	11,91,596	19.63	24.43	18.8
2001-02	12,50,754	21.64	27.61	19.5
2002-03	13,70,052	22.91	29.71	—
2003-04	14,95,671	24.57	32.57	23.30

Source: Calculated from various years of Annual Survey of Industries (ASI).

Globalization has resulted in an increased proportion of workers who do not receive secure wages or social security benefits either from the employers or from the state. Many informal workers live from one day to the next and are faced with the risk of various calamities that can throw them into the state of permanent indebtedness. UN insured risks among informal sector workers and their households are major contribution to poverty. Reduction in income security and social protection arises from the attempts of governments to promote competitiveness and to attract foreign investment. Competition to impose lesser taxes lead to further reduction in taxes, particularly on corporate profits, reduced the ability of governments to provide social protection.

Globalization has generated opportunities for local producers and entrepreneurs to reach international markets, it has at times intensified existing inequalities and insecurities for many poor women are usually the least able to seize the longer term opportunities offered. Further discriminatory practices in the labour market are reflected in the wages for women workers. They are not only concentrated in low paid occupations in the unorganized sector but are subjected to discrimination in payment.

Employment for longer period of time in the informal sector has been positively correlated with poverty and might also intergenerational consequences because the children were more likely to inherit their parent's poverty due to low educational achievement. Moreover with hardly any social protection in the informal sector, chances of old age poverty rise with informal employment (Shepherd, 2010).

V

Causalization of Employment

The quality jobless growth has become a specific feature of our economic reforms process. In this process the rural poor, the weaker sections, the downtrodden, the illiterate persons and the scheduled castes and tribes are the worst sufferers. Even the educated persons in a large number are without jobs and the economy could not succeed to have the proper benefit of demographic dividends. With the changing structure of the economy, employment effects have not been positive properly. Agriculture, with rapidly declining share in GDP still enjoys the top position with engaging about half of our working population, but this employment is distressed one with increasing casualization and low paid job opportunities with unfavourable work conditions and without upward mobility. The manufacturing sector has not come to our expectation and the knowledge and the skill requirements in the manufacturing and services sector have not allowed us to have the appropriate benefits.

The deteriorating quality of employment as signified by the rising share of casual labour, decreasing share of wage bill against rapidly rising profit share and worsening bargaining capacity of the working class, it is evident that the dream of inclusive growth remains a dream which has given way to quality jobless growth and in fact exclusive growth. Table 11.5 indicates that the share of regular wage and salaried group has shown slow but the consistent rise over the last three NSSO rounds which is a good thing, but the sharp rise in the share of casual labour from 130 million in 2004-05 to 151.6 million in 2009-10. It is worrisome as increase in share of casual labour means decreasing bargaining power of the labour, low wage rates and less social security.

Table 11.5: Different Categories of Workers (Casualization of Workforce) During (1999-2000 to 2009-10)

NSS, Rounds	*Workforce (in millions)*			*Share (%)*		
	SE	*RWS*	*CL*	*SE*	*RWS*	*CL*
1999-2000	209.3	58.2	130.3	52.6	14.6	32.8
2004-05	259	70	130	56.4	15.2	28.3
2009-10	233.2	75.3	151.6	50.7	16.4	32.9

Note: SE—Self-employment, RWS—Regular Wage and Salaried, CL—Casual Labour

Source: Rangarajan, C, Padma Iyer Kaul and Seema (2011) "where is missing labour force", *Economic and Political Weekly*, 24 September, Vol. xlvi, No. 39, p.71.

VI

Women Workers are at The Receiving End

Liberalization was predicted to increase participation of women, it becomes true but demand for women labour increased because it is cheaper than male labour. Most of the women compelled to do low productive, unskilled and insecure jobs, either to supplement family income or due to loss of jobs by the male bread earner. Women are able to get more jobs but the work they get is more casual in nature or is the one that men do not prefer to do or is left by them to move to higher or better jobs. In addition to agriculture the maximum number of women are earning from low qualitative informal jobs (bad jobs) like domestic work, construction work, factory work, street vending, rag picking, home work etc. All these works are very much insecure, neither support with minimum wages nor with minimum facilities at the place of work and at the place of residence. In most of these jobs (in case of self-employment) no employer at all, which causes self-exploitation of workers (Jayati Ghosh, 2004). Most of the women continue to remain marginalized as they are generally employed in a chain of work and seldom allowed independent charge of work, at the same time their burden of work has doubled inside and outside the home.

VII

The Decent Work and the ILO

Jobs in which core labour standards are not respected are treated as indecent jobs. If working conditions so hateful or harmful that it would be better for people not to work at all than to work in such damaging conditions. Decent work enhances national economic, social and labour market performance. In the 87th session of International Labour Conference in 1999, ILO Director General described decent work as "opportunities for women and men to obtain decent and productive work in conditions of freedom, equity, security and human dignity" (ILO, 1999, p. 3). The four core labour standards, i.e. Freedom of association, collective bargaining, elimination of forced or compulsory labour, an end to child labour and the elimination of discrimination – must be respected if work is to be decent. Along with other factors poverty result from insufficient employment, low pay, inability to work due to an uncompensated occupational injury, discrimination, lack of access to social protection, unavailability of a basic pension, or one of the many other labour market factors.

Decent work is a major driver of development it goes beyond the domain of economic issues and directly addresses social concerns. It incorporates agenda of poverty reduction, human development and social integration. It reasserts the role of employment as a development policy instrument. It validates informal economy and stresses the need to improve quality, productivity and remuneration of work in informal setting. It enlarges the prominence of the issue of gender in the world of work. Decent work applies not just to workers in the formal economy but also to unregulated wage workers, the self-employed and home workers. The composite index of decent work deficit (DWD) measure combines indicators of low hourly pay, excessive hours of work, unemployment, non-enrolment in school, youth unemployment, male-female gap in wages and labour force participation and old age without pension.

VIII

Policy Measures and Conclusion

Development strategies should integrate the economic, social and environmental dimensions. Economic policies have to be more explicitly directed towards the goal of decent work generation for achieving macroeconomic stability. Remunerative employment is the best form of social protection. Priority should be given for adopting labour intensive techniques. Informal labour need to be involved in formulating and implementing policies that will affect them. Workers in formal economy should extend support to workers in the informal economy, to organize, and develop the capacity of organizations. Strengthen law enforcement agencies to strictly implement labour laws by the employers. Informal labour are not homogeneous category, so that variety of programmes are required to suit the different sectors and sections. Improve household incomes by building assets and safeguard them against vulnerability arising from economic and other crises, through credit, provision of technology support, input supply, marketing need, insurance and other financial vehicles to achieve inclusive growth. Improve total factor productivity by enhancing investment in informal sector to increase skill formation, there of improvement in workers earnings will be possible. The resulting higher earnings not only improve (capabilities and entitlements) living standards but also provide them with the means for the education and the skill development among their children, which will pave the way for intergenerational upward mobility.

Note: In this paper informal sector and unorganized sector are used synonymously.

REFERENCES

Arjun Sen Gupta *et al.,* (2005). 'India's Common People—Who Are They, How Many are they and How do They Live?' *Economic and Political Weekly*. March 15, 2008.

Amitab Kundu and Niranjan Sarangi (2007). Dynamics of Labour Market Under Globalization. Changing Characteristics of Informal Employment in India'. *Indian Journal of Labour Economics*. Vol. 50, No. 2.

Amitab Kundu and Alak N. Sharma (2001). edit. *Informal Sector in India Perspectives and Policies*. Institute of Human Development and Institute of Applied Manpower Research, New Delhi.

Chen, M.A. (2007). 'Rethinking the Informal Economy Linkages with the Formal Economy and the Formal Regulatory Environment'. *Linking the Formal and Informal Economy, Concepts and Policies*, edit Basudeb *et al.*, Oxford University Press, New Delhi.

Jeemol Unni (2008). 'Women Workers in the New Economy'. *The Indian Journal of Labour Economics*. Vol. 51, No. 4.

Jayati Ghosh and C.P. Chandrasekhar (2006). 'Employment Growth; The Latest Trends, the results of the latest survey of the 61st round covering 2004-05' (17th November 2006 *Business Line*).

Kannan, K.P. (2008). 'Dualism, Informality and Social Inequality'. *Presidential address at golden jubilee conference of Indian society of Labour Economics.* December 13-15.

Kundu Amit (2006). 'Wage Employment Relationship In The Agriculture; Labour Market of West Bengal'. *Indian Journal of Labour Economics*. Vol. 49, No. 4, pp. 681-690.

Mahendradev. (2002). 'Growth Mediated and Support Led Social Security in the unorganized Sector in India'. *The Indian Journal of Labour Economics*. Vol. 45. No. 2.

Narasimha, Reddy D. (2005). 'Challenges of Decent Work In The Globalizing World'. *Indian Journal of Labour Economics.* Vol. 48. No.1.

NCEUS (2008). *Report on Conditions of Work and Promotion of Livelihoods in the Unorganized Sector*. Government of India, New Delhi. Also published by Academic Foundation, New Delhi.

Paola, T.S. (2004). 'Globalization, Employment and Social Protection, Emerging Perspectives for the Indian Workers'. *Indian Journal of Labour Economics*. Vol. 47. No. 3.

Patnaik, Utsa (2006). 'Poverty and Neo Liberalism in India', based on *Rao Bhaduri Kale Memorial Lecture* delivered at Ghokale institute of Politics and Economics, Pune, February 3.

Ruddar Datt. (2002). 'Employment Policies and the UN organized Sector'. *Indian Journal of Labour Economics.* Vol. 45, No. 2.

Ramaswamy, K.V. (2008). 'Globalization, Employment and Labour Market Flexibility'. *India Development Report 2008*. Oxford.

UNO (2005). *The World's Women.*

World Bank (2010). 'India's Employment Challenge, Creating Jobs, Helping Workers'. Oxford University Press, New Delhi.

Chapter 12

Globalization and Consumerism

Consequences for Transitional Economies

Devinder Pal Singh

Introduction

India's position as an emerging economy has been well recognized and corroborated by its remarkable economic resilience from the current economic slowdown. The growing economy coupled with rapid growth of income of citizens is an attractive proposition for the multinationals. The increase in disposable income of the citizens has led to transformation in the lifestyles, which has resulted in a dramatic increase in the demand for newer products. The MNCs attracted to these emerging economies are exporting western-style consumption patterns to emerging countries, which could prove disastrous to the environment (KPMG, 2008). This has resulted in the emergence of consumption culture which is a potent threat to sustainability. The article traces the trajectory of consumption culture with the onset of globalization. It highlights the various threats manifested in contemporary consumption patterns in light of lack of desired infrastructure for sustainability.

Consumerism: Consumer Culture

Culture has been identified as the fundamental determinant responsible for differences in behaviour. Culture is the software of mind and responsible for human behaviour (Hofstede, 1980). Culture constitutes the values, norms, rituals and myths as the elements of any social setting (Sheth and Mittal, 2003). Hofstede (2001) identifies values as the core element of culture. The invisible values along with three other visible elements—symbols, heroes, and rituals, constitute the total concept i.e. culture. Values are invisible but become evident in behaviour, while the other three are the visible manifestations of culture.

Consumption culture is the culture characterized by the primacy of consumption. Consumption culture means more goods, more air travel, more waste, pollution and more carbon dioxide emissions (Featherstone, 2007). Consumer culture is the dominant cultural orientation that guides people to find meanings, contentment and acceptance through what they consume (Assadourian, 2010). It leads people to associate high consumption with well-being, prosperity, and success. In most of the countries the birth of a child is greeted with profusion of gifts and the parents along with relatives demonstrate their joy through them, like the pain during the death of someone is demonstrated with flowers, condolence cards etc. (Sassatelli, 2007). Consumer culture values more wealth and more material possession as essentials to good life (Assadourian, 2010). The possession of variety of goods is the principal cultural aspiration and is the perceived route to happiness and prosperity.

The symbols of consumer culture are logos, jingles, slogans, mascots which influence behaviour at unconscious levels. Consumers recognize these symbols more easily as compared to wildlife species. Assadourian (2010) puts forth the studies which show that British children recognize more Pokemon characters than common wildlife species and that American two year olds cannot identify the letter 'M' but they can identify McDonald's M shaped golden arches.

Cultural norms are routine lifestyles of individuals of any culture. In contemporary consumer culture pantry shelves boast of processed foods, pastas, drinks in pet bottles, plastic packed cookies to maggie. The wardrobes are overloaded and walls are adorned with ostentatious symbols symbolizing the values of prosperity and success.

The heroes of consumer culture are the cartoon characters for children. For the youngsters the brand ambassadors who are usually celebrities are the heroes and role models. The media has transformed the role models for consumers which coax consumers to consume more.

Consumer culture has reduced the traditional rituals into extravagant occasions of display of wealth and success. Diwali no more marks the occasion of Ram's return to Ayodhya but an occasion of gift giving, feasting and consumption. Emerging economy society has been exposed to more rituals like Valentine's Day, Mother's Day, Father's Day etc. which further provide impetus to senseless consumption.

Drivers of Consumerism

WBCSD (2008) recognizes the population growth, rise of global affluence and culture of consumerism among the high income groups as the global drivers of consumption. China and India account for 40 per cent of the world's population (Savage, 2006). World population is expected to reach nine billion by 2050 (WBCSD, 2008).

World GDP is projected to grow by 325 per cent by 2050 and India's GDP is expected to come close to that of the US (WBCSD, 2008). The share of BRICS in the world GDP could rise to US $130 trillion in 2050 (WBCSD, 2009). Consumer culture which is the sign of economic success is centre to the expansion of Asian economies like China and India (Featherstone, 2007). McKinsey & Company's report (2007) shows that if India continues on its current high growth path for next two decades, the income levels will almost triple and the country will climb from its present position as the 12th largest consumer market today to the world's fifth largest consumer market by 2025. This fifth largest consumer economy is going to be one of the largest markets of the next two decades (Bhardwaj, Swaroop and Vittal, 2005; Beinhocker, Farrell and Zainulbhai, 2007). The consumer demand is growing three to four times faster than the overall economy (Zainulbhai, 2005). This rise in consumer demand is driven by the emerging middle class (Bhardwaj, Swaroop and Vittal, 2005). The burgeoning middle class and the changing consumption patterns (Singh, 2000; Das, 2002; Wessel, 2004; Chhokar, 2007) have made India one of the most coveted markets. Consumption culture is the centre to the expansion of asian economies like India (Featherstone, 2007). Consumer culture is the sign of economic success and so it is difficult to relinquish it, as it has become a major source of industrial production and employment. Curbing consumption is not a popular option which means politicians, seek out 'technological fix' solutions which will allow the economy to proceed at full speed, but somehow clean up or recycle pollution and waste (*ibid.*).

Concerns for Transitional Economies

The Transitional economies have a combined Gross Domestic Product (GDP) of over US$ 7 trillion and represent a major future growth market and their share of world GDP could rise to US$ 130 trillion in 2050 (WBCSD, 2009). Economic development requires the use of natural resources. As emerging economies like India, China, Brazil, and Russia rapidly industrialize; they will strain the planet for material and energy burden (Unruh, 2008). China, India, Brazil, and Russia are collectively already responsible for 30 per cent of global CO_2 emissions (Sustain Ability, 2007). The emerging markets account for over 40 per cent of the world's population. Increasing population makes increasing demand on such resources thereby leading to the degradation of the environment (Roy and Tisdell, 1999).

The Indian household incomes are set to almost triple over the next two decades but the consumer awareness about sustainable consumption is low (WBCSD, 2008). The high growth rate along with the increase in spending power has led to phenomenon of consumerism (Halepet and Iyer, 2008). The rapid growth of income of Indians and the transformation in the lifestyles has resulted in a dramatic increase in the demand for newer products. Traditionally there was a tendency to use and reuse a product (Ramachandran, 2000; Keller and Moorthi, 2003). Ball point pen was used till its physical destruction as ink refills were used. No more do the consumers refill the ball point pens as there is the emergence of tendency to use and throw. Now-a-days people's office tables, homes and cars display bunches of pens thus generating lot of plastic waste. The tendency to use and reuse is giving way to product personalization and planned obsolescence. The tendency to personalize products has also added to the concern as every individual within a family longs for personal TV, car, room, house etc. Planned obsolescence of consumer products leads to over use of energy and material resources (Dobers and Strannegard, 2005). By planned obsolescence the consumers cognitively feel the products as obsolete, even though the products can still be used. For example, products ranging from cars to home furnishings are replaced after short span of time. The analysis of consumption suggests that behavioural change on part of individuals and groups for sustainable consumption is limited. Planned obsolescence leads to overuse of energy and material resources. Material lifestyle and consumer culture has become widely accessible to an increasingly growing middle class through out the world. The consumer class is just 12 per cent of the total population in India but it will be disastrous as the consumer class grows.

Wessel (2004) observes that in the contemporary Indian society the relationships are superficial and are largely formed on the desire to prove one's worth to class fellows through conspicuous consumption. Products are not bought for their own sake but for their capacities as lifestyle carriers (Dobers and Strannegard, 2005). The sense of 'community' that is formed under such conditions is based in large part on the desire to prove one's worth to class fellows through conspicuous consumption (Wessel, 2004). Consumption becoming more fashion sensitive, dependent on aesthetics and well designed products and services brings serious ecological problems to the surface (Dobers and Strannegard, 2005). Aesthetics, taste and design are the drivers of consumption and impediments on the path to sustainability (*ibid.*).

Sustainable Consumption: Path to Sustainability

Sustainable consumption is a prerequisite for a more prosperous, safe and equitable global future within the resource constrained world (WEF, 2010). Considering the social and ecological costs that come with consumer culture it is imperative to intentional shift to a cultural paradigm where the norms, symbols, values, and traditions encourage just enough consumption to satisfy human well-being while directing more human energy toward practices that help to restore planet's well-being (Assadourian, 2010). Sustainable consumption requires widespread changes in behaviour at all levels of society to reduce environmental impacts of consumption (Seyfang, 2007). It requires transformation of consumer culture to sustainable consumption culture. Transforming cultures is not an easy task but it is possible if culture pioneers work tirelessly to redirect cultural-shaping institutions like business, media, government, education and religion (Assadourian, 2010).

Public policies can change the behaviours of many people and organizations in public sphere (Stern, 2000). The aggregate individual behaviours have significant impact on environment (*ibid.*). Consumption patterns need to be altered, lifestyles need to be changed and the ways the products and services are extracted, distributed and consumed need to change (Dobers and Strannegard, 2005).

Corporates must create new business models considering whether their business is able to adjust to alternative 'sustainable' service models that respect the environment as well as consumer needs. For example, lease products rather than sell units, encourage refilling rather than repurchasing, offer upgrades to an existing product rather than replacing it.

Conclusion

There is convergence of cultural values across the globe and consumer culture is the dominant cultural paradigm spread across the world.

Consumer culture is a grave threat to the sustainability and the future of the planet and humanity. This necessitates that consumer culture be transformed into sustainable consumer, culture. This transformation requires the proactive role of institutions like business, media, government, education and religion.

REFERENCES

Assadourian, E. (2010), *The Rise and Fall of Consumer Cultures in 2010 State of the World: Transforming Cultures*, The Worldwatch Resources Institute, www.worldwatch.org.

Beinhocker, Eric D., Farrel, Diana and Zainulbhai, Adil S. (2007), 'Tracking the Growth of India's Middle Class', *The McKinsey Quarterly*, 3, 50-83.

Bhardwaj, V.T., Swaroop, G.M. and Vittal, I. (2005), 'Winning the Indian consumer', *The McKinsey Quarterly*, Special Edition, 43–51.

Chhokar, Jagdeep S. (2007), 'India: Diversity and Complexity in Action,' in *Culture and Leadership Across the World: The GLOBE Book of In-Depth Studies of 25 Societies* (Chhokar, J.S., Brodbeck, F.C. and House, R.J., eds.), Lawrence Erlbaum Associates, Mahwah, NJ.

Das, G. (2002), *India Unbound*, New Delhi: Penguin.

Dobers, Peter and Strannegard, L. (2005), 'Design, Lifestyles and Sustainability: Aesthetic Consumption in a World of Abundance', *Business Strategy and the Environment*, 14, 324-336.

Featherstone, Mike (2007), *Consumer Culture and Postmodernism*, New Delhi: Sage.

Hofstede, G. (2001), *Culture's Consequences*, New Delhi: Sage.

KPMG (2008), Sustainable Development and Innovation, Sustainable Insight, October, pp. 1-6

Keller, Kevin Lane and Y.L.R. Moorthi (2003), 'Branding in Developing Markets', *Business Horizons*, (May-June), 49-59.

McKinsey & Co. (2007), The 'Bird of Gold': The Rise of India's Consumer Market. San Francisco, CA: McKinsey Global Institute.

Ramachandran, Raja (2000), "Understanding the Market Environment of India," *Business Horizons*, (January-February), 44-52.

Roy, K.C. and Tisdell, C.A. (1999), 'Conservation and prudent management are the key to the preservation of the environment: The case of water-resources, and the Indian situation', *International Journal of Social Economics*, 26(1/2/3), 274-289.

Sassatelli, Roberta (2007) *Consumer Culture: History, Theory and Politics*, New Delhi: Sage.

Seyfang, Gill, (2007), 'Growing Sustainable Consumption Communities: The Case of Local Organic Food Networks', *International Journal of Sociology*, Vol. 27, No. 3/4, 120-134.

Sheth, Jagdish N. and Mittal, Banwari (2003), *Customer Behaviour: A Managerial Perspective*, Thomson Learning, New Delhi.

Singh, Yogendera (2000), *Culture Change in India: Identity and Globalization*, New Delhi: Rawat Publications.

Sustain Ability (2007), *Raising Our Game: Can We Sustain Globalization ?* SustainAbility Ltd., Washingtion, www. sustainability.com

Unruh, G.C. (2008), 'The Biosphere rules', *Havard Business Review*, February, 97-104.

WBCSD (2009), *Thinking Globally, Acting Locally: The Regional Network*, Geneva: World Business Council for Sustainable Development. www.wbcsd.org

WBCSD (2008), *Sustainable Consumption: Facts and Trends*, World Business Council for Sustainable Development. www.wbcsd.org

WEF (2010), *Redesigning Business Value: A Roadmap for Sustainable Consumption*, Geneva: World Economic Forum.

Wessel, Margit Van (2004), 'Talking About Consumption How an Indian Middle Class Dissociates from Middle-Class Life', *Cultural Dynamics*, 16(1), 93-116.

PART II
GLOBALIZATION, INDUSTRY AND AGRICULTURE

Chapter 13

Globalization, Agrarian Crisis and Farmers Suicides in India

K. Gopal Iyer and *Jagdish Chander Mehta*

Causes of Widespread Agrarian Crisis

The causes of the widespread Agrarian crises are complex and manifold. The main causes are dominantly related to public policy. The agrarian crises can be linked to combination of macro liberalization and globalization polices of Central Government. For farmers the single most adverse effect has been the combination of low prices and output volatility for cash crops. The new liberal economic reform strategy led to financial liberalization measures, removal of restriction on internal trade in agricultural commodities and liberalization of external trade. The rural people have been left out of the process of globalization or have been marginalized or excluded. Debt burden itself is only a symptom of the wider malaise. The increase in the number of farmer's suicide and its proximate cause is the most dramatic sign of extreme despair and hopelessness. The most extreme manifestation of this crisis is in the suicide by farmers and agricultural labourers who are typically driven to desperate act by the inability to repay debt incurred in the process of cultivation. The burden has fallen disproportionately on small and marginal farmers and rural labour. The volatility of crop prices has been a major source of income instability and distress for farmers. A substantial part of price volatility has been related to external trade liberalization.

Globalization essentially means economic globalization. Free flow of goods, services, capital and technology under a competitive market was the core ingredient that provoked and spread globalization the world over. The detrimental effects of globalization (Bhagwati. 2004,) resulted in significant vulnerability and economic insecurity. The critics of globalization take a position that the process involves proliferation of capitalist development which is similar to the process of colonialism, weakening of the state in the developing world, and exposing the vulnerable to the worst disasters in the market. The vulnerability of the weak is one of the most dangerous impacts of globalization. The role of the state in the decision making process of the farmers is quite prominent and well entrenched. The process of marginalization becomes very demanding in some of the states.

One of the major changes in the agrarian structure has been a growing predominance of small and marginal farmers. This does not stop at the process of marginal size of land holding but manifests itself in 'marginalization' of the peasantry itself. Yet the state policy over the years has not taken serious cognizance of this. The highest incidence of farmers' suicides by various studies suggests the very neglect of the state policy towards this problem. However, the Green Revolution has served as a model of modern agriculture to trap the peasants in the market web thus inducing a range of new risks into the lives of farmers. The root of distress lies in the conditions arising from the wrong technology compounded by ill-formulated policy and social. structuring of the commercial agriculture. Neo-liberal policies accounts for the making of the crisis where agricultural issues and agriculturists are in a state of 'advanced marginalization'. Suicides are not the crisis or a form of crisis but are only symptoms and expressions of the deeper structural problems of Indian agriculture and the agrarian system itself.

The opening up of the international market for agricultural commodities was one such step. On one side it is well accepted that the Indian farmer needed to participate in the international market, but on the other it is also necessary to ascertain whether the farmer is ready for such transition. The question of linking the process of globalization to the agrarian distress is quite complex and one needs a clear understanding on both sides. It is true that the crisis deepened during the 1990s along with the introduction of the new economic policy. It cannot be denied that the externalities of globalization contributed to the deepening of the crisis. The scenario of the agriculture crisis in India, clearly indicates that the roots of the crisis are within the economy to which globalization has acted as an igniting factor. There is a dire need of formulating policies keeping in view the interest of small and marginal farmers. The states severely affected included Andhra Pradesh, Maharashtra, Karnataka, Kerala and Punjab. Later on suicides also engulfed the States of Madhya Pradesh and Chhattisgarh intriguingly; some of these States are among the most promising agricultural regions of the country where the potential loss to the economy is quite severe. There is clear evidence of marginalization of land base. Punjab has always served as the high point of India's achievement in agriculture. Farmers' suicide cases from Punjab have perturbed many researchers and policy makers of agriculture; the green revolution technology could be squarely attributed to the role of the state. 'Farmers operate in a self-created moral and social world, where dignity is of prime importance. If they are humiliated due to indebtedness, they prefer to commit suicide rather than facing continuous humiliation in the society.'

Further, the conditions deepening the crisis can be attributed to the following. First, the number of marginal and small farmers is increasing at a faster rate. The shrinking size of holdings is steadily imposing non-viability on the peasants. This is enhanced by the increasing cost of cultivation and technology. Second, the non-viability size of holdings compelled peasants to undertake commercial crops. They were attracted towards the new crops and varieties, recognizing the market-led instability. Third, the land market was more in favour of the large owners; this created marginalization of the farmers and weaker sections. Large number of farmers lost land under the pressures of this non-viability and non-affordable technology. Four, the restrictions on tenancy created an undercover tenancy market and this is much more exploitative. Erratic rainfall, attacks of the American bollworm pest, spurious seeds and pests and frequent droughts have resulted in low yields and crop failures, causing increasing costs of cultivation and heavy reduction in net income of the farmers. The presence of non-institutional credit suppliers and their nexus with traders led to hefty interests rates on one hand, while forcing farmers to sell their produce at the lowest prices to those traders on the other. This leads to aggravation of indebtedness among the farmers.

Gender, age and caste factors are also taken into consideration for the analysis of farmers' suicides. Studies probing into the factors causing recent farmers' suicides have identified indebtedness as one of the major underlying reasons. (Assadi, 1998; Revathi, 1998; Deshpande, 2002 and Mishra, 2006). Changes in the pace and composition of agricultural credit emerged as a significant issue in the context of the farmers' distress in various parts of the country. Indebtedness is not an overnight phenomenon that has occurred suddenly, but is the result of faulty credit policies followed over the years. *In the case of Rural suicides, it is the cumulative debt burden which has served as one of the important causes of suicide.*

The Political Economy of Corporate Globalization

Farmers suicides are the most tragic and dramatic symptom of the crisis of survival faced by Indian peasants. The rising costs of production and the falling prices of farm commodities are rooted in the policies of trade liberalization and corporate globalization. In 1998, the World Bank's structural adjustment policies forced India to open up its seed sector to global corporations like Monsanto, Syngenta, Cargill etc. This resulted in farm saved seeds being replaced by corporate seeds which needed fertilizers and pesticides and the farmers could not save these seeds. This shift from farm saved seed to corporate monopolies is a shift from biodiversity to monoculture crops in agriculture. Seed monopolies created crop monocultures of cotton, leading to disappearance of millions of nature's evolution and farmers' breeding. Monocultures and uniformity increased the risks of crop failure. When Monsanto first introduced Bt Cotton in India in the year 2002, the farmers lost rs. one billion due to crop failure. (Shiva, Vandana). The second pressure which the Indian farmers are facing is the dramatic fall in prices of farm produce as a result of free trade policies of the WTO. The WTO rules for trade and agriculture are in essence, rules for dumping (Gulati, 2003.) They have allowed an increase in agri-business subsidies. High subsidies combined with forced removal of import restrictions is a readymade recipe for rural suicides. The immediate cause of rural suicides has been attributed to economic liberalization (Christian Aid, 'The Damage Done: Aid, Death, and Dogma, 2005'). These liberalizing factors at both national and state levels, were the results of policies formulated by central government as also, the State Governments of Andhra Pradesh, Karnataka, Kerala, Maharashtra, and Punjab. These liberalizing factors were reinforced by the international financial institutions of the IMF and the World Bank primarily.

Trends of Farmers Suicides in India

"Farmers' suicides have to be viewed as a *national disaster*", the statement of the Prime Minister of India, himself a distinguished economist opens our eyes to the agrarian crisis that haunts the country today. Tens of thousands of farmers in different states of India have committed suicide. These suicides can no more be considered isolated cases of farmer's deaths but a symbol of deepening crisis of Indian agriculture. There is a debate regarding causes and number of deaths of farmers in the country. In the initial period of late

1990s when there were sporadic incidents of suicides across the country there was general indifference and apathy towards these incidents. But, when in early 2000 and onwards the number of farmers' deaths started rising fast in Andhra Pradesh, Karnataka, Kerala, Maharashtra and Punjab, the Governments started feeling the pinch of growing public wrath. While some Governments took immediate relief measures, some appointed commissions to probe into the truth of the matter. There are a few pertinent questions to be answered in the context of farmers' suicides in the country. These have been debated widely in parliament, state legislatures, academia and the press. There are differing views. There were also attempts to pass on the buck to sundry reasons like family conflict, alcoholism etc. by some reports, brushing aside the ground realities of agrarian crisis and the resultant tragedy of farmers' deaths. Due to series of difficulties faced by the farmers over a period of time, this phenomenon has acquired a serious dimension. Though farmers' suicides have been occurring since 1990 but it is alarming in the scale and spread to different states.

One of the most disquieting development in the era of the neo-liberal policy in India has been widespread occurrence of farmers' suicides in different parts of the country including not only the drought prone areas of Andhra Pradesh, Karnataka and Maharashtra but also a State of heavy rainfall like Kerala, as also a State like Punjab with large areas under irrigation. With the preoccupation of the Government with the rate of economic growth and promotion of the private sector in the secondary and tertiary sectors, that is, industrial and service sectors, the agricultural sector and the sector of rural development were neglected. The government did not wake up for many years to attend to this phenomenon. This is indeed a black mark on the economic performance of the government.

Table 13.1: Trends of Suicides in Four Major States

Year	*Maharashtra*	*Andhra Pradesh*	*Karnataka*	*Madhya Pradesh*	*Yearly total for Big Four*
1997	1917	1097	1832	2390	7236
1998	2409	1813	1883	2278	8383
1999	2423	1974	2379	2654	9430
2000	3022	1525	2630	2660	9837
2001	3536	1509	2505	2824	10374
2002	3695	1896	2340	2578	10509
2003	3836	1800	2678	2511	10825
2004	4147	2666	1963	3033	11809
2005	3926	2490	1883	2660	10959
Total 1997-2005	28911	16770	20093	23588	89362

Source: National Bureau of Crime Records, Ministry of Home Affairs, Government of India.

Maharashtra, Andhra Pradesh, Karnataka and Madhya Pradesh have together seen 89,362 farmers' suicides between 1997 and 2005 (Table 13.1).

On average, one Indian farmer committed suicide every 32 minutes between 1997 and 2005. Since 2002, that has become one suicide every 30 minutes. The frequency at which farmers are killing themselves in many regions is appalling. On an average, one farmer took his or her life every 53 minutes between 1997 and 2005 in just the States of Maharashtra, Andhra Pradesh, Karnataka and Madhya Pradesh (including Chhattisgarh). In Maharashtra alone, there was one suicide every three hours. It got even worse after 2001. It rose to one farm suicide every 48 minutes in these big four states, and one every two and a quarter hours in Maharashtra alone. The big four have together seen 89,362 farmers' suicides between 1997 and 2005, or 44,102 between 2002 and 2005. K. Nagaraj of the Madras Institute of Development Studies (MIDS), who has studied farmers' suicides between 1997-2005 based on the National Crime Records Bureau (NCRB) data, shows a high farmers' suicide rate (FSR) for the above four states that is suicides per 1,00,000 population. The NCRB data shows that Andhra Pradesh saw 16,770 suicides between 1997 and 2005.

Significant reporting on suicides among farmers in India began in the 1990s. One of the major reporters of these suicides was the Rural Affairs Editor of *The Hindu*, P. Sainath. The first state where suicides were reported was Maharashtra. Soon newspapers began to report similar occurrences from Andhra Pradesh. In the beginning it was believed that most of the suicides were happening among the cotton growers, especially those from Vidarbha. A look at the figures given out by the State Crime Records Bureau, however, was sufficient to indicate that it was not just the cotton farmers but farmers as a professional category were suffering, irrespective of their holding size. Moreover, it was not just the farmers from Vidarbha but all over Maharashtra who showed a significantly high suicide rate. The government appointed a number of inquiries to look into the causes of farmer's suicide and farm related distress in general. Subsequently Prime Minister Manmohan Singh visited Vidarbha and promised a package of ₹110 billion (about $2.4 billion) to be spent by the government in Vidarbha. The families of farmers who had committed suicide were also offered an *ex gratia* grant to the tune of ₹100,000 (about $2,000) by the government, though this amount was changed several times. In 2006, the State of Maharashtra, with 4,453 farmers' suicides accounted for over a quarter of the all-India total of 17,060, according to the National

Crime Records Bureau (NCRB). NCRB also stated that there were at least 16,196 farmers' suicides in India in 2008, bringing the total since 1997 to 199,132. According to another study by the Bureau, while the number of farm suicides increased since 2001, the number of farmers has fallen, as thousands abandoning agriculture in distress. According to government data, over 5,000 farmers committed suicide in 2005-2009 in Maharashtra, while 1,313 cases reported by Andhra Pradesh between 2005 and 2007. In Karnataka the number stood at 1,003, since 2005-06 till August 2009. According to NCRB database number of suicides during 2005-2009 in Gujarat were 387, Kerala 905, Punjab 75 and Tamil Nadu 26. In April 2009, the state of Chhattisgarh reported 1,500 farmers committed suicide due to debt and crop failure. At least 17,368 Indian farmers killed themselves in 2009, the worst figure for farm suicides in six years, according to data of the National Crime Records Bureau (NCRB). The farmer was also caught in a Scissors Crisis. In the late 1990s and early 2000s, public attention was drawn to suicides by indebted farmers in India following crop failures. As of 2009, 87 per cent of Indian cotton-growing land was used for Bt cotton. Various studies identify the important factors as insufficient or risky credit systems, the difficulty of farming semi-arid regions, poor agricultural income, absence of alternative income opportunities, a downturn in the urban economy which forced non-farmers into farming, and the absence of suitable counselling services. The Indian Council of Agricultural Research (ICAR) and the Central Cotton Research Institute (CCRI) stated that in the five years from 2007 to 2012 the cost of cotton cultivation had jumped, as a consequence of rising pesticide costs associated with Bt cotton production, while crop yield declined.

In 2008, a report published by the International Food Policy Research Institute, an agriculture policy think tank based in Washington DC, stated that there was no evidence for an increased suicide rate following the 2002 introduction of Bt cotton. The report stated that farmer suicides predate the official commercial introduction of Bt cotton by Monsanto Mahyco in 2002 (and its unofficial introduction by Navbharat Seeds in 2001) and that such suicides were a fairly constant portion of the overall national suicide rate since 1997. The report concluded that while Bt cotton may have been a factor in specific suicides, the contribution was likely marginal compared to socio-economic factors. More recently, in 2012 the ICAR and the CCRI stated that for the first time farmer suicides could be linked to a decline in the performance of Bt cotton, and they issued an advisory stating that "cotton farmers are in a deep crisis since shifting to

Bt cotton. The spate of farmer suicides in 2011-12 has been particularly severe among Bt cotton farmers. As of August 2012, technical experts appointed by the India Supreme Court have recommended a 10-year moratorium on all field trials of Genetically Modified (GM) food, as well as the termination of all current trials of transgenic crops. With giant seed companies displacing cheap hybrids and far cheaper and earlier traditional varieties with their own products, a cotton farmer in Monsanto's net would be paying far more for seed than he or she ever dreamed they would. Local varieties and hybrids were squeezed out with enthusiastic state support. In 1991, a farmer could buy a kilogram of local seed for as little as ₹ 7 or ₹ 9 in today's worst affected region of Vidarbha. By 2003, the farmer would pay ₹350 for a bag with 450 grams of hybrid seed. By 2004, Monsanto's partners in India were marketing a bag of 450 grams of Bt cotton seed for between ₹1,650 and ₹1,800. This price was brought down dramatically overnight due to strong governmental intervention in Andhra Pradesh, where the government changed after the 2004 elections. The price fell to around ₹900 still many times higher than 1991 or even 2003.

Farm suicides rose sharply by almost 450 in Maharashtra in 2012 to touch 3,786, the latest National Crime Records Bureau data show. (The State saw 3,337 suicides in 2011). That is the worst annual increase in seven years. It also brings Maharashtra's total tally since the NCRB began recording farm data in 1995 to a staggering 57,604 farmers' suicides. Andhra Pradesh also saw an upward surge. It logged 2,572 farm suicides in 2012. That is 366 higher than the previous year's figure of 2,206. Chhattisgarh's three-year average prior to its zero-declaration approach was 1,567. Indeed, the State's own data, prior to that shows it suffered 18,375 farm suicides between 2001 and 2010. The Big 5 states accounted for over 68.4 per cent of all farm suicides in the country in 2012. That is the highest ever since the recording of such data began. Among other major States, Kerala saw 1,081 farm deaths, a steep increase of 251 over its 2011 number of 830. The NCRB figures across 18 years for which data exist show that at least 2,84,694 Indian farmers have taken their lives since 1995. India saw 1,38,321 farm suicides between 1995 and 2003 at an annual average of 15,369. For the period 2004-12, the number is 1,46,373, at a much higher annual average of 16,264. The figures in the second half occurred against a steep decline in the numbers of farmers in India and are hence even worse than they appear.

In Maharashtra, for instance, the rate is 29.1 suicides per 100,000 farmers ('Main cultivators'). Which is over 160 per cent higher than that for all Indians excluding farmers. Such gaps exist in other States, too. In 1995, the 'Big 5' accounted for over half of all farm suicides in India. In 2011, they logged over two-thirds of them. Ten States show a higher farm suicide rate in 2011 than in 2001. That includes the major farming zones of Punjab and Haryana. A farmer in Maharashtra is two-and-a-half times more likely to kill himself than anyone else in the country. The Census records cultivators; the police count suicides. In listing suicides, the State governments and police tend to count only those with a title to land as farmers. However, in case of Punjab, NCRB could not correctly capture the farmer's suicides number and rate because between 1989 and 2013, the farmers committing suicides were afraid of police repression due to the continuity of militancy days and so they stealthily cremated the dead bodies secretively without the knowledge of police. This was done in any case with full community support. Hence, the figures of NCRB do not correctly reflect the actual number of farmer's suicides in their statistics. "Large numbers of farm suicides still occur," says Prof. Nagaraj. "Only that seems not to be recognised, officially and politically. Is the 'conspiracy of silence' back in action?" Others will doubtless do the same. Punjab and Haryana have in several years claimed 'zero' women farmers' suicides. (Though media and study reports in the same years suggest otherwise). This trend must at some point fatally corrupt the data. At least 270,940 Indian farmers have taken their lives since 1995, NCRB records show. This occurred at an annual average of 14,462 in six years, from 1995 to 2000, and at an yearly average of 16,743 in 11 years between 2001 and 2011.

A record number of 2.5 lakh farmers have committed suicide in India over the last 13 years. Agriculture Minister Sharad Pawar's home state Maharashtra tops the list. It has the worst record for the 10th consecutive year. According to the National Crime Records Bureau (NCRB) data, more than 2,16,000 farmers have committed suicide since 1997. P. Sainath, Rural Affairs editor for '*The Hindu*', says: Add figures for the years 1995, 1996 and 2010, the total figure crosses 2,50,000 UPA government says the problem is systemic. Agriculture Minister Sharad Pawar whose state has the worst figures for the 10th consecutive year has stopped quoting NCRB figures since 2007. A total of 290,740 farmers have committed suicide during 1995-2011 due to various reasons. Parliament was informed of this. "As per ADSI reports for relevant years, 290,470 self-employed persons in farming/agriculture committed suicide during 1995-2011, "Minister of State for Agriculture, Harish Rawat said in Rajya Sabha in a written reply to a question whether three lakh farmers committed suicide between 1995 and 2012 (till date). The Minister referred the data from the National Crime Records Bureau's (NCRB) latest Annual Report on suicides, the ADSI-2011 (Accidental Death and Suicides in India). Causes of suicides across professional categories mentioned in ADSI include family problems, illness, drug abuse addiction, unemployment, property dispute, bankruptcy or sudden change in economic status, poverty etc. The Minister said that Government has taken several steps to revitalize agriculture sector and improve condition of farmers. Implementation of rehabilitation package covered 31 districts in Andhra Pradesh, Karnataka, Kerala and Maharashtra under which an amount of ₹ 19,998.85 crore was released till September 30, 2011. Implementation of Agricultural Debt Waiver and Debt Relief Scheme, 2008, benefited about 3.69 crore farmers, involving debt waiver/relief of ₹ 65,318.33 crore. The seed sector of India was opened to global corporations like Cargill, Monsanto, and Syngenta due to the World Bank's structural adjustment policies. The global corporations changed the input economy overnight. Farm saved seeds were replaced by corporate seeds, which need fertilizers and pesticides and cannot be saved. The corporate globalization of seed sector resulted in the increase in indebtedness. The Situation Assessment Survey of Farmers Indebtedness of Farmer Households by National Sample Survey (NSS) 59th Round (January-December 2003) points out that at national level, on an average, 29 out of 100 indebted households borrowed from 'agricultural/professional moneylender'. Marriages and ceremonies accounted for 111 rupees per 1000 rupees of outstanding loans of farmer households. The most important source of loan in terms of percentage of outstanding loan amount from the banks was 36 per cent and from the moneylenders 26 per cent. The World Trade Organization (WTO) has a negative impact on the Indian farmers. The prices of agricultural products before the WTO agreement in India were lower than the international prices. But as a result of heavy subsidization of agricultural products by developed countries, the situation has changed. The prices of International Agricultural Products have become lower than the Indian agricultural prices.

The World Bank's structural adjustment policies forced India to open up its seed sector to global corporations. Farm saved seeds were replaced by corporate seeds. The poor peasants have to buy new seeds for every planting season and what was a traditionally a free resource, available by putting aside a small portion of the crop, becomes a commodity. This new expense increases poverty and leads to indebtedness. The cause of farmers suicides are associated with high level of indebtedness is popularly and even in some academic writings, seen as indicative of the Indian peasantry in general suffering from unbearable burden of debt and teetering on the brink of bankruptcy. The farmers are unable to cope up with the sudden changes in cropping patterns, market fluctuations, and use of pesticides to increase the yield. These are direct results of agricultural policy driven by market forces. When the crops fail, they are in debt, which they have no means to repay. They are unable to perform the role of provider for the family. All these factors are to be taken in to consideration while understanding an individual farmer committing suicide. was secure. The joint families in olden days were extending moral support to its members at the time of all crises. A person is almost certainly well insured morally when isolated and left to himself than when constantly under beneficent discipline of family surroundings. Failure of social institutions to instill and establish confidence among those who are on the verge of breakdown is one of the main factor responsible for the suicide among farmers. Contributing Factors for Farmers Suicides Apart from the views of the thinkers, mentioned above the following factors contribute to the suicides among farmers. Failure of Crops is due to the failure of rainfall, drought, destruction of crops due to pests and use of low quality seeds.

The Vidarbha region in Maharashtra was the first to get a ₹ 3,750-crore (₹ 37.50 billion) relief package from Prime Minister Manmohan Singh. As per the figures of farmers' suicide compiled by the Union Agriculture Ministry on the basis of reports sent by different states, Maharashtra stands third. From 2000-01 to 2005-06, around 8,600 farmers committed suicide in Karnataka, while the figures stood over 2,000 in Andhra Pradesh for the same period. In case of Maharashtra, the government reported 981 farmer suicides between 2001 and 2005. A sharp spurt in suicide cases was reported from Vidarbha. It was also much worse in Andhra Pradesh as per official figures — 1,068 farmers committing suicide in barely six months, from May 14, 2005 to November 11, 2005. These discrepancies raise several questions about the authenticity of the figures on farmers:' suicide in different parts of the country. The then Opposition Congress in Andhra Pradesh had made farmers' suicide their central plank in the year 2004 Assembly election to unseat the Telugu Desam Party. In July 2004, the Prime Minister visited Hyderabad and Kurnool districts to review the State Government's efforts to check suicides. The Prime Minister had left Hyderabad with the promise that he would personally go into farm-related issues. About two years hence, he was visiting Vidarbha while the crisis continued to worsen in Andhra Pradesh. Actually, most of the suicide cases in Andhra Pradesh were in Telangana region.

Farmers Suicide in Maharashtra

In recent years Vidarbha was in the media for a spate of farmer suicides ostensibly because of the falling Minimum Support Price for cotton. The problem is complex and root causes include lopsided policies of the World Trade Organization and developed nations' subsidies to their cotton farmers which make Vidarbha's cotton uncompetitive in world markets. Consequently, Vidarbha is plagued by high rates of school drop outs, penniless widows left in the wake of suicides, loan sharks and exploitation of the vulnerable groups. Traditionally cotton has been the cash crop for farmers in Vidarbha and adjoining districts. However, cotton profitability declined over recent years. Contributing factors were high subsidies by the US leading to price distortions, low import tariffs in India, and failure of the Monopoly Cotton Procurement Scheme (MCPS), which intended to stabilize prices but quickly became non-functional. The withdrawal of the State is evident from a declining public investment in agriculture, a poor agricultural extension service, and a diminishing role of formal institutions in rural financial market. Farmers started depending on input dealers for advice, leading to supplier-induced demand. Informal sources of credit meant a greater interest burden. Furthermore, water shortages and increased input quantities and prices (mostly fertilizers and pesticides) have meant many farmers have experienced both yield and price shocks. The state is facing socio-economic and agrarian crisis which heavily impacts on poor farmers. The important contributing factors are indebtedness, deterioration of economic status, family conflict, crop failure, a decline in social position, suicide in a nearby village, addictions, health problems, a recent death in the family, and a history of suicide in the family. These indicate structural factors—a socio-economic and agrarian crisis which is contributing to the observed increased rates of farmer suicides.

Approximately 3.4 million cotton farmers occupy the Vidarbha region which includes Akola, Buldana, Washim, Amravati, Nagpur, Chandrapur, Gondia, Bhandara, Yavatmal, Gadchiroli, and Wardha districts and 95 per cent of them struggle with massive debt, according to the Vidarbha Jan Aandolan Samiti (VJAS; Local Farmers' Support Network) Incidence of farmers ending their lives in this region had hit epidemic like proportions recently. In 2004, in response to a request from the All India Biodynamic and Organic Farming Association, the Mumbai High Court requested the Tata Institute to produce a report on farmer suicides in Maharashtra, and the institute submitted its report in March 2005. The survey cited "government apathy, the absence of a safety net for farmers, and lack of access to information related to agriculture as the chief causes for the desperate condition of farmers in the state". A new survey on farmer suicides in Maharashtra by the Tata Institute of Social Sciences (TISS), Mumbai had come up with a far greater estimate of farm deaths in the state than previously cited, either by the state government or by media reports. The survey found that 644 farmers committed suicide in Vidarbha, Marathwada and Khandesh regions of the state between January 2001 and December 2004. Worse, only 20 per cent of the suicide victims' families received any compensation from the Maharashtra government. The TISS survey cited government apathy, the absence of a safety net for farmers, and lack of access to information related to agriculture as the chief causes for the desperate condition of farmers in the state. Widely regarded as the most comprehensive survey on farmer suicides (it relied on both primary and secondary data), the survey focused largely on socio-economic variables such as family composition, education, history of agriculture, cropping pattern, landholding, input costs incurred, expected output, holding capacity, history of loans taken by the head of the household and causes for taking the loans, mental state of the person, addictions, and any other information the family wished to share.

Key Findings of the TISS Survey

- The suicides are not restricted to income level or landholding category. They occurred both among large landholding owners and the landless, and across all caste groups.
- The causes, however, are common — repeated crop failure, inability to meet the rising cost of cultivation, and indebtedness. In all cases, this extreme step was taken only after all avenues were exhausted.
- Understanding the profile of the victims in their social and economic contexts can help gauge the depth and spread of the tragic phenomenon.
- Fifty per cent of the total sample constituted small landholders who owned up to five acres, 43 per cent medium landholders who owned between five and 15 acres, and 5 per cent large landholders who owned more than 15 acres. The remaining 2 per cent did not own land. The overwhelming numbers are reflected in the small and medium-sized holdings across caste groups. This is suggestive of a problem that is widespread, cutting across caste and class barriers.

- Of the sample, 89 per cent were married. This indicates the pressure to provide for a household. A startling 81 per cent were literate, primarily because most of the people who committed suicide were men.
- Seventy per cent of the total number of suicide victims grew cotton as their primary cash crop. The cost of cotton cultivation is between ₹ 2,500 and ₹ 3,000 per acre. Another 5 per cent took up horticulture as the major occupation, while the remaining 20 per cent cultivated *tur*, *urad*, soybean, *jowar*, vegetables and sugarcane. Once again, the data suggests that cultivators of all sorts of crops are affected.
- The survey enumerates a host of interlinked reasons that put farmers in debt. Cost of cultivation of most crops has increased owing to higher input prices. Thus, the purchase of large quantities of inputs, and high cost of labour, has increased the demand for cash. The absence of a corresponding increase in the prices of produce affects the viability of farming. The complete mismatch between cost of production and low minimum support price and market price creates huge losses for the farmer.
- Money is also required for social needs such as marriages and education. In some of the cases studied, the debts were as low as ₹ 10,000. According to the report, the loans ranged from ₹ 10,000 to ₹ 3 lakh.
- In a detailed break-up of the loans, which includes size of land held by farmers and their sources of funds. The largest group of borrowers are the small and medium landholders. As most of the time the victims have run out of credit with the banks, the only other source of funds is private lenders who charge exorbitant interest rates as high as 5 per cent per month. Some even pledge their crop to the moneylender. If it fails there is little recourse left.
- The private lending component, which includes borrowing from relatives, accounts for about 50 per cent of the total lending. Primary agricultural credit cooperatives contribute 21 per cent of loans, and commercial banks and land development banks together contribute 18 per cent. The rest comes from a number of small sources. This lends itself to an argument that the largest off-take of credit is still being met by private sources. Essentially the resultant debt trap is due to the inadequate credit supply to

cultivators at affordable prices and due to the rising cost of production that cannot be met.

While discussing the links between farmer suicides and the larger economic scenario, the TISS report observes that heavy rural indebtedness is not a phenomenon that came about overnight but one that has its roots in the credit policy being followed by the country over time. Field data suggests that crops have failed repeatedly over the past four years. This was not entirely due to the failure of the monsoons. It occurred also because of a reduction in land productivity owing to overuse of fertilizers and pesticides, and the reliance on hybrid seeds and, to some extent, genetically modified seeds such as BT cotton. Crop failure becomes a cyclical phenomenon and not a one-time occurrence. Moreover, regions where suicides have occurred have little irrigation. Almost 60 per cent of irrigation projects cater to western parts of Maharashtra that produce sugarcane and account for just 30 per cent of the total area under agriculture in the state.

In its final recommendations to the High Court, the report suggests that a compensation of ₹ 2.5 lakh be given immediately to each of the bereaved families. It recommends the constitution of a committee comprising experts in the field, activists and government officials to distribute the funds. Since the investigations revealed that the suicides were not properly recorded and investigated by the government, the report suggests that a team put together a list of the deaths. It requests the court to direct government insurance agencies to create an insurance safety net assuring a minimum life support system to cultivators. The report asks the court to instruct the state to provide information about cultivation to farmers through e-networks. It says the government must be told to propagate alternative low-cost organic farming in these areas through its agencies and voluntary organizations. The report concludes: "Any relief is a short-term measure. Long-term measures should be the rehabilitation of a system, in this case the agrarian production system itself." Until the Indian government overhauls its agricultural policies, the situation will not improve, says the report. It suggests that the High Court Direct the Central Government to frame policies that encourage marginal and small farmers, as millions of them have no livelihood options outside the agricultural sector. These policies must support cultivation so that farmers stay out of the debt trap. The report recommends that the Court make the Indian government 'party' to the present suit so that it is forced to take cognizance of the magnitude of the problem.

In Maharashtra, the government neglected the phenomenon which was most striking in the Vidarbha area, until the High Court got seized of it and asked the Tata Institute of Social Sciences to study the subject. The Government of Maharashtra then woke up and asked the Indira Gandhi Institute of Development and Research to make a survey and submit its findings. The Planning Commission also sent a team at the instance of the Prime Minister to study the causes of farmers' suicides and propose suitable measures and programmes. The State Government under pressure made some provisions and after the Prime Minister's visit, the Central Government provided a financial package. Both these failed to stem the tide of farmers' suicides, suggesting that the package was not based on a correct understanding of the causes of farmers' suicides. As the general elections was drawing near, the Finance Minister, in his Budget speech, made a dramatic announcement of the write-off of loans of small and marginal farmers and made a provision of ₹ 60,000 crore which later increased to ₹ 71,000 crore to enable the banks to write off the loans. This still leaves out the farmers' debts to the private moneylenders, which are a substantial part of indebtedness. In the era of neo-liberalization since 1991, the nationalized banks started reducing their commitment below the prescribed 18 per cent, while the cooperative banks turned sick and failed to provide adequate credit. This forced the farmers to turn from institutional credit to the moneylenders, despite the usurious interest rates charged by them. It concentrates its research on the districts in the Vidarbha area, whose epicentre is the Yavatmal district. The study, based on a wealth of statistics and case studies, shows that farmers commit suicides because they are driven to do so by the desperate conditions in which they find themselves. These farmers belong to different caste groups and not only small and marginal farmers but even those owning larger holdings, which in the context of dry agriculture are not enough to enable the farmers' families to eke out livelihood. The suicide of the breadwinner, whether young or old, leave the families desolate and disrupt the social order. The causes of farmers' suicides are both economic and social.

The question arises as to why Vidarbha is home for approximately 3.4 million cotton farmers and 95 per cent of them are struggling with the massive debt. Most of the villages in Vidarbha are badly in need of basic social infrastructure like all-weather roads, drinking water, regular electricity, primary health care, and basic education. Majority of suicide cases are from cotton growing areas. The cotton farmers in India are paying more prices for inputs like seeds, pesticides, fertilizers, electricity, water, and labour whereas the price of cotton has gone down along with decreased productivity. In contrast to this picture in India, US Government is giving US$ 4.0 billion to cotton farmers and asking for further liberalization of cotton trade in USA. In Vidarbha (basically a low rainfall area), the major crop is cotton, *jowar*, and pulses and people rely more on dry farming. Irrigated farming is insignificant and seen only in very few pockets where major rivers provide water for the whole year. With the cumulative effect of these reasons coupled with environmental antagonism and exploitation of the farmers in all sectors made them pessimistic towards life resulting into development of suicidal tendency in them. The remedial measures undertaken by the government did not show any immediate positive effect in the attitude of the farmers.

Critics say that state government's guidelines for defining who is a farmer and what is a genuine farmer suicide has tended to be exclusive rather than inclusive. Women are not identified as farmers, especially because land is rarely bought or registered in their names. As costs rose, credit dried up. Debt went out of control. Subsidies destroyed their prices. Starving agriculture of investment (worth billions of dollars each year) smashed the countryside. India even cut most of the few, pathetic life supports she had for her farmers. The mess was complete. From the late-1990s, the suicides began to occur at what then seemed a brisk rate. Corporations do not as yet have direct control of Indian farming land and do not carry out day-to-day operations directly. But they have sewn up every other sector, inputs, outlets, marketing, prices, and are heading for control of water as well (which states in India are busy privatizing in one guise or another). The largest number of farm suicides is in the state of Maharashtra. In the state of which Mumbai is capital, there have been 40,666 farmers' suicides since 1995, with very little media attention. Farmers' suicides in Maharashtra crossed the 4,000-mark again in 2007, for the third time in four years, according to the National Crime Records Bureau. As many as 4,238 farmers took their lives in the state in 2007 the latest for which data are available, accounting for a fourth of all the 16,632 farmers' suicides in the country. ('Suicide of Farmers in Maharashtra: Background Papers, Submitted to the Government of Maharashtra', Srijit Mishra, Sangeeta Shroff, Deepak Shah; Vivek Deshpande, Anjali P. Kulkarni, Vinayak S. Deshpande, P.R. Bhatkule, Indira Gandhi Institute of Development Research, Mumbai, 26 January, 2006).

Intervention of M. S. Swaminathan Foundation

Of special mention here is the National Commission on Farmers (NCF) constituted by the Government of India. The NCF held several formal consultations across the country and also directly interacted with the farmers and other local stakeholders in some of the districts in the country. As Chairman of NCF, Professor M.S. Swaminathan visited Vidarbha region during October 2005 and interacted with several of the affected families, farm leaders, social activists, non-governmental organization representatives, politicians, government officials, Academican and media representatives. These interactions brought to light the dire plight of the suicide affected families. Young school going children of many of these families were forced to take up the responsibility of contributing to the family's income to make both ends meet. Following a field visit to Vidarbha region, the M. S. Swaminathan Research Foundation (MSSRF) initiated an Education Support Programme (ESP) in 2006 for school children from suicide-affected farmer's families in Wardha district. The programme was started with the aim of providing financial support to the children of affected families to continue their education. The interaction with the mothers of children covered under ESP brought out the high degree of vulnerability in the lives and livelihoods of the women farmers in the region. The nature of agriculture in Vidarbha is marked by backwardness and adversity. Agriculture is practiced under unfavourable agro-ecological conditions with low levels of irrigation and modernization, leading to high levels of instability and vulnerability of the production system. The women farmers, in particular suicide victims, struggling to eke out a livelihood in an agricultural domain which is wrought with such adversities need emotional, economic and technical support. Their capacities need to be built up to help them take informed scientific decisions and perform their role as farmers effectively. Moreover, in spite of being actively engaged in farming and farm-related activities for sustenance, women farmers are not recognized as farmers. Women also lack ownership rights to the land on which they toil. Support in the form of access to credit, technology, infrastructure and markets would go a long way in empowering women farmers. MSSRFs bio-village paradigm focuses on enhancing lives and livelihood of the communities through appropriate on-farm and off-farm interventions. Its focus on ICT based intervention has resulted in grassroots women knowledge holders taking a key leadership role in rural areas. MSSRF has enabled many women leaders who now occupy elected positions in the local bodies and have represented their community in several regional, national and international fora.

The Mahila Kisan Sashaktikaran Pariyojana Programme

Mahila Kisan Sashaktikaran Pariyojana (MKSP), a Programme for Empowerment of Women Farmers, was launched in 2007 by MSSRF to address some of the concerns of women farmers in Vidarbha region of Maharashtra. MKSP endeavours to bring about positive change in the lives of women farmers through mobilising them into collectives, helping generate an independent identity as farmers, building their skills and capacities as farmers and in problem-solving more generally, facilitating their increased involvement in decision making in their families and facilitating formation of community-based institutions which will emerge as a support and pressure group. The strategy adopted under MKSP has two prime foci to ensure the sustainability of the programme: the institution building aspect of the programme; the extension and scaling up aspect of interventions. Women farmers are trained on organization management skills to build their capacities to run women farmer collectives. These include training on recordkeeping, accounting, communication, mobilization and building linkages with local administration at all levels. - Sustainable agriculture: Natural Resource Management in the women farmers' field is done through soil and water conservation structures such as contour bunding. Soil health management is done through continuous monitoring of the Food and nutrition security: Capacity building on household food and nutrition security are taken up on a life cycle approach. Awareness creation on issues relating to health and sanitation are also addressed with the members of the women collectives. Locally suitable food crops, horticultural crops, and backyard kitchen gardens are promoted to increase household consumption of local food grains, vegetables, and fruits among the members. Periodic health camps are conducted to address the health needs of the group members. Better access to the various government schemes related to food, nutrition and health is also facilitated under this component.

Empowerment Through Access to Entitlements

Lack of access to entitlements is a serious issue among women farmers. Facilitation to access to entitlement using household entitlement card is a unique strategy adopted by MSSRF to reach these entitlements to the target households. Household entitlement cards provide information on various schemes implemented by different departments of the Central and State Governments. For each one of the schemes listed in the entitlement card, information on eligibility criteria, documents required at the time of application, the department responsible for sanctioning the scheme, the contact person and address of the department etc. are provided. Facilitation to access to the government schemes pertaining to agriculture, food and nutrition and health are taken up with women farmers using this entitlement card. ICT is used as a tool for rural development, womens empowerment and bridging the urban-rural digital divide. This small initiative started in Vidarbha has now become a national programme under the same title, viz., Mahila Kisan Sashaktikaran Pariyojana and special provision has been made in the union budget of 2010-11 for expanding this programme on a national scale. This marks the beginning of a new era where women farmers and farm women are enabled to play their rightful role in strengthening national food security and agrarian prosperity. The programme has had both tangible and intangible results. The direct tangible outcome of the initiative so far is currently all 795 members of MKSP have received awareness and training on different sustainable agricultural practices, food and nutrition security issues and on organization management. About 2200 hectares of land have been brought under one or the other sustainable agriculture practice for which the women farmers have received training. Adoption of best practices in member's field has created demonstration effects in MKSP villages resulting in demand by non-members for capacity building on these issues. The institution building strategy involves mobilization of women farmers into collectives, and building their capacities to better their lives and livelihoods. MKSP will eventually create community based organization to institutionalize the ongoing activities under the initiative. This envisages a three-tier structure consisting of women farmer groups at the village level, cluster of 8-10 women farmers groups at the block level, and federation of all the women farmers groups at the district level. The federation of women farmers will be a registered body to take up services like credit and market linkages. The federation will serve as an aggregator and source inputs collectively for its members as well take up collective marketing on behalf of its members. The members will benefit from the economies of scale those results from the bulk purchase and sale of inputs and produce. Federations will also be able to approach commercial banks for credit. The evolution of the community based organization with the federation of women farmers as the apex body is the ultimate step towards ensuring sustainability of the programme.

Impetus of Liberalization to Agrarian Crisis and Rural Suicides in Andhra Pradesh

Among all the Indian states, the maximum use of pesticides is in Andhra Pradesh and a major portion of this is used in cotton and chilli cultivation. The cotton crop is quite susceptible to a range of Pests and diseases. During the year 1997-98, the problem was very severe in the Telangana region of Andhra Pradesh and the pests attacked the standing crops in the fields of which the most affected crop was cotton followed by chilli and ground nut (Shiva, Vandana, 1998). In Andhra Pradesh, there were several companies that were selling spurious and low quality chemicals. The two pests that attacked the cotton crop in 1997-98 were 'heliothis and spodoptera.' The consequences of crop loss was the over burdening debts among the farmers of Andhra Pradesh and the accumulated debts also led to distress sale of kidneys by many farmers.

In Andhra Pradesh, hundreds of cotton farmers resorted to commit suicide since 1987. The trend continued and the situation became alarming since 2000 when the state continuously faced drought situation. This phenomena continued even after the new state government took over in May 2004. The government took steps by announcing relief measures, but the spate of death continued unabated. Diversification of food crops to non-edible commercial crops, increased cost of agricultural production and falling price of farm commodities, failure of financial institutions in reaching the small and marginal farmers, exploitative role of private moneylenders and traders in agriculture, replacing the farm saved seeds with corporate high cost inputs, neglected surface irrigation facilities, failure of agriculture extension services and neglected non-farm employment led to subsistence crisis among many small and marginal farmers in the state and forced some of them to commit suicide. Expenditure on life cycle ceremonies, health and education, and absence of any social security measures added to the distress of these farmers ultimately leading them to commit suicide. Small and marginal farmers especially those who leased in the land from others were not eligible for institutional credit and crop insurance. The situation had helped in strengthening the merchant capital. Traders-cum-moneylenders had the fortune in the absence of institutional mechanism. Market driven mono-cropping had damaged the soil and did not yield as expected. The entry of commercial crops brought major changes in the farmers lives and agricultural practices. The distressed economic situation and failure of institutions in safeguarding the interests of small and marginal farmers forced them to commit suicide.

Revathi (1998) analyzed some missing issues in farmers' suicides and identified the non-inclusion of irrigation as a major factor for the tragedy in Andhra Pradesh. Second missing point was the source of credit. Other major problem was tenancy. She observed that Telangana district of AP was precursor of many peasants movements. However, defeatist tendencies like suicides by the farmers were quite new phenomena to the region. More than sociological reason like alienation of individual from family and society, it was the politics and economics of a neglected region for decade that was the cause of the suicide deaths. A study conducted by AWARE (1998), an NGO in Andhra Pradesh, has presented empirical data relating to farmers' suicides in Andhra Pradesh. The study has covered 17 districts in AP (focusing more on Telangana districts where the incidence of suicides was very high during 1997-1998). Totally a sample of 92 out of 307 reported cases of suicides has been covered under this study. This study provides a good database on the deceased farmers and their households. Generally, this study has highlighted the distress conditions of the farmers that led them to commit suicide. The main reason for the strain on the cotton peasant was the growing indebtedness of the agriculturist to the moneylender-cum-dealer. A number of factors were cited as reasons for suicides. There were adverse rain fall and low yields, adverse prices, rise in cost of cultivation and particularly cash components, indiscriminate use of pesticides and high cost of cultivation, poor position of cooperative credit agencies and commercial banks, growing power of moneylender. Citizen report (1998), based on the sample of 50 cases of deceased farmers in Warangal district, the study concluded that, the new agriculture technology initiated in mid-sixties on irrigated land tenures which helped in raising production in food grains, led to severe pressure on crucial resources like soil and water in the semi-arid region like Warangal. In the second phase, the expansion of commercial crops like cotton and chilly on small holdings in a situation of meagre physical and financial resources and the intermittent fluctuations in crop yields, superimposed by exploitative input and output linked markets had highly destabilized the small farm economy culminating in large scale suicides. In Andhra Pradesh, over 2200 farmers committed suicide. The government has recognized only 144 farmer's suicides as 'genuine' and eligible for compensation. The rest of the families got no compensation.

R.M. Vidyasagar and K. Suman Chandra (2004), "Farmers' Suicides in Andhra Pradesh and Karnataka—NIRD study" have observed that about 3,000 Andhra Pradesh farmers committed suicide owing to debt trap, drought and crop failure. The Government of Y.S. Raja Shekhar Reddy announced free electricity for agriculture, waiver of electricity dues and a ₹ 150,000 financial assistance for the relatives of the farmers who committed suicide. This study has identified a suicide belt consisting of districts in Andhra Pradesh and Karnataka states where instances of farmers' suicide continue unabated for last five to six years. This belt falls mainly in the arid and semi-arid zones of the Royalaseema region and in certain other districts in northern Karnataka that are contiguous to Royalaseema region. Within this region, farmers' suicides have become a persisting feature for last five years in Anantapur district of Andhra Pradesh. Certain districts adjoining Anantapur but falling in Karnataka are also taken up where it is observed that suicides are taking place or have taken place. The northern districts of Karnataka bordering to Royalaseema region share the same agricultural background as Anantapur district. Drought condition is not something strange to Anantapur as this is one of the two districts in the country having lowest rainfall. Thus, low rainfall and drought conditions alone do not explain why farmers should take recourse to such extreme step while the farmers have already built enough resilience to drought conditions. One of the striking features of changes in cropping pattern is that over a period of time Anantapur district has almost become a mono-crop district. It is seen that the area under groundnut has tremendously increased during last two decades, from a mere 16 per cent of the gross cropped area 1930-31 to 70 per cent in 1999-2000. The increase is sharper from late 1980s. Local varieties of cereal crops (coarse grains) were also drought resistance to a greater extent and dependency on market for inputs was not much. But at present the mono-culture of groundnut has completely transformed socio-economic life of people. This is the crucial factor in understanding the phenomenon of farmers' suicides. Resilience to drought is broken due to mono-culture of groundnut. A recent study done by the Government of Andhra Pradesh reported that more than 55 per cent of the farmers are not getting the Minimum Support Price (MSP). This is true in the case of Anantapur also. Most of the farmers are tied to the traders and middlemen who are dealing in agricultural inputs. This depresses the price that farmers are to get for their output. The cost of cultivation is increasing manifold in the 1990s. Available data (Agricultural Census, 1995) on land holdings in Anantapur district shows that about 90 per cent of the holdings are small and marginal holdings. They are under great pressure owing to their dependency on vagaries of market and non-institutional forces that control input, credit and output markets. Karnataka in general has a vast tract of drought-prone area. It is said that the state has a disproportionate share of drought-prone areas in the country. The northern districts of Karnataka are considered backward compared to other parts of the state. The crop pattern has been tilting in favour of commercialization and hence the risk of crop loss increased due to higher proportion of purchased inputs and technology. There was also a tendency to adopt mono-culture and consequent over-exploitation of land.

This compels them to remain in the village and somehow improve their income. Removal of QR under WTO regime have created havoc and exposed the farmers to the volatility of international market and prices. This situation has helped in strengthening the merchant capital and the traders-cum-moneylenders have their fortunes in the absence of supportive institutional mechanisms. Market driven mono cropping has damaged the fertility of the soil and created ecological imbalances. All these factors along with the usual social pressure have made many small and marginal farmers to throw up their hands. This process is intensifying during the last decade under the regime of liberalization and globalization. The Human Rights Forum (HRF) demands that the government take immediate steps to ensure that the families of farmers who have committed suicide are duly compensated and rehabilitated as envisaged under GO 421.

In view of the immense pressure from the activists and intellectuals, the Government of Andhra Pradesh announced compensation and rehabilitation *vide* its G.O.Ms. No. 421 dated 1st June, 2004 which are as follows:

1. An *ex-gratia* of ₹ 1.00 lakh (Rupees one lakh only) in cases of suicide provisionally arises out of farm income related issues shall be provided to the family/next of kin of the deceased farmer, as an economic support, besides loan settlement up to a ceiling of ₹ 50,000 (₹ fifty thousand only) as one time settlement to creditors.
2. The loan settlement up to a ceiling limit of ₹ 50,000 (₹ fifty thousand only) shall be paid as one time settlement.
3. The following measures to provide social cushion will also be taken up:
   (a) Admission of children in Social Welfare schools and Hostels.
   (b) Allotment of houses under I. A.Y. Scheme.
   (c) Economic support under Government schemes.
   (d) Pensions etc.
4. These compensations measures were applicable to all the cases

of suicides primarily arising out of farm income related to suicides from 1-7-1998. The Government of Andhra Pradesh paid compensation to the suicides committed from 1998 to 12-11-2013.

5. Under P.M.'s. Packages an extent of ₹ 50 lakh were given to each district for extending benefits to the families of farmers who committed suicide.
6. Maximum relief to any single family should not exceed ₹ 10,000.
7. Educational expenses of children may be supported where the families have to incur expenses in pursuing studies.
8. A total amount of ₹ 7,42,46,620 was disbursed by Collectors of 16 districts to 8833 cases in the entire Andhra Pradesh.

Farmers Suicide in Karnataka

While it is difficult to pin-point precise numbers, according to the Karnataka State Crime Record Bureau, the total number of suicides in Karnataka among farmers during the period of 1996-2000 was 10,959 (8,728 male and 2,231 female). The year-wise figures were 2,079 for 1,996, 1,832 for 1997, 2,039 for 1998, 2,379 for 1999 and 2,630 for year 2000. Press reports indicated that at least 3,000 farmers had taken their lives between 2000 and 2003. Regional and local press reported an average of about four farmer suicides per week. Over 276 farmers have committed suicides in Karnataka within a span of five and a half months from April 1, 2003. The suicides were intense between August to September 2003. There was an average of five suicides for every two days. Of late the Karnataka Government has accepted the fact of farmers' suicide and revealed that 708 in 2003-04, 271 in 2004-05 and 143 farmers in 2005-06 did commit suicide (Anonymous, 2006). Successive droughts and untimely rains have seriously affected farmers for past four to five years. Crop losses caused by four successive years of inadequate rainfall and then diminishing presence of institutional credit forced a large number of Karnataka farmers into the debt trap. Some of them choose death as a way out. The paradox is that the suicides, far from being phenomena of drought-prone regions, have spread to fairly prosperous regions and irrigated belts also. During 1999, Government of Karnataka appointed a Joint House Committee to enquire into causes of farmers' suicides. The committee concluded that only one out of sixty cases examined had crop loss and in rest of the cases, the committee categorically stated that, the suicides were on account of "personal and domestic problems rather than crop loss". And hence the committee recommended no compensation. But, later in view of the growing public concern about farmers' suicides the Government appointed an Expert Committee to conduct a scientific study of suicides in the state. The Commission called Veeresh Committee completed and presented its report in 2002. But in conclusion the Committee observed that agrarian distress caused in the districts of Karnataka is a fact. However, connecting the spate of suicides directly to any single cause will be erroneous. It was observed that typical social factors like family composition, failure of social situations, habits, alcoholism, social security etc. contributed to suicides.

A number of reports on farmers' suicides appeared not only from Bidar district but also from other districts particularly from Northern Karnataka. A joint house committee of Karnataka under the Chairmanship of G.B. Shivakumar, Former Member of Legislative Assembly examined whether crop failure and repayment of crop loans were the major causes for suicides. Farmers have had a harrowing time in Karnataka, having had to content with continuous drought and ever-increasing agriculture input costs. This has driven many farmers to suicide, with the number of deaths touching 100 in the last financial year (2012-13). More than 16 per cent of sowed crops were affected due to erratic rainfall. The State government declared 157 talukas in 28 districts as drought-hit. A total of 2,986 farmers ended their lives in the last one decade (2003-04 to 2012-13). As many as 187 farmers committed suicide in 2011-12 and 242 in 2010-11. Farmers commit suicide primarily due to agrarian distress caused by debts, high farming cost, particularly fertilizers, and low returns due to faulty policies, says R.S. Deshpande, Director, Institute for Social and Economic Change (ISEC), Bangalore. Observers note that the contribution of the agriculture sector to the economy has been declining without commensurate decline in the workforce in agriculture. The State's Economic Survey (2012-13) noted that the agricultural sector is likely to register a growth of 1.8 per cent while the food grain production is expected to touch 12.5 million tonnes as against the target of 13.65 million tonnes. Per capita availability of food grains is steadily declining. Per capita availability of food grains in 2003 was 27 kgs less than \what it was in 1991. Farmers indebtedness was one of the main causes of distress in the agriculture sector. Almost half of (49%) India's farmer households are indebted. The small and marginal farmers get the loan at a higher rate of interest from private money lenders due to non-availability of institutional credit. As a result they are unable to clear of the loan of the private moneylenders and the farmers enter into vicious debt trap.

According to Viresh Committee there were multiple factors which accounted for the farmers suicides, e.g., the crop failures resulting from drought, scant or no rainfall, and pest attacks; increasing prices of chemical fertilizers and other essential inputs; poor quality of seeds, fertilizers and pesticides etc. Consequent to the recommendations of the Expert Committee the Government of Karnataka announced package of ₹ 840 crores for the rehabilitation of the farmers in distress and also payment of compensation to the members of the victim's family. The farmers were exempted from the payment of interest on crop loans. Further, they were exempted from the payment of water tax and land revenue. Arrangements were made to supply the seeds at the subsidized rates to the small and marginal farmers.

Farmers Suicide in Kerala

One State outside the Big Four that has seen high numbers of farmers' suicides is Kerala. It saw a total of 11,516 in 1997-2005. Worse, many of these occurred in small districts such as Wayanad. Kerala shows a fluctuating but declining trend over the nine-year period. The years 1998 to 2003 were clearly its worst period. More than 70 per cent of its farm suicides occurred in those years. From 2004, the numbers begin to drop. So much so that unlike the Big Four, it shows no increases in farm suicides for the whole period. Kerala created a "Debt Relief Commission" soon after the change in government there in 2005. The Commission held a case by case scrutiny of the debt problem, while the government halted aggressive loan recovery measures by banks and moneylenders. On the Commission's advice, the government also decided to declare the entire Wayanad revenue district distress-affected. The improvement is quite fragile and could easily see a downturn. Kerala's farm suicide rate for the period is very high, and the State remains vulnerable to volatility in the prices of, for instance, coffee, pepper, cardamom or vanilla. A fragility enhanced by the fact that major relief on the debt front requires Central help. Besides, State bureaucracies are extremely hostile to debt relief for farmers. Also, India's free trade agreements with nations and neighbours that produce the same cash crops as Kerala hurts badly. The State's balance on the farm suicides front is very delicate. Complacence would be, literally, fatal.

In Wayanad, since suicide statistics are directly linked to the payment of compensation through the Revenue Department, the number of farmers' suicides stagnated during the years 2006 to 2008. 'Safe Farmers Campaign' (SFC), a consortium of eight, mostly Catholic, NGOs (including Shreyas), in 2007 began a large-scale investigation into farmers' suicides that ran parallel to the state's efforts of enumeration and classification. Taking police reports of suicides as a starting point and following up all cases from 2000 to March 2008 they have come up with a total number of 1,690 farmers' suicides (Kerala Social Service Forum 2009). That is nearly four times the figure of 435 officially recognized farmers' suicides. The latter number is also the number of beneficiaries of the Chief Minister's (CM) relief fund.

Trends of Rural Suicides in Punjab

A number of studies on farmers' suicides in Punjab, their nature and causes, have been undertaken. These studies have captured and analysed the phenomenon in a unilinear manner. The increase in suicide rate in Punjab has been sharp after 1992. While in 1998 the suicide rate in Punjab was 0.57; it rose to 0.95 in 1993 and 2.03 in 2001. It came down to 1.38 in 2005 (Punjab Police Data, 1988-2001). The incidence of suicide in Punjab rose by 33.68 per cent in 1992 over 1998. After this there was a sharp increase in the number of suicides when it rose to 418 in 1997, a three times increase over 1992. The number of suicides remained static till 2001 after which the decline started; the decrease in 2005 was 18.64 per cent over 2001.

In India the incidence of suicides increased by 24.71 per cent in 1992 over 1998. After this came a decline by 19.56 per cent from 1992-1997. Further, the number of suicides again declined by 2.16 per cent from 2001 to 2003 at the India level. The increase in the incidence of suicides in post-terrorism Punjab (1992-1997) was significant, and it stabilized over the next four years (1997-2001) and declined thereafter (2002-2005). Punjab has experienced an uneven spread of suicides. Its occurrence is localised. There are six districts which have recorded a higher number of suicides as compared to their share of the population in the state. The geo-cultural spread of the incidence of suicides shows that there are located in the Malwa districts, i.e. Mansa, Sangrur, Bhatinda, Ferozpur, Ludhiana and Moga. These six districts contributed around 70 per cent of the total suicides that took place in the State.

The highest contribution of grain to the national pool has been the State of Punjab which has now got a notorious distinction of having one of the highest rates of farmer suicides among all the states. Though the rural suicides in Punjab started in 1990, but in 1997-98 it became very severe and today it has acquired an alarming proportion. According to

Vandana Shiva it has crossed the suicide rate of Andhra Pradesh and Karnataka as well (Vandana Shiva, Jafri *et al.*, 1998). The Punjab Government was not ready to acknowledge that the suicides were occurring in the State. Among the various studies, on suicide in rural Punjab, one of the initial ones were conducted by the Institute of Communications and Development, Chandigarh in 1998 which confirmed that there has been an increase in the number of suicides in the state since 1998. In 1992-93, the suicides in Punjab increased by 51.97 per cent, in 1993-94 by 14 per cent, 1994-95 it increased by 57 per cent. The study notes with concern that the suicide rates has been steadily increasing in the state from 0.57 in 1988 to 2.06 in 1997. The study admits that the rate of suicides of cultivator farmers has been on the rise in Punjab since 1993. The state government of Punjab, however, was reluctant to accept the large scale suicide taking place in Punjab and as per the State's Chief Minister reply, during the June-July Assembly Session in 1998 (Question no. 1087), had observed that during 1996, 1997, and 1998 there were only three suicides of farmers and agriculture labourers in Punjab.

The increased number of farmer suicides in Punjab need to be understood in the context of changes in the agrarian policy during the era of globalization, which contributed to the decline in the farmers' income, increased cost of production, crop failures, and crop loss as also due to the monoculture of wheat-paddy cultivation. Mr. Prakash Singh Badal, the then Chief Minister of Punjab, had commented that agriculture had become a pain in the neck of the farmers. It is not profitable at all for those who own less than 10 acres. The statistical data shows that the farmers of Punjab consume 10 per cent of the total fertilizers of the country, 11 per cent of the pesticides and 55 per cent of the herbicides. There is also heavy induction of farm machinery in Punjab agriculture. The productivity and production of cotton decreased in the state from 19.25 lakh bales in 1996-97 to 9.45 lakh bales in 1997-98 due to the pest attack and crop failures. Pests had emerged as a very serious menace to Punjab agriculture. There has been consistent increase in the prices of inputs and labour which pushed the cost of production between 1980-2010, 6 times for wheat, 7 times for cotton, and 10 times for paddy. It also led to increased indebtedness among the farmers. The level of mechanization also increased the cost of cultivation and Punjab today is the highest mechanized agricultural state in the country. There are over 4 lakh tractors in Punjab. Even farmers with 5-6 acres of land buy tractors in the state which is not economically stable. This has given rise to a second hand market of tractors and a 'tractor mela' (market) is held in more than 15 different places in Punjab. Farmers buy new tractors on loan and within a month sell it in the market at ₹ 50,000-60,000 less than the actual price, due to the distressed economic condition and to repay the loans borrowed from local *Arthies* (commission agents). The reason for suicides by farmers in Punjab were attributed mainly to high indebtedness. "Indebtedness among the farmers and farm labourers in Punjab has reached epidemic proportions. Landless agriculture labourers, small and marginal farmers are more vulnerable than large farmers. Large farmers are able to sell portions of their holdings to pay off debts, which acts as a buffer. The major thrust of small and semi medium farmers is to borrow primarily for agriculture and marriage purposes. The lending agencies not only pressurize the farmers to clear the outstanding loans, but also humiliate them. They experience loss of prestige and are forced to commit suicide" (Iyer and Manick, 2000).

There is unique co-incidence of Rural Suicides simultaneously taking place in the agriculturally advanced States in the country, e.g. Andhra Pradesh, Karnataka, Kerala, Punjab and Vidarbha (Maharashtra) during the era of globalization commencing from 1990 onwards. The advent of Globalization has accentuated the agrarian crisis and agrarian distress as the basic causative factors of rural suicides which has squeezed the agricultural labourers, marginal and small farmers within its stranglehold (Iyer and Manick, 2000; Parmod Kumar, S.L. Sharma and Varinder, 2000; Sidhu, M.S., Singh Sukhpal, Bhullar, A.S., 2011 and Jaijee, Inder Singh, 2011). Studies probing into the factors causing recent farmers' suicides have identified indebtedness as one of the major underlying reasons (Assadi, 1998; Revathi, 1998; Deshpande, 2002 and Mishra, 2006). Changes in the pace and composition of agricultural credit emerged as a significant issue in the context of farmers' distress in various parts of the country. Indebtedness is not an overnight phenomenon that has occurred suddenly, but it is the result of faulty credit policies followed over the years. *The central issue of farmer's suicide was the debt trap.* Small and marginal farmers especially those who leased in the land from others were not eligible for institutional credit and crop insurance. The situation had helped in strengthening the merchant capital. Traders cum moneylenders had the fortune in the absence of institutional mechanism. Farmers operate in a self-created moral and social world, where dignity is of prime importance. If they are humiliated due to indebtedness, they prefer to commit suicide rather than face continuous humiliation in the society.

It would be necessary at this point to highlight the findings of the Census Study on Rural Suicides conducted by Government of Punjab.

Table 13.2: Magnitude and Proportion of Rural Suicides in 20 Districts of Punjab based on Census Enumeration Number of Suicides in Punjab conducted by Punjab Agriculture University (2000-2008)

Sr. No.	*District*	*Due to Debt*		*Total*	*Due to Non-Debt*		*Total*
		Farmers	*Agricultural Labourers*		*Farmers*	*Agri-cultural Labourers*	
1.	Mansa	599	414	1013	133	188	321
2.	Barnala	322	210	532	90	54	144
3.	Moga	191	101	292	114	184	298
4.	Ludhiana	195	149	344	106	188	294
5.	Bhatinda	550	277	827	223	206	429
6.	Sangrur	738	394	1132	246	258	504
	Total	2595	1545	4140	912	1078	1990
	Conducted by Punjabi University, Patiala (2000-2011)						
7.	Faridkot	21	06	27	01	00	01
8.	Fateghgarh Sahib	30	17	47	11	02	13
9.	Hoshiarpur	06	01	07	00	00	00
10.	Mukatsar	50	52	102	08	12	20
11.	Mohali	09	00	09	02	00	02
12.	Patiala	65	61	126	02	02	04
13.	Roop Nagar	03	01	04	03	00	03
	Total	184	138	322	27	16	43
	Conducted by GND University, Amritsar (2000-2011)						
14.	Amritsar	48	15	63	08	20	28
15.	Gurdaspur	24	13	37	23	18	41
16.	Taran Taran	28	05	33	07	05	12
17.	Jalandhar	08	02	10	15	39	54
18.	Kapurthala	08	02	10	04	08	12
19.	S.B.S. Nagar	04	07	11	01	19	20
20.	Ferozpur	44	16	60	14	28	42
	Total	164	60	224	72	137	209
	Grand Total	2943 (62.80%)	1743 (37.20%)	4686 (100.00)	1011 (45.09%)	1231 (54 91%)	2242 (100.00)

Source: The Government of Punjab had entrusted the Study of Rural Suicides in Punjab based on Census method to three universities of the State, namely, the Punjab Agriculture University Ludhiana, GNDU, Amritsar and Punjabi University, Patiala.

As per the findings of PAU study, the total number of suicides due to debt was 4140 and due to non-debt it was 1990. The figures of Punjabi University Patiala point that in 7 districts the suicides due to debt was 322 and due to non-debt it was 43. The study of GNDU indicates that suicides due to debt were 224 and due to non-debt it was 209. *Thus the total number of suicides due to debt in the 20 districts of Punjab was 4686 and suicides due to non-debt were 2242. The total number of suicides was 6928 out of which 67.64 per cent due to debt was entitled for compensation where as 32.36 per cent was excluded from compensation.* This is an arbitrary distinction which is a violation of human rights and deprives nearly one-third of the suicide victims from compensation. This is a virtual denial of social justice to them by Punjab Government.

It needs to be pointed out that the incidence of suicides of agricultural labourers in such high percentage is unique and specific to Punjab unlike the states of Andhra Pradesh, Karnataka, Kerala and Vidarbha. Economic distress emerged as the most important determinant of suicides. The distressed condition of these families highlights the critical economic position of such households with respect to their capacity to cope with economic distress in the context of commercialization of agriculture and market connectivity. *Debt was found to be positively associated with suicides. The failure of cotton crop between 1997-2003 was attributed as one of the important reasons for the cumulative debt. The amount of debt was much higher than their income. While debt was attributed as the major cause of suicide; apart from this low income, crop failure especially in case of cotton, sale of assets like land were the important factors leading to suicide; the social factors associated with suicides were domestic conflict, prolonged illness due to cancer, permanent disability of the victim* etc. *The PAU study included the economic factor as 'suicides due to debt' and the 'social factors' as non-debt related suicides.* The suicide victim farmers' households tried to repay the debt by selling their assets like Land, Machinery, Gold etc. *Over 40 per cent of the farming families sold the land and other assets and were reduced to the status of agricultural labourers.* The PAU study points out that fall in income and increase in farm investments were the two most important factors which cause economic squeeze of the farming household. In the Malwa region of Punjab cotton was one of the prominent Kharif crop occupying 50 per cent of the area and its productivity drastically fell during the period of 1997-2002 causing erosion in farm incomes. *The productivity of cotton declined due to the severe attack of American Boll Worm.* Such losses shattered their economic sustenance and their dependent on credit increased manifold. Besides this the continuous fall in water table compelled farmers to deepen their wells at regular intervals putting financial pressure on small and marginal farmers. This region of Punjab is also considered as socially and culturally backward. The suicides of farmers had adverse gender effect as over 70 per cent of the families lost their main bread-winner placing the surviving widows to become not only the new bread-winner but also to take care of the livelihood of the other family members, health care, childrens' education and marriage of the grown up daughters. The Punjab Government had announced monetary support of ₹ 2 lakh to the families of suicide victims, but it is only in February 2013 that they dispersed the compensation amount of ₹ 1 lakh to the families of suicide victims. Rest of ₹ 1 lakh is to be paid during the financial year 2013-14. It is necessary to mention here that Sri Prakash Singh Badal, Chief Minister of Punjab had announced payment of compensation of ₹ 2.50 lakh ten years back which is now equivalent to ₹ 5 lakh by adjusting it in terms of the increase in inflation over the years.

Specific Findings of PAU Study

Suicides by Farmers

1. The suicides among farmers have been committed mostly by marginal and small farmers.
2. Consuming insecticides and pesticides have been the major mode of committing suicides followed by hanging, jumping in front of running train, drowning in canal etc.
3. Indebtedness happens to be the major reason for committing suicides which has been taken mostly from the commission agent followed by banks, cooperative societies and relatives. The loans invariably carry 24 per cent annual interest. The chief characteristics of indebtedness are that they are cumulative in nature.
4. Loan has been taken for economic reasons including the cost of agriculture production, crop failure, low returns from crops, high land rental value etc. The social reasons include the marriage of daughters and sons, medical treatment and to repay the outstanding loans.
5. There are also cases of pauperization and proletarianization of Jat Sikh farmers as acute indebtedness has led to sale of lands. Some of the farmers have been reduced to the status of agriculture labourers which is a new emerging phenomenon.
6. It is mostly the young and middle aged persons who have committed suicides. They are either illiterate or have very low modicum of education.

7. Though the suicide is predominantly by male members but there are also cases of young girls committing suicides.

Suicides by Agriculture Labourers

1. 45.2 per cent of the suicides in rural Punjab were those of landless labourers.
2. For the surviving families it is the beginning of another battle.
3. For the children of labourers, the absence of a father meant a childhood stolen.
4. The average annual income of the labourers was ₹ 19,410 but the average debt owed is ₹ 70,036. *The average debt-income ratio is 3.63.*
5. Due to heavy mechanization of Punjab agriculture, the agriculture labourers get hardly ten-fifteen days of work in a month.
6. Among the agriculture labourers the major reasons for committing suicides is the loan contracted from land owners, shop keepers, moneylenders and relatives at the rate of 24 per cent annual interest.
7. Both casual daily wage labourers as also bonded labourers have committed suicides. The linkage between bondage and suicides is a special feature of rural suicides in Punjab.
8. The agricultural labourers are not indebted to banks and cooperative societies because of their lack of assets and hence outside the pale of bankability. The banks maintain the relations of Exclusion with the agricultural labourers. This makes agriculture labourers and bonded labour quite vulnerable to social compulsions and depend for loan on private sources like landlords, moneylenders and traders.
9. Youth are the major victims of suicides among bonded labourers and agriculture labourers. They are invariably illiterate and at most having a very low level of education.
10. One of the special features of suicides among agricultural labourers is the bonded debt which they owe to the landlords. Due to the acute poverty conditions, there are also cases of women bondage who are mostly employed as cattle shed cleaners in the house of the landlords.
11. The major victims of suicides committed by farmers and agriculture labourers are their young widows who are required

to shoulder the economic responsibility, educate the children, manage the marriage of their daughters, meet the medical treatment and also carry the mental agony of clearing the accumulated loan.

12. The farmers and agriculture labourers in Punjab are the victims of discrimination both by the Government of Punjab and the Central Government.

It needs to be pointed out that Central Government have announced assistance to the next of kin of the persons committed suicides in the States of Andhra Pradesh, Karnataka, Kerala and Vidarbha (Iyer and Arora, 'Land Reforms in India Volume 12', Sage, 2010, pp. 285-286) but similar compensation and rehabilitation efforts have not been undertaken in Punjab. Due to continuous pressure exerted by Farmers Organizations and MASR (under the leadership of Mr Inderjit Singh Jaijee) compelled the Punjab Government to conduct studies on Rural Suicides initially by Centre for Communication and Development (Kumar Pramod *et al.*, 2006) and later on (Census enumeration of rural suicides) by the three universities of Punjab (PAU, Ludhiana, 2009). The Punjab Government has announced that the bereaved families will get compensation of ₹ 2 lakh in two instalments (₹ One lakh in the Fiscal Year 2012-13 and another ₹ One lakh in the next Fiscal year 2013-14). It earmarked ₹ 30 crore for this purpose in the state budget for the Fiscal Year 2012-13. Amount of ₹ 1 lakh has been distributed by the authorities concerned for disbursement to the affected families (*The Tribune*, Sangrur, February 9, 2013).

Impact on Women Farmers and Women Labour

Ranjana Padhi (2009) in her paper on '*Women Surviving Farmer Suicides in Punjab* '(EPW, 9th May 2009, Vol. 44) has analyzed as to how have women been coping in the aftermath of farmer suicides in Punjab? This article is based on detailed interviews with 32 women in three districts of the state. The tradition restricts Jat women's mobility from taking on wage work. Despite getting pushed into indebtedness and without often being able to clear the principal amount, they are in no position to think of wage work. This internalized taboo also prevents them from seeing any other future for their daughters other than marriage, ensuring, in turn, the drudgery of housework and other additional responsibilities for the next generation of women too. The poor in Punjab are paying a heavy price in the form of dowry; many suicides are related either directly or indirectly to increased indebtedness because of this burden. In a situation of total helplessness, debts are incurred to install a tube well, purchase land or an electric pump, meet the expenses of weddings and the demands of a dowry. Even for families where suicides have taken place, the minimum expectation of the amount of dowry was ₹ 2 lakh; landless households have to pay over ₹ 60,000 in such marriage settlements. Women, whose husbands have committed suicide, have also been taking loans more than once in order to get their daughters married. Despite participating in every household activity and helping with livestock and crops, daughters are viewed as burdens as there is no salvation unless one mobilizes the requisite amount of money for a dowry to get them married. The identification of women with the family and housework remains uncannily intact with the traditional burden that a patriarchal set-up foists on them (Ranjana, 2004). The widows are coping with a set of newer responsibilities of running fatherless families. The sending of money to the daughter's house continues even after marriage. The birth of a grandchild means spending more money. Even a dalit landless labourer has to incur a debt of ₹ 50,000. *Even for the marriage of daughter, they have to take a loan of ₹ 1.5 lakh for the marriage; more daughters to marry means more debt burden. However, meeting the wedding expenses of a son is also impossible without getting into debt or selling assets.*

Most school-going children seemed far more serious and often a bit grim too. Most mothers stated that how cooperative the children were and how obedient too. Constant financial difficulties, the harassment of agents, the children's education, etc., used to worry them all the time. The girl children are also keen to study and work. But they are deeply disturbed by the family's economic plight. The reality of quiet and obedient young children is peculiarly offset by the older boys and young men who have taken recourse to drugs and other addictions. Many women shared their agony of illnesses and surgeries that have pushed them into indebtedness, often after the death of their husbands and sometimes after being in steep debt already. Indebted families take loans to meet the expenses of treatment and hospitalization of the elderly that they continue to repay after the aged pass away. The most bizarre manifestation of commercial healthcare is witnessed in Punjab as private clinics take advantage of the situation when dying farmers are rushed in emergency by desperate families. The expectations voiced by these women revolve largely around the future of the children in terms of school fees, technical training and employment. The most obvious ways in which they assert themselves is in the upbringing of the children, undertaken with deep concern and hopes for the future. Yet the deafening silence surrounding the struggles of the poor to 'run' families or 'maintain' families emanates to a significant extent from an insufficient engagement with issues concerning class, caste and patriarchy, and the weakening of strategies of resistance. Those who own little land as well as the large section of the landless that is dependent on wage labour in the agricultural economy have much at stake both in the struggle for a life of dignity as well as a future for their children.

Fresh Case Studies of Rural Suicides (conducted by Dr. K. Gopal Iyer during 2012-13)

The author undertook in-depth case studies of suicide affected families who were bonded labourers, agricultural labourers, marginal farmers and small farmers in three districts of Punjab, namely, Sangrur, Bathinda and Mansa.

Methodology

Table 13.3: No. of Case Studies covered in Three Districts

Sr. No.	*District*	*Number of suicide victims cases covered*				
		Farmers	*Agricultural Labourers*	*Bonded Labourers*	*Others*	*Total*
1.	Sangrur	3	4	9	00	16
2.	Mansa	23	8	4	2	35
3.	Bhatinda	00	11	2	2	15
	Total	26	23	15	4	66

Findings of Case Studies in Punjab

Case No.1: Bonded labour commits suicides—both husband and wife—Bonded-Case of Sh. Avtar Singh.

Sh. Avtar Singh, Bonded Agricultural Labour of Village Ganduan, District Sunam was bonded to the landlord Baaru Singh. He was bonded for 3 years due to the loan amount of ₹ 25,000 from his employer. Absence from work meant deduction of ₹ 200 per day from wages. His wife Jasbir Kaur was a female bonded labour to the same landlord. They had also taken a loan of ₹15000 for House construction which was added to the bonded debt. Avtar Singh was severely beaten by his employer for being absent from the work. He became semi-conscious and died while under treatment on 11th August, 2012. His wife borrowed ₹7000 for cremation of the dead body of her husband. On 15th September, 2012, Baaru Singh asked Jasbir Kaur to continue to work as bonded labour which she refused. DDVA has represented her case to NHRC.

Case No. 2: Gurdeep Singh, Village Ganduan. District Singo.

Mr. Gurdeep Singh committed suicide in the year 2007 due to bonded debt of ₹2 lakh borrowed from his employer for house construction. The rate of interest was 24 per cent per annum. His wife Chanderpal was also a bonded labour to the same landlord. Her six year old son studied in Class 1. She is not receiving widow pension though she has become a widow after her husband commited suicide. Now she is the head of the household managing the livelihood requirement and education of the children.

Case No. 3: Najar Singh, Village Ganduan, District Sangrur.

Najar Singh was bonded to a commission agent. He committed suicide during 2002 at the age of 35. He had taken a loan of ₹1.20 lakh + 25 per cent interest. His two sons aged 19 and 21 years were also working as bonded labour to the same commission agent. The young widow is shouldering the responsibility of economic maintenance of the family, education of the children and marriage of the daughter.

Case No. 4: Harpal Singh, Vazigarh, Scheduled Caste, Bhawanigarh, District Sangrur

Harpal Singh, committed suicide on 9th August, 2002 by handing due to excessive debt burden. His debt burden is indicated below:

(i) Land owner - ₹ 70,000 + 24 per cent interest.
(ii) Shop keeper - ₹ 10,000 + 24 per cent interest (buying baffalow)
(iii) Second land owner - ₹ 80,000 + 24 per cent interest.
(iv) Cooperative Society - ₹ 25,000 + Interest.

His wife also died due to Electric shock. Two sons aged 16 and 17 are working as masons and goat rearing. Marriage of a grown up girl is the impending problem for the family.

Case No. 5: Two suicides in the same family.

Both the widows are female household head with responsibility of children's education and marriage of their daughters.

1. Naib Singh – Committed suicide on 31-10-2008 by consuming pesticides.
2. Jagjeet Singh– 40 years, committed suicide in 2005 by consuming pesticides.

The surviving members are Paramjeet Kaur, widow aged 35 years and Sukhwinder Kaur, aged 34 years. Paramjeet Kaur has dependent mother-in-law, four daughters who are respectively studying in class 8, 9, 11 and 16. They have an outstanding bonded debt of ₹ 50,000. Sukhwinder Kaur, widow of Jagjeet Singh is aged 34 years with two sons aged 15 and 17 years who are studying in Class 8 and 10 and her daughter of 18 years is studying in class 10. The outstanding bonded debt for this family is ₹ 30,000. Both the widows are working as labourers and they are the main bread earners. Due to the financial stringency the children have discontinued their studies. The widows are very much concerned about the money to be taken loan for the marriage of their daughter. Both widows are working as wage labour which is the main source of the livelihood. The old debt continues to be outstanding.

Case No.6: Suicide by a Young girl – Harjinder Kaur aged 16 years, Village Kheri Jattan, Bhatinda.

Harjinder Kaur belongs to Ramdasia caste and she committed suicide by burning herself in 1999. Her mother died due to Cancer in the year 2000. Her Sister Amandeep Kaur committed suicide in anticipation of likely debt burden due to her marriage. She has a brother aged 17 years, who left his study after class 8th and is working as wage labour. The family has an outstanding loan of ₹ 1.03 lakh which was taken for marriage purpose at 24 per cent interest.

Case No. 7: Suicide by another young Girl–Kaki Kaur of 14 years.

Kaki Kaur belongs to Mazhabi caste (Scheduled Caste) who committed suicide by consuming pesticides. Her reason for committing suicide was also due to the sensitivity that her marriage would cost heavily to the family. Her father is a Rickshaw puller and her mother is domestic servant of two land owners. Earlier 3 sisters were married and their loan of ₹50,000 + interest is still outstanding.

Case No. 8: Jat Sikh – Pauperization and Proletarianization.

Harmeet Singh, Village Singo, Block Talwandi Saboo, District Bhatinda had committed suicide on 10th Oct. 2005. He owned 12 acres land but sold all of that during last few years to clear the outstanding loan. He had taken a loan of ₹2.00 lakh for the marriage of daughter aged 22 years and another loan of ₹ 1 lakh to marry his sister of 21 years. The surviving members include his mother 68 years and his son of 24 years. His son is the main bread earner who works as an agricultural labour.

Next five cases also relate to the Jat Sikh family who committed suicide due to outstanding loan by selling their lands. The details are given below:

Case No. 9: Maggar Singh, Village Tamkot, District Mansa, committed suicide on 10th January 2008 at the age of 50 years by Electrocutting himself. He had sold 1.75 acres to clear the outstanding loan. Now the family is left with 0.75 acres land. His son is working as wage labour.

Case No. 10: Two persons of the same family, namely Soma Singh aged 45 years, and Sukjeet Kaur aged 18 years committed suicide. Soma Singh committed suicide in the year 2005 due to the continuous pressure exerted by the commission agent and the bank to return the outstanding loans. Sukhjit Kaur committed suicide due to heavy debt burden of ₹ 2.00 lakhs from the bank, ₹ 2.80 lakhs from the commission agent, and ₹ 1.50 lakhs from the relative.

Case No. 11: Nazar Singh–Village Tamkot, District Mansa. He committed suicide in 2005 when he was 45 years old. He drowned himself in Canal water. He had a loan of ₹1.15 lakh from the bank, ₹ 1.00 lakh from commission agent, and ₹1.00 lakh from his relatives. There was constant pressure on him from the bank to return the loan. He also sold 0.25 acres of his land. The surviving members include his widow and four adults sons. The outstanding loan now stands as ₹ 7.00 lakh for which ₹ 4.5 lakh is from the Bank and ₹2.5 lakh is from the commission agent.

Case No. 12: Gurdass Singh, Village Tamkot- He committed suicide at the age of 50 years due to the debt burden of ₹ 3.5 lakh (₹ 1.50 lakh from the bank and ₹ 2.00 lakh from the commission agent). One of the reason for the debt burden was the marriage of her daughter though he had also sold 1 acre land for this purpose. Now they are left with 2.50 acres land. The present outstanding loan is ₹ 6.5 lakh of which ₹ 4.5 lakh is from the bank and ₹ 2.00 lakh is from the commission agent.

Case No. 13: Two suicides from the same family. Two brothers Bappa Singh aged 26 years and Resam Singh aged 24 years committed suicide by consuming pesticides during the year 1991 and 1995. They had an outstanding loan of ₹2.50 lakh from the commission agent and ₹3.00 lakh from the bank. Part of this amount was taken for marrying their two sisters. The commission agent pressurized them for returning the loan and also files case in the court.

Government Action at All India Level

Suicides are only one extreme symptom of the larger crisis looming over the agriculture sector. The situation of the people who are surviving in the deceased families and others still on the margin is no different. The crisis is also manifested in terms of large scale migration, unemployment and underemployment of agriculture workers, pauperization, malnutrition, ill health, and other social problems. The government is expected to take a holistic view and address the issue. The reality seems to be very different.

1. The Central and State Governments have initiated measures to address the crisis but the crises seem to be deepening rather than coming under control. In many states the numbers have significantly increased after 2002 which only shows that the measures taken are not effective. For example, in Maharashtra suicide have increased in a time when the loan was maximum from Government; from 2006 to 2008 altogether a sum of 20,000 crore (is the maximum till date) was given as relief from various Government sources but in 2006, 2007 and 2008 **the suicides number increased to 12,493. These 600 deaths are more than the previous worst, 2002-2005**. It means the very architecture of compensation was flawed.
2. **Playing deaf to Committee reports:** The Central Government and various State Governments and independent organizations have appointed various commissions/committees /teams to look into the issues of crises and make recommendations. About 53 committees have submitted their report on how to address the agrarian crisis. Notable of them are the National Farmers

Commission chaired by Dr. M.S. Swaminathan, Jayati Ghosh Commission in Andhra Pradesh and Narindra Jadav Committee in Maharashtra. Many of the recommendations by these committees were never implemented.

3. **Relief Measures:** Governments are invariably in denial mode in accepting suicide in the state which increases the miseries. In Maharashtra a compensation of ₹ One lakh was provided and in Andhra Pradesh ₹ One lakh as compensation to the family and ₹ 50,000 to repay the pending loans were announced. Both these initiatives have dubious category called **'Genuine Farmer Suicides'** which establishes the eligibility of the family for the compensation. In Bundelkhand Relief Package, there is no component which takes care of immediate distress of the bereaved families. In AP among the total 33,326 farmer's suicides reported only 5241 are recognized as genuine. Similar situation is reported from Maharashtra as well. In Maharashtra, to avoid the paying of compensation, state made two categories *eligible and non-eligible and only those who are eligible for compensation comes under the category of farmer suicide.* Chhattisgarh also suffers from Government denial on suicide rate in the state which increases the miseries of the farmers multifold. Similarly, in Punjab distinction has been made between Debt related suicides and non-Debt related suicides.

4. **Addressing Indebtedness:** Increasing indebtedness is seen as one of the major reasons behind the crisis. In the fact finding visits, it was also found that all the farmers' families are in deep debt trap. In 2004 the UPA government came up with a loan waiver programme. Still majority of the farmers are not covered under institutional credit and depend on moneylenders for high cost loans. The loans to farming have reduced after 1990 with changes in the bank priorities.

Remedial Measures: Farming in India needs a complete paradigm shift:

A comprehensive relief and rehabilitation package needs to be evolved to address the distress conditions of bereaved families.

(a) This package should be enough to take care of the problems related to immediate debt relief (public and private), release of land from mortgage, livelihood support (agriculture and non agriculture), education of the children and health needs of the family.

(b) A widow pension to the tune of ₹ 2000 per month to meet the survival needs of the family would take care of major part of the requirement.

(c) There are gaps in; the packages of "Andhra Pradesh and Maharashtra, and of Bundelkhand which need to be modified to cover the major needs of the farmers and not only their distress situation.

(d) The categorization of suicides into "genuine" and "not genuine" as also between 'eligible' and 'non-eligible' should be immediately removed.

(e) All the victim families should be entitled to existing government schemes like MGNREGA, PDS and Food Security Schemes.

(f) Government should also identify the families in extreme distress conditions like under excessive debt, land under mortgage or sale.

(g) The Government should formulate policies to protect the livelihood of marginal farmers, small farmers and agricultural labourers.

(h) MSPs should be commensurate along with remunerative prices and undertake procurement of grains wherever it is needed.

(i) Tenant farmers and other farmers with concealed tenancy should be entitled to institutional loans.

(j) It is also necessary to formulate long term policy measures to address the root causes of agrarian crisis.

Recommendation and Follow Up Actions Specifically for Punjab Compensation and Rehabilitation

1. The Punjab Government should send the census figures of rural suicides in the state to the Government of India.
2. The Central Government should declare Punjab *as a suicide affected state*, similar to Andhra Pradesh, Karnataka, Maharashtra, and Kerala.
3. The Central Government package should be announced to Punjab as well on the same pattern as the states of Andhra Pradesh, Karnataka, Maharashtra, and Kerala.
4. Punjab Government should undertake the following steps for suicide victim families:

   (a) Increase the compensation amount from ₹ 2 lakh to ₹ 5 lakh to suicide victim families

(b) The census survey of rural suicides should also include suicide victim families between 1990 and 1999 and such families should also be eligible for compensation and rehabilitation package.
(c) 'Non-debt suicides' are also genuine suicide cases. They should also be entitled to compensation and rehabilitation from the Punjab Government.
(d) The children of suicide affected families should be granted scholarships for continuing their education.
(e) There should be complete rehabilitation of suicide victim families with respect to their livelihood, children's education and their healthcare.
(f) Widow, old age, and handicapped children should invariably be given monthly pension of a minimum amount of ₹ 1500 per month.
(g) A vocation based rehabilitation scheme needs to be systematically worked out for targeting all the suicide affected families, including vocational training for their educated youth, both boys and girls.
(h) There should be complete waiver of principal and interest amount for the suicide affected families.
(i) The existing debts of the suicides affected families should be completely waived including the loans of moneylenders, commission agents and other private lenders.

Strategies to Prevent Farmer Suicides

(a) Government should declare waiver of overdue accumulated interest of agriculture labourers, marginal and small farmers with respect to institution and non-institutional loans.
(b) Waiver of loans to agriculture labourers, marginal and small farmers, up to ₹ 2 lakhs.
(c) Overdue agricultural loans should be rescheduled, enabling the farmers to avail fresh credit from the banks.
(d) The Government should focus the agricultural policy to protect the interest of agriculture labourers, marginal and small farmers.
(e) Special financial assistance should be given to marginal farmers and small farmers for inducting submersible pumps.
(f) Every agriculture labour family should be allotted to a minimum

extent of two acres of cultivatable land to secure their livelihood base.

(g) Every landless widow, women headed households and destitute women should be allotted 2 acres land.

(h) The houseless families should be allotted to a minimum extent of ten decimal lands for their housing purpose, maintaining live stock and kitchen gardening.

(i) Free education to all agriculture labour children and vocational training and skill enhancement programme for the youth (both boys and girls).

REFERENCES

Aman Sidhu and Jaijee Inderjeet Singh (2011), *Debt and Death in Rural India—The Punjab Story*, Sage Publications, New Delhi.

Assadi, Muzaffar (1998), "Farmers Suicides: Signs of Distress in Rural Economy", *Economic and Political Weekly*, 33(13): 747-48

Bhagwati, Jagdish, (2004), *In Defense of Globalization*, Oxford University Press, New York.

Bharati, Vishab (2011), "Indebtedness and Suicides: Field Notes on Agriculture Labourers of Punjab", *Economic and Political Weekly*, Vol. XLVI, No. 14.

Bhullar, A.S. and Singh, Sukhpal (2011), "Farmers Suicides in Punjab: Census Survey of The Two Most Affected Districts", *Economic and Political Weekly*, Vol. XLVI, No. 26-27.

Deshpande, R.S., (2002), "Suicide by Farmers in Karnataka- Agrarian Distress and Possible Alleviatory Steps", *Economic and Political Weekly*, 37(26): 2601-10.

Singh, Sukhpal *et al.* (2011), "Farmers and Agricultural Labourers Suicides due to Indebtedness in the Punjab State", (Pilot Survey in Bhatinda and Sangrur Districts, Department of Economics and Sociology, Punjab Agricultural University, Ludhiana), Punjab, April, 2009.

Gulati, Ashok and Narayan, Sudha (2003), *The Subsidy Syndrome in Indian Agriculture*, Oxford University Press, Oxford.

Iyer, K. Gopal and Manick, Mehr Singh (2000), *Indebtedness, Impoverishment and Suicides in Rural Punjab*, Indian Publishers, New Delhi.

Iyer, K. Gopal, and Arora, Saroj (2010), "Indebtedness and Farmers' Suicides," in Deshpande, R. S. and Arora, Saroj, *Agrarian Crisis and Farmer Suicides*, Sage Publications, New Delhi.

Kalamkar, S.S. and Shroff, Sangeeta (2011), "Impact of Rehabilitation Package in Suicides Prone Districts of Vidharba", *Economic and Political Weekly*, Vol. XLVI, No. 5.

Kumar, Pramod, Sharma, S.L. and Varinder (2006), *Suicides in Rural Punjab*, (IDC), Punjab State Farmers' Commission, Government of Punjab, Chandigarh.

Kumari, B. Ratna (2011), *Farmers Suicides in India: Impact on Women*, Serials Publication, New Delhi.

Mishra, Srijit, (2006), *Suicide of Farmers in Maharashtra*, Mumbai: IGIDR.

Nayer, Peter (2010), *Suicide and Society in India*, Routledge, London and New York.

Ranjana, Padhi, (2009), "How have Women been Coping in the Aftermath of Farmers Suicides in Punjab", *Economic and Political Weekly*, Volume 44, 9th May, 2009

Revathi, E. (1998), "Farmers' Suicide: Missing Issues". *Economic and Political Weekly*, 33(20): 1207.

Sidhu, M. S., Sukhpal Singh, A.S. Bhullar, (2011), "Farmers Suicides in Punjab: A Census Survey of the Two Most Affected Districts", *Economic and Political Weekly Supplement*, Vol. XLVI, Nos. 26-27, pp. 131-137.

Singh, Sukhpal (2005), *Institutional and Policy Aspects of Punab Agriculture: A Small Holder Perspective*, Vol. XLVII, No 4.

Vandana, Shiva *et al.* (1998), *Seeds of Suicide: The Ecological and Human Cost of Globalization of Agriculture*; Research Foundation for Science, Technology, and Ecology, New Delhi.

Vandana, Shiva (2000), *The Suicide Economy of Corporate Globalization*, Research Foundation for Science, Technology, and Ecology, New Delhi.

Vidyasagar, R. and Chandra, K. Suman, (2001), *Farmers Suicides in Andhra Pradesh and Karnataka*, National Institute of Rural Development, Hyderabad.

Appendix-1

Social Characteristics of Rural Suicide Victims in Bathinda District

(Village Giana, Block/Tehsil, Talwandi Saboo, District Bhatinda)

Sr. No	*Name of person committing suicide*	*Age*	*Education*	*Caste*	*Occupation*	*Year and date of committing suicide*	*Mode of committing suicide*	*Reason for committing suicide*
(1)	(2)	(3)	(4)	(5)	(6)	(7)	(8)	(9)
1.	Pyara Singh S/o. Inder Singh	20	Class V	Mazhabi Sikh	Handicapped	20 years back 1992	Jumped under the Train	Debt burden of parents
2.	Thandu Singh	35	Illiterate	-do-	Siri	2005	Consumed pesticides	Debt burden
3.	Already covered Bir Pal Singh S/o. Jagga Singh (Village Tarkhanwala)	22	Illiterate	Bauria sikh	Labour	12.12.2005	Consumed pesticides	Debt burden Rs.45,000+ 24 interest-Siri
4.	Kake Kaur d/o. Hargobind Singh (Village Tarkhanwala)	14	Class V	-do-	Rickshaw puller	2003	Consumed pesticides	Debt burden
5.	Paramjit Singh S/o. Gurcharan singh (Village Phullo-Kheri)	22	Illiterate	-do-	Siri – 12 years (Mukhtiar Singh)	2001	Consumed pesticides	Debt burden-sisters marriage Rs.25000

(*Contd.*)

Appendix 1 (*Contd.*)

(1)	(2)	(3)	(4)	(5)	(6)	(7)	(8)	(9)
6.	Hardev Singh S/o. Lilu Singh (Village Kanakwal)	22	Illiterate	Ramdasiya Sikh	Labour	2001	Consumed pesticides	Debt burden (Rs. 90,000+ 24% interest from land owners.
7.	Gurmail Singh S/o. Nahar Singh	24	Illiterate	Mazhabi Sikh	Labour	20.2.2006	Jumped before a running Train	Mental Tension due to debt burden Rs. 60,000 +24% interest
8.	Harmit Singh S/o. Tekh Singh (Village Singo) Already covered.	32	Illiterate	Mazhabi Sikh	Labour	17.10.05	Consumed pesticides	Debt burden
9.	Bikar Singh S/o. Sukhdev Kaur (Village Singo)	40	Class IX	Ramdasiya Sikh	Labour	23.10.08	Hanged	Debt burden (3.70 lakh land owners)
10.	Major Singh S/o. Maggar Singh (Village Kalalwala)	45	Class IV	Mazhabi Sikh	Petty shop-keeper	2001	Hanged	Debt burden (Rs. 1.00 lakh from land owners)—Marriage
11.	Veer Singh S/o. Jagga Singh, Village Tarkanwala	35	Illiterate	Mazhabi sikh	Labour	12.12.2005	Consumed pesticides	Debt burden
12.	Sadha Singh (Village Jeevansinghwala)	46	Illiterate	Mazhbi Sikh	Labour	10.2.2007	Hanged	Debt burden (Rs. 2.20 lakh + 24% interest)

(*Contd.*)

Appendix 1 (*Contd.*)

(1)	(2)	(3)	(4)	(5)	(6)	(7)	(8)	(9)
13.	Pappu S/o. Jal Kaur	22	Class VII	Mazhabi Sikh	Labour	2007	Consumed pesticides	Debt bondage to brick kiln
14.	Gurditta Singh S/o. Pritam Singh village Behman Kaur Singh	28	Illiterate	Ramdasiya Sikh	Agricultural labour	27.5.2006	Hanged	Debt burden Rs.1.5 lakh land owners.
15.	Jagga Singh S/o. Ram Singh Village Tarkanwala)	24	Illiterate	Ramdasiya Sikh	Agricultural labour	1.5.2010	Consumed pesticides	Debt burden.

Appendix-2

Social Characteristics of Rural Suicide Victims in Mansa District

(Village Tamkot, Block/Tehsil Mansa, District Mansa)

Sl. No.	*Name of person committing suicide*	*Age*	*Education*	*Caste*	*Occupation*	*Year and date of committing suicide*	*Mode of committing suicide*	*Reason for committing suicide*
(1)	(2)	(3)	(4)	(5)	(6)	(7)	(8)	(9)
1.	Mela Singh	30	Illiterate	Ramdasia	Agri. labour	18 years back (1994)	Consumed Insecticide	Debt burden
2.	Tej Singh	50	-do-	-do-	-do-	12 years back (2000)	-do-	Debt burden
3.	Gurtej Singh	45	-do-	Jat Sikh	Agirculture	5 years back (2007)	-do-	All lands sold for marriage of 5 daughters
4.	Maggar Singh	50	-do-	-do-	Agriculture	10.01.08	Deliberately applied Electric shock	Debt burden
5.	Sukhjit Kaur and Soma Singh	18 45	-do- -do-	-do- -do-	Agriculture -do-	2000 2005	Hanging consumed spray	Loan from bank and Debt burden
6.	Jasbir Singh	24	9	Jat Sikh	Agricultre (6 acres)	19-1-2007	Consuming pesticides	Debt burden

(*Contd.*)

Appendix 2 (*Contd.*)

(1)	(2)	(3)	(4)	(5)	(6)	(7)	(8)	(9)
7.	Roop Singh	50	Illiterate	Jat Sikh	Siri (bonded labourer)	1993	-do-	-do-
8.	Sita Singh	42	Illiterate	Ramdasia	Agricultural labour	6-5.2010	-do-	-do-
9.	Nazar Singh	45	-do-	Jat Sikh	Agriculture (2.50 acres)	2005	Drowned in flowing canal water	-do-
10.	Kulwant singh	20	-do-	Mazhabi Sikh	Siri (bonded labour)	2004	Consuming pesticides	Debt burden
11.	Gurdas singh	50	8th	Jat sikh	Agriculture (3.5 acres)	2008	Consuming pesticides	Debt burden Sold 0.50 acres
12.	Gurpratap singh	48	10	Jat Sikh	Agriculture (9 acres)	2011	Consuming pesticides	Debt burden
13.	Nazar singh	45	Illiterate	Jat Sikh	Agriculture (2.50 acres)	2005	Consuming pesticides	Debt burden
14.	Resham Singh Beppa Singh	25 20	Illiterate -do-	Jat Sikh -do-	Agriculture (2.50 acres)	1991 1993	Consuming pesticides	Debt burden
15.	JoginderSingh	20	Illiterate	Jat Sikh	Agriculture (5 acres)	1997	Consuming pesticides	Debt burden
16.	Kewal Singh	38	8	Jat Sikh	Agriculture (2.50 acres)	2009	Consuming pesticides	Debt burden

(*Contd.*)

Appendix 2 (*Contd.*)

(1)	(2)	(3)	(4)	(5)	(6)	(7)	(8)	(9)
17.	Jasbir Singh	30	Illiterate	Jat Sikh	Agricultre (6 acres)	2002	Hanging	Debt burden
	Sukhjit singh	70	-do-	-do-	-do-	2007	Consuming pesticides	-do-
18.	Gurdev Singh	40	-do-	Jat sikh	Agricultural	2002	Applied electric current	-do-
19.	Harinder Singh	40	-do-	Jat Sikh	Agriculture (4 acres)	2010	Consumed pesticides	-do-
21.	Maggar Singh	50	-d0-	Jat Sikh	Agriculture (2 Acrers)	10.01.2008	Applied electric current	Debt burden
22.	Gurtej singh	42	Matric	Jat Sikh	Agriculture (4 acres)	13.1.2008	Drowned in canal	Heavy debt
23.	Pala Singh	47	Illiterate	Mazibir Singh	Agriculture Labour	3.6.2008	Jumped in to the well	Debt burden
24.	Ram Singh	25	Illiterate	-do-	Agriculture Labour	2008	Consuming pesticides	Debt burden
25.	Mithu Singh	35	Illiterate	Ramdasia Sikh	Siri	3.3.2008	Consumed pesticides	Debt burden
26.	Ajit Singh	38	10th	Jat Sikh	Agriculture	14.3.2008	Took poison us tablet	Debt burden
27.	Pritpal Singh	23	Illiterate	Jat Singh	Agriculture	26.6.1998	Hanged	Sale of all land by his father

(*Contd.*)

Appendix 2 (*Contd.*)

(1)	(2)	(3)	(4)	(5)	(6)	(7)	(8)	(9)
28.	Ravinder Singh	30	10th	Jat Sikh	Agriculture	2008	Consumed pesticides	Debt burden
29.	Gursewak Singh	20	8th	Jat Sikh	Agriculture	20.2.1999	Consumed pesticides	Debt burden
30.	Pala Singh	45	Illiterate	Mazhabi Sikh	Siri	9.12.2008	Consumed pesticides	Debt burden
31.	Amarjit(Women)	27	Illiterate	Jat Sikh	Agriculture	29.9.2010	Consumed spray	Debt burden
32.	Jagraj Singh	34	Illiterate	Jat Sikh	Agriculture	22.10.2002	Consumed pesticides	Debt burden
33.	Sarabjit (Female)	25	Illiterate	Mazhabi Sikh	Agriculture Labour	2011	Burnt herself	Debt burden
34.	Nachhatar Singh-Village Burj dhilawan	28	Illiterate	Thori (Backward)	Sevadar	2008	Consumed pesticides	Debt burden
35.	Major Singh	45	V	Ramdasia Sikh		2008	Consumed pesticides	Debt burden

Appendix-3

Social Characteristics of Rural Suicide Victims in Sangrur District

Sr. No	Name of person committing suicide	Age	Education	Caste	Occupation	Year and date of committing suicide	Mode of committing suicide	Reason for committing suicide
(1)	(2)	(3)	(4)	(5)	(6)	(7)	(8)	(9)
1.	Ram Singh	35	Illiterate	Ramdasiya	Siri (Bonded Labour)	2002	Consuming pesticides	Due to Coercion by Landlord
2.	Nikka	19	Illiterate	Ramdasiya	Siri (Bonded Labour)	2002	Jumped under a running train	Debt burden—Coercion by Landlord
3.	Bittu	18	Illiterate	Majhabi	Siri (Bonded Labour)	2002	Consuming pesticides	Accumulated debt burden
4	Gurdeep Singh	22	Illiterate	Majhabi	Siri (Bonded Labour)	5-10-2007	Consuming pesticides	Debt burden—Coercion by Landlord
5.	Satpal Ram	32	Class 7	Brahmin	Driver	2003	Consuming pesticides	Family Pressure-debt burden
6.	Najar Singh	35	Illiterate	Ramdasiya	Siri (Bonded Labour)	2002	Consuming pesticides	Debt Burden of the commission agent
7.	Amarjit Kaur W/o Najar Singh	25	illiterate	Ramdasiya	Housewife	1995	By Burning herself	Child Physically Handicapped
8.	Gurjit Singh	22	Class 8	Ramdasiya	Casual Worker	2003	Electrocuted	Debt Burden

(*Contd.*)

Appendix 3 (*Contd.*)

(1)	(2)	(3)	(4)	(5)	(6)	(7)	(8)	(9)
9.	Bhola Singh	45	Illiterate	Ramdasiya	Siri (Bonded Labour)	1-4-1999	Burnet Himself	Accumulated Debt Burden
10.	Bhagwant Singh	33	illiterate	Ramdasiya	Siri (Bonded Labour)	19-7-1999	Consumed Poison	Debt Burden
11.	Swroop Singh	35	Class 8	Ramdasiya	Siri (Bonded Labour)	15-8-2008	Consumed Poison	Not Known
12.	Didar Singh	19	illiterate	Majhabi	Siri (Bonded Labour)	2001	Consuming pesticides	Bonded Debt Burden
13.	Harpal Singh	25	Illiterate	Bazigar	Agricultural Labourers	9-8-2002	Hanged Himself	Debt Burden
14.	Husband of Surjeet Kaur and Gurmail Kaur	35	illiterate	Jat	Agricultural Labourers	1999	Consuming pesticides	Heavy Debt Burden
15.	Naib Singh	36	Illiterate	Ramdasiya	Agricultural Labourers	2008	Consuming pesticides	Cumulative debt burden
16.	Jagjit Singh	40	Illiterate	Ramdasiya	Agricultural Labourers	2005	Consuming pesticides	Cumulative debt burden

Chapter 14

Agrarian Crisis in the Era of Globalization in India

Rajiv Bhatia and *Renu Sharma*

The direct contributions of the agriculture sector to the functioning of the national economy are reflected by its participation in total GDP, its foreign exchange earnings and its role in supplying savings and labour to other sectors. The development literature in the 1950s is now viewed as generally pessimistic with respect to this sector's potential for productivity and export growth. There was a presumption that the sector was insensitive to incentives and the significant linkages of agriculture with other sectors did not exist. This set of stylized facts led to the conclusion that spurring agricultural growth was a low priority in the search for policies that would stimulate national economic development.

It is now well known fact that development economists have reassessed the efficiency of agricultural producers and the sector's growth potential, especially following the work of Schultz (1964) and otheothers. The reassessment followed the results of econometric analyses suggested that agriculture in developing countries was as responsive as in developed countries, and the sector was both capable of productive growth and responsive to technological change. With respect to the links between agriculture and the rest of the national economy, the evidence demonstrated that the farm sector could have significant multiplier effects and, therefore, that agricultural growth could be propagated to other sectors in the economy.

Although agriculture occupies a shrinking share of India's national economy, achieving rapid growth in agriculture remains a major policy concern nationwide. The contribution of agriculture to India's gross domestic product (GDP) fell from 40 per cent in 1980-81 to 14 per cent in 2009-10. However, 72 per cent of India's population lives in rural areas, and three-fourths of the people making up these rural populations depend on agriculture and allied activities for their livelihoods. The agricultural sector is the main source of employment in India, comprising 57 per cent of the country's population engaged in agriculture in 2009-10. Indian economy is still predominantly rural, with slow urbanization but growing rural-urban disparities in income and levels of living. Agriculture continues to be the most important economic activity in the countryside with a disproportionate retention of high share in the total workforce, but with a fast declining share in the national product.

The agricultural sector evolves as the one with preponderance of self-employed small-farms in terms of land holdings, and growing proportion of hired-casual labour awaiting the spread of appropriate technology for a breakthrough towards improved productivity. Even after fifty years of planned development strategy, the Indian economy towards the end of the Twentieth Century still remained predominantly rural. The rural India, however, was never closed or isolated but had its own dynamism and was on a steady path of articulation with the rest of the Indian economy and the world at large. Since India's Independence and in the planning period Indian agriculture has passed through various phases experiencing a lot of policies and programmes for raising productivity and contribution. The 1950s saw state governments introducing land reform measures to attain the objectives of growth and equity. Land Reform was an institutional revolution in India trying to resurrect Indian agriculture from its then low ebb to a higher plane by putting the agrarian relations in order.

The growth rate in agriculture which was a mere 0.3 per cent before the introduction of planning, reached 3.3 per cent during the first decade of planning. The amount of reduction in inequalities obfuscates the differentiation of the peasantry and the emergence of a neorich class consequent on land reforms. With little aid from production and market structures, 'free and fair' situation for agriculture was elusive. It was realized that land reform is necessary but not a sufficient condition for agrarian development. Technological changes came in the form of New Agricultural Strategy with HYV seeds as the nucleus. The mid-60s ushered in the era of green revolution in India with similar spectacular achievements in some other South Asian and Latin American countries too.

The institutional and technological changes initiated the process of agricultural transformation in India, visible and quantifiable in terms of input as well as output. The farmers in that era were the representatives of the new agrarian economy of India and are among the significant contributors to the progress of the Indian economy. The 1980s saw government's efforts to extend and strengthen the agricultural inputs and services delivery mechanisms in the country. Special programmes for eastern states, establishment of technology mission were taken up during this period. The GDP of agriculture increased at more than 3 per cent per year during the 1980s, a period of satisfactory performance of the sector. Agricultural growth rate picked up to reach a respectable level of 3.9 per cent in 1981-91, before dipping down to 2.8 per cent in 1990.

In 1991 began the era of global economic reforms, i.e. World Trade Organization (WTO), General Agreement on Trade in Services (GATS), Trade Related Intellectual Rights (TRIPS) etc. put an end to restrictive trade, even in agriculture.

The main forces underlying this process of globalization include:

- International trade liberalization.
- Free flow of capital and investment.
- Technological advance in communications and transportation
- Convergence towards market-friendly economic management systems.
- Development of global media and business practice standard.
- The formation of regional and other supranational trade and cooperation entities.

Liberalization created an unprecedented demand in all sectors of trade including agriculture. Government had to introduce reforms in agricultural sector too. Reforms in agricultural policies were felt necessary for achieving trade liberalization in the agricultural sector. Much of this transformation was well under a series of development programmes where the state had a dominant protective as well as promotional role. During the last two decades, especially since the early 1990s, as a part of the neo-liberal wave of globalization aided by the revolution in information and communication technology (ICT), which has compressed time and space drastically, the rural India too is exposed to the surge towards integration into the global market economy.

Important Measures of Economic Liberalization in Indian Agriculture

Although in 1991, when India officially went along the structural adjustment path and introduced a series of neo-liberal economic reforms, there was apparently not much explicitly by way of reforms in agriculture. But very soon, at least by mid-1990s when the WTO was in place, there did unfold many policy reforms directly addressed to agriculture. The internal and external market liberalization involved the following:

- Reduction or abolition of export taxes and quotas.
- Reduction or elimination of government controls on agricultural trade, and disbanding of state marketing agencies or boards.
- Reduced import tariffs and elimination of import licensing, quotas or prohibitions.
- Elimination of internal market regulations and restrictions on the private sector in product and input marketing.
- Decline in public production and infrastructural services including research and extension, product distribution, input supply and agricultural credit.
- Beginning with 1997, all Indian product lines are placed under Generalised System of Preferences (GSP).
- By 2000 all agricultural products are removed from Quantitative Restrictions (QRs) and brought under tariff system.
- Channelization of trade in agricultural commodities through state trading agencies was almost removed and most of the products brought under Open General Licensing (OGL).
- The average tariffs on agricultural products, which stood at over 100 per cent in 1990, was brought down to 30 per cent by 1997 and targeted to come down further.
- The National Seed Corporation established in 1963, and later, a network of State Seed Corporations established since 1975 had virtual monopoly and responsibility of developing and distributing better and high yielding variety (HYV) seeds in collaboration with the agricultural universities. Though trade in seeds was opened to private trade in 1980s. 100 per cent foreign equity was allowed in seed industry in India in the year 1991 and restrictions on import of seeds were relaxed.
- Gradual reduction of fertilizer subsidies since 1991.
- Power sector opened for private sector.
- Water rates increased in some State and Participatory water management was sought to be introduced through Water Users'.

In order to understand the implications of liberalizing trade in agriculture, it is important to take into account the closer links between trade liberalization and growth in Agriculture. While it has been empirically demonstrated earlier that countries with liberal agricultural strategies can experience economic benefits or net social welfare gains, it is not clear whether the rapid agricultural growth can be achieved with successive liberalization attempts. In this connection, it becomes crucial for countries to identify the channels through which trade liberalization in agriculture can potentially impact on their rural economies. It is possible that the liberalization can encourage the commercialization of agriculture and also lead to the diversification of agriculture by impacting on the production and marketing of high-value commodities, viz. floriculture, fisheries, marine products, etc. As regards the crucial issue about the influence of international trade liberalization on economic growth, there has been some studies which provided important insights on the subject (Feder, 1982; Levine and Renelt, 1992; Wacziarg, 2001). According to these studies, trade impacts on growth through creating new investments, positive external effects, technology transfers, inflow of foreign direct investments, productivity growth, etc. Trade liberalization may also provide other benefits such as scale economies due to increased market size, knowledge of demand characteristics in foreign market and quality improvement in products due to international competitiveness.

Agricultural exports from India demonstrated signs of growth following the devaluation and successive deprecation of the exchange rates during the reform years in early 1990s. The exchange rate convertibility on trade account also enabled many farm based products to become internationally competitive. Globalization, however, is gradually eroding the scope for autonomous, national agricultural policy making. Global competitiveness will more and more determine the nature and scope of agricultural opportunities. As technological innovation has long been the principle means of improving competitiveness, agricultural research will play an increasingly important role. A powerful engine of growth, globalization promises ample rewards for those most able to take advantage of new technologies and expanding market opportunities.

Challenges before Small Peasantry and Agrarian Crisis in the Era of Economic Reforms

It is well known that the rural poor are characterized by insufficient asset holdings, low returns to their assets, numerous market failures, unfavourable terms of market participation, large institutional gaps, and lack of access to public goods and services resulting in not only poverty but also vulnerability to risks of change in their biophysical and economic environments. Natural and human disasters disproportionately affect poor farmers and marginal areas, often causing irreversible loss of productive assets and long-run impacts on human capital through short-term illness, malnutrition and withdrawal of children from schools.

Farming systems have been undergoing shift from crops based on traditional variety to high-yielding varieties to hybrids crops. The shift to high value but high-risk hybrid crops is also accompanied by increasing exposure to market dependence for seeds, which may also carry *sui generis* kind of intellectual property right for which farmers end up paying exorbitant price. There has been significant change in the structure of costs of production in the last two decades, reflecting the changes in technology and relative prices of inputs (Sen and Bhatia, 2004).

Land degradation due to excessive use of chemical fertilizers, and soil erosion due to extension of cultivation to marginal lands are problems that are more familiar. The answers, in the form of shift towards organic farming and crop rotation, are not easy options particularly to small farmers unless accompanied by appropriate institutional support systems.

More challenging, is the pressure on water resources. The problems of water-logging, salinity and reduction of wastage are some of the problems often addressed in the context of command areas. The serious crisis is depletion of ground water resources, especially in dry and drought prone areas as a consequence of over-exploitation. A study by activist scholars draws attention to the fact that at present 57 per cent of total irrigated area in the country is dependent on ground water resources and it is likely to increase to unsustainable levels of over 70 per cent, which would spell high risk and ruin farmers. (Narendranath, Uma Shankari and K. Rajendra Reddy, 2005).

The institutional sources of credit and other inputs like fertilizers, pesticides and seeds have been on the decline over the years. Most of the small-marginal farmers are driven to depend on unregulated and unscrupulous sources. A nation-wide survey (NSS, 2005; Report, 498) also brings out the grave agrarian situation in terms of farmer indebtedness. Almost 50 per cent of the farming households are indebted, but it is much higher in states like Andhra Pradesh (82.0%), Tamil Nadu (74.5%), Punjab (65.4%) and Kerala (64.4%), which are also States with relatively higher investment. More than 50 per cent of the borrowing is for investment in agriculture, but it is much higher in Andhra Pradesh (77%), Maharasthra (83%) and Karnataka (73%).

The economic reforms in the Indian agriculture intensified the process of public and private-resource crises brewing from the mid-1980s. Gross Capital Formation (GCF) in Indian agriculture declined drastically. Contrary to the expectations, the reform measures did not stimulate much increase in private investment. On the contrary there was deceleration of growth of private investment in agriculture. The overall GCF in agriculture as a share of total capital formation in the country, declined by half during the last two decades.

Initially, the reforms did result in improvement in terms of trade for agriculture. Indian agriculture witnessed a small acceleration in the growth rate. The country had successfully overcome the food crisis. The growth rate in agriculture and allied sectors had risen from 3.3 per cent in 1951-61 to 3.9 per cent in 1981-91 (after a low of 1.7 per cent in 1971-81), reached 5.8 per cent in 1992-93 but the euphoria was short-lived. In 1993-94 it fell to 4.1 per cent, rose to 5.0 per cent in 1994-95 before falling to -0.9 per cent in 1995-96 and -2.4 per cent in 1997-98. In 2006-07 it was 2.7 per cent and for the entire period 2005-10 it was only 3.1 per cent (Datt and Sundharam, 2011). The export of agricultural products has grown subsequently but only at a slow rate. The phenomenon that exports have lagged behind the imports leading to gradual erosion of the traditional surplus in agricultural trade is an outcome of the fact that the growth rate of domestic agricultural production has been below that of the effective demand.

Removal of Quantitative Restrictions (QRs) and recent fall in the global cotton prices has turned India into an importer of cotton, which depressed domestic prices of cotton and has been the cause of serious losses to cotton farmers. According to an estimate, most of the global agricultural commodity prices in 2002 were lower than in 1994, and particularly cotton prices were 30 per cent less (Vamsi, 2005). Farm Business Income (FBI), the difference between the value of output produced and the costs actually paid out, started declining. The "real FBI per cultivator may actually have declined in Andhra Pradesh, Bihar, Gujarat. Consumer Price Index for Agricultural Labour (CPIAL) continued to be rising while the farmers' income languishes. This has also resulted in widening of disparities between agricultural and non-agricultural incomes.

Unemployment in the agricultural sector has been a bane during the reform period as agriculture was not profitable due to the fall in the price of farm products. When the number of people employed in the primary sector and the area under cultivation decreased it caused a decline in rural employment. According to the National Sample Survey, the annual rate of growth of the employment in the rural areas was 2.07 per cent in 1987-1984, while it declined to a mere 0.66 per cent in 2000-2007, which corresponds to the period of liberalization. (Hans, 2008).

Farmer's suicides an all India phenomenon emanating largely from severe indebtedness has pushed Indian agriculture to a critical condition. The National Sample Survey Organization (NSSO) Report released in 2005 states that 1 in 2 farm households are in debt and only 10 per cent of the debt was incurred for nonproduction purposes. 32.7 per cent of farmers still depend on money lenders. The National Crime Records Bureau reports that 1,56,562 farmers committed suicide between 1997-2007. Nearly 60 of them took place in the 4 progressive states, viz., Maharashtra, Andhra Pradesh, Karnataka and Madhya Pradesh. More than 20 per cent of suicides have taken place in Karnataka The cases in Punjab are also rising. (Pushap, 2007, Kumaraswamy, 2008).

Conclusion

It is a cruel paradox that the country is agriculturally self-sufficient and the policy makers have designs and dreams about high export growth of agricultural commodities including food grains but farmers who are the architects of these surpluses are allowed to die out of distress. There is no instance of small-marginal farmers earning adequate livelihood with appropriate social security and economic support. These farmers in dry regions are the most vulnerable but least cared for in the economic reforms framework. It is the policy neglect that has been forcing these farmers to shoulder all the costs and risks of high investment including land and water resource development with borrowed capital at usurious interest rates.

Some agricultural reforms have already been carried out but these are highly inadequate. Primacy must be given to the agriculture sector in all future reforms related to rural industrialization and overall rural development. Both on-farm and off-farm employment potential must be fully exploited. This will raise incomes of farmers and rural labour on a sustainable basis and provide a much-needed boost to demand for industrial products and services, thus spurring all-around economic growth. There is an urgent need to raise public investment in agriculture substantially. Areas needing investment include: irrigation; watershed development; rural infrastructure. This will help raise the productivity of Indian agriculture to international levels and help in promoting rural prosperity in India. Second-generation reforms must reduce the perennial anti-agricultural bias by permitting free exports of all primary products. This will provide a major boost to India's exports consistent with the rules set by the World Trade Organization. Simultaneously, India must improve its marketing infrastructure. Agricultural reform will unleash high growth rates in agriculture, on which nearly sixty per cent of India's population is still dependent for employment.

REFERENCES

Aerthayil, Mathew (2008), "Agrarian Crisis in India is a Creation of the Policy of Globalization", *World Bank Economic Review*, Vol. 46(13).

Datt, Ruddar and Sundharam, K.P. M. (2011), *Indian Economy*, New Delhi: *S. Chand & Company, Ltd.*

Ghosh, Jayati (2005), "Trade Liberalization in Agriculture: An Examination of Impact and Policy Strategies with Special Reference to India", *Human Development Report Office Occasional Paper 2005/12,* Background Paper for HDR 2005, UNDP.

Globalization, *The Journal of World Intellectual Property Rights*, Vol. 3(1-2), 159-183.

Gupta, Smita (2005), "The Crisis of Indian Agriculture under Neo-Liberal Policy", *Working Paper No. 24*, Institute for Human Development, New Delhi.

Hans, V. Basil (2008), "Inclusive Strategies under Globalization Challenges and Opportunities for India" 'National Seminar on 'Social Exclusion, Poverty and Livelihood of Marginalized Groups in India – Need for Effective Strategies', September 24-25, *Centre for Study of Social Exclusion and Inclusive Policy (CSEIP)*, Mangalore University, Mangalagangothri.

Kumar, Kiran Jayasheela and Hans, V. Basil (2008), "Indian Agriculture in the Post-Economic Reforms Period", *Journal of Development Research*, Vol. 1(1): 29-42.

Kumaraswamy, D. M. (2009), "Agriculture in Karnataka" (Keynote Address), State level Seminar on Agriculture in Karnataka: Issues and Challenges, *Sri Dhavala College*, Moodbidri, January 23, 2009.

Levine, R. and D. Renelt (1992), "A Sensitivity Analysis of Cross-Country Growth", *American Economic Review*, Vol. 82 (4).

Mohan Rao, J. and Storm, S. (2000), "Agricultural Globalization in Developing Countries: Rules, Rationales and Results" in Jayati Ghosh and C.P. Chandrasekhar (eds).

Narendranath, G. Uma Shankari and K. Rajendra Reddy (2005), "To Free or

Not to Free Power: Understanding the Context of Free Power to Agriculture", *Economic and Political Weekly,* Vol. 15(5).

Pursell, G., and A. Gulati (1995), "Liberalizing Indian Agriculture: An Agenda for Reforms", in Robert Cassen and Vijay Joshi [Ed.]: *India: The Future of Economic Reforms,* Oxford University Press: Delhi.

Pushap, P. (2007), "Agriculture – India's backbone Industry and its Plight in the wake of Globalization", *The Journal of World Intellectual Property Rights*, Vol. 3(1-2), 159-183.

Sen, Abhijit and M.S. Bhatia (2004), "State of the Indian Farmer: A Millennium Study – Cost of Cultivation and Farm Income", Vol. 14, *Academic Foundation*, New Delhi.

Wacziarg, R. (2001), Measuring the Dynamic Gains from Trade, *World Bank Economic Review*, Vol. 15 (3).

Chapter 15

Globalization and Challenges Before Indian Agriculture

Savita Saini and *Shilpa Gupta*

Introduction

Agricultural sector is the mainstay of the rural Indian economy around which socio-economic privileges and deprivations revolve, and any change in its structure is likely to have a corresponding impact on the existing pattern of social equality. Agriculture occupies a prominent position in Indian policy-making not only because of its contribution to GDP but also because of the large proportion of the population that is dependent on the sector for its livelihood. One of the major economic issues faced by the country in the era of globalization is that agriculture is the sector which is the main source of livelihood for about 54 per cent of Indians till date today in Globalization World agriculture is not well developed and faces lots of problems resulting into low productivity of crops.

As 43 per cent of land in India, is used for farming but contributes only 18 per cent of the nation's GDP. The poor condition of agriculture in the country is the point of concern for Indians. The rural farmers in India suffer from poverty and most of them are illiterate so there is lack of good extension services.

Another major problem faced by Indian farmers is their dependency on nature and poorly maintained irrigation systems. Current agricultural practices are neither economically nor environmentally sustainable and India's yields for many agricultural commodities are low.

Poorly maintained irrigation systems and almost universal lack of good extension services are among the factors responsible. Poor roads to market from village, rudimentary market infrastructure, and excessive regulation are few of the other concerned points for the agriculture sector in India.

Research Objectives

(i) To know the reasons for weaknesses of Indian agriculture in the global scenario.
(ii) To know what can be done to overcome these weaknesses.
(iii) To analyze the government efforts for agricultural growth.

Research Methodology

For the fulfilment of the above objectives, data is collected basically on secondary basis. The secondary data for the study was collected from different sources such as trade journals, articles, internet, books. The study is basically descriptive in nature. The period and data of the study is selected on convenience basis in order to fulfil the objectives of the study.

Challenges of Globalization for Agriculture Sector in India

Globalization has brought forward many weaknesses of Indian agriculture. These weaknesses have come up as a challenge for the Indian agricultural sector to cope up with the globalized scenario.

Urbanization: India's agriculture sector faces a crisis because of declining productivity due to urbanization, and the latest technologies are failing to reach many of its farmer. "The agriculture sector faces a critical situation of low productivity—young people running away to the cities," P. Chengal Reddy, Secretary General of the Consortium of Indian Farming Associations, said in an address to a conference. "In India, the land is shrinking because of urbanization." Chengal Reddy said "Policy-makers had neglected agriculture in India and the latest technologies were failing to reach many of the country's 600 million farmers. There is need to build bridges between various sectors." Chengal Reddy, speaking at the February 4-7(2012) Kingsman Dubai Sugar Conference, urged increased private investment in Indian agriculture and infrastructure to help raise yields and living standards.

Poor Information Technology: In the context of agriculture, the potential of information technology (IT) can be assessed broadly under two heads: (a) as a tool for direct contribution to agricultural productivity and (b) as an indirect tool for empowering farmers to take informed and quality decisions which will have positive impact on the way agriculture and allied activities are conducted. Precision farming, popular in developed countries, extensively uses IT to make direct contribution to agricultural productivity. The techniques of remote sensing using satellite technologies, geographical information systems, and agronomy and soil sciences are used to increase the agricultural output. This approach is capital intensive and useful where large tracts of land are involved. Consequently it is more suitable for farming taken up on corporate lines. The indirect benefits of IT in empowering Indian farmer are significant and remain to be exploited. The Indian farmer urgently requires timely and reliable sources of information inputs for taking decisions. At present, the farmer depends on trickling down of decision inputs from conventional sources which are slow and unreliable. The changing environment faced by Indian farmers makes information not merely useful, but necessary to remain competitive.

Illiteracy: Indian farmers are uneducated. An agriculturist needs to be educated to avail of the facilities made available to him by government. He needs to keep account of various figures. Because of illiteracy farmers in India are not able to do bank dealings.

Decline in the growth rate of food grains: The rate of growth of agricultural output was gradually increasing in 1950-1990, and it was more than the rate of growth of the population. In the 1980s the agricultural output grew at about four per cent per annum. Thus India became self-sufficient in food and started exporting wheat and rice. But during the 10-year period after the start of liberalization, the rate of growth declined to two per cent. According to the Mid-term Appraisal of the Tenth Five Year Plan (2002-07), the rate of growth of the GDP in agriculture and allied sectors was just one per cent per annum during the years 2002-05. As a result, per capita availability of foodgrains decreased; the growth rate of population became higher than that of foodgrains, and India started to import foodgrains at a much higher price than that in the domestic market.

Water crisis: Prof. Jeffrey D. Sachs, Director, The Earth Institute, Columbia University and Special Adviser to the Secretary-General, United Nations, at the Delhi Sustainable Development Summit said Indian agriculture was not sustainable because of the water crisis. "Farming methods need to be changed, particularly in Green revolution areas such as Haryana and Punjab, where the water tables have fallen" (February 2012). Inadequate irrigation facilities and dependence of farmers on monsoon season, where good monsoon results in a vigorous growth while a poor monsoon leads to a sluggish growth for the economy as a whole.

Lack of credit: Farm credit is regulated by NABARD, which is the statutory apex agent for rural development in the country. Farmers are indebted in India. There has been minimal financial support from the government for small farmers.

Suicides: When agriculture was not yielding remunerative income, the life of the farmers became very desperate. Many of them committed suicide as a last resort. As revealed by Sharad Pawar, the Union Agriculture Minister, in the Lok Sabha in 2004, over one lakh farmers committed suicide in India after the economic reform, started. According to the National Crime Records Bureau, 17,060 farmers committed suicide in the country in 2006 with Maharashtra having the highest number of (4453) suicide deaths. Punjab is the latest in the list of States having farmers' suicide. This is a record in the agricultural history of India. It points to the acute nature of the problem which has affected the vast majority of the population, and which has created a real crisis. But unfortunately, the government and the people do not consider it a crisis; their lack of seriousness and lukewarm response to the problem points to this reality.

Trends of Farmers Suicides

Farmers Suicides in India

Year	*Maharashtra*	*Andhra Pradesh*	*Karnataka*	*Madhya Pradesh & Chhattisgarh*	*Total of 5 states*	*All India*
1997	1917	1097	1832	2390	7236	13622
1998	2409	1813	1883	2278	8333	16015
1999	2423	1974	2379	2654	9430	16082
2000	3022	1525	2630	2660	9837	16603
2001	3536	1509	2505	2824	10374	16415
2002	3695	1896	2340	2578	10509	17971
2003	3836	1800	2678	2511	10825	17164
2004	4147	2666	1963	3033	11809	18241
2005	3926	2490	1883	2660	10959	17131
2006	4453	2607	1720	2858	11638	17060
2007	4238	1797	2135	2356	11026	16632
2008	3802	2105	1737	3152	10797	16196
Total	41404	23279	25685	32454	122823	199132
Average	3450.33	1940	2140	2704.5	10235.3	16594.3

Source: www.inditogether.org- Date: 3/11/2011
Indian Streams Research Journal / 113.

Poor-infrastructure: India's rapidly growing economy has been placing huge demands on power supply, roads, railways, ports, transportation systems, water supply and sanitation. But, bottlenecks in agricultural infrastructure have been eroding the country's competitiveness. The Government of India has increased infrastructure investments under the Eleventh Five Year Plan. However, with India's low taxation base – only some 15-16 per cent of GDP is collected as taxes in India as compared to 25-40 per cent in developed countries—the country is unable to invest the required amounts through its budgetary resources.

India suffers an estimated food grain and agriculture produce loss of ₹ 50,000 crore every year due to the lack of adequate post-harvest infrastructure and inefficient supply chain management by the country's farmers. According to the country's Ministry of Food Processing Industries' Secretary P.I. Suvrathan, one of the biggest challenges for India is to find ways to organise farmers who may not have any idea about supply chain management and to create institutional mechanisms to empower them (2007).

Increasing Costs: Lack of increase in the prices of agricultural products as compare to agricultural inputs. Indian farmers are facing the dramatic fall in prices of farm produce as a result of the WTO's free trade policies.

Poor Processing: According to Foodpro 2007 Chairman and Aditya Birla Retail CEO Sumant Sinha, barely two per cent of fruits and vegetables grown in India are processed as against 80 per cent in the US. India's share in international food trade is still as low as 1.5 per cent and the rate of value addition to foods by processing is just 8 per cent.

Lack of Marketing Facilities

The defective marketing system also poses difficulties to the farmers. The farmers do not get a due reward from the sale of his produce. The middleman takes away portion of their profits. Unless farmers are guaranteed fair and remunerative prices there is little inducement for agricultural output to increase. Indian marketing has no facilities of godowns and warehousing where the cultivators may keep their produce for a better price. Moreover, they lack transportation facilities. This results in low price of the produce.

Agricultural Research

Undoubtedly, a huge amount of money is spent on agricultural research;

still the fruits do not reach to the poor cultivators. There is a lack of co-ordination between laboratory and the farm.

Remedies

1. Quantitative restrictions should be imposed on import of agricultural products. Since the import policy was the major reason for the crash in prices of many agricultural products, there should be restrictions on the quantity and customs duty of such products. Necessary import duty and quantitative restrictions should be imposed on imported goods to protect our farmers who should be given priority to the discipline of the WTO.
2. Subsidy and concessions are given to agriculture but removed in the post-reform period should be restored. This is a must to make agriculture remunerative. India should assert its right to give sufficient subsidy to its farmers to offset the rising cost of cultivation and protect their livelihood.
3. Bank loans should be easily made available to the farmers, especially since the input cost of agriculture has gone up. The government should seriously think of restoring the low rate of interest to farmers given by banks and other financial institutions as it had done before the reform period. In fact, the M.S. Swaminathan Commission for Agriculture has recommended a low rate of four per cent interest for the farmers.
4. The government should augment its investment and expenditure in the farm sector. One reason for the agricultural stagnation is low government expenditure. Investment in agriculture and its allied sectors, including irrigation, transport, communication and farm research, should be drastically increased, and the government should aim at integrated development of the rural areas. Effectual Implementation of National Rural Employment Guarantee Scheme can also become a means of revival of the rural economy.
5. There is a need for periodic revision of the procurement prices for farm produce making those remunerative. This will help the farmers to meet the increasing expenses for farm inputs and ensure at least remunerative income. According to the Swaminathan Commission, unless agriculture is made a profitable enterprise, its present crisis cannot be solved. The Commission has suggested 50 per cent more of the total production cost as supportive price for foodgrains.

6. The government should revise the policy on Special Economic Zones as it goes against the interest of farmers and the agricultural sector. It should not acquire fertile agricultural land for SEZs. When it does take over land for essential public utilities, it should give just compensation and initiate comprehensive rehabilitation measures. The recommendations of the Swaminathan Commission not to acquire land suitable for agriculture for non-agricultural purposes, to give adequate compensation for the acquired land and to distribute surplus land to the landless farmers should be seriously taken into account when the policy of SEZs is reframed. Over and above the policy of SEZs, there is a need for constitutional structures and mechanisms which will mandate the government, both Central and States, to implement the policy of relief and rehabilitation of people displaced due to SEZs and other developmental projects.
7. Bold steps should be taken to implement land reforms which were not implemented in most States. Feudal structures and landlordism based on large holdings of land by high caste and upper class people even now tend to keep a majority of the people, especially Dalits and backward castes, in the rural areas under their control and domination. Neo-liberal policies with privatization will only reinforce and strengthen these unjust and exploitative structures. Therefore, there is a need for conscious efforts and positive steps from the government side to implement land reforms. Surplus land acquired thus should be distributed to the Dalit and adivasi farmers. According to Amartya Sen, the Nobel Laureate, though the economic growth rate of India is impressive, India cannot play a significant role in the global economic scenario unless it completes land reforms.
8. The rural economy, particularly agriculture, will be greatly benefited if programmes meant for economically backward sections, including the Integrated Child Development Schemes, mid-day meals for school children and the National Rural Employment Guarantee Scheme, are effectively implemented. Food security of the poor will be ensured if the public distribution system is efficiently run. All these programmes will increase the purchasing power of the rural people and indirectly help agriculture itself.

Steps Taken by the Government under Various Programmes

Crops

- Intensive Cotton Development Programme (ICDP) under Mini-Mission- II of Technology Mission on Cotton.
- Minikit Programme for Rice, Wheat and Coarse Cereals.

Technology Mission on Oilseeds and Pulses

- Oilseeds Production Programme (OPP).
- Accelerated Maize Development Programme (AMDP).
- Sub-programme on Maize-based Cropping Systems for Food Security in India under GOI-UNDP Food Security Programme.
- National Pulses Development Project (NPDP).
- Oil Palm Development Programme (OPDP).
- Post-Harvest Technology in Oilseeds, Pulses and Maize.
- National Oilseeds and Vegetable Oils Development Board (NOVOD) – (On-going Scheme).

Horticulture

- National Horticulture Board Schemes.
- Coconut Development Board.
- Technology Mission for Development of Horticulture in North Eastern Region including Sikkim.
- Human Resource Development in Horticulture.
- Integrated Programmes for Development of Horticulture in Tribal/Hilly Areas.

Seeds

Central Sector Scheme on Transport Subsidy for the movement of Seeds to the North-Eastern States, Sikkim, Himachal Pradesh, Jammu & Kashmir, Uttarakhand and Hill Areas of West Bengal.

Pilot Scheme on Seed Crop Insurance

- Quality Control Arrangement on Seeds.

- Central sector scheme for establishment and maintenance of seed bank.
- Central sector scheme for implementation of legislation on plant varieties and farmers rights protection.

Fertilizer

- National Project on Development and Use of Biofertilisers.
- Strengthening of Central Fertilizer Quality Control and Training Institute and its Regional Labs.

Plant Protection

- Promotion of Integrated Pest Management.
- Implementation of Insecticides Act, 1968.
- Expansion of Plant Quarantine Facilities in India.
- Locust Control and Research.
- Training in Plant Protection.

Machinery

- Strengthening of Farm Machinery Training and Testing Institutes at Budni (MP), Hissar (Haryana), Garladinne (A.P.) and Biswanath Chariali (Assam).
- Establishment of Farm Machinery Training and Testing Institute in Tamil Nadu.
- Conducting study and formulating long term Mechanization strategies for each Agro-Climatic Zone.
- Productionising of Industrial Design of Agricultural Implements.

Rainfed Farming System

- Watershed Development Council (WDC).

Natural Resources Management

- National Land Use and Conservation Board (NLCB).
- EEC assisted project for Reclamation and Development of Alkali Soils in Bihar and Uttar Pradesh.

- Watershed Development Project in Shifting Cultivation Areas (WDPSCA).
- All India and Land Use Survey and application of Remote Sensing Technology.

Credit

- Investment in Debentures of State Land Development Banks (SLDB)/State Cooperative Agriculture and Rural Development Banks (SCARDB).
- Centre for International Cooperation in Agricultural Banking (CICTAB).
- National Agricultural Insurance Scheme (NAIS).

Cooperation

- Cooperative Education and Training.
- Assistance of National Cooperative Federations.
- Development of Multi-State Cooperative Societies and Strengthening of the Cooperation Division.
- Integrated Cooperative Development Projects in Selected Districts (ICDP).
- Cooperative Marketing, Processing, Storage etc. programmes in cooperatively under/least developed States.
- Share Capital participation in Cooperative Sugar Factories.
- Share capital participation in growers cooperative spinning mills
- Development of Rural Growth Centres in Bihar EEC.
- EEC assisted Coconut Development Project in Kerala.
- Assistance to National Agriculture Cooperative Marketing Federation of India (NAFED).

Directorate of Extension

- UNDP-funded Programme on National Food Security.
- Human Resource Development Training Support to Agriculture.
- Information Support/Management Information System.
- Innovations in Technology Dissemination Component of National Agriculture Technology Project (NATP).
- Central Sector Scheme of Women in Agriculture.

- Strengthening of Agricultural Extension Services Sub-components.

Directorate of Economics and Statistics and Agriculture Census

- Assistance to the States/UTs for the conduct of Livestock Census
- Timely Reporting Scheme (TRS).
- Establishment of an Agency for Reporting of Agricultural Statistics (EARAS).
- Improvement of Crop Statistics (ICS).
- Crop Estimation Survey for Fruits and Vegetables (CES-F&V).
- Strengthening of Agricultural Statistics and Policy Formulation
- Quarterly Estimation of Agriculture Production for Special Data Dissemination Standards (SDDS).
- Agro-Economic Research Scheme.
- National Centre for Crop Forecasting (NCCF).
- The Comprehensive Scheme for Studying the Cost of Cultivation of Principal Crops in India.
- Decentralization of Planning-Evaluation/Research Studies of CACP.
- Agricultural Census.

Agriculture Marketing

- Agmark Grading and Standardisation.
- Scheme for Estimation of Marketable Surplus and Post-Harvest Losses of Food grains in the country.
- Scheme for Market Survey, Investigation and Research Grants in the field of Agricultural Marketing.
- Agricultural Markting Information Network.
- National Institute of Agricultural Marketing (NIAM).

Information Technology

- Promoting Use of Informatics in Agriculture.

Policy and Plan

- Macro Management of Agriculture 'Supplementation/Complementation of States' Efforts through Work Plan'.

- Policy and Management in Agriculture "State of the Indian Farmer—A Millennium Study".

Trade

- Small Farmers' Agri-Business Consortium.

Natural Disaster Management

- Natural Disaster Management Programme.

Conclusion

The agriculture sector in India is facing a crisis today. The globalization process, which started in the 1990s, is the main reason for this crisis. The solution of the problem is not in a few "packages" but in drastic changes in the present economic policies related to agriculture. For this, the government should be ready to take bold steps. Farmers, agricultural labourers and people's organisations in civil society should work collectively to assist and persuade the government to make the necessary changes. It is high time that the government and the people realized that India can become a real "superpower" only when the vast majority of the people, especially the farmers in the rural areas, become prosperous and are really empowered. The words of Dr. M.S. Swaminathan are relevant here: "In a country where 60 per cent of people depend on agriculture for their livelihood, it is better to become an agricultural force based on food security rather than a nuclear force."

REFERENCES

Chandra S.P. (2007), *Economic Survey of India 1947-48 to 2008-09*, New Century Publication. New Delhi.

Kothari, C.R. (2003), *Research Methodology*, Wishwa Prakashan, New Delhi.

Deshmukh, (February 2011) "Farmers suicide in India", *Indian Streams Research Journal*, 113-117. http://agro.indiamart.com/agro-programme-schemes/

Economics Times, 5/2/2012.

http://www.igovernment.in/site/poor-infrastructure-costs-india-rs-50000-crore-agri-loss-every-year/

Chapter 16

The Façade of Globalization

Agrarian Crisis in Punjab

Sunaina Jain

Introduction

Human societies across the globe have tried to establish closer contacts with each other over the past few centuries but the pace with which the world has transformed into a 'global village' has been remarkable during the last few decades. The unprecedented merger and mobility of cultural, social, political and economic aspects of life and the pace of global integration has been largely due to the advancements in the field of communication, media, transportation, computer technology, coupled with the free-trade ideology of international financial institutions backed by elite Northern countries. In India, Globalization had its impact on almost all the sectors including religion, culture, law, society, and most importantly, our economy.

Agriculture sector, the backbone of Indian economy, is the source of livelihood of majority of its population. However, in the wake of liberalization and globalization policies, agricultural sector underwent a major transitional phase which contradicts the prevalent narrative of India being one of the fastest growing economies of the world. The present paper seeks to exemplify and ascertain the true impact of globalization on Indian agriculture with special focus on the North-Western state, Punjab. Has Globalization been able to keep up the promise of growth in the agricultural sector of Punjab? Or is it a mere false pretext, a kind of neo-colonialism, which has devoured the 'bread-basket' of India, and reduced this state to pauperization and marginalization? The questions which need to be answered are whether the condition of farmers in these states has improved or deteriorated with the rapid rise in industrialization of agriculture; whether crop productivity has actually increased as per the tall claims made by various transnational corporations; whether the methods and policies of these institutions are conducive to environment, or are they eroding the natural resources of these states keeping all safety norms and rules at bay with the sole purpose of reckless pursuit of profit? The present paper would use empirical evidence and factual findings to rule out skewed analysis and to ensure transparency.

The seeds of globalization in agriculture were sown during 1960s when India was facing major mass famine crisis and Punjab was chosen as a site to try the new crops by the Indian government because of its reliable water supply and a history of agricultural success. India began its own Green Revolution Programme of plant breeding, irrigation development, and financing of agrochemicals. It may be said to be the first phase of 'Agricultural Globalization' due to the inroads made by such international institutions like the International Maize and Wheat Improvement Centre, the International Rice Research Institute, and multinational seed corporations. Vandana Shiva, a renowned environmental thinker and activist and director of 'Navdanya' and the Research Foundation for Science, Technology, and Natural Resource Policy, and winner of Alternative Peace Prize in 1993, has assessed and critiqued the socio-economic and cultural impact of the Green revolution in Punjab. According to Vandana Shiva, Green Revolution posed a massive threat to the preservation of genetic biodiversity due to the 'monoculture' programme of concentrating only on a few profit-making crops (wheat-rice cropping pattern was adopted in Punjab, replacing the diversified cropping pattern before the advent of the Green Revolution) and the self-renewability of food crops due to the introduction of commercialized and privatized seeds. It was assumed that the Green revolution could be the 'panacea' for all the problems as it would meet the food requirements, and be beneficial for the farmers by increasing per hectare yield many folds, and lead our country to a new phase of development. However, the fact file of peasants' condition shows an entirely disturbing and a conflicting picture as the agrarian sector in Punjab is reeling under deep financial crunch. Furthermore, Vandana Shiva (2010) maintains that the Agriculture Agreement of the WTO and the structural adjustment programmes of the World Bank have been the most important instruments for the globalization of agriculture.

Let us assess how the high promises of Green Revolution backlashed in Punjab, the farming heartland of India. According to a study conducted by Sucha S. Gill in his paper *Economic Distress and Farmers' Suicides in Rural Punjab*, the rural areas of Punjab witnessed a spurt in their prosperity in the years immediately following the Green Revolution. However, the potentials of Green revolution technology soon began to be exhausted in the mid-1980s which resulted in economic distress among the farmers of Punjab. With the Green revolution, agriculture became more and more commercialized, and the commodification of food production turned agriculture from a subsistence sector to a mere profit-generating enterprise. The high productivity associated with it required the input of hybrid and HYV seeds, intensive use of chemical fertilizers and pesticides, mechanization, and large scale irrigation; in short, it became more capital-intensive and resource-intensive. Vandana Shiva is critical of this industrialized growth in agriculture and strongly believes that the method of mixed cropping is better than monoculture as it is "part of the adaptation of nature's ways in which cereal crops like millet, wheat, barley, and maize are mixed with pulses, providing nutrition to each other, and thus, a balanced diet to people" (SA107). Punjab witnessed a major shift in cropping patterns when global agricultural strategies reduced the production of pulses and oilseeds, and replaced them with wheat-rice production only. Relying on the statistical data collected by the Statistical Abstract of Punjab, Sucha S. Gill in *Economic Distress and Farmers' Suicides in Rural Punjab* maintains that the share of cereals in the total cropped area was 45.65 per cent, food grains was 64.73 per cent whereas pulses accounted for 19.08 per cent in 1960-61. However, all other crops except wheat and rice showed a major decline in their share. The share of cotton which had been above 9 per cent from 1960-61 to 1999-2000, fell down to 5.96 per cent in 2000-01. Similarly, the contribution of pulses in the total cropped area dropped down to 0.69 per cent in 2000-01 as compared to 19.08 per cent in 1960-61.

Vandana Shiva argues that the so-called 'inferior' grains like *bajra, ragi, jowar*, milled wheat, and milled rice are actually superior in content as compared to HYV varieties of wheat and rice. Moreover, rice and wheat bran which are eaten in home-processed grain are destroyed by mechanized milling, hence turning the most nutritious part of the food into waste. She cites an example of *bathua*, a green leafy vegetable with very high nutritive value which grows as an associate of wheat. However, it has been declared as a 'weed' that is killed with herbicides and pesticides, thus depriving rural peasants of a free source of nutrition. Another ironical fact is that the introduction of HYVs has made crops more vulnerable to insects and pests resulting in increased use of insecticides and pesticides, thus increasing the input costs even more. The stakes are significantly higher with genetic engineering. Paul Goettlich states that genetically engineered crops are not only designed to resist pesticides but those pesticides are quite necessary for the crops to grow. He further says that Monsanto has even been approved by EPA (The U.S. Environmental Protection Agency) to have a greater residue of its most popular pesticide, Roundup, on crops, and Roundup has been shown to be an endocrine disruptor and a carcinogen. Long term side-effects of the use of GM crops have not been evaluated by the firms who endorse the use of it, thus risking the health and safety of people. At the same time, the use of insecticides, herbicides, and pesticides are jeopardizing the health of consumers as well as farmers.

Rachel Carson, an environmentalist and a social critic, had imagined an ecological 'dystopic' world society fifty years back in her book 'Silent Spring', which documented detrimental effects of pesticides on the environment, particularly on birds. Carson accused the chemical industry of spreading disinformation, and public officials of accepting industry claims uncritically. The same analysis holds true in current situation as today, it is the people of Punjab who are becoming silent victims of cancer menace aggravated due to indiscriminate use of pesticides, insecticides, and other related causes. An article "Fear, Myths and a Disease" by Dharminder Kumar published in *The Indian Express* on February 17, 2013 presents a shuddering picture of the cotton belt of Punjab, from Ferozepur to Mansa district, "where cancer has become an evil which thrives in a web of silences." Though the Health Minister, while releasing the survey report maintained the excessive use of pesticides to be the cause of cancer, the Government has conducted no definitive study yet that links pesticides to cancer. The fear of '*bimari*' or '*doojibimari*' (the other disease), as they call it, has made people silent as they do not even want to name it or talk about it, fearing social or business exclusion, or "as if it were a phantom that would turn on them if they even named it." According to a survey in 2009, there were 7,738 cancer patients in Punjab. The figures have shown a steep rise as according to 2012 survey, the number rose to 23,874. The article also reveals that in addition to more than 33,000 deaths from cancer-related causes in the last five years, around 18 a day, and 84,453 suspected cases, according to the latest statewide door-to-door survey conducted by the state government. The concluding lines of the article paint a poignant picture of Punjab: "In an ironic mirroring of meaning, cancer, the malignant growth of cells, has become an apt metaphor for what has happened to agriculture in Punjab."

The toxic legacy of pesticides has killed people and animals, poisoned water, air and soil, caused the bankruptcy of many thousands of farmers, and forcing them to kill their own lives by consuming pesticides. Isn't it paradoxical that the very pesticides designed supposedly to ensure increased productivity of crops of farmers have become the very source to end their lives? In the current situation of alarming suicide cases among farmers of Punjab, it seems that the 'monster' of globalization is rapidly gobbling up the farmers' lives as well as exhausting the physical resources of this state. The leading newspapers like *The Economic Times, The Hindu, The Indian Express,* and *The Tribune* have been publishing reports of suicide cases by farmers of other states including Punjab. In an article published in *The Tribune* on May 27, 2012, it was reported that forced by financial crunch, an estimated 5,000 farmers and farm labourers committed suicide in the agrarian state of Punjab, popularly known as grain bowl of India, in the last decade—2000 to 2010. This works out to 500 suicides a year or three suicides every two days. The report also confirmed that of these 5,000, about 3,000 have committed suicide in just two districts—Bhatinda and Sangrur, and these were the startling findings of a state government commissioned survey conducted by three universities of the state—Punjabi University, Patiala; Punjab Agricultural University, Ludhiana; and Guru Nanak Dev University, Amritsar. According to the findings of MASR (Movement Against State Repression), an NGO founded by Indeljit Singh Jaijee in 1987, and working in Southern Punjab for more than past two decades, there were 1,738 suicides recorded in 91 Punjab villages from two sub-divisions of district Sangrur between 1988 and 2010. The question remains how is increased mechanization and industrialization responsible for farmers' suicides? As a result of introduction of HYV varieties, input costs shot up due to high demands of chemicals, insecticides, and pesticides which could yield high production. At the same time, irrigation costs also showed a steep hike as the HYV varieties needed at least three times more supply of water as compared to traditional farming patterns. The worst hit with these raised costs were the small and marginal farmers of Punjab who had to take heavy loans to cope with the demands of new technology. However, Vandana Shiva explains: "After a few years of bumper harvests with the green revolution in Punjab, crop failures were reported at a large number of sites, despite liberal applications of NPK fertilizer" (145).

Hence, it is clear that the rising cost of production and commercialization has made farming in Punjab high cost and risk sensitive as crop failure due to floods, pest attacks, etc. has been repeatedly reported. Citing the research conducted by R.S. Sidhu and S.S. Johl, Sucha S. Gill explains that with the rising costs in production, the rise in Minimum Support Price (MSP) at which the market clearance takes place in Punjab, has not compensated the agricultural sector. He further maintains that leaving aside the case of wheat which continues to give a rising rate of return per hectare, return on rice declined from ₹684 to ₹298 in 1995-96 at constant prices, and that of cotton fell down from ₹1418 in 1991-92 to ₹217 in 1995-96. According to a study conducted by Gaurang R. Sahay titled *Globalization, Liberalization, and Agrarian Distress: A Study of Suicides among Farmers in India*:

> With the reduction of subsidies on these inputs following fiscal reforms farmers' reliance on the market for these inputs increased substantially. Since the market prices of these inputs have risen considerably in the recent past, there is a sharp rise in the overall cost of cultivation. For example, the price per tonne of urea, diammonium phosphate (DAP) and muriate of potash (MOP) were ₹ 2350, ₹ 3600 and ₹ 1300 respectively in 1990-91, which increased to ₹ 4830, ₹ 9350 and ₹ 4455 respectively in 2003-04.

According to a survey conducted by H.S. Shergill in 1998 (*Rural Credit and Indebtedness in Punjab*, IDC, Chandigarh, 1998), the debt burden on farmers stood at ₹5,700.91 crore in 1997, and it has been mounting since then as is inevitable due to the rising instances of suicide cases in Punjab. According to reports, Sangrur, Mansa, and Bhatinda belt of Punjab has been found to be the most vulnerable. Are we ready to incur the costs of globalization at the cost of lives of our farmers? The State and Central Governments seem to be apathetic about the plight of farmers as nothing substantial has been done so far by them. The compensation to the surviving family of a suicide victim is not enough, and is not the solution to this problem. The government may have to do more than just allocate funds. The study of PAU has highlighted declining farm incomes as the main underlying cause for suicides. The article 'Punjab budgets for farm suicides' published in *The Indian Express* on June 22, 2012 expressing the impassive attitude on the part of State government says: "On tackling rural debts, the Badal government has stone walled the advice of its own advisory body, Punjab Farmers

Commission, which has cited the system of payment to farmers through commission agents as a root cause of vicious debt cycle, saying agents pay farmers for their produce after deducting loans and interest calculated at rates much higher than market rates. But in the last five years, the government has shown little political will to usher in this reform owing to pressure from the powerful lobby of commission agents." The Central Government, too, does not seem to acknowledge the magnitude of the problem. Though it realizes the gravity of the same situation in other states like Maharashtra and Karnataka, not much attention has been paid to the state of Punjab. It is the urgent need of the hour to ensure new policy implementation keeping in mind the interests of the farmers, and helping them in coming out of the vicious cycle of debt.

Besides the adverse social and economic impact, Globalization has posed serious threat to environment and the physical resources of Punjab. Vandana Shiva (2010:146) shows her concern about the crisis of desertification and death of soils caused due to mechanization of agriculture:

> The disturbance of the nutrient balance in the soil takes place through either depletion of trace elements or their excess. The green revolution has also resulted in soil toxicity by introducing excess quantities of trace elements in ecosystems. In Hoshiarpur district of Punjab, boron, iron, molybdenum and selenium toxicity has built up with green revolution practices and is posing a threat to crop production as well as animal health.

Due to intensive irrigation, more water has been introduced into ecosystems than the natural drainage capacity of soils leading to rise in the water table, i.e. water logging. Several areas in the state of Punjab are affected by water-logging and salinity. Vandana Shiva (2010:147) cities the research done by G.S. Hira and V.V.N. Murty ('An Appraisal of the Water-logging Problems in Punjab', Ludhiana: PAU, 1985) that "the major problem of water-logging is in the south-west districts of Punjab i.e., Faridkot, Ferozepur and Bhatinda. Faridkot and Ferozepur districts alone have about a metre depth of 2.14, and are affected by salinity. Bhatinda is the next badly affected district, where it has been estimated that about 0.7 lakh hectares are severely salt-affected and produce either no or poor crop yields". Groundwater is drying up in many regions of Punjab because it has been over-exploited to feed cash crops. The Malwa region, according to Shiva, once known for its abundance of water, is today dry, both above and below ground. While, earlier, water was normally struck at 80 ft., it is now difficult to find water even after drilling 300 ft. below the ground. The proliferation of tubewells has lowered the water table to a great extent. The past few decades have seen an increase in private investment in exploiting ground-water resources through the digging of borewells. In the article "Fear, Myths and a Disease", Dharminder Kumar tells that as far back in 1995, a study conducted by the Guru Nanak Dev University, Amritsar, there were alarming amounts of uranium in water samples from Bhatinda and Amritsar districts. Moreover, South African toxicologist CarinSmit found unusually high uranium in hair samples of children in Faridkot district in 2009.

All these studies and surveys reveal the true social, economic, and environmental impact in the wake of Globalization, and the facts cannot, and should not be negated, considering the urgency of the current situation in Punjab. Hence, whatever gains accrued to Punjab in the short run after the Green Revolution are being counter-balanced by a significant rise in the problems related to it. Albert Einstein once remarked that, "You can´t find a solution to a problem by employing the same thinking that moved you into the problem in the first place." Globalization related problems cannot be sorted out with the same rational, linear thinking. It is time to move beyond corporate-controlled agriculture to restore health back to air, soil, water, and very importantly, to our farmers as well as general population. The focus of the Farmers is slowly shifting to Organic Farming, and "Organic Farming Council of Punjab" has been formed to promote and develop Organic Farming on a large scale, and to advise the State Government regarding policy initiative on Organic Farming and Value Addition of the crops produced under the programme. In order to ensure the adoption of a vigorous package of practice to support Organic Farming, Consultants/Experts in organic farming have been engaged to give on-farm training and guidance and also guide them for the production of in house organic inputs like Vermiculture, Bio-dynamic composts and other home-made pesticides etc. using common herbs and plants. To supplement the income, farmers are encouraged to shift from high volume crops to high value crops, 3 to 4 crop rotation system and exhaustive crops to restorative crops.

As Gandhiji reminded us, "The Earth has enough for everyone's needs, but not for some people's greed." So, we need to explore alternatives to check the growth of multi-national corporations taking control of our agricultural economy.

REFERENCES

Gill, Sucha. S. (2005), "Economic Distress and Suicides in Rural Punjab." *Journal of Punjab Studies* 12 February : 219-38. Print.

Goettlich, Paul (2000), "The Green Revolution: A Critical Outlook". mindfully.org. 10 October, Web. 1 January 2013.

Kaur, Sukhdeep (2012), "Punjab budgets for farm suicides". *The Indian Express*, 22 June, Chandigarh. Print.

Kumar, Dharminder (2013), "Fear, Myths and a Disease". *The Sunday Express* 17 February, Chandigarh, Sunday edition. Print.

Sahay, Gaurang R. "Globalization, Liberalization and Agrarian Distress: A Study of Suicides among Farmers in India". Paper for VI. Global Labour University Conference, Berlin.

Shiva, Vandana (2010), *Staying Alive: Women, Ecology, and Development.* NY: South End Press, Print.

Shergill, H.S. (1998), *Rural Credit and Indebtedness in Punjab.* Arihant Print 'N' Graphics, Print.

Vasdev, Kanchan (2012), "In Punjab, three farmers kill selves every two days". *The Sunday Tribune*, 27 May, Chandigarh, online edition. Web.

Chapter 17

Globalization: A Boon for Micro, Small and Medium Enterprises in India

Pramod Bhargava

Introduction

Globalization has integrated the world into one huge market. It takes off the borders among the countries and providing several things to several people from one place to another. The process of globalization takes place through three channels, i.e. trading, capitalization and financing. In Indian aspect the Globalization means 'incorporate' the economy of the country with the world economy. In India the concept of Globalization was initiated in the new economic policy introduced by the Government of India in July 1991. But the introduction of globalization has also brought its side effects which ultimately effected domestic industries. Globalization has had a huge impact over the small business industry. The small scale sector is a vital part of overall industrial sector of the country. It forms a dominant part of Indian industry and contributing to a significant proportion of production, exports and employment. The effects of globalization over small businesses are wide and diverse moreover; in the bigger picture globalization is advantageous for small businesses.

The Aim of Globalization

Globalization can be defined as the process of change, increasing interconnectedness and interdependence among countries and economies, bringing the world closer through better world-wide communication, transport and trade links. This process is changing the world dramatically and quickly, affecting economic, social, political and cultural aspects of life. Globalization refers to an advanced stage of development where capital, technology, labour, raw materials, information and transportation, distribution and marketing are integrated or interdependent on a globe scale.

Positive Effects of Globalization Over Small Businesses

The first positive effect of globalization is that small businesses can also now compete on an International scale. Small businesses are now better equipped when it comes to competing against big players in the industry. With the advent of globalization, small businesses are now able to compete in International markets against even large multinational companies. Earlier the international business was dominated by MNCs. However, just because of globalization, small businesses can now not only enter the International market but also challenging a tough competition to big business houses. Globalization has, took both, the MNCs and SSCs as counterpart and levelled the playing field between small businesses and their MNCs. Secondly, Globalization provides an endless opportunities for a wider, more global audience. Before the era of globalization, small businesses are limited in terms of territorial boundaries. They do business within the scope of their area or community. Globalization opened the barriers that separate domestic and International markets. Furthermore, globalization created a single, global market for goods and services. Every business firm, regardless of its size, is given an equal opportunity to succeed in such global market. Small businesses can access different available avenues to reach such global market. Thirdly, Globalization also enhances the communication and network systems between domestic small businesses to overseas partners, customers and suppliers. Similarly, the Internet also plays a crucial role in such effective communication and networking system. Small businesses can search for better opportunities through their overseas networks. These opportunities may take the form of cheaper raw materials, outsourcing strategies and other important first-hand industry knowledge. Small businesses can also take advantage of newer and better technologies introduced by their overseas partners. In order to impart more vitality and growth to small scale sector, a separate policy statement is announced for small, tiny and village enterprises on 6th August, 1991. This policy statement was a leap-forward because it was the first time that Government had issued a separate policy statement for the small and decentralized sector.

The fact that Government considered it necessary to make a separate policy statement for small enterprises was a welcome recognition to the dynamic and vibrant nature of the sector. This policy statement proposed some path-breaking measures to mitigate the handicaps that were faced up by small enterprises in respect. Government of India introduced a large number of innovative promotional measures to uplift the growth of small scale sector. Major features of the Small Industrial policy of 1991:

1. Emphasis to shift from cheap credit to adequate credit.
2. Equity participation by other undertakings (both domestic and foreign) up to 24 per cent.
3. Introducing factoring services by banks.
4. Marketing of mass consumption goods under common brand name.
5. Setting up of sub-contracting exchanges.
6. Establishment of technology development cell.
7. Opening of quality counselling and technology information centres.

Table 17.1: Development of MSME

Year	*Total MSMEs (lakh number)*	*Fixed Investment (Rs. Crore)*	*Production (Rs. Crore)*	*Employment (Lakh persons)*	*Exports (Rs. Crore)*
2001-02	105.21 (4.07)	154349 (5.11)	282270 (8.03)	249.33 (4.44)	71244 (2.07)
2002-03	109.49 (4.07)	162317 (5.16)	314850 (11.54)	260.21 (4.36)	86013 (20.73)
2003-04	113.95 (4.07)	170219 (4.87)	364547 (15.78)	271.42 (4.31)	97644 (13.52)
2004-05	118.59 (4.07)	178699 (4.98)	429796 (17.90)	282.57 (4.11)	124417 (27.42)
2005-06	123.42 (4.07)	188113 (5.27)	497842 (15.83)	294.91 (4.37)	150242 (20.76)
2006-07	261.01 (111.48)	500758 (166.20)	709398 (42.49)	594.61 (101.62)	182538 (21.50)
2007-08	272.79 (4.51)	558190 (11.47)	790759 (11.47)	626.34 (5.34)	202017 (10.67)
2008-09	285.16 (4.53)	621753 (11.39)	880805 (11.39)	659.35 (5.35)	N. A.
2009-10	298.08 (4.53)	693835 (11.59)	982919 (11.59)	695.38 (5.47)	N. A.
2010-11	311.52 (4.51)	773487 (11.48)	1095758 (11.47)	732.7 (5.29)	N.A
Average growth rate	16.1	24.1	14.5	14.4	16.6

Source: Reserve Bank of India and Ministry of Micro, Small and Medium Enterprises, Government of India.

Indian small scale industry is playing an imperative role in the economic expansion of the country and have vast approaching for employment generation. Increasing small scale sector units also results in decentralized industrial development, better distribution of wealth and investment and entrepreneurial talent. The government has initiated several policies for the growth and development of small scale industries. Post-liberalization economic ćonditions have created immense growth prospect for the small scale industries. The Micro, Small and Medium Enterprises in India are acting as power and spirit of economic growth in the 21st century.

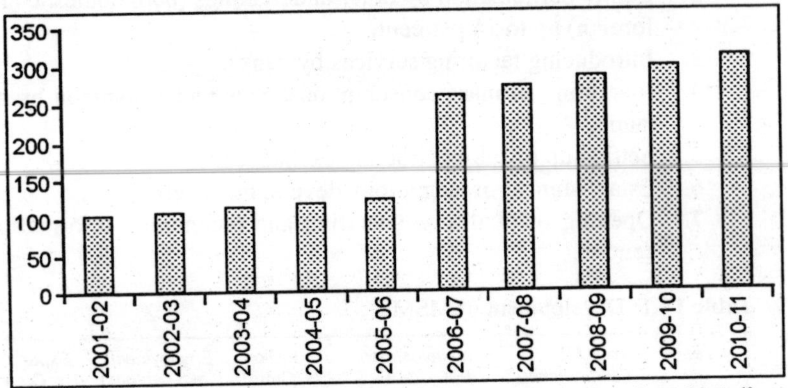

Source: Reserve Bank of India and Ministry of Micro, Small and Medium Enterprises, Government of India.

Chart 17.1: Number of MSME in India

The small scale sector has played an extremely essential role in the socio-economic development of the country during the past 50 years. It has significantly contributed to the overall growth in terms of Gross Domestic Product (GDP), employment generation and exports.

The Micro, Small and Medium Enterprise (MSME) sectors contributes significantly to manufacturing output, employment and exports of the country. It is estimated that in terms of the value, the sector accounts for about 45 per cent of the manufacturing output and 40 per cent of the total exports of the country. The sector is estimated to employ about 69 million persons in over 26 million units throughout the country. There are over 6000 products ranging from traditional to high tech items which are being manufactured by SSEs in the country. It is well known that SSE sector provides maximum opportunities for both self-employment and job outside agriculture sector.

Conclusion

MSME had played a vital role in Indian economy but from the last two decades it is remarkable. Globalization which was considered as a curse for SSIs, is now turned and performed as a boon. At one fold it facilitated SSIs open access of world market and on the other hand it boosted up the SSIs performance by generating competition. The overall performance and contribution of small scale industries to Indian economy is described in terms of its absolute growth in units, employment, production and exports. The MSMEs Development Act of 2006 perhaps is the most crucial of these recent policy changes. The small scale sector has grown rapidly over the years. In the period of liberalization and the development, the MSMEs sector constituted an important segment of our economy.

MSMEs are a very important segment in the Indian industrial sector and would continue to play a crucial role in the Indian Economy in the future. It also brought in huge amounts of foreign investments into the country and provided employment opportunities for many people in the country which in its turn helped reduce the level of poverty in the country. A rewarding feature of economic development in India is due to impressive growth of modern MSMEs.

REFERENCES

Banerjee, P. (2005). Corporate Governance and Competence in SME's in India, National Institute of Science, Technology and Development Science (NISTADS), *CACCI Journal,* Vol. 1.

Das, B.; Shil, N.C.; Pramanik, A. (2007). *Strengthening SMEs to make export competitive*, Munich Personal Re-PEc Archive (MPRA).

Gupta, R. (2006). *Scope of Cottage and Small Scale Industry in West Bengal in the Early 2000*, IBS Research Centres, Kolkata.

MSME (2007), Micro, small and medium enterprises in India an overview. Ministry of Micro, Small and Medium Enterprises (MSME), Nirman Bhavan, New Delhi.

MSME. (2007-08). Ministry of Micro, Small and Medium Enterprises, Government of India, *Annual Report 2007-08*, Chapter I.

MSME. (2008-09). Ministry of Micro, Small and Medium Enterprises, Government of India, *Annual Report 2008-09*, Chapter I, p. 1.

Chapter 18

Small Scale Industry in India under Globalization

Harneet Kaur

Introduction

Small scale industry occupies a place of strategic importance in Indian economic structure due to its considerable contribution in terms of output, exports and employment. By the end of March 2002, there were 3.4 million small industry units, accounting for more than 40 per cent of the gross value of output in the manufacturing sector, about 35 per cent of the total exports and provided employment to over 19.2 million persons, which is second only to agriculture (Planning Commission, 2002). This much contribution has emerged despite the sector being exposed to intensifying competition during the decade since 1991. Small scale industry in India has been confronted with growing competitive environment since 1991 due to (1) liberalization of investment regimes in the 1990s, favouring foreign direct investment (FDI) at the international level, particularly in socialistic and developing countries, (2) the formation of World Trade Organization in 1995 forcing its member countries (including India) to drastically scale down the quantitative and non-quantitative restrictions on imports and (3) domestic economic reforms (Bala Subrahmanya, 2002b).

In order to impart more vitality and growth to small scale sector, a separate policy statement has been announced for small, tiny and village enterprises on 6th August, 1991. This policy statement was a leap-forward because it was the first time that Government had issued a separate policy statement for the small and decentralized sector. In the past, small scale sector merited only two or three paragraphs in the more general industrial policy statements. The fact that Government considered it necessary to make a separate policy statement for small enterprises was a welcome recognition to the dynamic and vibrant nature of the sector. This policy statement proposed some path-breaking measures to mitigate the handicaps that were faced up by small enterprises in respect. Government of India introduced a large number of innovative promotional measures to uplift the growth of small scale sector. Major features of the Small Industrial Policy of 1991:

1. Emphasis to shift from cheap credit to adequate credit.
2. Equity participation by other undertakings (both domestic and foreign) up to 24 per cent.
3. Introducing factoring services by banks.
4. Marketing of mass consumption goods under common brand name.
5. Setting up of sub-contracting exchanges.
6. Establishment of technology development cell.
7. Opening of quality counselling and technology information centres.
8. New technology upgradation programmes.

Globalization

For the purpose of the argument in this paper, as well as understanding some of the responses to globalization, it is important to define what mean by globalization. This is all the more crucial because even if we leave out the unambiguous supporters of globalization in its present form— those who hold that it is purely beneficial, and the benefits will 'trickle down' automatically to the poor—there are still widely differing conceptions of this process. Those who either oppose globalization, or are anxious about its potentially detrimental effects on employment and poverty, encompass a wide political spectrum. The extreme right oppose it from the standpoint of economic and cultural nationalism, and liberals might deplore the loss of national sovereignty because it reduces the effectiveness of state intervention to regulate capital and labour, alleviate poverty and so forth. Globalization is the process of integrating various economies of the world without creating any hindrances in the free flow of goods and services, technology, capital and even labour or human capital. The term globalization has, therefore, four parameters:

1. Reduction of trade barriers to permit free flow of goods and services among nation-states;
2. Creation of environment in which free flow of capital can take place among nation-states;
3. Creation of environment, permitting free flow of technology; and
4. Last, but not the least, from the point of view of developing countries, creation of environment in which free movement of labour can take place in different countries of the world.

Small Scale Industry and Its Importance

Economic development of a country is directly related to the level of industrial growth. The expansion of industrial sector leads to a greater utilization of natural resources, production of goods and services, creation of employment opportunities and improvement in the general standard of living. India has also been striving to develop the country's industrial base over since independence. It has framed various policies aimed at development of industries in the public and private sectors. Special emphasis has been laid on small-scale industries. Small-scale industries play a key role in our planned development with its advantages of low investment, high potential for employment generation, diversification of the industrial base and dispersal of industries to rural and semi-urban areas. The small-scale industries sector has been appropriately give a strategic position in our planned economy towards the fulfilment of the socio-economic objectives particularly in achieving equitable growth. P.N. Dhar and H.F. Lydall in introduction to their book, "The Role of Small Enterprise in Indian Economic Development" have observed that 'The promotion of small scale industries has been widely recommended as one of the most appropriate means of developing industry in over-populated backward countries.' The definition of small scale sector is broadened from small-scale industries to small scale enterprises that include all business enterprises in the services sector which provide service to industrial sector in addition to small scale industries taking into account all these factors, at present, Reserve Bank of India uses an expanded definition of small scale industries which include: (i) Small scale industrial undertaking which are engaged in the manufacturing, processing and preservation of goods in which the investment in plant and machinery not to exceed ₹ 5 crore. These would include units engaged in mining or quarrying servicing and repairing of machinery. (ii) Tiny enterprises whose investment in plant and machinery do not exceeds ₹ 25 lacs. (iii) Power looms. (iv) Traditional industries which require high workmanship and techniques and also village and household industries producing common goods of consumption predominantly by using simple tools. (v) The decentralized and informal sector like handlooms and handicrafts. (vi) The industry related to services/business enterprises. (vii) Food and agro-based industries. (viii) Software industry. The development of small scale industries is being given due importance by the Government in order to achieve the following objectives:

1. To provide additional employment opportunities.
2. To mobilise resources of capital and skill from various parts of the country.
3. To provide a more equitable distribution of national income.
4. To provide a helping hand to large industries and facilitate them in their work.

Need and Objectives of the Study

Small Scale Industry in India has been confronted with an increasingly competitive environment due to: (i) liberalization of the investment regime in the 1990s, favouring foreign direct investment at the international level, particularly in socialistic and developing countries; (ii) the formation of the World Trade Organizations (WTO) in 1995, forcing its member-countries (including India) to drastically scale down quantitative and non-quantitative restrictions on imports, and (iii) domestic economic reforms. The cumulative impact of all these developments is a remarkable transformation of the economic environment in which small industry operates, implying that the sector has no option but to 'compete'. To compete in the international market, the Indian Government Announced a separate Industrial Policy for Small, Tiny and Village Industries on 6th August, 1991 and started some development programmes for the development of Small Scale Sector. The main objective of the present study is to analyze the impact of globalization on the growth of small scale industries.

Database and Methodology

In the present study an attempt has been made to analyze the impact of globalization on the growth of small scale industries. For this, the growth pattern and some aspects of productivity in SSI sector in India have been calculated. The study has been conducted with reference to the data related to Performance of Small Scale Industries in India. The SSI sector has been studied with the belief that they hold the largest share of Industrial Sector in India. The reference period for the analysis of the data has been taken from 1973-74 to 2006-07. The study period has been divided into two parts: pre-liberalization (1973-74 to 1989-90) and post-liberalization (1990-91 to 2006-07) to know the impact of globalization after liberalization. For this, a comparative analysis of Average Annual Growth Rates for pre- and post-globalization periods has been carried out for key growth and performance parameters like number of units, production, employment and exports. The study has been based on secondary information. The data for the study purpose has been taken mainly from 'Ministry of Micro, Small and Medium Enterprises, Government of India' published by Reserve Bank of India in 'Handbook of Statistics on Indian Economy'.

Review of Literature

Various studies have been conducted from time to time in different states of India on different aspects of small-scale industries. The most of the studies are related to financial aspect, growth of small scale industries, entrepreneurship in SSIs, WTO regime and small scale industries and also related to small industry and globalization. A review of imported studies is presented below:

Mathew, M.C. (2004) highlighted the reason for panic in all India census report on small scale industries. The study observed that the vibrancy and dynamical of the sector anticipated under an era of deregulation and de-reservation remaining largely unrealized. The study stated that the country needs a strong small and medium enterprises policy, which was closely linked to its international commitments. The study suggested that at the strategy level, there were need to be mechanism by which the demography of small and medium enterprises sector itself becomes a matter of public security.

Rajyalakshmi, N. (2004) reviewed the productivity awareness among SSI units in Visakhapatnam district of Andhra Pradesh at micro level and explored small-scale entrepreneurs, how they measured productivity in their units. The study based on primary data collected by using structured schedule through personal interviews. A sample of 200 SSI units has been selected for the study. The study found that Chemical units were more capital intensive and it was low in food and agro units. Productivity awareness was not noticed in the SSI units. The study concluded that success in small industry will be best achieved if the productivity culture will be clearly understood by all the employees.

Subrahmanyabala, M.H. (2004) highlighted the impact of globalization and domestic reforms on small-scale industries sector. The study stated that small industry had suffered in terms of growth of units, employment, output and exports. Researcher highlighted that the policy changes had also thrown open new opportunities and markets for the small-scale industries sector. The author suggested that the focus must be turned to technology development and strengthening of financial infrastructure in order to make Indian small industry internationally competitive and contribute to national income and employment.

Sudan, F.K. (2005) described the challenges in Micro and Small Scale Enterprises Development and policy issues by arising different questions related to Micro and Small Enterprises. The study explained the meaning, advantages, problems and policy options of MSE sector. The study concluded that all the policies which were opted by GOI were the efforts to form a dynamic MSE sector and a diversified economy providing expanded employment opportunities to absorb all new labour force and offer exciting career opportunities.

Rathod, C.B. (2007) described the importance of small scale industrial sector and also the contribution of Indian small scale entrepreneurs in world economy. The main objective of the study was to study the growth and pattern of the SSI sector and identify the reasons for success/failures, to evaluate the impact of globalization on SSIs and export opportunity, to identify the barriers and constraints that SSIs were facing to cope with globalization. The study analysed that SSI sector in India has been exhibiting a striking export performance; export had grown up to double digit from the last ten years. The study concluded that both opportunities and challenges were raised as the impact of globalization on Indian Industry as a whole and the small scale sector in particular. The study found that a major portion of our exports would have to gear up to the new era of boundary-less economy. The study has suggested that there was need for simplified legal and regulatory framework, good governance, sufficient and accessible finance, suitable infrastructure and competitive environment.

Global, National and Sectoral Policy Changes: Implications for Small Industry

The 1990s was an eventful decade in terms of policy changes, nationally as well as internationally. Since the beginning of 1990s policy changes have been taking place at three different levels—global, national and sectoral, which have implications for small industry functioning and performance in India. The first and the foremost development is the "globalization" process at the international level. Globalization would mean free movement of factor inputs (both labour and capital) as well as output between countries. According to Stiglitz, J. (2002), globalization is the closer integration of the countries and peoples of the world which has been brought about by the enormous reduction of costs of transportation and communication, and the breaking down of artificial barriers to the flows of goods, services, capital, knowledge, and (to a lesser extent) people across borders. However, the developments that have been taking place since the early 90s are mostly with reference to the free movement of only one of the factor inputs, i.e. capital, commonly known as Foreign Direct Investment (FDI) and free movements of goods, particularly from the developed to the developing countries.

The liberalization of FDI regimes and the strengthening of international standards for the treatment of foreign investors allow foreign firms greater freedom in making international location decisions (UNCTAD, 2001). On an average, 58 countries have introduced changes in their investment regimes annually during 1991–2000. In 2000 alone, 69 countries made a total of 150 regulatory changes, out of which, 147 (98%) were more favourable to foreign investors (UNCTAD, 2001). As a result, global FDI inflow increased to US $ 1271 billion in 2000 from US $ 209 billion in 1990. The rate of growth of FDI inflow increased to about 21 per cent in the early 1990s as compared to 17.4 per cent in the 1980s and further increased to about 41 per cent in the late 1990s. The increased inflow of FDI has led to its greater share in gross capital formation in all industries together as well as manufacturing industries (Table 18.1). The increase was more significant in developing countries. This would have led to intensifying competition in the national as well as international markets for small firms.

The formation of World Trade Organization (WTO) in 1995 has only accelerated the process of scaling down of tariff and non-tariff restrictions on imports. India, as a member of the WTO has substantially done away with its quantitative and non-quantitative restrictions by April 1, 2001 (Ministry of Finance, 2002). As a result, industry will have to face much stronger international competition (Planning Commission, 2002). The process of removal of quantitative and non-quantitative restrictions across countries has led to free movement of goods between countries including

India. As a result, world exports grew in dollar terms at an average rate of 5.9 per cent during 1990-99 as against 5.2 per cent during 1980-90 (Ministry of Finance and Company Affairs, 2003). The reduction of restrictions on the movement of goods between countries and the subsequent increase in world exports would have benefited Multinational Corporations much more than small enterprises.

Table 18.1: FDI in Capital Formation: 1980, 1990 and 1998

Region	*FDI as a % of Gross Capital Formation (All Industries)*	*FDI as a % of Capital Formation in Manufacturing*
World		
1980	2.3	9.0
1990	4.7	14.0
1998	11.1	21.6
Developing Countries		
1980	1.2	11.7
1990	4.0	22.3
1998	11.5	36.7

Source: UNCTAD (2000).

This has to be viewed along with the process of economic reforms launched by the Government of India at the national level. This has resulted in considerable freedom for enterprises, domestic as well as foreign, to enter, expand or diversify their investments in Indian industry. India's economic reforms have two major outcomes, among others: Firstly, the growth of the public sector has come down considerably since 1991 as compared to the earlier period in terms of not only investment and employment but also production (Table 18.2). Public sector has been a major customer of small enterprises in India. The curtailed growth of PSUs would have resulted in reduced growth or even absolute reduction in public sector demand for small industry products in the 90s. The relative role of the public sector as a distinct entity will decline further in the course of the Tenth Five Year Plan (Planning Commission, 2002). This will most probably bring down public sector demand further for small industry products.

Secondly, there has been a rapid increase in FDI inflow into diverse sectors of Indian industry. FDI inflow increased from ₹ 3,514.3 million in 1991 to ₹ 161, 344.4 million in 2002 (which excludes ADRs/GDRs/ FCCBs, stock swapping, etc.) at the rate of about 42 per cent per annum

Table 18.2: Growth of Public Sector Enterprises in India: 1973-74 to 1997-98

Year	*Investment (₹ Million)*	*Employment (Number in '000)*	*Production (₹ Million)*
1973-74	64,700	13,650	32,190
1990-91	777,900	23,230	7,55,680
1997-98	1,439,550	23,880	1,795,870
Period	*Compound Average Growth Rate*		
1973-74 to 1990-91	15.75	3.17	20.39
1990-91 to 1997-98	9.19	0.39	13.16

Source: EPW Research Foundation (2002).

(SIA, 2003). This would have created not only threats through greater competition, particularly in non-durable consumer goods industries but also opportunities for outsourcing in durable consumer goods and capital goods industries, to small enterprises. The introduction of an exclusive policy for small industry, which laid emphasis on imparting more vitality and growth impetus to the sector, is the sectoral dimension of the major policy changes relevant to small industry (Ministry of Industry, 1991). The policy marked: (i) the beginning of an end to protective measures to small industry, and (ii) promotion of competitiveness by addressing the basic concerns of the sector, namely technology, finance and marketing (Bala Subrahmanya, 1998). Subsequently, the number of items reserved exclusively for small industry manufacturing has been gradually brought down from 842 in 1991 to 675 in 2003. Of course, the contribution of this policy to small industry growth was nothing much to talk about (Bala Subrahmanya, 1995). Concessional element in lending rates for small industry has been largely withdrawn during the 1990s (RBI, 2003). The number of products reserved exclusively for purchase from small industry by Directorate General of Supplies and Disposals for the public sector has been changed to 358 items from 409 items after deleting items having common nomenclature and making the entries more generic as well as addition of new items (DCSSI, 1999). The price preference scheme (up to 15% over the lowest quotation of the large scale units) has remained the same. On the whole, the protection emphasis of India's small industry policy has undergone dilution since 1991. Thus, policy changes that have occurred at the global, national and sectoral levels have radically changed the environment for the functioning of small industry in India. The growth of small industry in the country has to be analysed with this backdrop.

Small Industry Performance in the Globalization Era

The overall performance and contribution of small industry to Indian economy is generally described in terms of its absolute growth in units, employment, production and exports. Equally important is its relative contribution, which can be analysed in terms of small industry share in national income, total exports and total organized sector employment. Thus, the growth performance of small industry can be evaluated in two ways:

1. To compare the growth rates of units, employment, output and exports of small industry in the 1990s with that of the 1980s.
2. To ascertain the change in small industry's relative contribution to GDP, exports and organized sector employment.

This will reveal how the sector is coping up with challenges and changes in the intensifying competitive environment emerging since 1990-91. The growth of small industry in terms of units, employment, production and exports is estimated based on the figures given in *Economic Surveys* (Ministry of Finance). The share of small industry in National Income is arrived at as follows: The Gross Value Added (GVA) of units having investment more than that of the small industry investment limit is deducted from the manufacturing sector's contribution to Gross Domestic Product (GDP) and the remainder is the contribution of small industry to GDP. It represents the contribution of the entire small industry sector and not just the modern small industry sector. This value is calculated as a percentage of the total GDP. *Annual Survey of Industries* (EPW Research Foundation, 2002) and *Hand Book of Statistics on Indian Economy* (RBI, 2001) are used for the purpose. The share of small industry exports in total exports is calculated in rupee terms based on the figures available in the *Economic Surveys* (Ministry of Finance). Similarly, the quantum of employment of small industry is calculated as a percentage of total organized sector employment based on *Economic Survey* figures. Strictly speaking, small industry employment comprises employment generated by both organized and unorganized sectors and therefore, is not directly comparable to total organized sector employment. However, here the purpose is to show the importance of small scale industry in terms of employment generation as compared to the employment of entire organized sector.

The growth rates of small industry in terms of units, employment, output and exports for the 1980s and 1990s are presented in Table 18.3. It is clear that the growth of small industry in the transitional period of 1990s has come down in terms of not only units and employment but also output. This could be an indication that increasing competition in the globalization period does affect the growth of Indian small industry adversely. However, the growth rate of exports has actually increased marginally. To probe the growth pattern further, growth rates are estimated for five-year periods for both 80s and 90s. They also broadly correspond to India's five-year plans: sixth, seventh, eighth and ninth respectively. The scenario does not differ much, except for exports (Table 18.3). The growth rates of units and employment have steadily come down. But the growth rates of output and more importantly, exports have fluctuated. In fact, the growth rate of output increased in the late 80s as compared to the early 80s but then declined in the early 90s and further in the late 90s. Whereas, the growth rate of exports increased steadily till the early 90s but then declined considerably (see Figure 18.1).

Table 18.3: Growth of Small Scale Industry: 1990s *vs.* 1980s

Sl. No.	*Period*	*Units*	*Employment*	*Output*	*Exports*
I	1980s	8.40	5.84	18.66	19.38
	1990s	5.62	4.00	15.31	20.62
II	1980-81 to 1985-86	9.18	6.21	16.88	11.00
	1985-86 to 1990-91	7.63	5.47	20.46	28.40
III	1990-91 to 1995-96	6.88	4.02	18.05	30.42
	1995-96 to 2000-01	4.37	3.99	12.62	11.56

The other dimension of small scale industry performance is its relative contribution to national income (GDP), exports and employment. The contribution of small scale industries is considered for three periods of time: 1980-81, 1990-91 and 2000-01 (Table 18.4). The share of small scale industry in national income increased in the protection period of 80s but declined considerably in the transitional period of 90s. The share of small industry in exports and its employment in relation to organized sector employment have consistently increased both in the protection period and in the transitional period. But, the increase in the share of small industry in total exports was more significant in the protection period of 1980s as compared to the transitional

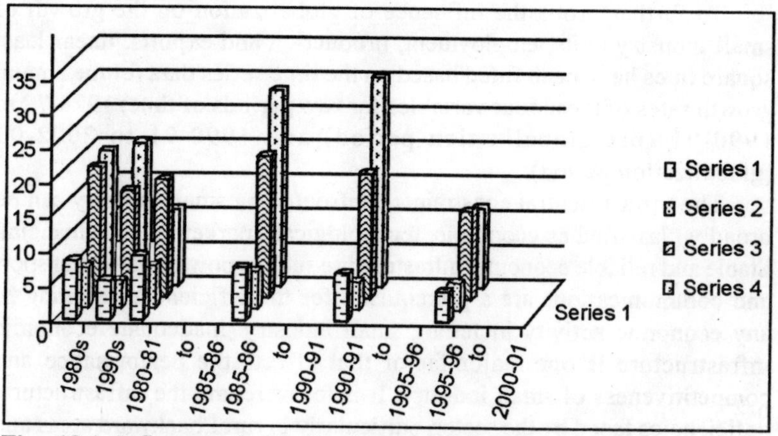

Fig. 18.1: Influence of globalization on small scale industries

period of 1990s. However, the increase in the relative share of small industry employment was more significant in the 1990s as compared to the 1980s. Small industry employment (which included partly unorganized manufacturing sector employment as well) was equivalent to about 31 per cent of the total organized sector employment in 1980-81. It went up to nearly 48 per cent of the organized sector employment in 1990-91. By 2000-01, small industry employment increased to the level of two-thirds of the organized sector employment. That is, though the growth rate of small industry employment has come down in the 1990s, small industry employment has increased more than proportionately in the period of globalization as compared to the protection period, with respect to other sectors of the Indian economy. As a result, its size relative to organized sector employment has gone up.

Table 18.4: Small Industry in National Income, Exports and Employment (in %)

Year	*National Income*	*Exports*	*Employment*
1980-81	9.2	24.5	31.0
1990-91	11.0	29.7	47.6
2000-01	7.8*	30.9	66.4

Sources: *For the year 1997-98.

1. Government of India (1998)
2. Government of India (2002)
3. Reserve Bank of India (2001)
4. EPW Research Foundation (2002)

To further probe the influence of globalization on the growth of small industry units, employment, production and exports, linear least square lines have been fitted based on the time series data for the annual growth rates of these four variables for two periods of time: 1978-79 to 1990-91 (pre-globalization period) and 1990-91 to 2002-03 (globalization period).

The infrastructural constraints confronted by small industry can be broadly classified as economic, technological, marketing and financial. Stable and reliable economic infrastructure such as power, water, transport and communications are a prerequisite for the efficient functioning of any economic activity including small industry. Inadequate economic infrastructure is one major factor that affects the performance and competitiveness of small industry. It is to overcome the infrastructural deficiencies faced by the sector, particularly in rural/backward areas and to strengthen linkages between agriculture and industry that the Government introduced the Integrated Infrastructure Development (IID) Scheme in 46 centres in 1994 (DCSSI, 1999). The IID scheme proposes to contain developed sites, power distribution network, water, telecommunications, drainage and pollution control facilities, road, banks, raw material depots, storage and marketing outlets, common facilities and technological back-up services (DCSSI, 1999). Thus, IID scheme aims at providing not only economic but also technological, marketing and financial infrastructure for the development of small industry. However, the IID scheme has not made much headway even after almost a decade. So far only 58 IID centres have been approved and 50 more centres have been proposed for development in the 10th Plan (Planning Commission, 2002). But a small number of IID centres will not make any major impact on small industry performance. Recently, the Prime Minister has proposed to extend IID scheme to the entire country (Planning Commission, 2002). However, it is not clear how and when the scheme will be extended to cover the entire country.

Technological obsolescence has been a characteristic of small industry in India across a wide variety of sectors. In the early 90s, two survey-based studies have brought out that technological obsolescence of small industry affect quality and productivity adversely. These empirical studies indicated that small industry in general, is characterized by technological obsolescence and therefore, inferior quality as well as low productivity (Awasthi, Krishna and Sebastian, 1993; NCAER, 1993). Subrahmanian, K.K. (1995) had also highlighted the lack of technological dynamism in Indian small industry.

However, the need for improving the competitive strength of small industry through technology improvement and modernization was recognized as early as in the 1950s with the setting up of Small Industries Development Organization (SIDO) and a network of Small Industries Service Institutes (SISIs), National Small Industries Corporation (NSIC) and National Research Development Corporation (NRDC). Since then, over a period of time, particularly in the 1990s exclusive technology infrastructure has come up for small industry to facilitate technology transfer (Bala Subrahmanya, M.H., *et al.*, 2002). Thus, Policy Makers in India have considered technology development in small industry only from a single dimension, that is, through institutional technology transfer. This implies that small industry in India is perennially external technology dependant.

How far technological infrastructure meant for small industry has helped the sector is another issue. For example, the Technology Bureau for Small Enterprises (TBSE) which was set up in 1995 through the collaboration of United Nations' Asian and Pacific Centre for Transfer of Technology (UN-APCTT) and Small Industries Development Bank of India (SIDBI), as an endeavour to bridge the technology gap, attended so far to a total of 5793 enquiries, facilitated 29 technical collaborations and helped 124 small enterprises in identifying indigenous technologies, among others (SIDBI, 2002). Of course, the network of 28 Small Industries Service Institutes (SISIs) and 30 branches of SISIs have 45 common facility workshops spread across the country and they provide technical support services, among others (SIDO website). But they do not undertake any technology upgradation programme. The Integrated Technology Upgradation and Management Programme (UPTECH), which was launched in 1998 by SIDO, covers all the facets of technological improvements but the scheme was approved only for 12 clusters for implementation during the IX Plan (DCSSI, 1999). State Bank of India (SBI) has implemented Project Uptech scheme to catalyze technology upgradation in 19 small industry clusters and approved its implementation in another four clusters (Anantha Swamy, 2003). In addition, SIDBI has identified about 25 small industry clusters for structured intervention including technology upgradation (SIDBI, 2002). But India has 361 small and medium enterprise (SME) clusters (which are overwhelmingly predominant with small industries and the share of medium and large industries is nominal) and 1656 artisan clusters (SIDO website). Given this, it is not difficult to comprehend that the technology infrastructure would have made, at the most, only a marginal impact on the sector as a whole.

Timely availability of adequate finance is another issue, which crucially determines the survival and growth of small firms. Small firms are largely dependent on bank credit to meet their financing requirements while the big firms have alternative sources of finance (RBI, 2003). To ensure better financial infrastructure, Small Industries Development Bank of India (SIDBI) was set up in 1990. Today, SIDBI operates through the head office, five regional offices and 36 branch offices across the country (SIDBI, 2002). In addition, based on the recommendations of Nayak Committee set up by RBI (1992), 370 exclusive bank branches for small industry were set up by Public Sector Banks by 1998 (DCSSI, 1999). Further, as per Nayak Committee recommendations, Reserve Bank of India has directed banks to meet the working capital needs of small industry at the rate of 20 per cent of annual output subject to an individual upper limit of ₹ 20 million (DCSSI, 1999). However, despite the development of exclusive financial infrastructure for small industry, the growth in the amount of bank credit extended to small industry declined in the 1990s as compared to that of the 1980s (Table 18.5). In fact, the decline in the growth rate was more pronounced relative to total priority sector, medium and large scale industry sector and total non-food bank credit. As a result, credit to small industry as a percentage of non-food gross bank credit increased marginally from about 14 per cent in 1980-81 to 15.14 per cent in 1990-91 but decreased to 13 per cent in 2000-01. Further, the total bank credit extended to small industry as a percentage of small industry output declined marginally from about 9.4 per cent in 1993-94 to 8.7 per cent in 2000-01 (Table 18.6). This brings out that despite policy support, credit flow to small industry has actually declined relatively in the1990s.

Table 18.5: Sectoral Deployment of Non-Food Gross Bank Credit (Outstanding)

(₹ Millions)

Year	*Priority Sector **	*Small Industry*	*Medium and Large Industry*	*Non-Food Gross Bank Credit*
1980-81	85040	32290	99600	230450
1990-91	429150	171810	445080	1135130
2000-01	1544140	560020	1628370	4291620
Period	*Compound Average Growth Rate (%)*			
1980-81 to 1990-91	17.57	18.19	16.14	17.28
1990-91 to 2000-01	13.66	12.54	13.84	14.22

* Priority sector includes small industry, among others.

Source: RBI (2001).

Table 18.6: Bank Credit to Small Industry

(₹ Millions)

Year	*Bank Credit extended to Small Industry*	*Small Industry Output*	*Bank Credit as % of Output*
1993-94	226170	2416480	9.36
1997-98	435080	4626410	9.40
2000-01	560020	6454960	8.68

Marketing has been identified as one of the major problem areas of the small scale sector and it has been ranked, according to the Second Census of small scale industries, as the second most important reason for the closure of small industry units (SIDBI, 2002). It is quite logical and obvious. If small firms do not have access to reliable and efficient economic infrastructure, suffer, in general, from technological obsolescence and credit flow is not sufficient, they will not be able to produce quality goods and productivity will not be high either. In such a case, small firms will not be able to penetrate markets, national or international, even if marketing support is coming forth from government agencies.

In the 1990s, two major steps have been taken by the government to promote small industry marketing:

1. The scheme of establishing Sub-Contracting Exchanges (SCXs) by Non-Government Organizations (NGOs) and Industry Associations was launched in February 1995 (DCSSI, 1999). As a result, during 1995-2001, 27 such sub-contracting exchanges have been set up, in addition to the already existing 34 SCXs in the SISI network (SIDO website). One of the major objectives of sub-contracting exchanges is to develop sub-contracting relationship between small and large firms.
2. With a view to ensure that exporters from small scale sector exhibit their products in the International Exhibitions, required assistance and support is provided. Expenditure on account of space rent, handling and clearing charges, insurance and shipment charges etc. are met by the Office of the Development Commissioner (Small Scale Industries) under one of the plan schemes (SIDO website). In 2000-01, SIDO has participated in seven international trade fairs/exhibitions (SIDO website). During 1996-2001, SIDBI has conducted/participated in 18 trade

fairs/exhibitions, nationally as well as internationally (SIDBI, 2002). Both these schemes would have helped those small firms, which are modernized, efficient and produce quality goods. However, the proposed marketing of mass consumption items under common brand names by National Small Industries Corporation (NSIC) has not taken off at all even after 12 years of exclusive policy announcement for small industry, which contained the proposal.

Future Prospects of Small Scale Industry in India

The central issue of concern for the future growth of small industry is how to strengthen its competitiveness? First of all, if small industry has to thrive steadily, infrastructural bottlenecks must be overcome to enable them to compete on their own based on their inherent potential. And it is the responsibility of the Government to remove any structural bottleneck for small industry performance especially when market forces are given prominence through the removal of "protective elements". It is essential to provide the much-needed "level playing field" to small enterprises through infrastructure development. But overcoming the infrastructural bottlenecks for small enterprises is easier said than done.

Small enterprises in India have come up in an unplanned, uncontrolled and haphazard manner (CPCB, 2001). They have emerged anywhere and everywhere—closer to the location of resources as well as markets—in clusters as well as in a dispersed manner, in industrial, commercial and residential areas. Of these, the 2000 and odd small industry clusters vary in size with a population ranging from hundred to thousand units. Approximately, these clusters would account for 1/3 to 1/2 of the total small industry units in the country. A considerable majority of these clusters are natural and traditional skill based. By and large, these clusters lack reliable and efficient infrastructural facilities such as power, road, water, transportation and communications, information, technical inputs, etc.

Finally, irrespective of the degree of support extended by the government and irrespective of the amount of efforts put in by small industries and their associations, India is going to experience the emergence of small industry sector, which is qualitatively superior, technologically vibrant and internationally competitive, in the next five to ten years because the 'inefficient ones' are likely to vanish gradually. The objective of the Policy Makers as well as small industry associations should be to enable the sector to emerge vibrant and competitive without a considerable reduction in its size and thereby enable it to make a sustainable contribution to national income, output and exports.

Table 18.7: Swot Analysis of Indian Small Scale Industrial Sector

Strengths	*Weaknesses*
• Flexible Manufacturing system	• Inadequate capital for investment/ expansion
• Lower cost of production	• Inadequate working capital
• Low level of capital investment per unit of output and employment	• Expensive bank loan
• Utilization of local resources	• Technologically weak due to inadequate capital
• Inherent ability to innovate	• Weak bargaining power
• Ability to make quick adjustments to the changing economic and trading scenario	• Absence of brand equity for Made in India labels
• Operational Flexibility	• Lack of Development policy framework
• Knowledge of internal markets	• Product Reservation Policy
Opportunities	*Threats*
• Untapped exports potential in sectors such as computer software, leather and leather products, light engineering products, hand tools and implements, auto components and ancillaries, garments including hosiery	• Technological Obsolescence
	• Inadequate use of information and communication technologies
	• Slow adoption of quality culture
	• Poor infrastructure support
• Growing service sector	• International environmental agenda which is in stark contrast to low emphasis by Indian firms
• Sector and stability of access under the WTO regime	• Non-compliance with non-tariff barrier particularly environment, health and safety standards
• Tariff reduction by all countries	
• Phasing out of MFA	
• Establish backward forward linkages, both nationally and internationally	

Summary and Conclusions

Small industry in India finds itself in an intensely competitive environment since 1991, thanks to globalization, domestic economic liberalization and dilution of sector specific protective measures. As a result, its growth in terms of units, employment, output and exports has come down. This has resulted in less impressive growth in its contribution to national income and exports though not in terms of employment in the 90s. Lack of reliable and stable economic infrastructure, reduced growth of credit inflow and technological obsolescence, which together would have led to inferior quality and low productivity are the major banes of small industry in India.

But at the same time, international and national policy changes have thrown open new opportunities and markets to Indian small industry. Concerted efforts are needed both from the government and more importantly, from small industry itself to imbibe technological dynamism into Indian small industry. Technological upgradation and in-house technological innovations and promotion of inter-firm linkages need to be encouraged consciously and consistently. The benefits and need to go for technology development through either technology transfer or technological innovations or inter-firm linkages should be emphasized in the light of dimensions of global competition and its negative fallouts as well as positive opportunities, to small industry entrepreneurs through seminars and workshops at the local level. Financial infrastructure need to be broadened and adequate inflow of credit to the sector be ensured taking into consideration the growing investment demand including the requirements of technological transformation. Small industry should be allowed to come up only in designated industrial areas for better monitoring and periodic surveys through DICs should enable policy corrections from time to time. A technologically vibrant, internationally competitive small industry should be encouraged to emerge, to make a sustainable contribution to national income, employment and exports.

REFERENCES

Abid Hussain (Chairman) (1997): *Report of the Expert Committee on Small Enterprises*, New Delhi, January.

Anantha Swamy, M.K. (2003): "Incentives and Support for Technological Upgradation of SMEs", in Seminar on Technology Upgradation of SMEs, Background Paper, Kanara Chamber of Commerce, Mangalore, January.

Asian Development Bank (1997): *Korea: Study of the Manufacturing Sector with Special Reference to New Technology-Based Small & Medium Industries*, Programmes Department (East), Manila, December.

Awasthi, Krishna and Sebastian (1993): *Research Report on Impact of New*

Economic Policies on Small and Tiny Industries Sector, Entrepreneurship Development Institute of India, Ahmedabad.

Bala Subrahmanya, M. H. (1995): "Reservation Policy for Small Scale Industry: Has it Delivered the Goods?", *Review of Industry and Management, Economic and Political Weekly*, Mumbai, Volume XXX, No. 21, May 27, pp. M 51-M 54.

Bala Subrahmanya, M.H. (1998): "Shifts in India's Small Industry Policy", Small Enterprise Development, *An International Journal*, London, Vol. 9, No. 1, pp. 136-154.

Bala Subrahmanya, M.H. (2002a): "Small Scale Industry in the Liberalization Era: Emerging Dimensions of Needs for Finance" in (ed) N. Meenakshisundaram, *Financial Management in Small Enterprises*, Kanishka Publishers, Distributors, New Delhi.

Bala Subrahmanya, M.H. (2002b): "Small Industry in India in the Transitional Age-Coping with Challenges and Changes" paper presented at APO Symposium on Adaptation of SMEs in a Transitional Age-Coping with Challenges and Changes, held during 27-30 August 2002, at Taipei, Taiwan, Republic of China.

Bala Subrahmanya, M.H., M. Mathirajan, P. Balachandra, M.N. Srinivasan and Laxman Prasad (2002): *R&D and Technological Innovations in Small Scale Industries*, Allied Publishers (P) Ltd., New Delhi.

CPCB (Central Pollution Control Board) (2001): *Pollution Control in Small Scale Industries: Status and Needs*, Ministry of Environment and Forests, Government of India, New Delhi, December.

DCSSI (Development Commissioner, Small Scale Industries) (1999): Small Scale Sector, Department of SSI and A and RI, Ministry of Industry, Government of India, New Delhi.

Economic and Political Weekly (2003): "Automotive Components: New Rising Star", Editorial, Volume XXXVIII, No 27, July 5-11, pp. 2785.

Mathew, M. (2004), " Small Industry and Globalization", *Economic and Political Weekly*, Vol. XXXIX, No. 20, 15 May 2004, p. 1999-2000.

Nag, B. (2000), "WTO Regime and Its Implications for Indian Small and Medium Enterprises Sector", *SEDME*, Vol. 27, No. 3, September 2000, pp. 1-17.

Chapter 19

Globalization and the Banking Industry

Harneet Kaur

Introduction

The economic reforms undertaken by the Government of India in last two decades have their genesis in the diverse intellectual and political agenda of the developed nations which had looked for the market for their products worldwide. Such agenda aims at radically transforming the social and economic institutions throughout the globe.

The globalization can thus be described as a set of socio-economic changes so as to align with international practices and benchmarks leading to a transformation of economic conditions and institutions through the process of widening and deepening of international flow of trade, technology, capital, information and Human Resources within single integrated global market.

Globalization has changed the entire market dynamics across sectors. It is observed that the focus of gloablization is on the developing countries led by Brazil, Russia, India, China and South Africa popularly known as BRICS nations. It is mainly because the BRICS nations offer huge market potential for the proponents of globalization. The ideology of the champions of globalization is quite dominant It influences the thinking and the style of the policy makers in the target nations while also influencing political practices across the world spectrum. The proponents of globalization believe that the globalization would produce the best outcome for the growth and well being of humanity. The globalization as a tool supports convergence in international activities such as increasing the production of foreign goods and services, increase in consumer demand in emerging markets, railing barriers in international trade, rapidly changing technology and so on. Globalization has created mutual dependence between various countries in the global economy. The financial sectors including banking have been significantly influenced by the globalization of the world economy.

The important components of globalization include the following:

- Social Reforms
- Economic and financial Reforms
- Trade Reforms
- Institutional Reforms
- Market Reforms
- Regulatory Reforms
- Liberalization
- Privatization
- Technology Innovation and Development
- International Acquisition and Mergers
- Global Takeover and Buyouts

The process of reforms carried out in India has transformed the business of banking substantially. The business models of the Banks in India have undergone a shift from plain Vanila Banking to Universal Banking, manually driven to technology driven, regulated regime to deregulated regime, urban banking to rural banking and so on. On the other hand the process of globalization has greatly transformed the models of business in different sectors of the economy having linkages with the Banks. All these reforms have created a need for newer skill sets to manage the change caused by the globalization.

Basel III Framework: A Road to Resilient Banking System

Banks performs a function of financial intermediation, i.e. accepting deposits from the savers and lending to the borrowers, and, in the process, facilitate efficient allocation of funds. In their role as financial intermediaries, banks undertake transformation—of risk, size and maturity, and play a catalytic role in the economic growth. Banks are a critical link in the transmission mechanism of monetary policy and enable efficient transmission of policy actions. Thus, banks play a very important role in the overall economy. Banking in India has a long history and its evolution makes an interesting case study. It has evolved over a period into a resilient system and has received international acclaim for surviving the Global crisis without any major impact.

A strong and resilient banking system is the basis for sustainable economic growth, as banks are at the centre of the credit intermediation process between savers and investors. Moreover, banks provide critical services to consumers, small and medium-sized enterprises, large corporate firms and governments who rely on them to conduct their daily business, both at a domestic and international level (Bank for International Settlements, 2011). The international regulatory authorities have taken several measures over the period of time in the form of Basel I and Basel II to make the global banking system sound and stable.

But the financial crisis that began in 2007 in U.S. and had spill-over effect infecting many countries of the world revealed the weakness in global regulatory framework (Basel II) in maintaining the soundness of the banking system. There are many reasons responsible for the occurrence of crisis and the most significant ones are inadequate quantity and quality of capital, insufficient liquidity buffers, excessively leveraged financial institutions, inadequate coverage of certain risks, absence of a regulatory framework to address systemic risks in the financial system, poorly understood financial products, vicious incentive structure in securitization process and inadequate regulation and supervision (Sinha, 2011).

To plug the loopholes in capital rules and address the market failures revealed by the crisis, the Basel Committee has introduced a number of fundamental reforms in the form of Basel 'III' to make the banking sector more resilient. Basel III has been designed to address all the shortcomings that have surfaced in the wake of the crisis including the very important issue of systemic risk.

On 16 December, 2010, the Basel Committee on Banking Supervision (Basel Committee) had published the Basel III rules with an objective to reducing the probability and severity of future crisis. 'Learning the shock absorbing capacity of each and every individual bank as the first order of defence and in the worst case scenario, if it is inevitable that one or few banks have to fail, Basel III has measures to ensure that the banking system as a whole does not crumble and its spill-over impact on the real economy is minimized' (Mahapatra, 2012).

Nout Wellink, Chairman of the Basel Committee on Banking Supervision and President of the Netherlands Bank, described the Basel in Framework as "a landmark achievement that will help to protect financial stability and promote sustainable economic growth. The higher levels of capital, combined with a global liquidity framework, will significantly reduce the probability and severity of banking crises in the future" (Bank for International Settlements, 2010). These reforms are intended to reinforce the bank-level or micro prudential regulation, which will help to raise the resilience of individual banking institutions in the periods of stress. Basel III also covers the macro prudential aspect, addressing system-wide risks that can build up across the banking sector as well as the procyclical amplification of these risks over time. Clearly these micro and macro prudential approaches to supervision are interrelated, as greater resilience at the individual bank level reduces the risk of system-wide shocks (Bank for International Settlements, 2011).

Basel III is typically an enhancement to Basel II (shown in Figure 19.1) as it is built on three pillars of Basel II in framework. Basel III has tinkered the various existing requirements (risk weighted assets, capital structure etc.) and added a host of new ones. Basel III elevates both the quality and quantity of the regulatory capital base and augments die risk coverage of the capital framework along with more strengthened market discipline.

Key Features of Basel III

Basel III incorporates several new measures on the existing Basel III framework. New elements in the form of liquidity requirements/leverage ratio, procyclicality measures have been introduced and it also involves enhancement of minimum capital requirements and risk coverage to make the financial system stronger. Basel III combines both micro and macro-prudential reforms to address both institution and system level risks. So, the focus is on financial stability of the system as a whole along with micro regulation of individual bank. These quantitative capital requirements will be reinforced by more stringent qualitative capital standards. The key features of Basel III have been summarized in Table 19.1.

Micro-prudential Regulations

The Basel III framework incorporates various reforms to deal with bank-level or institution-level risks and changes:

- **Global liquidity standard:** Many financial institutions experienced liquidity difficulties during 2007 financial crisis, despite meeting their regulatory capital requirements. Moreover,

Table 19.1: Key features of Basel III Framework

Nature of Regulation	*Features*	*Key Aspects*
Micro-prudential	Global Liquidity Standard	Liquidity Coverage Ratio (LCR) Net Stable Funding Ratio Set of Common monitoring metrics
Micro-prudential	Enhanced Minimum Capital Requirements	Increasing the quantity and enhancing the quality and transparency of capital base Tier I capital must consist predominantly of common equity and retained earnings Common Equity Tier I must be at least 4.5% of risk-weighted assets Tier I Capital must be at least 6.0% of risk-weighted assets Tier III capital instruments are eliminated
Micro-prudential	Enhanced Risk Coverage	Higher Capital requirements for trading and securitization activities Enhancements to Pillar 2's supervisory review process and Pillar 3's market discipline, particularly for trading and securitization activities Capital requirement for certain counterparty credit risk exposures based on stressed inputs Incorporation of IQSCO's Code of Conduct Fundamentals for Credit Rating Agencies to mitigate the reliance on external ratings of the Basel II framework Capital charge for potential mark-to-market losses Additional standards to strengthen collateral risk management practices
Macro-prudential	Leverage Ratio	A non-risk-weighted minimum leverage ratio of Tier I Capital to Total exposure is introduced as a supplementary measure to enhance the risk absorbency of individual banks and address the concern about leverage in the financial system
Macro-prudential	Addressing Procyclicality	Forward looking provisions prescribed Introduction of Capital Conservation buffer Introduction of Countercyclical buffer Addressing systematic risks and interconnections

Source: Compiled from "Basel III: A Global Regulatory Framework for More Resilient Banks and Banking Systems", BIS, 2011.

there were no internationally agreed and harmonized liquidity standards. The financial crisis highlighted the importance of liquidity risk and now it is viewed as a risk as grave to a financial institution as credit, market, and operational risk (Gassmann *et al.*, 2011). So, Basel III introduces two new liquidity ratios to manage the pressure on liquidity in a stress scenario:

(i) ***Liquidity Coverage Ratio***: Liquidity Coverage Ratio (LCR) is introduced to promote resilience to short term liquidity disruptions over a 30-day horizon. At a minimum, the stock of liquid assets should enable the bank to survive until 30th day of the stress scenario, by which time it is assumed that appropriate corrective actions can be taken:
Liquidity Coverage Ratio = Stock of high quality liquid assets/Net cash outflows over the next 30 days *100 > 100 per cent.

(ii) ***Net Stable Funding Ratio:*** Net Stable Funding Ratio (NSFR) intends to strengthen the banks' resilience to long term liquidity crisis. The NSFR is designed to ensure that long term assets are funded with at least a minimum amount of stable liabilities in relation to their liquidity risk profiles (Reserve Bank of India, 2012).
Net Stable Funding Ratio = Available Stable Funding (ASF)/ Required Stable Funding (RSF) *100 >100 per cent
Such a stringent approach to liquidity risk supervision is indeed rather new in the regulatory framework (Barua *et al.* 2010). Monitoring metrics are also introduced in relation to specific areas like contractual maturity mismatches and concentration of funding.

- ***Enhanced Minimum Capital Requirements:*** Definition of capital has been redefined under the new framework. Basel III framework emphasizes that the predominant form of Tier 1 capital must comprise of common shares and retained earnings and Common Equity Tier 1 component has been raised from 2 per cent to 4.5 per cent. Deductions from capital and prudential filters have been harmonized internationally and Tier 3 capital instruments are eliminated. Minimum Tier 1 capital as a percentage of risk-weighted assets is raised from 4 per cent to 6 per cent—thereby improving the overall level of high quality capital in banks.
- ***Enhanced Risk Coverage:*** One of the major focuses of the Basel III is to strengthen the risk coverage in response to shortcomings of the Basel II accord. So, Basel III framework covered various strands of risks not addressed or partially addressed under Basel II. It stipulated higher capital requirements for trading and

securitization activities and introduced new risk weights to better capture risks in trading portfolios. Moreover, it also stipulated enhanced guidelines on Pillars 2's supervisory review process and Pillar 3's market discipline, particularly for trading and securitization activities. Under new framework, banks must determine their capital requirement for counter party credit risk under stressed inputs. Further, banks will be subject to a capital charge for potential mark to market losses (i.e. credit evaluation adjustment-CVA-risk) associated with deterioration in the creditworthiness of counterparty.

The Basel Committee also assessed and introduced number of measures to mitigate the reliance on external ratings of the Basel III framework. The measures include requirements for banks to perform their own internal assessments of externally rated securitization exposures, the elimination of certain "cliff effects" associated with credit risk mitigation practices, and the incorporation of key elements of the IOSCO Code of Conduct Fundamentals for Credit Rating Agencies into the Committee's eligibility criteria for the use of external ratings in the capital framework (Bank for International Settlements, 2011). Thus, the Basel III framework will have enhanced risk coverage.

Macro-prudential Regulations

The Basel Committee has incorporated certain macro-prudential regulations under the Basel III framework to address the concerns about financial system as a whole that will lean against the wind to take care of issues relating to the systematic risks (Mahapatra, 2012).

The macro-prudential regulations covered under Basel III are:

- ***Leverage Ratio:*** The Basel Committee has introduced a non-risk-weighted minimum leverage; ratio of Tier 1 capital to total exposures (including on-balance sheet and off-balance sheet items) to constrain leverage in the banking sector, thus helping to mitigate the risk of the destabilizing deleveraging processes which can damage the financial system and the economy (Bank for International Settlements, 2011). This measure will affect all business areas that are perceived as low-risk but that inflate the balance sheet (for example, the repo business). During a test period from 2011 to 2017, the ratio will be set at 3 per cent.

Then, after a final review, a new ratio will be set for 2018 onward (Gassman *et al.*, 2011).

- ***Addressing Procyclicality***: One of the most destabilizing elements of the crisis has been the procyclical amplification of financial shocks throughout the banking system, financial markets and the broader economy (Bank for International Settlements, 2011). The Basel III framework also contains the measures like capital conservation and countercyclical capital buffer to reduce the cyclical effects of Basel III. The primary objective to introduce such measures is to ensure that banking sector serves as a shock absorber instead of transmitter of risks to financial economy.
    (i) ***Capital conservation buffer***: The minimum amount of capital conservation buffer of 2.5 per cent of common equity Tier 1 will be maintained thus, bringing the total common equity capital requirements to 7 per cent. In times of financial stress, banks can draw on the buffer provided that, if they do so, earnings distributions such as bonuses and dividends are limited and when buffer is drawn banks must find ways to rebuild it.
    (ii) ***Counter cyclical capital buffer***: The countercyclical capital buffer is aimed at ensuring that banking sector capital requirements take account of the macro-financial environment in which banks operate. To address the procyclicality additional countercyclical buffer-that could range from 0 per cent to 2.5 per cent of risk-weighted assets are to be built to protect the banking sector from system-wide risks arising out of excessive credit growth. Furthermore, banks will be subjected to the restrictions on distributions also if the capital-level (capital conservation buffer this countercyclical buffer) falls below the required levels during the periods when the countercyclical capital buffer is in force.
    (iii) ***Additional requirements for systemically important financial institutions***: Basel Committee will group G-SIB (Globally Systematic Important Banks) with assets of US $ 100 bn or more into different categories of systematic importance based on the score produced by the indicator based measurement approach. Systemically important financial institutions could be subject to additional

requirements and tighter supervision based on the risks their failure poses to financial system.

All the elements incorporated under Basel III framework are intended to make banks more resilient. These measures are considered important to strengthen the regulation of banking sector. Mr. Nout Wellink, Chairman of the Basel Committee and President of the Netherlands Bank, stated that "these measures will result over time in higher capital and liquidity requirements and less leverage in the banking system, less procyclicality, greater banking sector resilience to stress and strong incentives to ensure that compensation practices are properly aligned with long-term performance and prudent risk taking" (Bank for International Settlements, 2009).

Implementation of Timeline Basel III framework was endorsed by Group of Governors and Heads of Supervision of member countries at the September 12, 2010 meeting of the central bank governors. The phase in period for implementation of guidelines will begin from January 1, 2013 while its full implementation is expected to be achieved till 2019. On January 1, 2013 minimum common equity ratio will be raised from current 2.5 per cent to 3.5 per cent and Total Tier I up to 45 per cent. The capital conservation buffer will be phased in between January 1, 2016 and the end of 2018. The market expects banks to comply with Basel III before the regulatory deadline pushing them to faster implementation (Bank for International Settlements, 2010).

Basel III Framework in Indian Banking Scenario

In order to make the Indian financial system safer from the impact of any potential global financial crisis, the RBI is fully committed to the objective of Basel III framework and it has also released draft regulations of Basel III for Indian banking sector on 30 December 2011 and 21 February, 2012, respectively. RBI has adopted a bit conservative approach in India as compared to its international counterparts, by setting more demanding schedule for Basel III. Implementation of Basel III in India is proposed to be fully implemented by March 31, 2017 as compared to January 1, 2019 deadline proposed by the Basel Committee for its implementation around the globe. The minimum regulatory requirement of CRAR in India at present 9 per cent, higher than BIS norm of 8 per cent and Indian Banks are required to maintain Tier 1 capital at 6 per cent.

Key Elements of RBI Draft Guidelines on Basel III Framework

- Minimum Tier I capital of 7 per cent of Risk Weighted Assets (RWAs) to be maintained by banks on an ongoing basis.
- Banks have to maintain Common Equity Ratio of at least 5.5 per cent, and a minimum total capital of at least 9 per cent of RWAs on an ongoing basis.
- Additional capital conservation buffer (CCB) in the form of common equity will be build up to2.5 per cent which is proposed to be achieved by banks till March 2017. Hence, the total capital requirements would be 11.5 per cent of Risk Weighted Assets.
- Instruments which no longer qualify as regulatory capital instruments will be phased-out during the period beginning from January1, 2013 to March 31, 2022.
- Two minimum global regulatory standards, viz. LCR and NSFR, will become binding from 1 January, 2015 and 1 January, 2018, respectively.
- For the first time banks will need to maintain a leverage ratio, which will limit their ability to leverage. Banks will be expected to operate at a minimum Tier 1 leverage ratio of 5 per cent between 2013 and 2017 (www.economictimes.com).

The Reserve Bank has projected stricter norms for banks in India as part of a plan to migrate to the Basel III framework to create a healthier and safer banking system. According to the Report published by S&P on RBI's Basel III guidelines, Basel III may have negative effect on the credit growth of a few banks in India. But, if the guidelines are implemented in proper sense it will benefit Indian banks' credit profiles. In the view of International credit rating agency 'Moody', draft guidelines by RBI reflects its policy of ensuring that Indian banks have extra stress absorption capacity if the operating environment worsens.

Implications of Basel III Framework in India

- Additional capital Infusion
- Data Issues
- Substantial Impact on Return on Equity
- High Compliance Cost
- Liquidity Issues
- Macroeconomic Costs
- Sound Risk Architecture

Conclusion

New Basel III framework is an opportunity to make the global financial system more secure and stable. The feature that distinguishes Basel III from previous attempts to improve the financial system is its focus on structurally improving the balance sheets of financial institutions. If Basel III is implemented in principle, it will improve the banks' competitiveness in every aspect, but the task of integrating it is challenging.

Basel III requirements expose banks across the globe to major challenges regarding their capital and liquidity requirements, as well as their risk management. The prime challenge for affected banks will be to act upon the actions mandated by Basel III to create stronger capital and risk structures. So, there is need to adopt several measures to enhance the ability of banks for its envisaged application. Banks need to consider the Basel III as an opportunity to put their houses in order and adopt world class risk management practices, instead of taking a technical approach towards framework around meeting compliance requirement. For every bank, designing the most cost-effective model for implementing Basel III will be a critical issue.

Banks should develop data systems based on common data inputs to derive market, credit and liquidity risk. There should also be an integrated reporting approach across risk types to give senior managers and investors a consistent view across the enterprise of the impact of different types of risk. The Basel III norms require more risk sensitivity, and, hence, more complex measurement techniques and sound regulatory framework to create a healthier banking system.

Implementing the proposed Basel III norms will strengthen the core banking sector and improve its resilience to systemic shocks in the economy.

REFERENCES

Bank for International Settlements (2012), "Consultative Proposals to Strengthen the Resilience of the Banking Sector", retrieved from: http://www.bis.org/press/ p091217.htm on Dec 15,2012

Economic Times: economictimes. indiatimes.com

CRISIL (2012), RBI's Basel guidelines to strengthen Banks Capitalization-Press Release.

rbidocs./rbi.org.in/rdocs/bulletin/PDFs/IOSPBULO90412.pdf

rbi.docs.rbi.org.in/rdocs/notification/PDFs/70BIIIMC010713.pdf

Barua; R., Battaglia, F., Jagannathan, R., Mendis, J., Onorato, M. (2010), Basel III: What's new? Business and technological challenges. Algorithmics.

Sinha, A. (2011), "Macroprudential policies—Indian Experience" address at 11th Annual International Seminar in Policy Challenges for the Financial Sector, co-hosted by the Board of Governors of the Federal Reserve System, IMF and the World Bank, Washington.

Chapter 20

Globalization and Its Impact on Retail Sector in India

Gaurav Vats

Introduction

Retailing consists of the sale of goods or merchandise for personal or household consumption from a fixed location such as a shopping mall or store. Retail means selling goods and services in small quantities directly to customers. Retailing consists of all activities involved in marketing of goods and services directly to consumer for their personal, family and household use. The Indian retailing industry is becoming intensely competitive, as more and more players are looking for the same set of customers. Although still at a nascent stage, organized retailing in India is witnessing a radical transformation. The increase in the number of retail chains across the country is an indication that organized retailing is emerging as an industry and will boom in a big way in the near future.

Retailers are at the end of the supply chain. Marketers see retailing as part of their overall distribution strategy. Retail comes from the French word retaillier which refers to "cutting off, clip and divide" in terms of tailoring. It first was recorded as a noun with the meaning of a "sale in small quantities" in 1433 (French). In both Dutch and German it refers to sale of small quantities.

International trade and commerce has existed for centuries and played a very important part in the World History. However, International Retailing has been in existence and has gained ground in the past two to three decades. The economic boom in several countries, coupled with globalization has given way to organizations looking at setting up retailing across borders. The advent of internet and multimedia has further changed the dimensions as far as International Retailing is concerned. International Retailing and branding has been one of the sectors that is seeing exponential growth. With increase in standard of living and disposable income, people in developing countries are getting exposed to international brands. Rise of internet and multi-media has further provided impetus to the dream of people to aspire for branded consumer goods. Along with the rising awareness and aspirations of the people, the opening up of economies and foreign direct investment opportunities have fuelled the growth of international retailing business.

Review of Literature

Bhel (2012) aimed to highlight the present scenario of retail in India. Further, efforts have been made to analyse growth sector-wise organised retail market in India and suggest policy implications to accelerate the growth in Indian retail market.

Mehta (2009) attempted to identify retailers challenges in two broad groups, namely 'inherent challenges' and 'external challenges' which a retailer comes across and develop strategies to face them under two broad groups, namely maintenance and motivation strategies.

Leknes & Carr (2004) aimed to study retail internationalization from a strategic perspective. Despite being developed on the basis of a study of manufacturing industries, Calori's framework of strategic configurations has proved reasonably applicable to retailing, though we also found it helpful to incorporate McKinsey's 'global shaper' configuration. Combined with performance data, the analysis suggested insights on international strategic options for clothing retailers and practical recommendations. Study's most confident statistical result is clothing's much greater profitability in comparison to that of other retail sectors. This endorses Varner Gruppen's decision not to consider diversification out of clothing. Other significant statistical results suggest that worldwide specialists, global luxury niche players, geographic niche players and quasi-global players are less profitable to the extent of 32 per cent, 24 per cent, 8 per cent and 7 per cent respectively, compared to all other strategic configurations.

Burt (2011) analysed IKEA's marketing strategies in three countries from a standardisation/adaptation perspective. The study has systematically assesses the degree of standardization (and adaptation) of four commonly identified retail marketing mix activities—merchandise, location and store format, the selling and service environment, and market communication—within three countries. The data upon which the comparison is based was generated from personal interviews, in-country consumer research, company documentation and third party commentaries. The conclusions suggested that whilst IKEA operates a standardized concept, degrees of adaptation can be observed in customer facing elements, and in the supporting 'back office' processes which support these elements. Boyle (2006) observed that Wal-Mart is going on the offensive when it comes to ethics. They have recently established a Global Ethics Office and staffed it with 10 individuals to oversee potential ethical issues within the business. Burns (2007) presented a study of collegiate students' opinions regarding ethical issues from both developed and non-developed countries. Each student was presented with a questionnaire detailing several retail situations and was asked for their opinion to determine the outcome. The study also discussed the various perceptions of ethics and how they vary from culture to culture.

Evolution of Retail Market in India

Retail sector in India has evolved to support the unique needs of our country, given its size and complexity *Haats, Mandis* and *Melas* have been a part of Indian Retail market. The Public Distribution System (PDS) as the single largest retail chain existing in the country, the origin of PDS in India in "*Rationing System*" introduced by the British during World War II. It was started in 1939 in Bombay and extended to other cities and towns. There was rapid increase in the ration shops called as Fair Price Shops.

The *Khadi and Village Industries* (KVIC) was also set up post-independence. The cooperative movement was again boosted by the government.

In recent trends, Indian market place has transformed dramatically. However, from 1950s to the 1980s investment in various industries was limited due to low purchasing power of consumers and the government's policies favouring the small scale sector.

Retailing is one of the biggest sectors and it is witnessing a revolution in India. The new entrant in retailing in India signifies the beginning of retail revolution. The Windows of Opportunity shows that Retailing in India was at opening stage in 1995. India has started emerging as a new market for all the global players because of changing demand and growing economy. The economy is one of the biggest magnetic factors which is

Evolution of Retail in India

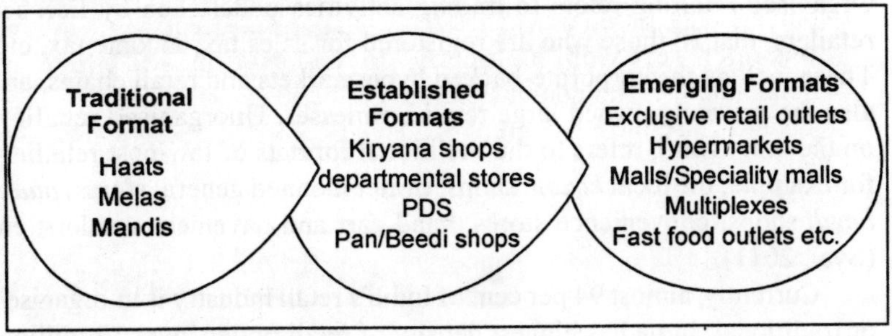

pilling every major retail player outside this economy to enter and get the biggest possible bite of the cake as the cake called Indian market is the most tempting one today.

India presents a large market opportunity given the number and increasing purchasing power of consumers, there are significant challenges as well given that over 90 per cent of trade is conducted through independent local stores. Challenges include: Geographically dispersed population, small ticket sizes, complex distribution network, little use of IT systems, limitations of mass media and existence of counterfeit goods.

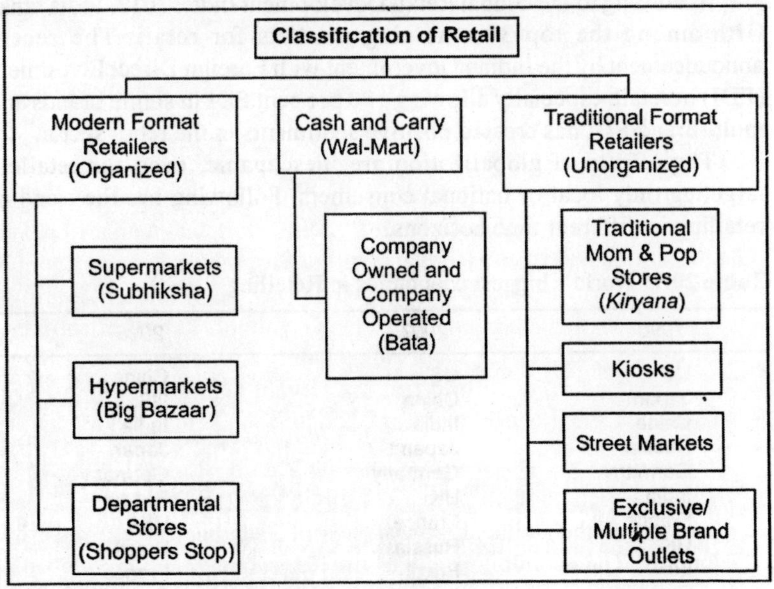

The retail industry is divided into organised and unorganized sectors. Organised retailing refers to trading activities undertaken by licensed retailers, that is, those who are registered for sales tax, income tax, etc. These include the corporate-backed hypermarkets and retail chains, and also the privately owned large retail businesses. Unorganised retailing, on the other hand, refers to the traditional formats of low-cost retailing, for example, the local *kirana* shops, owner manned general stores, *paan/ beedi* shops, convenience stores, hand cart and pavement vendors, etc (Syal, 2011).

Currently, almost 94 per cent of India's retail industry is unorganised or traditional. India has highest density of retail outlets over 12 million. The retail sector contributes about 10-11 per cent to Indian GDP (Behl, 2012). In contemporary scenario the relevance of completive advantage comes from emerging malls and modern format stores opening up, not only in the fast moving metros but also in the bustling smaller cities and towns which are far closer to what is the real India.

Retail industry, being the fifth largest in the world, is one of the sunrise sectors with huge growth potential and accounts for 14-15 per cent of the country's GDP. Comprising of organized and unorganized sectors, Indian retail industry is one of the fastest growing industries in India, especially over the last few years.

According to the Global Retail Development Index 2012, India ranks fifth among the top 30 emerging markets for retail. The recent announcement by the Indian Government with Foreign Direct Investment (FDI) in retail, especially allowing 100 per cent FDI in single brands and multi-brand FDI has created positive sentiments in the retail sector.

The effects of globalization are inescapable, even for retailers targeting only local or national consumers. Following has the trend of retailing in different time horizons.

Table 20.1: World's biggest economies in Retailing

1990	*2007*	*2025*
US	US	China
Japan	China	US
China	India	India
Russia	Japan	Japan
Germany	Germany	Germany
India	UK	Russia
France	France	UK
UK	Russia	Brazil
Italy	Brazil	France
Brazil	Italy	South Korea

Table 20.2: 2012 Global Retail Development Index

2012 Rank	*Country*	*Region*	*Market attractive-ness (25%)*	*Country Risk (25%)*	*Market saturation (25%)*	*Time Pressure (25%)*	*GRDI Score*	*Change in rank compared to 2011(1)*
1	Brazil	Latin America	100.0	85.4	48.2	61.6	73.8	0
2	Chile	Latin America	86.6	100.0	17.4	57.1	65.3	0
3	China	Asia	53.4	72.6	29.3	100.0	63.8	+3
4	Uruguay	Latin America	84.1	56.1	60.0	52.3	63.1	–1
5	India	Asia	31.0	66.7	57.6	87.9	60.8	–1
6	Georgia	Central Asia	27.0	68.7	92.6	54.0	60.6	N/A
7	United Arab Emirates	MENA	86.1	93.9	9.4	52.9	60.6	+1
8	Oman	MENA	69.3	98.3	17.4	50.4	58.9	N/A
9	Mongolia	Asia	6.4	54.4	98.2	75.1	58.5	N/A
10	Peru	Latin America	43.8	55.5	62.9	67.2	57.4	–3
11	Malaysia	Asia	56.7	98.1	18.9	54.8	57.1	+8
12	Kuwait	MENA	81.1	88.7	36.4	20.3	56.6	–7
13	Turkey	Eastern Europe	78.8	69.3	32.3	33.1	53.4	–4
14	Saudi Arabia	MENA	63.1	81.8	35.4	33.0	53.3	–4
15	Sri Lanka	Asia	12.7	68.3	79.0	51.3	52.8	+6
16	Indonesia	Asia	39.6	61.6	47.0	62.4	52.7	–1
17	Azerbaijan	Central Asia	19.2	41.5	93.6	53.2	51.9	N/A
18	Jordan	MENA	45.8	65.3	69.5	23.8	51.1	N/A
19	Kazakhstan	Central Asia	31.5	47.5	75.5	47.5	50.5	–5
20	Botswana	Sub-Saharan Africa	44.4	88.1	42.7	23.7	49.7	N/A
21	Macedonia	Eastern Europe	34.6	46.5	55.9	56.6	48.4	+8
22	Lebanon	MENA	60.2	30.2	48.9	54.2	48.4	–10
23	Colombia	Latin America	47.8	70.1	36.7	36.6	47.8	+1
24	Panama	Latin America	53.4	68.8	42.0	25.2	47.4	+2
25	Albania	Eastern Europe	24.6	47.6	74.8	39.9	46.7	–12
26	Russia	Eastern Europe	80.2	53.6	19.6	32.2	46.4	–15
27	Morocco	MENA	23.5	58.2	48.2	49.2	44.8	–7
28	Mexico	Latin America	71.9	70.0	15.1	20.3	44.3	–6
29	Philippines	Asia	28.3	54.6	52.5	38.3	43.4	–13
30	Tunisia	MENA	35.7	55.4	65.0	14.4	42.6	–12

Emerging Areas in Retail Industry

Some sectors that occupy a prominent position with the retail industry are:

Apparel Retail: Everybody understands the impact of fashion and textiles on the environment. Almost $19.5 billion were spent on online apparel shopping in the year 2009 and increasing since then.

Fashion and Lifestyle Retail: In India the vast middle class and its almost untapped retail industry are the key attractive forces for global retail giants wanting to enter into newer markets, which in turn will help the retail to grow faster.

Food and Beverage Retail: Backed by huge potential and changing lifestyles, the food and beverage retail market is growing at a robust 30-35 per cent per year.

Pharmaceutical Retail: Driven by therapies like anti-diabetic, vitamin, anti-infectives and dermatology, it accounted for a robust 15 per cent growth in 2011.

E-commerce or E-tailing – the next big revolution: With the advent of e-commerce in the retail industry, retail stores are facing stiff competition from e-stores. The rising demand for e-shopping has lead to a new debate cropping up in the world.

Table 20.3: Porter's Five Forces to influence Retail Industry

Supply	Players are now moving to Tier II and Tier III cities to increase penetration and explore untapped markets as Tier I cities have been explored enough and have reached a saturation level.
Demand	Healthy economic growth, changing demographic profile, increasing disposable incomes, changing consumer tastes and preferences are some of the key factors that are driving and will continue to drive growth in the organised retail market in India.
Barriers to entry	Reforms by India in opening up its economy have greatly improved trade prospects, but major barriers still exist such as regulatory issues, supply chain complexities, inefficient infrastructure, and automatic approval not being allowed for foreign investment in retail. But, some of these are set to change with FDI in multi-brand retail set for approval.
Bargaining power of suppliers	The bargaining power of suppliers varies depending upon the target segment, the format followed, and products on offer. The unorganised sector has a dominant position, still contributing 95 per cent of the total retail market. There are few players who have a slight edge over others on account of being established players and enjoying brand distinction. Since it is a capital intensive industry, access to capital also plays an important part for expansion in the space.
Bargaining power of customers	High due to wide availability of choice. With FDI coming in, this will increase further.
Threat/Competition	High Competition is characterised by many factors, including assortment, products, price, quality, service, location, reputation, credit and availability of retail space etc. New entrants (business houses and international players) are expected to further intensify the competition and so would the foreign players' entry.

The Five Forces that shape Industry Competition

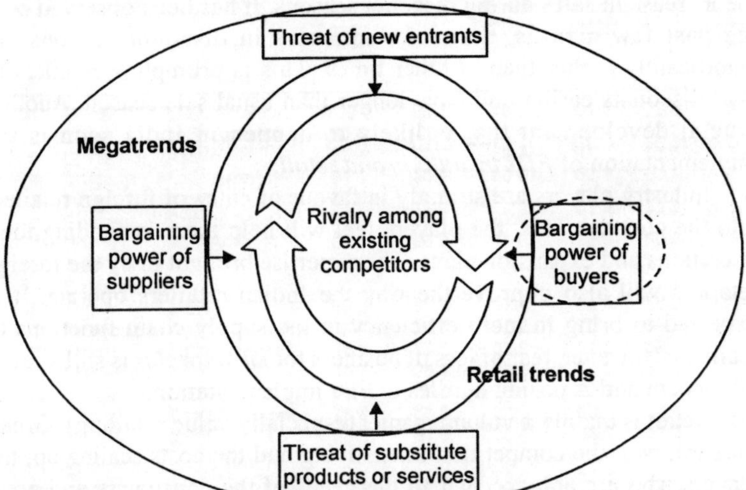

Source: *Adapted from*: The Five Competitive Forces That Shape Strategy" by Michael E. Porter, *Harvard Business Review*, January 2008, page 80.

Factors Driving Growth Rate are:

- Emergence of nuclear families.
- Falling real estate prices.
- Growing trend of double-income households.
- Increase in disposable income and customer aspiration.
- Increase in expenditure for luxury items.
- Large working population.
- Low share of organized retailing.
- Growing liberalization of the FDI policy in the past decade.

Conclusion, Future Prospects and Challenges in Retail Industry

Retail industry has been on a growth trajectory over the past few years. With the economy back on track, retailers are executing their expansion plans. The industry is expected to grow at a rate of 12 per cent per annum for the next 5 years.

Retail industry has been on a growth trajectory over the past few years. The industry is expected to grow at a rate of 12 per cent per annum for the next 5 years. A significant new trend emerging in retail sector is the increase in sales during discount seasons. It has been observed over the past few months, that sales numbers in discount seasons are significantly higher than at other times. This is prompting retailers to start discounts earlier and have longer than usual sale season. Another crucial development that is likely to happen in India soon is the implementation of *FDI in multi brand retail*.

Industry players are strongly in favour of entry of foreign retailers into the country. This, the players feel will help them in funding their operations and expansion plans. The expertise brought in by the foreign retailers will also improve the way the Indian retailers operate. It is expected to bring in more efficiency in the supply chain functions of retailers. However, fear of loss of business for *kiranawalas* is still a cause of concern and is posing hurdles in FDI implementation.

Retail is mainly a volume game, (especially value retailing). Going forward, with the competition intensifying and the costs scaling up, the players who are able to cater to the needs of the consumers and grow volumes by ensuring footfalls, while being able to reduce costs, withstand downturns, and face competition will have a competitive advantage.

Luxury Retailing is gaining importance in India. This includes fragrances, gourmet retailing, accessories, jewellery among many others. Indian consumer is ready to splurge on luxury items and is increasingly doing so. The Indian luxury market is expected to grow at a rate of 25 per cent per annum. This will make India the 12th largest luxury retail market in the world.

Rural retailing is now the focus for many retailers. It is observed that the rural regions registered saw consumption even during the economic slowdown. Rural India accounts for 2/5th of the total consumption in India. Thus, the industry players do not want to be left out and are devising strategies suited especially to the rural consumer.

Challenges in Retailing

There are various reasons for changing customer needs and preferences:

1. Single family concepts,
2. Dual Income concepts,
3. Limited to One children concepts,
4. Willing to spend concepts,

5. Brand Preference concepts, and
6. Personal and Health Care concepts.

Retailing sector need to be improved at a faster pace, following are some barriers in the way of system itself:

- A long way to meet international standards,
- Lack of efficient supply-chain management,
- Lack of required retail space,
- No fixed consumption pattern,
- Shortage of trained manpower, and
- Lack of proper infrastructure and distribution channels.

REFERENCES

Behl, S. (2012), "The New Retail Tale in Global Scenario", EXCEL *International Journal of Multidisciplinary Management Studies*, Vol. 2 (9): pp. 44-56.

Boyle, M. (2006). Wal-Mart: desperately seeking ethics. Retrieved January 27, 2006, from Business Source complete database.

Burns, D. Retail ethics as appraised by future business personnel in Malaysia and the US. Retrieved January 24, 2007, from Business Source Complete database.

Burt, S., Johansson U., Thelander A. (2011), "Standardized marketing strategies in retailing IKEA's marketing strategies in Sweden, the UK and China", *Journal of Retailing and Consumer Services*, Vol. 18, pp. 183-193.

Leknes, H.M. and Carr C. (2004), "Globalisation, International Configurations and Strategic Implications: The Case of Retailing", *Long Range Planning*, Vol. 37, pp. 29-49.

Mehta, J.D. (2009), "Overcoming the Challenges of the Changing Retail Scenario in India to Gain Competitive Advantage", *Management & Change*, Vol.13 (1): pp. 89-97.

"Retailing Sector Analysis Report", www.equitymaster.com

Syal, H. (2011), "Retailing in India-Future Perspective", *International Journal of Research in Finance & Marketing*, Vol. 1(8): pp. 66-75.

www.retailtrafficmag.com

www.chainstorage.com

Chapter 21

Changing Face of Business Ethics in Globalization

Manjit Kour

Introduction

The market economy has become increasingly global. Leaders in business, government, and non-governmental organizations (NGOs) now see global economic development as "the best way to increase prosperity within and among countries, and to create opportunities for millions of people, especially in the developing world, to secure a decent life for themselves and their children." The challenge is to find the right balance between emerging global norms, values, and standards and local cultures, business practices, and community needs. Businesses in emerging market economies face many challenges For example, although no society *approves* of paying or accepting bribes, in societies where workers receive lower than subsistence-level pay, "expediting fees" (also known as "bribes") often become unapproved but *accepted* behaviour under local custom. In such societies, bribery is so common that even law enforcement officials pay bribes to gain their positions.

We live in an age of innovation, the growth of free markets, and a world economy. New technologies, roles for government, and players on the global scene offer challenging opportunities, demands, and constraints. More peoples and nations are working together to spread freedom and democratic principles; to nurture free markets; to protect individual property rights; and to encourage respect for human rights, the rule of law, and the environment. With increasing urgency, market and social forces are rewriting the roles and responsibilities of business as well.

Though the profit motive of business is understood and accepted, people do not accept it as an excuse for ignoring the basic norms, values, and standards of being a good citizen. Modern businesses are expected to be responsible stewards of community resources working toward then: growth and success of both their companies and their communities. Businesses are at the strategic centre of a civil society, and they have a stake in their communities. They depend on free markets and good public governance for their growth and success, but they are also authors of their own destiny. Through responsible business conduct, they contribute to the essential social capital of trust and fairness that makes good governance and free markets possible.

Globalization

Globalization is the new buzzword that has come to dominate the world since the nineties of the last century with the end of the cold war and the break-up of the former Soviet Union and the global trend towards the rolling ball. Globalization has brought in new opportunities to developing countries. Globalization involves the diffusion of ideas, practices and technologies. It is something more than internationalization and universalization. It isn't simply modernization or westernization. It is certainly isn't just the liberalization of markets. Anthony Giddens (1990: 64) has described globalization as 'the intensification of worldwide social relations which link distant localities in such a way that local happenings are shaped by events occurring many miles away and *vice versa*'. This involves a change in the way we understand geography and experience localness. As well as offering opportunity it brings with considerable risks linked, for example, to technological change.

Over many centuries, human societies across the globe have established progressively closer contacts. Recently, the pace of global integration has dramatically increased. Unprecedented changes in communications, transportation, and computer technology have given the process new impetus and made the world more interdependent than ever. Multinational corporations manufacture products in many countries and sell to consumers around the world. Money, technology and raw materials move ever more swiftly across national borders. Along with products and finances, ideas and cultures circulate more freely. As a result, laws, economies, and social movements are forming at the international level.

Greater access to developed country markets and technology transfer hold out promise improved productivity and higher living standard. But globalization has also thrown up new challenges like growing inequality across and within nations, volatility in financial market and environmental deteriorations. Another negative aspect of globalization is that a great majority of developing countries remain removed from the process. Till the nineties the process of globalization of the Indian economy was constrained by the barriers to trade and investment liberalization of trade, investment and financial flows initiated in the nineties has progressively lowered the barriers to competition and hastened the pace of globalisation

Business Ethics

Ethics has also been called the study and philosophy of human conduct, with an emphasis on determining right and wrong. *The American Heritage Dictionary* offers these definitions of ethics: "The study of the general nature of morals and of specific moral choices; moral philosophy; and the rules or standards governing the conduct of the members of a profession." Business ethics is the study of business situations, activities, and decisions where issues of right and wrong are addressed. One difference between an ordinary decision and an ethical one lies in "the point where the accepted rules no longer serve, and the decision maker is faced with the responsibility for weighing values and reaching a judgment in a situation which is not quite the same as any he or she has faced before." Another difference relates to the amount of emphasis that decision makers place on their own values and accepted practices within their company. Consequently, values and judgments play a critical role when we make ethical decisions.

Globalization and Business Ethics

Considerations about business ethics are derived from the desire for the application of basic moral codes in the conduct of the different aspects of business. As such, the relationship between business ethics and globalization refers to the manner in which the concept of globalization and its application to business operations can benefit from the practice of proper business ethics. Since the growth of globalization has led to a rise in the branching out of companies into various counties in the world, ethical business standards help ensure that such operations are rooted in integrity and applicable values. The challenge in the subject of business ethics and globalization is derived from the fact that while some basic moral codes are understood to be universal, some of the specific ethical standards are dictated by the environment, making it essential for companies to understand their market and the ethical requirements that may be unique to that area.

Business enterprises today are expected to meet standards of responsible business conduct that go beyond what had been expected traditionally. Although people more often than not still speak of business in terms of products, jobs, and profits, it is understood and accepted across the globe that a business enterprise remains a member of its community. The pursuit of profits and economic progress is not a licence to ignore community norms, values, and standards of respect, integrity, and quality. Improved business performance, profits, and economic progress come to those who effectively and efficiently foster and meet the reasonable expectations of their primary stakeholders—customers, employees, suppliers, investors, and the environment, as well as the owners and managers themselves. Success for any business is ultimately measured in profits and losses, and the socially responsible business generates the capital and revenues required to operate and stay in business over the long haul. The socially responsible business must generate enough revenue to cover the real cost of capital, the risks and uncertainties of future economic activity, and the needs of its workers and pensioners.

For the enterprise in an emerging market economy struggling to make payroll, not to mention a profit, global economic development is, at once, an opportunity, a risk, and a challenge. As an opportunity, it offers tantalizing prospects for new markets and access to international capital. The risk, however, is heightened competition and capital flow reversals from the slightest perceived political, economic, or social threat. The challenge is to learn from the experiences of successful businesses in market economies and to adapt them to overcome the legacies of the command economy. By learning from others' experiences (including the mistakes), enterprises in emerging markets can contribute to the development of their own market economies and can join the global market place.

The current financial crisis has raised questions about the effects of globalisation. Ethical failures certainly played a role. While it remains to be seen whether and how many people blatantly broke the law, there are abundant signs of various forms of potentially unethical behaviour. These include greed, unreasonable amounts of leverage, subtle forms of corruption (such as ratings agencies that appear to have had a conflict of interest), complex financial instruments that no one really understood, and herd behaviour where people just followed along and failed to exercise independent judgment.

It is difficult or impossible to regulate against greed and against many of the other ethical shortcomings that have been seen. What can be done is to force greater transparency and accountability, a process which began with Sarbanes-Oxley and is expected to continue with new regulations of the financial system.

Factors Leading to Unethical Behaviour Globally

The factors that precipitated the unethical behaviour globally are identified as:

- ***Shareholder greed.*** While much ink is spilled regarding excessive CEO compensation as the symbol of greed, the greed and short-term orientation of many shareholders are to blame. These shareholders don't care about the company; they are looking simply to make a short-term gain.
- ***Increased moral ambivalence***. The past 20 years or so "We've cloaked things we used to call 'corrupt' in language that makes it seem okay. We've lost the ability to discern what's really not right".

One example is how credit rating agencies, which seem quite culpable in the current scandal, have gotten into debt advisory businesses. At the very least, this creates a significant appearance of a conflict of interest.

- ***Financial instrument complexity***. The complexity of the innovative financial instruments masked conflicts of interest, incapacitated regulation, and facilitated self delusion—presenting many ways to justify to oneself actions that were morally ambiguous. These products were not created for corrupt reasons but did end up facilitating corruption.
- ***An insufficient emphasis on reasonableness***. CEOs are pressured to push the limits. How much debt can their organization take on? How much can earnings grow in the next quarter? At all times the expectation has been to push the limits, with a razor-thin margin for error. Needed are more reasonableness, more long-term perspective, and acting with decency.
- ***Failure of understanding risk.*** The lending markets are supposed to identify, call out, and prevent the assumption of

unacceptable risk. The reality is that in the past several years, investors have been unable or unwilling to see risk levels for what they really were. Whether self-delusion was at fault or simply a failure of understanding is debatable.

- ***Herd behaviour***. This is when everyone appears to suspend judgment because it seems that everyone else has bought into some idea. It is often hard to distinguish between herd behaviour, greed, stupidity, and corruption.

Implementing Values and Ethics in Globalized Business

Markets become free and remain free if their players are responsible and respect the basic values of honesty, reliability, fairness, and self-discipline. The alternatives to responsible business conduct are inefficient markets and costly government regulation. Free flows of capital, talent, knowledge, and creativity are possible where communities are known for transparency, respect for property, a market-oriented legal framework, and reliable dispute resolution mechanisms. The alternatives are a lack of capital, high transaction costs, limited markets, underdevelopment, and poverty.

Business ethics and globalization are firmly rooted in the concept of diversity among people and practices as well as the fact that such diversity need not be an impediment since it can be channeled by the company in question into a source of competitive advantage. As such, companies that diversify into other countries and cultures must necessarily develop a master plan that is aimed towards providing a general framework establishing the ethical views of the company and integrating it into the culture of the corporation. This master plan will only be a general guide that will also make provisions for situations where beliefs and societal practices in place in some areas call for a variation of the ethical code. A good example of this can be seen in the case of a company that provides an equal playing field for everyone, regardless or belief or gender.

Owners and managers must temper the competitive aspects of capitalism with concerned citizenship. They must take individual responsibility for the decisions and activities of their enterprises and their impact on the culture of their enterprise and its stakeholders. A business needs committed, productive employees, agents, and suppliers to create goods and services. It needs loyal, satisfied customers and consumers to make a profit. It needs people who believe in it and in its prospects enough to invest. It needs to take the long view and to respect the physical environment and the prospects of future generations. Businesses around the world are designing and implementing business ethics programmes to address the legal, ethical, social responsibility, and environmental issues they face. By addressing these issues in a systematic way, enterprises can improve their own business performance, expand opportunities for growth, and contribute to the development of social capital in their markets. They can realize specific business benefits, such as:

- Enhanced reputations and goodwill.
- Reduced risks and costs.
- Protection from their own employees and agents.
- Stronger competitive positions.
- Expanded access to capital, credit, and foreign investment.
- Increased profits.
- Sustained long-term growth.
- International respect for enterprises and emerging markets.

Enterprises that excel in these areas create a climate of excellence for their employees, shareholders, and communities, and contribute to the economic wellbeing of their countries.

Conclusion

Today's global business world requires companies to take into account its peoples values and to follow through with ethically sound practices. Companies form their organizational values in light of what its employees' value. From a company's organizational values comes a universal code of conduct which is tried and revised until it results in successfully resolving situations demonstrating solid ethics. Personal values, just like cultural values, need to be considered when a company is forming its policies. Personal values are linked closely to cultural values and need to be viewed as such by a company. Generally, if a company is compliant with its employees' cultural values, so also it will be with its employees' personal values. While personal values are just that personal, many personal values are shared in a way that cultural values are shared.

Given the country and industry differences found, from a managerial perspective, it appears to be a mistake to expect all corporate ethics policies to look alike. Careful thought should be given to tailoring the policy to the particular firm, industry, and country. Large multinational firms operating in a number of countries need to consider the general applicability of a code of ethics or ethics training that was developed in the country in which the firm's headquarters is located. If ethical concerns differ by country, then imposing a set of standards developed for one country on another country may be counterproductive. Similarly, expatriates working for multinational firms need to be aware that their own perception of ethical issues may not match that of their native fellow employees.

REFERENCES

Barrett, D. (2009, January). "Corporate social responsibility and quality management revisited." *The Journal for Quality & Participation,* 24-30.

Barry, Vincent (ed.). 1979. *Moral Issues in Business.* Belmont, CA: Wadsworth.

Beauchamp, Tom and Norman Bowie (eds.). 1979. *Ethical Theory and Business.* Englewood Cliffs, NJ: Prentice Hall.

Bekaert, Geert, Campbell R. Harvey and Christian Lundblad (2002). "Does Financial Liberalization Spur Growth?", presented at the World Bank Conference, *Financial Globalization: A Blessing or a Curse*? May: 30-31.

Bowen, H. (1953). *The social responsibilities of the businessman.* New York: Harper & Row.

Donaldson, Thomas. 1991. *The Ethics of International Business.* New York: Oxford University Press.

Edwards, Sebastian (1998). "Openness, Trade Liberalization, and Growth in Developing Countries," *Journal of Economic Literature*, 31, 3 (S eptember), 1358-1393.

Guru Nanak Nishkam Sewak Jatha (GNNSJ), Nishkam Puran Institute (NPI): A Technical Training Facility with a faith input for the youth of Kericho, Kenya, GNNSJ, 4th October 2002, Birmingham.

Joseph, Ella, 'We can't just leave it to business to be good', *The Observer*, 1st December, 2002.

Mofid, Kamran, *Business Ethics, Corporate Social Responsibility and Globalistaion for the Common Good,* Shepherd Wawyn (Publishers) Ltd.

Weber, Max. 1970. *Protestant Ethic and the Spirit of Capitalism.* New York: Scribner.

Willmore, Ian, 'How to make corporations accountable', *The Observer*, 14th July, 2002.

PART III
GLOBALIZATION AND SUSTAINABILITY

Chapter 22

Globalization Led Clean Development Mechanism Based Developmental Projects

A Threat to Natural Ecological Order

Mohinder Kumar Slariya

The Concept of Globalization

Humans have interacted over long distances for thousands of years. The overland Silk Road that connected Asia, Africa and Europe is a good example of the transformative power of international exchange that existed in the "Old World". Philosophy, religion, language, the arts and other aspects of culture spread and mixed as nations exchanged products and ideas. Early in the 19th century, the development of new forms of transportation (such as the steamship and railroads) and telecommunications that "compressed" time and space allowed for increasingly rapid rates of global interchange.

Rourke and Williamson (2000) has asserted that in the 20th century, road vehicles and airlines made transportation even faster, and the advent of electronic communications, most notably mobile phones and the Internet, connected billions of people in new ways leading into the 21st century.

Rodhan and Martin (1990) has rightly defined in his book, Globalization, Knowledge and Society, *Globalization* is the process of international integration arising from the interchange of world views, products, ideas and other aspects of culture. The term *globalization* is derived from the word *globalize*, which refers to the emergence of an international network of social and economic systems. One of the earliest known usages of the term (as the noun) was in 1930 in a publication entitled *Towards New Education* where it denoted a holistic view of human experience in education.

By the 1960s, both terms began to be used as synonyms by economists and other social scientists. It then reached the mainstream press in the later half of the 1980s. Since its inception, the concept of globalization has inspired competing definitions and interpretations, with antecedents dating back to the great movements of trade and empire across Asia and the Indian Ocean from the 15th century onwards.

Roland Robertson, Professor of Sociology at University of Aberdeen, was the first person to define globalization as *"the compression of the world and the intensification of the consciousness of the world as a whole."*

Sociologists Martin Albrow and Elizabeth King define globalization as:*... all those processes by which the peoples of the world are incorporated into a single world society.*

In *The Consequences of Modernity*, Anthony Giddens uses the following definition:

> Globalization can thus be defined as the intensification of worldwide social relations which link distant localities in such a way that local happenings are shaped by events occurring many miles away and *vice versa.*

In *Global Transformations* David Held *et al.* study the definition of globalization:

> Although in its simplistic sense globalization refers to the widening, deepening and speeding up of global interconnection, such a definition begs further elaboration. ... Globalization can be located on a continuum with the local, national and regional.

Concept of Clean Development Mechanism

Kyoto Protocol (IPCC, 2007) has defined Clean Development Mechanism (CDM) as one of the "flexibility" mechanisms. The Article 12 of the Protocol defined CDM which aims to meet the two most important objectives round the globe. The first objective is to assist parties not included in Annexure-I in achieving sustainable development and in contributing to the ultimate objective of the United Nations Framework

Convention on Climate Change (UNFCCC), which is to prevent dangerous climate change; and the second is to assist parties included in Annex I in achieving compliance with their quantified emission limitation and reduction commitments (greenhouse gas (GHG) emission caps). "Annex I" parties are those countries that are listed in Annex I of the treaty, and are the industrialized countries. Non-Annex I parties are developing countries. This is to be achieved by allowing the Annex I countries to meet part of their caps using "Certified Emission Reductions" from CDM emission reduction projects in developing countries (Carbon Trust, 2009:14). This is subject to oversight to ensure that these emission reductions are real and "additional". The CDM is supervised by the CDM Executive Board (CDM EB) and is under the guidance of the Conference of the Parties (COP/MOP) of the United Nations Framework Convention on Climate Change (UNFCCC).

The CDM allows industrialized countries to invest in emission reductions wherever it is cheapest globally (Grubb, 2003: 159). During the first year of project through renewable energy, energy efficiency, and fuel switching (World Bank, 2010: 262). Carbon capture and storage (CCS) was included in the CDM carbon offsetting scheme in December 2011. However, a number of weaknesses of the CDM have been identified (World Bank, 2010: 265-267). Several of these issues are addressed by a new modality, the Programme of Activities (PoA) that moves away from accrediting single projects but bundles all projects of one type of activity and accredits them together.

Under the CDM, the developer can make a deal for carbon credit. Under the UNFCCC, charter any company from the developed world can tie up with a company in the developing country that is a signatory to the Kyoto Protocol. These companies in developing countries must adopt newer technologies, emitting lesser gases, and save energy. A portion of the total earnings of carbon credits of the company can be transferred to the company of the developed countries under CDM. At present Indian stand on CDM projects (Table 22.1):

India comes under the third category of signatories to United Nations Framework Convention on Climate Change (UNFCCC). India signed and ratified the Protocol in August, 2002 and has emerged as a world leader in reduction of greenhouse gases by adopting Clean Development Mechanisms (CDMs) in the past few years. As it is evident from the above table that all countries of South Asia are having CDM projects and India and china are countries with maximum projects. In India, Himachal Pradesh is a state having maximum projects (11).

Table 22.1: Showing CDM Based Projects in Hind-Kush Region

Country	*State*	*No. of Projects*	*Capacity (in MW)*
Afghanistan	Not defined	0	0
Bhutan	State not defined	2	1314
China	Gansu	60	3116
	Guizhou	25	1128
	Hunan	46	2260
	Quinghai	10	392
	Shaanxi	11	955
	Sichuan	141	9497
	Xinjlang	19	1898
	Yunnan	124	6346
	Total	436	25,574
India	Himachal Pradesh	11	2076
	Jammu and Kashmir	2	89
	Meghalaya	1	84
	Sikkim	6	2111
	Uttarkhand	8	818
	Total	28	5178
Mayanmar	Kachin	1	240
Nepal	Not Specified	1	15
Pakistan	Khyber Pakhtunkhwa	1	15
	Azad Kashmir	1	84
	Total	2	99
Total HKH Region		470	32,420
HKH Share of total Value		58.60%	60.60%

Source: CDM pipeline, 1 April, 2011, UNEP Rise Centre, 2011.

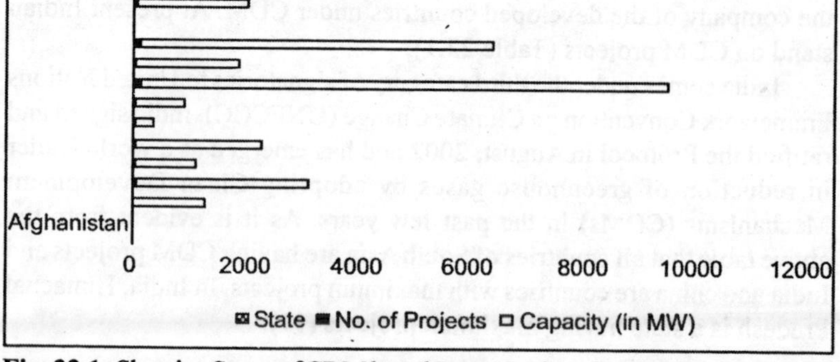

Fig. 22.1: Showing Status of CDM based Power Projects in Hind-Kush Himlayas

According to Report on National Action Plan for operationalizing Clean Development Mechanism (CDM) by Planning Commission, Government of India, the total CO_2—equivalent emissions in 1990 were 10,01,352 Gg (Giga gram), which was approximately 3 per cent of global emissions. If India can capture a 10 per cent share of the global CDM market, annual CER revenues to the country could range from US$ 10 million to 300 million (assuming that CDM is used to meet 10-50 per cent of the global demand for GHG emission reduction of roughly 1 billion tons CO_2, and prices range from US$ 3.5-5.5 per tonne of CO_2). As the deadline for meeting the Kyoto Protocol targets draws nearer, prices can be expected to rise, as countries/companies save carbon credits to meet strict targets in the future. India is well ahead in establishing a full-fledged system in operationalizing CDM, through the Designated National Authority (DNA).

The Indian market is extremely receptive to Clean Development Mechanism (CDM). Having cornered more than half of the global total in tradable certified emission reduction (CERs), India's dominance in carbon trading under the clean development mechanism (CDM) of the UN Convention on Climate Change (UNFCCC) is beginning to influence business dynamics in the country. Analysts claim if more companies absorb clean technologies, total CERs with India could touch 500 million. Out of the 391 projects sanctioned, the UNFCCC has registered 114 from India, the highest for any country. India's average annual CERs stand at 12.6 per cent or 11.5 million.

India being Annexure-I country and signatory of the Kyoto Protocol can invest in projects that both reduce GHGs and contribute to sustainable development in non-Annex I countries. A CDM project provides certified emissions reductions (CERs) to Annex I countries, which they can use to meet their GHG reduction commitments under the Kyoto Protocol. Article 12 of the Kyoto Protocol in Indian perspective sets out three goals for the CDM:

- To help mitigate climate change;
- To assist HIND-KUSH Region countries to attain their emission reduction commitments; and
- To assist developing countries in achieving sustainable development.

Current Status of CDM in India

As per the Basic Information provided by *www.igesorg.ip* up to

1 November, 2011 the number of CDM projects registered with executive board in India is 738 and projects which are at and after validation stage is 1022. Out of these 83 projects are of hydro power based projects. Following is the detail of CDM projects in India as on 1st November, 2011:

Table 22.2: CDM Projects in India

Type of Project	*Registered CDM Projects*					*Rejected*
	No. of Projects	*Avg. Annual Emission Reductions (t-CO_2)*	*Total ERs by 2012 (t-CO)*	*Amount of Issued CERs (t-CO)*	*Review Requested*	
Wind Power	233	32,055	33,996,009	9,854,826	56	8
Biomass	180	38,613	37,839,697	8,617,197	61	15
Hydro Power	83	88,199	20,586,368	2,877,343	23	5
Energy efficiency	75	113,814	13,099,874	1,385,897	21	8
Waste gas/heat Utilization	70	76,220	35,541,907	11,577,767	33	8
Fuel switch	20	358,053	27,760,522	7,637,476	7	0
Cement	17	114,708	16,806,437	1,382,047	2	4
Biogas	16	28,218	2,551,228	695,884	4	0
Methane avoidance	13	82,138	2,433,170	47,795	3	0
Afforestation and Reforestation	7	72,246	5,828,972	0	1	0
HFC reduction/ avoidance	7	1,577,424	82,691,940	74,813,284	2	0
Other renewable Energies	6	18,503	419,763	0	2	0
N_2O decomposition	5	406,915	6,137,291	155,115	3	0
Transportation	3	211,355	1,065,277	82,317	0	0
Methane recovery and Utilization	2	94,254	1,174,219	88,873	0	0
PFC reduction	1	433,551	1,301,367	33,624	0	0
Total	738	82,915*	289,234,041	119,249,445	218	48

Source: Basic Data for Registered CDM Projects in India as of 1 November, 2011.

Since the establishment of the Indian DNA (Designated National Authority) in 2003, it has approved a significant number of projects. 738 projects have been registered by the CDM executive board, which account for about 21 per cent of all the registered projects (as of 1 November, 2011).

In the initial stage of CDM development in India, biomass utilization projects, waste gas/heat utilization projects, and renewable energy (wind, hydro) projects were mainly being implemented. Other than those projects, India has various types of registered CDM projects that include energy efficiency (cement, steel and etc.), fuel switch, HFC reduction, N_2O decomposition, afforestation and reforestation, and transportation. Recently, a number of Wind Power projects were registered having a highest share in the Indian projects.

CDM promotion cells have been established at a state level. They conduct supportive activities such as information dissemination on CDM and coordination between local and national governments.

One of the features of CDM in India is its large share of unilateral CDM projects, CDM project developed by Indian stakeholders without the involvement (finance, technology) of Annex I countries. Indian project developers implement the project by bearing the transaction costs of CDM and taking on the risks of the projects.

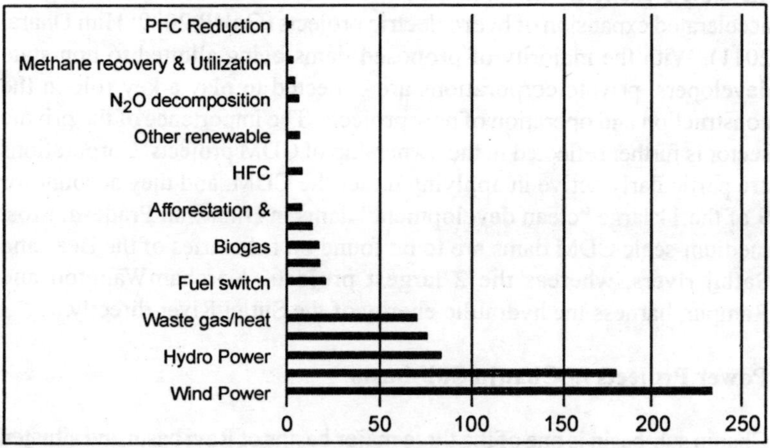

Fig. 22.2: Figure showing Number of CDM Projects

Therefore, the price of credits issued by unilateral CDM projects tends to be higher than bilateral or multilateral CDM projects:

1. The number of registered unilateral CDM projects (at the time of registration) (as of 1 November, 2011)= 603 (82%)
2. The number of CDM projects registered at the CDM executive board (as of 1 November, 2011) = 738

India as a signatory of this protocol have been registered 2313 projects up to August 2010, out of these, 64 projects are of hydro power generation and power projects in Chanju sub-basin are one of the CDM project in India.

CDM Projects in Himachal Pradesh

Most CDM dams can be found in the north-western state of Himachal Pradesh. Encompassing the upper reaches of the Satluj, Beas, Chenab, and Ravi rivers, the total hydropower potential of Himachal Pradesh is estimated at more than 23,000 MW, out of which 6460 MW has been tapped so far (GoHP, 2009: 68). After decades of comparatively modest hydropower expansion, state authorities plan to more than double the installed capacity by 2017 "to develop Himachal Pradesh as the 'Hydro-Power State' of the country" (GoHP, 2010: 56). Because of the lucrative "export" of peak demand electricity to urban and industrial centres in the Gangetic plains, hydropower is playing an increasingly important role in the state's economy, and the CDM is considered to be facilitating the accelerated expansion of hydroelectric projects (GoHP, 2009; Him Dhara, 2011). With the majority of proposed dams being allotted to non-state developers, private corporations are expected to play a key role in the construction and operation of new projects. The importance of the private sector is further reflected in the ownership of CDM projects. Corporations are particularly active in applying under the CDM, and they account for 9 of the 11 large "clean development" dams in Himachal Pradesh. Most medium-scale CDM dams are to be found on tributaries of the Beas and Satluj rivers, whereas the 2 largest projects, KarchamWangtoo and Rampur, harness the hydraulic energy of the Sutlej River directly.

Power Projects in Chanju Sub-basin

Chanju sub-basin is one of the three major basins of Ravi basin and situated below the Drati pass of the Peer Panjal range of middle Himalayas ranging from the elevation of 15,000 feet to more than 22,000 feet. Chanju sub-basin is a part of Baira-Suil basin, which is situated in the western Himalayas in 32° 47″ and 33° 2″ North Latitude and longitude of 75° 57″ to 76° 23″ in Chamba district of Himachal Pradesh, India and spread almost in 35 kms towards Drati pass touching the inter-district boundary of Chamba and Kullu. The people of this basin are very poor and mostly depend on these rivulets/nallas for their livelihood, which are the main sources of ecosystem services and these services, are raring 6000 people of the valley since ages. The water mills, who are serving the people of the valley are being threaten by the installation of these power projects (Fig. 22.1) and putting a question mark on the livelihood of the people for 67 MW power (Table 22.4).

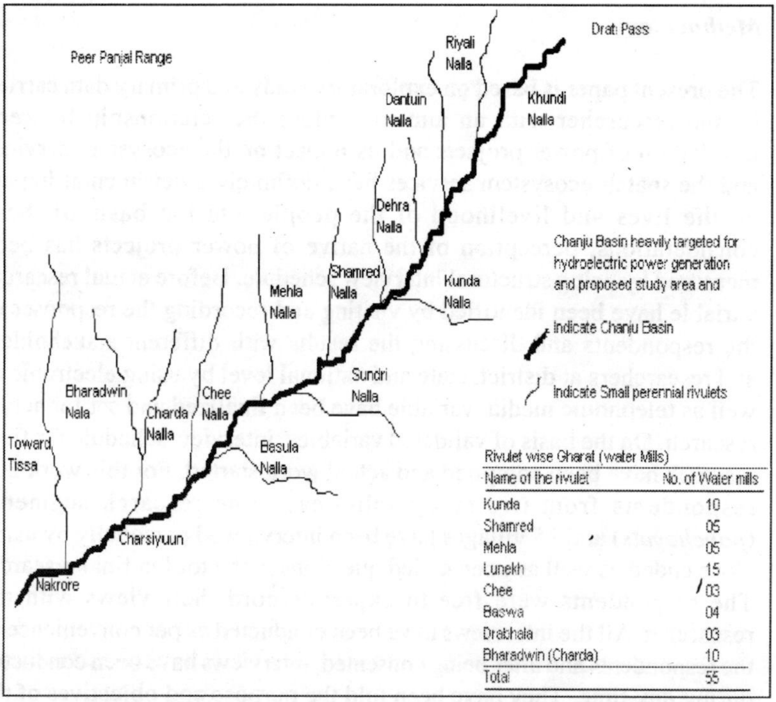

Rivulet wise Gharat (water Mills)

Name of the rivulet	No. of Water mills
Kunda	10
Shamred	05
Mehla	05
Lunekh	15
Chee	03
Baswa	04
Drabhala	03
Bharadwin (Charda)	10
Total	55

Source: *Author's compilation on the basis of first visit in August 2010*

Fig. 22.3: Showing rivulets/nallas and watermills in Chanju sub-basin on which small/mini power projects are proposed

This basin has eight perennial small and big rivulets whose installation capacity has been assessed 80 MW. On these rivulets there are more than 55 water mills that are serving the valley since ages and are the carrier of ***Hatt and Gharat Culture*** of Indian village community and at present raring more than 6000 people of the valley.

The present paper is an attempt of the researcher to record the perception of people regarding the viability of power projects in Chanju basin in specific and in whole hilly areas of Himalayas in general. The Chanju sub-basin can be divided in two parts, i.e. Chanju and Charda because of two streams. The native of catchment area of these two sub-basins have been selected for the study.

Methodology

The present paper is based on exploratory study and primary data carried by the researcher with an aim to explore the relationship between installation of power projects and its impact on the ecosystem services and the snatch ecosystem services have definitely a detrimental impact on the lives and livelihood of the people. On the basis of these considerations, perception of the native of power projects has been measured by using structural interview schedule. Before actual research, variable have been identified by visiting and recording the responses of the respondents and discussing the results with different stakeholders and researchers at district, state and national level by using electronic as well as telephonic media, variable have been finalized and set for actual research. On the basis of validated variables, interview schedule for final research have been compiled and actual work started. For this work 200 respondents from two study sub-areas, nine research segments (*panchayats*) and 35 villages have been interviewed personally by using close ended as well as open ended questions in the tool in final research. The respondents were free to express/record their views with the researcher. All the interviews have been conducted as per convenience of the respondents and after being consented, interviews have been conducted during day-time. They have been told the purpose and objectives of the research before the starting of the interview.

Methods of Data Collection

The present paper is being an attempt of the researcher to explore the relationship of installation of power projects with the people of area; exploratory research method has been used. The participant observation and questionnaire methods to collect data has been used to record the perception of the natives of Chanju sub-basin by participating in their routine activities and the ecosystem services used by the local people has been recorded, quantified and an assessment has been made about the supposed impacts of the installation of small power projects in this backward area by developing a suitable psychometric scale.

Sampling

This basin is spread over 50 small and large villages, which can be categorized in 9 administrative panchayats with approximate 5500

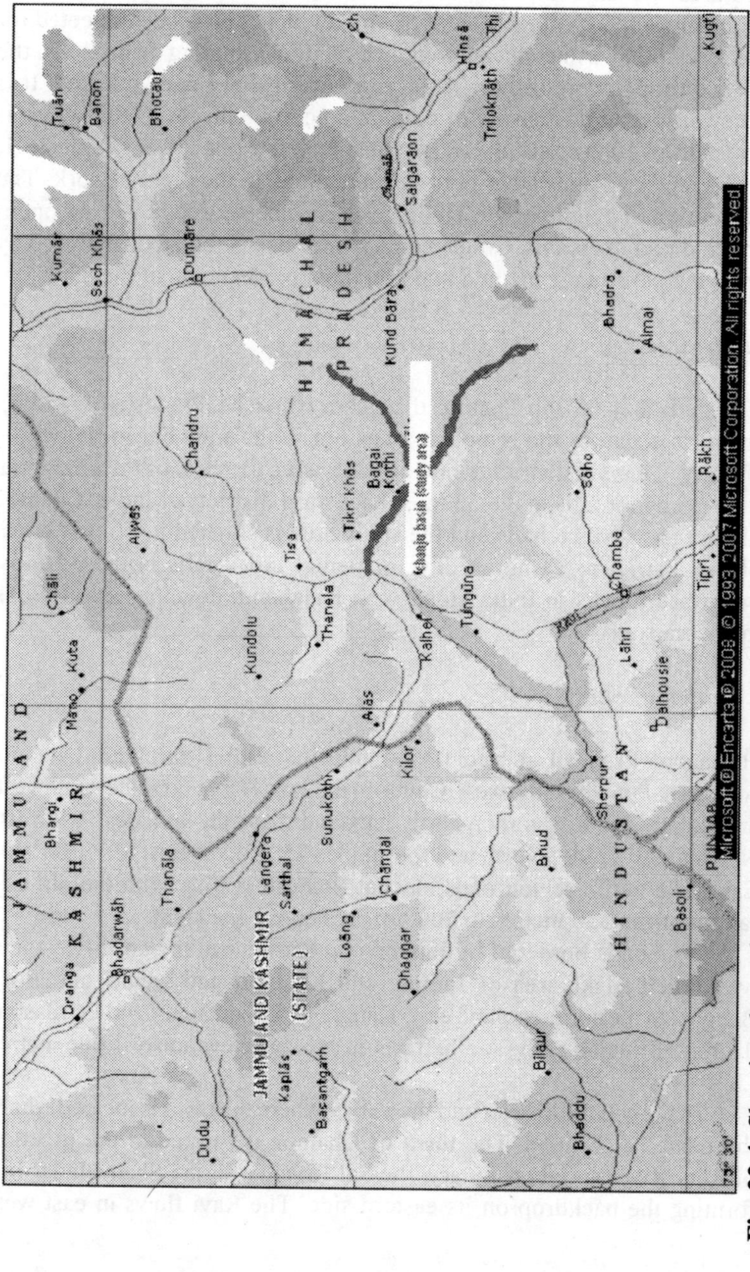

Fig. 22.4: Showing the study area: red line indicates Chanju basin, study area

population. For the present study whole study area was divided in two sub-areas (Chanju and Charda), 9 administrative panchayats (research segments) and 35 villages out of 50 small villages have been selected for the research by using cluster convince random sampling method. On the basis of population of the village, respondents have been selected. It is noteworthy that the density of population of the villages of study area is varies from 10 persons to 300 persons. As it is evident from Table 22.1, all 35 study villages have got representations in the present work. The perception of people of these villages has been recorded by using open-ended direct questions. Collected data have been tabulated, analyzed by applying percentage method and graphical presentation of the data.

Study Area

The study area falls in Chamba district of Himachal Pradesh (Fig. 22.4), India. It is one of the remotest areas not in the state but in the whole country. Chamba district is one of the twelve districts of the Himachal Pradesh and it falls in the 55 most backward districts of India. Chamba district has seven tehsils and the study area is situated in Churah tehsil of the district and Churah developmental block falls in the 35 most backward blocks in India along with Kalahandi developmental block in Orissa state.

Location of Study

Himachal Pradesh shared its boundaries with Uttarakhand on the southeast, Punjab on the west, China on the east, Haryana on the southwest, and Jammu and Kashmir on north. It extends from the latitudes 30°22′40″ North to 33°12′40″ North and longitudes 75°45′55″ East to 79°04′20″ East. The entire region of Himachal Pradesh is hilly with the altitude ranging from 350 metres to 7000 metres above sea level.

Chamba is bordered by Jammu and Kashmir to the north-west and west, the Ladakh area of Jammu and Kashmir and Lahaul and Bara Banghal to the north-east and east, Kangra to the south-east and Gurdaspur district of Punjab to the south. It has an average elevation of 1,006 metres (3,301 ft).

The town, the district and the valley where the town is located, share the name of Chamba. The town of Chamba is located at the junction of Ravi River and its tributary, the Sal River, with the Shah Madar hill forming the backdrop on its eastern side. The Ravi flows in east-west direction forming deep canyons. During the spring and summer months, the levels of the river rise significantly from snow melt and pose a flooding risk. Record levels were experienced in early July 2005, when the National Hydroelectric Power Corporation was forced to shut down the power generation on its 300-MW Chamera Power Station. Located on the right bank of the Ravi river valley, built on successive flat terraces, the town is bounded topographically by the Dhauladhar and Zanskar ranges, south of the inner Himalayas. Chamba, despite its hill location, is well connected by road to the rest of the state and country, including Shimla, Delhi and Chandigarh along several routes. The nearest broad gauge railway stations are at Chakki Bank and Pathankot, the latter of which is 120 kilometres (75 mile) away by road.

The temperatures in summer vary between 38°C (100°F) and 15°C (59°F) and in winter: 15°C (59°F) and 0°C (32°F). The maximum temperature recorded in summer is 39°C (102°F) and the minimum temperature in winter is 1°C (30°F). Climatically March to June is said to be the best period to visit Chamba, which is a well-known hill station. The average annual rainfall in the town is 785.84 millimetres (30.939 in).

Present paper is based on the study conducted by the researcher located at Chanju *nallah*, a tributary of Baira *nallah* and sub-tributary of the River Ravi. The access distance of the project site from is State Capital (Shimla) is 495 km, from district headquarter it is 70 km and the nearest rail head is 190 km (Pathankot) and nearest airport is Jammu (240 km). The geographical co-ordinates of the study are are: Longitude: 76°12′06″ E to 76°14′52″ E Latitude: 32°44′14″ N to 32°45′43″ N.

Results and Interpretations

As *David Inouye* of Ecological Society of America, has righty stated that *'The cereal we eat in the morning is being brought by the wind, or that the glass of clear, cold, clean water drawn from we faucet have been purified for us by a wetland or perhaps the root system of an entire forest? Trees in front of our house are always at work and trap dust, dirt, and harmful gases from the air we breathe to sustain our life. The fire of oak logs keep us warm in the cold nights and moreover, medicines we take to get relief from pain of an ailment come to us from Nature's warehouse of services.* Furthermore, natural ecosystems perform fundamental life-support services upon which human civilization depends. Unless human activities are carefully planned and managed, valuable ecosystems will continue to be impaired or destroyed. Moreover, ecosystem services are the processes by which the environment produces resources that we often take for granted such as *clean water, timber, and habitat for fisheries, and pollination of native and agricultural plants.*

Any developmental project aiming to bring prosperity in the lives of people must take care of these components, if not, then it put the native of that vary area into psychological traumatic conditions and put their livelihood options at stake and they start dying every minute, every hour, everyday and on the basis of which viability of the said development projects can be tested/measured. Same is the case with the projects which have been studied by the researcher to arrive at conclusion.

Table 22.3: Showing different Eco-system Services being used by the Respondents

Sl. No.	*Eco-system Service(s)*	*No. of Response*			
		Yes	*%age*	*No.*	*%age*
1.	Fuel wood collection	199	99.50	1	5.00
2.	Grazing and fodder for cattle	199	99.50	1	5.00
3.	Timber wood for House construction	198	99.00	2	1.00
4.	Clean drinking Water	199	99.50	1	5.00
5.	Fishing in rivulets	199	99.50	1	5.00
6.	Purification of water and air	200	100.00	—	—
7.	Mitigation of Drought and Flood	194	97.00	6	3.00
8.	Detoxification and decomposition of waste in the Nalla	197	98.50	3	1.50
9.	Make use of rivulets for burning of dead bodies	200	100.00	—	—
10.	Use for religious purposes (for Rites and Rituals)	200	100.00	—	—
11.	Use for eco-tourism/recreational purposes	200	100.00	—	—
12.	Swimming in the rivulets	—		200	100.00
13	Taking stone, sand etc.	200	100.00	—	—
14.	Irrigational channels	200	100.00	—	—

The eco-system services provided by the nature can broadly be divided in four major components: ***Provisioning, Regulating, Supporting and Cultural*** which further can be seen as stabilization of climate, regulating of hydrological cycle, pollination, maintenance of nutrient cycle, water purification and decomposition of wastes etc. As it has been narrated by different scholars in available literature, the eco-system services are the primer determinants of lives of people.

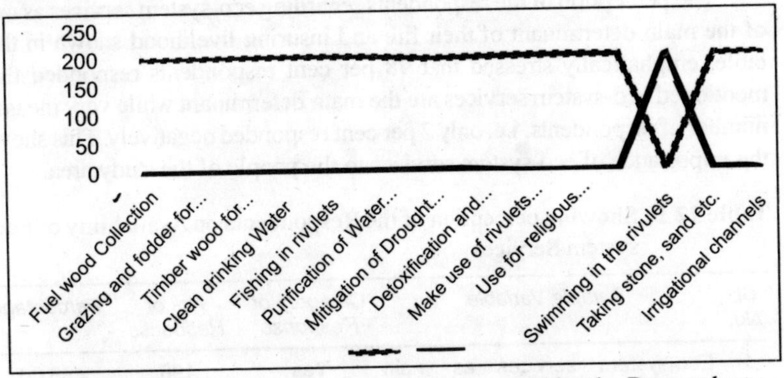

Fig. 22.5: Showing Eco-system Services being used by the Respondents

Availability of eco-system services in any area is a guarantee of sustainable and secure living standard and sustainable future. Area under study is self-reliant and self-sufficient and having no any dependency on outside of the villages. The available services are rearing the population of whole area. To assess the availability of eco-system services in the area 14 ecosystem services have been taken to get response of the respondents. As it is evident from above table the respondents are using 13 out of 14 eco-system services.

Few eco-system services related to mention four categories have been chosen to see the impact on coming power projects on them. On the basis of the data collected during the first phase (variable identification stage) of the research, these eco-system services have been recorded and found mostly prevalent and determining lives of people by giving meaning to them. Maximum number of respondents, i.e. more than 97 per cent is of the view that they are using mentioned eco-system, which shows their direct dependence on the natural system which has been provided by the nature to man as free gift and now man has to use them sensibly with futuristic sustainable approach.

Table 22.4: Showing Response of the Respondents regarding their perception of eco-system services as main determinant of their life and livelihood

Sl. No.	*Type of Response*	*No. of Responses*	*Percentage*
1.	Yes	196	98.00
2.	No	004	02.00
	Total	200	100.00

The perception of the respondents regarding eco-system services as one of the main determinant of their life and insuring livelihood shown in this table, emphatically stressed that 98 per cent respondents responded that mentioned eco-system services are the main determinant while very meagre number of respondents, i.e. only 2 per cent responded negatively. This shows the importance of eco-system services to the people of the study area.

Table 22.5: Showing perception of the Respondents on Availability of Eco-system Services

Sl. No.	Sample Variable	Category of Response	No. of Response	Percentage
1.	Eco-system services as main determinant of lives and livelihood	Yes	196	98.00
		No	4	2.00
2.	Available eco-system services being used by the Respondents	Yes	192	96.00
		No	8	4.00

Availability of ecosystem services in any area is a clear indication of sound and healthy environmental surroundings. The availability of ecosystem services in natural form which is gifted by nature, but it is not necessary that people living there might be aware about the existence of these services. Same is the case with the respondents of the study area. As indicated in the table, two variables have been used to measure the perception of the respondent. The first variable received 98 per cent response which indicates that ecosystem services are the main determinant of lives and livelihood of the people/respondents and 96 per cent respondents responded positively that they are using eco-system services in their daily lives. On the basis of responses received, it can be stated that people of study area are aware of ecosystem services and they are using these services since ages.

Table 22.6: Showing perception of Respondents regarding the Impact on lives and Livelihood

Sl. No.	Sample Variable	Category of Response	No. of Response	Percentage
1.	Knowledge of installation of power projects	Yes	200	100.00
2.	Perception of the Respondents regarding possible impacts on life and livelihood	Positive	20	10.00
		Negative	174	87.00
		No impact	6	3.00
3.	Views regarding the viability of power projects in chanju basin	Viable	84	42.00
		Un-viable	116	58.00

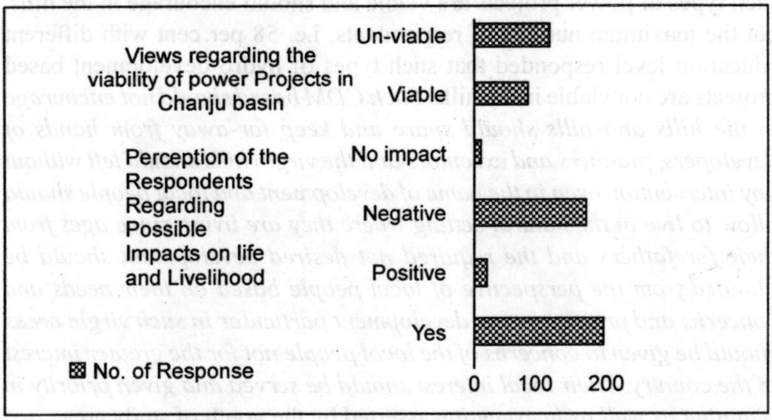

Fig. 22.6: Showing perception of Respondents regarding the Impact on lives and Livelihood

In view of above table and graphical presentation, it can be stated emphatically that the respondents at micro level and native at macro level are aware of the fact that this area is going to have power projects. Reasons responsible for this is people are very poor and are without employment and any opportunity they are knowing they rush behind that and try to grab it without knowing the positive/negative impacts.

Poor people have been allured by the representatives of corporate houses, at present they are very happy, but what would happen when they confronted with real situation. When they have been briefed about the possible impacts of forthcoming power projects, they were voiceless, then they respond to next question asked by the researcher and the question was related to the perception of the respondents regarding the possible impacts on life and livelihood and they have given three options, i.e. positive impact; negative impacts and no-impact. 10 per cent respondents responded positively, 87 per cent negatively and 3 per cent stated that there would be no impact.

Respondents also have been asked the question of viability of such Clean Development Mechanism (CDM) based small power projects in the hills. The illiterate people have no any idea about CDM, they don't know the concept of carbon neutrality and they don't have any concern with the theoretical jargons of the concepts, they only know how such types of proposed developmental initiatives are going to affect their lives and livelihood.

In view of such considerations, 42 per cent respondent responded that such types of power projects are viable and should encourage in the hills, but the maximum number of respondents, i.e. 58 per cent with different education level responded that such types of hydro development based projects are not viable in the hills. *Such CDM based should not encourage in the hills and hills should spare and keep far-away from hands of developers, planners and executors and the virgin hills should left without any intervention even in the name of development and local people should allow to live in the natural setting where they are living since ages from their forefathers and the required not desired development should be planned from the perspective of local people based on their needs and concerns and priority in any development particular in such virgin areas should be given to concerns of the local people not for the greater interest of the country. Their local interest should be served and given priority in planning as well as in execution* asserted by the youth of study area.

Recommendations for Policy Implications

The present paper is based on recently completed research project, submitted to UGC, New Delhi, India. To meet the aims and objectives of the project variables have been identified and later on developed in structured interview schedule and administrated on the respondents of two research segments. The compiled data reveals that respondents in particular and people of Chanju valley in general are using ecosystem services since ages and these services are corner stones of their lives and they are every inch dependent on them.

With the coming up of these development projects lives of people of Chanju basin is going to be affected to greater extent, though there is no direct physical displacement because of geographical reasons, but the ecosystem services which are corner stones of their lives, are going to affect badly. People of the area have been allured by the developers that they have been given employment, and their concerns will be taken care of first of all and compensation is to be given. The question remained unattended and answered that if employment, for how many days? And to how many?

Mere providing monetary compensation is not going to help the people of study area and their livelihood options cannot be compensated by mere allocation of funds. It needs an intensive strategic plan to restore the services and must give them skill upgradation options so that they can live happily and with respect. People are hardily concern with the carbon credit or CDM considerations of the policy makers, they are not knowing anything about these technical jargons, they are simple people concerned with their small world which confined up to their families and extended up to the village only. They are very happy and would be happier if they are not disturbed even in the name of proposed development.

The researcher is aware of the fact the natural resource based development cannot be stopped for the sake of negative impacts on the lives of the people as these are *sine quo non* of any developing economy. The researcher strongly recommended his proposed model of development, i.e. Benefit Sharing Participatory Model (BSPM) as an answer to existing lobbyist pressurized model of development. The benefit drawn developmental project should be shared with the local people and their concerns should be listen and taken care of first of all, I mean before the initiation of any development project and possible impact must be studied first of all not by the executing agency but by independent research team comprises engineers, sociologists, ecologists, environmentalists, economists and local people. The team would decide how and where benefits are to be distributed and what would be mechanism of distribution. This distribution should be of such types that native of any development project should participate and contribute in positive way and extend their cooperation to the executing agencies which will help both stakeholders. The executors will justify their CSR and better rapport with the local people and reciprocally the local people will be benefited and they will realised the benefits of such types of developmental project and can realise the meaning of independence.

REFERENCES

"About Chamba", Himachal Pradesh Tourism Department, Retrieved 2009-10-28.

Al-Rodhan, Nayef, R.F. and Gérard Stoudmann. (2006, 19 June). "Definitions of Globalization: A Comprehensive Overview and a Proposed Definition."

Albrow, Martin and Elizabeth King (eds.) (1990). Globalization, Knowledge and Society, London: Sage. ISBN 978-0803983243, p. 8. "...all those processes by which the peoples of the world are incorporated into a single world society."

"Access to Chamba", National Informatics Centre: Government of Chamba district, Retrieved 2009-10-29.

"Carbon capture and storage (CCS) accepted as UN-based carbon offsetting scheme, paving way for developing country finance". Global CCS Institute, Retrieved 2011-12-14.

"Chamba Hill station" Retrieved 2009-10-29.

"Chamba- Himachal Pradesh", Hill Resorts in India, Retrieved, 2009-10-29

"Chamba Tourism". *India Line* Retrieved 2009-10-28.

"Chamera power station shut down", *The Tribune* (Himachal Pradesh) 2005-07-06. Retrieved 2010-04-06. Bhatnagar (2008), p.40 Bharati (2001), p.16.

Carbon Trust (March 2009). "Global Carbon Mechanisms: Emerging lessons and implications (CTC748)". Carbon Trust website, Retrieved 2010-03-31.

Fisher, B.S. *et al.* (2007). "3.1.3 Development trends and the lock-in effect of infrastructure choices In (book chapter): Issues related to mitigation in the long term context. In: Climate Change 2007: Mitigation Contribution of Working Group III to the Fourth Assessment Report of the Intergovernmental Panel on Climate Change (B. Metz, *et al.* Eds.)". Print Version: Cambridge University Press.

Cambridge, U.K., and New York, N.Y., U.S.A. This version: IPCC website. Retrieved 2010-03-18.

Government of Himachal Pradesh, (2009), Economic Survey 2009-10. Shimla, India Finance Department.

Government of Himachal Pradesh, 2010 Annual Plan 2010–11. Shimla, India Planning Department.

Goldemberg, J. *et al.* (1996). *Introduction: scope of the assessment. In: Climate Change 1995: Economic and Social Dimensions of Climate Change. Contribution of Working Group III to the Second Assessment Report of the Intergovernmental Panel on Climate Change* (J.P. Bruce *et al.* eds. Cambridge University Press, Cambridge, U.K., and New York, N.Y., U.S.A.doi:10.2277/0521568544. ISBN 9780521568548

Grubb, M. (July–September 2003). "The Economics of the Kyoto Protocol" *World Economics* 4 (3): 143–189. Retrieved 2010-03-25.

Haites, E.,M. Duan, and S. Seres (2006), Technology transfer by CDMprojects. *Climate Policy* 6 (3): 327–344. CrossRef.

Haya, B. (2007) *Failed Mechanism How the CDM is Subsidizing Hydro Developers and Harming the Kyoto Protocol.* Berkeley, CAIRN [International Rivers Network].

High Court of Himachal Pradesh (2010). Report of the One Man Committee to Monitor Environmental Compliance of Hydel Projects in CWP No. 24/09. Shimla, India, High Court of Himachal Pradesh

Him Dhara [Environment Research and Action Collective] (2011). In the Name of Clean Energy: A Report on Asian Development Bank Financed Hydropower Projects in Himachal Pradesh www.sandrp.in/hydropower/ Report AdbFinanced_HEPs_HP210511.pdf, accessed on 27 May 2011.

Hydro Tasmania (2007), India River Basin Development Optimization Study Final Recommendations Report. Hobart, Australia Hydro Tasmania.

ICIMOD [International Centre for Integrated Mountain Development] (2011), Hindu Kush–Himalayan Region www.icimod.org/index.php?page=43; accessed on 6 May 2011.

IPCC (2007), "Glossary J-P In (book section): Annex-I in: Climate Change 2007: Report of the Intergovernmental Panel on Climate Change (B. Metz *et al.* Eds.)". Cambridge University Press, Cambridge, U.K., and New York, N.Y., U.S.A. Retrieved 2010-04-23.

IPCC [Intergovernmental Panel on Climate Change] (2011), Hydropower In: IPCC Special Report on Renewable Energy Sources and Climate Change

Mitigation. Cambridge, United Kingdom Cambridge University Press.

International Rivers Network 2008 Mountains of Concrete: Dam Building in the Himalayas. Berkeley, CA IRN [International Rivers Network] Jaypee (2011), Jaypee Karcham Hydro Corporation Limited www.jalindia.com/ under exec karcham.htm; accessed on 6 May 2011.

McCully, P. (2001), *Silenced Rivers: The Ecology and Politics of Large Dams* London, United Kingdom Zed Books.

National Environmental Engineering Research Institute, (2004), Comprehensive EIA for 1000 MW Karcham–Wangtoo Hydroelectric Project, Dist. Kinnaur, Himachal Pradesh. Final Report (Revised): Volume 1. Nagpur, India NEERI.

O'Rourke, Kevin H. and Jeffrey G. Williamson. (2000), "When Did Globalization Begin?" NBER Working Paper No. 7632.

South Asian Network on Dams, Rivers and People, 2003 Comments on the EIA of the KarchamWangtoo HEP in Himachal Pradesh, Delhi, India, SANDRP.

Sathaye, J., *et al.* (2001). "Barriers, Opportunities, and Market Potential of Technologies and Practices In: Climate Change 2001: Mitigation. Contribution of Working Group III to the Third Assessment Report of the Intergovernmental Panel on Climate Change (B. Metz, *et al.*, Eds.)" Cambridge University Press, Cambridge, U.K., and New York, N.Y., U.S.A. Retrieved 2009-05-20.

Sutter, C. (2003), *Sustainability Check-up for CDM Projects: How to Assess the Sustainability of International Projects under the Kyoto Protocol*. Berlin, Germany WissenschaftlicherVerlag.

Toth, F.L. *et al.* (2001), "Decision-making Frameworks. In: Climate Change 2001: Mitigation. Contribution of Working Group III to the Third Assessment Report of the Intergovernmental Panel on Climate Change (B. Metz *et al.* Eds.)" Cambridge University Press, Cambridge, U.K., and New York, N.Y., U.S.A. Retrieved 2010-01-10.

United Nations Environment Programme Risø Centre 2011 CDM Pipeline Overviewwww.cdmpipeline.org; accessed on 10 April 2011.

UNESCO [United Nations Educational, Scientific and Cultural Organization] (2009). The United Nations World Water Development Report 3. Paris, France UNESCO.

UNFCCC [United Nations Framework Convention on Climate Change] (1998), Kyoto Protocol to the United Nations Framework Convention on Climate Change http://unfccc.int/resource/docs/ convkp/ kpeng.pdf; accessed on 28 January 2011.

UNFCCC [United Nations Framework Convention on Climate Change] (2007), Project Design Document Allain Duhangan Hydropower Project http://cdm.unfccc.int/filestorage/ MTMwNTk4MzIxOC42 |0TZ4FHqlqusg-QBDl8apP97j4JY=; accessed on 28 January 2011.

United Nations Framework Convention on Climate Change, (2008), Project Design Document. Hydroelectric Project in Kinnaur District in Himachal Pradesh http://cdm.unfccc.int/filestorage; accessed on 28 January 2011.

World Commission on Dams, (2000), Dams and Development- A New Framework for Decision-Making. London, United Kingdom Earthscan.

World Bank (2010), "World Development Report 2010: Development and Climate Change". The International Bank for Reconstruction and Development / The World Bank, 1818 H Street NW, Washington DC 20433. Retrieved 2010-04-06.

Chapter 23

Globalization and Corporate Responsibility in Sustainable Development

Sandhya Rohal

Sustainable Solutions by Corporate Towards Protecting the Environment

1. To explore innovative forms of capitalism those are non-extractive. To include anti-pollution and resource protection clauses in all contracts with substantial consequences for violations.
2. Avoid dumping of hazardous materials, destruction of wetlands, and over fishing of endangered marine species.
3. Tree planting programmes, recycling, promotion of carpooling and bicycling and auto-free zones, and encouragement to public transport systems.

Buying consciously contributes directly to rebuilding the environment. This includes selecting products that are recycled, patronizing companies with proven environmental records, and simply consuming less[1].

A New Global Eco Label will be Launched at the Business for Environment Global Summit in Jakarta

Global Standards and Technical Guidance towards sustainable development have been enhanced by the establishment of a new standards setting organization—Global Environmental Choice. The organization was launched today at the Business for Environment conference in Jakarta, Indonesia. The organization publishes standards, guidance frameworks and a certification solution for green products, commodities, services, agricultural produce and environmental technologies. The global market for green goods and services is $750 Billion in 2011, with an annual growth rate of 3 per cent. Global Environmental Choice is to become a global membership based organization of professionals, scientists, industry and researcher institutes that are involved in the collaborative development of standards and guidance materials specifically delivering technical solutions to defining environmentally preferable and sustainability outcomes. The objectives of the organisations are to:

1. Provide transparency to the market of the environmental performance of commodities, products, services and companies.
2. Undertake research and review of fundamental aspects of markets related to environmental performance and outcomes.
3. Create and publish transparent and scientifically rigorous environmental and sustainability performance standards for commodities, products, services and companies through an international standard setting framework based on international best practice.
4. Promote and recognise sustainability leadership in the market.
5. Enhance the cultural and technical knowledge available to industry and governments in delivering sustainable solutions to the market.
6. Empower individuals, corporations, governments and institutions to make environmentally preferable purchasing and consumption choices.
7. Undertake technical assessments of the absorptive capacity of the natural environment to support economic activity.

Work with partner organisations to deliver market incentives for the transformation of our societies to a sustainable state.[2]

Bangladesh Paridesh Andolan Vice President Prof. Wahid Uddin Mahmud said protecting the environment should be a key element of sustainable development in a disaster-prone country like Bangladesh. If loss of environment is calculated in economic terms, the country's Gross Domestic Product may reduce from six per cent to four percent, he said while addressing a press conference. Bangladesh Paribesh Andolan organized the press conference titled 'Want environment-friendly budget, want transparent use of allocated fund' at Dhaka Reporters' Unity auditorium in the city. Giving proper allocation in environment is indeed essential for protecting existence of human beings, he added. Shahjahan stressed on transparent use of funds allocated to protect the environment.[3]

International Environmental Standard for Transnational Corporations

To achieve the goals of environmental protection and development, a committed participation from the governments, international corporations, industrial enterprises, environmental groups and private citizens is needed.[4]

Transnational Corporations operate a wide range of pollution intensive and hazardous industries that have products or processes can harm the environment or negatively impact human health. Transitional Corporations are also active in resource development industries, such as mining, petroleum, and agri-business, which can seriously affect environmentally sensitive areas. The general standard of environmental performance of Transitional Corporations is, therefore, matter of significant international concern. Several factors may include or enable Transitional Corporations to evade national control of environmental, health and safety matters, particularly in developing countries. Transitional Corporations possess flexibility, mobility, and leverage which local companies do not enjoy; tend to maintain corporate secrecy about the hazards associated with particular products and processes; and obtain the benefit of legal uncertainties concerning the liability of parent Transitional Corporations of their affiliates, activities. Environmental concern: the two Transitional Corporations activities most commonly identified as raising environmental concerns are the export of hazardous products and export hazardous processes or technologies. International trade in products such as pesticides, pharmaceuticals, toxic chemicals, and hazardous waste has been an issue for some years specially when it involves sales in developing countries. Both domestic and international measures have been developed and respond to the problems arising from such trade. Domestic measures have included export control, with particular emphasis upon the concept of prior informed consent. This concept requires a national authority in the importing country to agree before products or technologies which can cause injuries to human health or environment are exported. Transitional Corporations export hazardous processes by establishing highly polluting industries outside home countries, thus creating potential problems with pollution control, disposal of hazardous wastes, workers, health and safety, and the risk of major accidents. The accidents at Bhopal, India; and Basel, Switzerland demonstrate the serious consequences that arise when Transitional Corporations inadequately manage chemical manufacturing plants[5].

Developing Environmental Standards for Transitional Corporations

(a) **International law as a source of environmental standards**—Considerable support has been expressed in recent years for the development of international environmental standards. For example, Agenda 21, global action plan for environmental management adopted at the United Conference on Environment and Development in Rio de Janerio in 1992, states as one of its specific objectives: 'to promote through the gradual development of universally and multilaterally negotiated agreements, international standards for the protection of the environment that takes into account the different situations and capabilities of countries.' However, there is growing body of opinion, which Agenda 21 recognizes, that international environmental standards should not be of a uniform nature[6].

(b) **International environment standards: uniform or minimum**—Uniformity could work against sustainable development by forcing inappropriate priorities on developing countries. For example, developing countries do not need 'high levels of environmental protection against cancer at the expense of basic human need such as protection from high infant mortality and rampant malnutrition.' Criticisms based on economic analysis suggest that uniform standard would not equalize the international competitive position of Transitional Corporation and would not be economical efficient. Differences in the national environmental standards can be justified by arguing that the differences reflect geographic, ecological, and demographic variations among countries and hence differing capabilities to assimilate pollution[7].

(c) **Prospectus for the setting of International Environmental Standards**—In the only statistical sampling done to date on Transitional corporation and environmental performance, two-third of Transitional Corporations thought that the United Nations should work towards the standardizing national environmental rules and regulations. A majority also felt that United Nations should be active in setting international policy guidelines. Transitional Corporation would prefer to see national laws brought more closely into line, perhaps through 'soft law' mechanism that provide guidance to states but do not entail firm obligations, rather than have standards prescribed by international agreement. The extensive promotion of 'self regulation' by corporations and individual Transitional Corporation coupled with some stem resistance even to certain 'soft law' measures such as the draft United Nations Code of Conduct for Transnational Corporations highlights the fragility of any support alleged to exist among Transitional Corporation for the development of International Environmental Standards. Thus despite the emerging interest in the concept of minimum international environmental standards, and the precedents for international regulation where transboundary or global common issues are involved, the reality in that the prescription of detailed process standards for environmental, health, and safety matters through legally binding international agreements does not currently appear to have widespread governmental or industrial support[8].

Standardization Through the Use of Soft Law Instruments

There are no applicable "hard law" and little "soft law" in relation to transnational corporate accountability. nearly all the "non-binding" declarations are emerging "soft law". "Hard law" is to use what the lawyer at a domestic level. There are very less international law regulating corporations. Some of the most overlooked and powerful non-governmental actors in the human rights arena are transnational corporation's and other business enterprises. There are very less international law regulating corporations. Some supporters of international regulation also attach considerable importance to the role of soft law instruments, particularly since they may be addressed directly to Transitional Corporation unlike formal international agreements. Rather than place emphasis on legal form, it is argued that the more important consideration is the political commitment of those states who endorse particular instruments. Although soft law instruments impose no firm obligations on signatories, they may provide a basis for incorporation into domestic law and eventually achieve the status of international customary law binding on all countries through resulting changes in state practice and expressed intent. In particular, they provide an avenue for the development of standards in a way which could lead, through their adoption by states, to greater harmonization of domestic standards. A fundamental difficulty with soft law instruments is that they often constitute a compromise consensus has not yet been reached on particular measures. They may not enjoy the support of a large majority of nations and their language may be particularly open-ended or diluted to accommodate differences of opinion. The recent developments of the international community to impose on transitional corporations legal responsibility are regarded to be the first steps to ensure that human rights are not just ideals but also a reality. Now to conclude it by saying that Bhopal and the other accidents should not be treated as grim reminders of destiny and should not be forgotten as still mere episode of the cost-benefit era.[9]

The ISO 14000 Environmental Management Standard

The ISO 14000 environmental management standards exist to help organizations:

(a) Minimize how their operations (processes etc.) negatively affect the environment (i.e. cause adverse changes to air, water, or land).
(b) Comply with applicable laws, regulations, and other environmentally oriented requirements.
(c) Continually improve in the above.

ISO 14000 is similar to ISO 9000 quality management in that both pertain to the process of how a product is produced, rather than to the product itself. As with ISO 9000, certification is performed by third-party organizations rather than being awarded by ISO directly. The ISO 19011 audit standard applies when auditing for both 9000 and 14000 compliance at once.[10]

In some nations, legal requirements for social accounting, auditing and reporting exist (e.g. in the French bilan social), though international or national agreement on meaningful measurements of social and environmental performance is difficult. Many companies now produce externally audited annual reports that cover Sustainable Development and Corporate Social Responsibility issues ('Triple Bottom Line Reports'), but the reports vary widely in format, style, and evaluation methodology (even within the same industry). Critics dismiss these reports as lip service, citing examples such as Enron's yearly 'Corporate

Responsibility Annual 'Report' and tobacco corporations' social reports. In South Africa, as of June 2010, all companies listed on the Johannesburg Stock Exchange (JSE) were required to produce an integrated report in place of an annual financial report and sustainability report. An integrated report includes environmental, social and economic performance alongside financial performance information and is expected to provide users with a more holistic overview of a company. However, this requirement was implemented in the absence of any formal or legal standards for an integrated report. An Integrated Reporting Committee was established to issue guidelines for good practice in this field.[11]

International Environmental Laws to Promote Corporate Social Responsibility and Sustainable Development[12]

The United Nations environment programme helps in developing and applying national and international environmental law, advancing national and regional implementation of environmental objectives, and bridging major groups and governments in policy development and implement processes. Genesis of international environmental law started mainly with the the United Nations efforts in early 1970s. Therefore, it could be analysed in four parts[13], i.e. International environmental law in the first decade (1970-1980), International environmental law in second decade (1980-1990), International environmental law in third decade (1990-2000), and International environmental law in fourth decade (2000-2010).

(a) International environmental law in the first decade (1970-1980)

Main efforts made by the international community and the United Nations during this decade are:

(1) **Trial Smelter Arbitration, 1941:** It is first significant event in the development of international environmental law where sulphur dioxide fumes produced in Canada were causing damages in the United States of America. The arbitration tribunal decided that allowing the use of one's territory by a state in such a way which causes injury to another state is prohibited under international law.

(2) **Stockholm Declaration on Human Environment 1972:** First International Conference on Human Environment was convened from June 5-16, by the United Nations at Stockholm, Sweden after considering the negative impact of the pollution of air, water and environment. This

conference was the outcome of the consequences of the public awareness about growing environment pollution particularly in North America. An important outcome of Stockholm Conference was the establishment of United Nations' Environment Programme. It has four main components:

- **The Governing Council:** This main body has to submit its report through United Nations' Economic and Social Council to General Assembly.
- **Environment Secretariat:** Having its headquarter at Nairobi, it is headed by an executive director elected by the United Nation's Secretary General.
- **Environment Coordination Board:** It was established to ensure proper cooperation among all the bodies of United Nations' having a mandate for environmental programmes. It functions under the auspicious of the United Nations' administrative committee and coordination under the chairmanship of United Nations executive director. It is responsible to the United Nations environmental programmes in reporting annually.
- **Environment Fund:** It is established to enable the United Nations governing council to fulfil its obligations regarding direction and coordination of environmental activities undertaken by the United Nations.

(3) **The UN Convention on International Trade in Endangered Species of Wild Flora and Fauna, 1973:** As it was realised that international trade, destruction, land conversion of habitats and pollution are the main causes of loss in biodiversity, therefore, convention on international trade was adopted by the United Nations in 1973. It was the first wildlife treaty to provide express obligation and monitoring along with the lists of species which were threatened with the extinction and which might become threatened.

(4) **Cocoyoc Declaration on Environment and Declaration, 1974:** The United Nations environment programme was held at Cocoyoc in Mexico in October 1974 where Cocoyoc Declaration was adopted. The term sustainable development was used first time in this declaration. It identified the economic and social factors inherent in environmental degradation and laid emphasis on "development without destruction".

(b) International Environmental Law in Second Decade (1980-1990)

Main efforts made by the international community and the United Nations during this decade are[14]

- **Nairobi Declaration 1982:** It was adopted at Nairobi Conference convened for celebrating 10th anniversary of Stockholm Conference on Human Environment in 1972. It is recommendable to note that global nature of this problem transcends national boundries and should be resolved for the benefit of all through consultations amongst states and joint international action.
- **World Charter for Nature, 1982:** Adopted by the General Assembly in 1982. World Charter for Nature avoided the activities that cause the irreversible damage to nature. In each such activity it is unavoidable then it must be carried on so as to maximize the potential adverse effects.
- **The Montreal Protocol on Substance that Deplete Ozone Layer, 1987:** The Monetreal Protocol, an international agreement adopted as Ozone Treaty in 1982 impose obligation on states to reduce production and consumption of ozone depleting substances like chloro-fluoro-carbons. It mainly aimed at the elimination of choloro-fluoro-carbons at a uniform rate irrespective of the development status of a country.
- **Brundtland Commission, 1983:** The World Commission on Environment and Development was setup by General Assembly of United Nations in 1983. In 1987 in it's report "our common future" it gives two key concepts of sustainable development, i.e. concept of need and idea of limitation apart from giving a simple and clear definition for sustainable development.

(c) International Environmental Law in Third Decade (1999-2000)

Main efforts made by the international community and the United Nations during this decade are[15]:

- **The Earth Summit 1992:** The United Nations Conference on Environment and Development, 1992, commonly known as the Earth Summit, was held at Rio de Janeiro. This Summit forced the people worldwide to rethink how their lives affect natural resources and to confront a new environment that determines the surroundings in which they live.

- **Two Main Conventions:** Convention of Bio-diversity, 1992 and United Nations Convention on Climate Change, 1992.
- Convention of Bio-diversity, 1992, provided for conservation of biological diversity, sustainable use of its components and fair and equitable sharing of the benefits arising out of the use of biological resources, knowledge and for matters connected therewith.
- United Nations Convention on Climate Change, 1992 requires the states to take steps to reduce their emission of gases which are believed to contribute to global warming. Main objective of this convention was to achieve a stabilization of greenhouse gas concentration in the atmosphere as to prevent dangerous anthropogenic interference with the climate change. This Convention defined climate change as a change which is attributed directly or indirectly to human activity which alters the composition of global atmosphere.
- **Earth Summit Plus Five, 1997:** A special session of United Nations General Assembly at New York on environment was held in 1997 known as "Earth Summit Plus Five" as it was after five years from "earth summit" in Rio de Janeiro in 1992. Here representatives of various nations reviewed the progress in achieving the goal of sustainable development and to save the planet earth from further deterioration.
- **Kyoto Protocol and Pact on Global Warming (Green House Conference), 1997:** The United Nations Climate Conference in Kyoto (Japan) was held in 1997 and adopted Kyoto Protocol which supplemented the Convention on Climate Change 1992. Kyoto Protocol requires the industrialized countries as a whole to reduce their average annual emission of six green house gases like carbon dioxide, methane and chloro-fluoro-carbon by 5.2 per cent from 1990 levels between the years 2008 and 2012. Main objectives of Kyoto Protocol were to achieve stabilization of green house gas concentration in atmosphere by interference with the climate change to ensure that food production is not threatened and enable economic development to proceed in a sustainable manner.

(d) International Environmental Law in Forth Decade (2000-2009)

Main efforts made by the international community and the United Nations during this decade are:

- **The Sixth Conference of Parties to Kyoto Protocol (cops-6), 2001:** In Bonn Germany, parties to Kyoto Protocol agreed on a package of measures that would operationalise the Kyoto treaty and meet the 2008-12 targets by cutting developed countries emission of green house gases to 5.2 per cent below the 1990 levels. It further provided that the countries which do not meet their commitment by 2012 would make emission reduction during 2013-2017 of an additional 30 per cent on their unfulfilled targets and also pay financial penalty.
- **Delhi Declaration on Climate Change and Sustainable Development, 2002:** It was adopted in the eighth conference of parties (cops-8) to the United Nations framework convention on climate change in 2002 in New Delhi. It is considered to be a landmark and a new approach to the issues of climate change. It provided that sustainable development will be a success only if varieties of climate change such as change in weather, global warming, alteration of rainfall and temperature pattern are addressed[16].

Motives for Corporate Social Responsibility

Some critics believe that Corporate Social Responsibility programmes are undertaken by companies such as British American Tobacco, it is a global tobacco company headquartered in London, United Kingdom. It is the world's second largest tobacco company by global market share, with a leading position in more than 50 countries and a presence in more than 180 countries. Its brands include Dunhill, Kent, Lucky Strike and Pall Mall, the petroleum giant British Petroleum which is a global oil and gas company headquartered in London, United Kingdom. It is the third-largest energy company and fourth-largest company in the world measured by revenues and one of the six oil and gas 'super majors'. British Petroleum has operations in over 80 countries, produces around 3.8 million barrels of oil equivalent per day and has 22,400 service stations worldwide. Its largest division is British Petroleum America, which is the biggest producer of oil and gas in the United States and is headquartered in Houston, Texas. As at 31 December, 2010 it had total proven commercial reserves of 18.07 billion barrels of oil equivalent. The name 'British Petroleum' derives from the initials of one of the company's former legal names, British Petroleum. British Petroleum's track record of Corporate Social Responsibility has been mixed. The company has been involved in a number of major environmental and safety incidents and received criticism for its political influence. However, in 1997, it became the first major oil company to publicly acknowledge the need to take steps against climate change, and in that year established a company-wide target to reduce its emissions of greenhouse gases. British Petroleum currently invests over $1 billion per year in the development of renewable energy sources, and has committed to spend $8 billion on renewable energy in the 2005 to 2015 period[17].

NOTES

1. Jyoti Rattan, "Sustainable Development and Genesis of International Environmental Law: An Assessment," *Panjab University Research Journal* (Arts), p. 156.
2. Available at http://www.thedailystar.net/newDesign/news-details.php?nid=185711 accessed on 24.05.2011.
3. *Ibid.*
4. Current Blaze, "International Environmental Standards for Transitional Corporation", *Lawz*, p. 28, (June, 2011).
5. *Ibid.*
6. Rustam Singh Thakur, (2011), Transnational Corporations and Environmental Damages, p. 91.
7. Current Blaze, (2011), "International Environmental Standards for Transitional Corporation", *Lawz*, p. 91-92 (June).
8. *Ibid.*, p. 93.
9. *Ibid.*, p. 95.
10. Available at http://en.wikipedia.org/wiki/Quality_management accessed on 16.05.2011.
11. *Ibid.*
12. *Ibid.*
13. *Ibid.*, p. 153-154-155.
14. Altman, Mathew C. (2007), "The decomposition of the corporate body: What can't contribute to business ethics", *Journal of Business,* 74, p. 156 @ springer 2007.
15. *Ibid.*, pp. 156-159.

16. Its available at http://en.wikipedia.org/wiki/Our_Common_ Future, accessed on 16.03.2011.
17. Available at http://www.reuters.com/article/2010/04/13/bp-altenergy-idUSN1310080220100413 accessed on 12.06.2011.

REFERENCES

Altman, Mathew C. (2007), "The decomposition of the corporate body: what can't contribute to business ethics", *Journal of Business,* 74, pp. 253-266 @ Springer 2007.

Barbara, Parker (2005), Introduction to Globalization and Business Relationship and Responsibility, by Response Book (adviser of Sage Publication) New Delhi.

Biag, M.A. (1996), *A Environmental, Law and Justice*, by Regency Publication, New Delhi.

D'Amato and Henderson, (2009), *A guide to leadership task and functions,* by North Corolina, 1st edition.

Jain, Ashok K. (2005), *Law and Environment, Ascent Law for Society Series*, by Ascent Publication, Delhi.

Matten, Dirk and Moon, Jeremy (2004), "Corporate social responsibility education in Europe", *Journal of Business Ethics*, 54, pp. 323-337, by Kluwer Academics Publishers printed in Netherland.

Moon, Jermy (2007), "The contribution of corporate social responsibility to sustainable development" *Sustainable Development,* 15, pp. 296-306, published on line in Wiley Interscience, Noltinghang University Business School, U.K., available at www.interscience.wiley.com.

Routedge, C.J. Barrow *Environment Management (Principle and Practices)*, 1st published in 1999, by 11 New Felterlane, London.

Stivers, R. (1976), The Sustainable Society: Ethics and Economic Growth. by Philadelphia: Westminster Press.

Thapar, Radhika (2010), *Insight: Legal Essay*, by Shreeram's Law House, 2nd edition.

Werther, William B. Chandler, J.R. David, (1977), Corporate Social Responsibility, by University of Miami, Sage Publications.

Chapter 24

Water Resource Management of Kuhls of Kangra

Declining Community Participation

Rajan Bhandari and *Bharti*

Introduction

Kuhl is a man-made irrigation channels which carries water for irrigation as well as domestic purposes from sources like springs and glaciers. Irrigation in hilly reaches take place from small diversion put across streams and water diverted through channels commonly called *kuhls* (Planning Commission, 1966: 25). Such man made gravity-fed irrigation channels are found throughout the world but most common type is found in Central Asia (Fourniau, 2000: 36). Huge number of such channels exists in Himachal Pradesh (*Kuhls*) and Uttrakhand (*Ghuls*) in the Western Himalaya of India. From centuries, farmers in Kangra valley, in the Western Himalayan state of Himachal Pradesh, India, have constructed, maintained, and managed, one of the largest network of community-based irrigation system in the world. (Baker, 2005). In Kangra valley, the maximum numbers of *kuhl* exist in the Palampur tehsil (Kayastha, 1964: 82).

Kangra valley is occupying very dense network of *kuhls* which provides water not only for irrigation purposes but also for other domestic needs. There are around 750 large *kuhls* and 2500 small *kuhls* in the valley. Some *kuhls* are very large, irrigate more than 50 villages and many of small *kuhls* irrigate at least one village. According to Himachal Pradesh Development Report 2004, about 47.5 per cent of total irrigated area of the state was under *kuhls* and other sources whereas, 87 per cent of this (47.5%) area was irrigated by *kuhls*. In Kangra district 93.4 per cent of total irrigated area was under *kuhl* irrigation (Statistical Outline of Himachal Pradesh, 2002). The credit for success of *kuhl* of Kangra goes to its people and their community participation. The overwhelming perception among the local communities and NGOs is that the traditional system of "private" *kuhls* was, and wherever they still exist, is far more effective than the ones taken over by the government (Sengupta, 2003: 62).

Kuhls of Kangra valley represent a perfect illustration of participatory management and functioning as a common property from centuries. More than 150 years old traditional community-based *kuhl* in Himachal Pradesh are based on an elaborate and well-defined system of rules, rights, and responsibilities of water allocation between various upstream and downstream villages (Sengupta, 2003: 8).

Kangra valley provides most suitable physical and socio-cultural conditions for the setup of *kuhl* network. Some of these are mentioned below:

- Dhauladhar range, which separate Kangra district from Chamba district, followed by gently sloping valley, river terraced characterised by snow fed streams, has provided suitable conditions for *kuhl* construction in the valley. The scope of underground water for irrigation is low as compare to gravity flow irrigation systems, locally termed as *kuhl,* built 200 years ago by the farmer's ancestors without state patronage (B. Emmanuel, 2000: 6). Perennial rivers provide ample water for the regular supply of water for the development of *kuhls*.
- Scattered settlements in Kangra valley, mostly situated on the top of small spurs, had dependency on springs (locally known as *Bawries*) found in relatively low lying sites (generally more than one kilometre away from settlement). Sources like *Bawrie* were serving small water needs, usually drinking water due to its concentrated nature at particular point. *Kuhls,* due to elongated character could serve for distances, were useful for irrigation purposes. Such a pattern of scattered settlements inspired ancestor to construct *kuhls,* to serve larger area for domestic as well as irrigation purpose.
- Local irrigation means like *kuhl* were required for the cultivation of rice and wheat as most of the annual total precipitation (75%) occurs in the monsoon season. For rice cultivation large quantity

of water is needed in May-June months and for wheat it is required in case of drought.

- Before electrification in the region large numbers of water mills were functioning on these man-made channels. Many *kuhl*s were constructed for the gravity flow required for water mills and further serve as irrigation channels.

Objectives of the Study

The main objective of the study is to focus on the problem of declining importance of *kuhls* despite community participation in different tasks related to management, maintenance and water distribution. Present study has been divided into three parts. In the first part management and role of community participation in the maintenance of *kuhl*s and water distribution has been discussed; followed by, uses of *kuhl* water over the time; and lastly, causes of decreasing role of *kuhl*s and suggestions for its sustainability have been discussed. With the help of one case study all aspects regarding management, problems and solutions have been highlighted. Sapruhl *kuhl* of Palampur tehsil in Kangra District has been selected for present investigation for the following reasons:

- Sapruhl *Kuhl* is the longest among community managed *kuhls* of Neogle watershed system. Sapruhl *kuhl* got its origin at 1290 m. above mean sea level and covers a downward distance of around 22 km. up to Kharoth (910 Mtrs. above mean sea level).
- Sapruhl *kuhl* also put forth an instance of river water linking centuries back.
- Author has first hand experience of more than two decades.

Sapruhl *kuhl* was constructed more than two centuries back, mainly for the irrigation purpose. The *kuhl* got its name from *Sparu* clan of Kharot village, a down-stream village. According to folklore, Sapruhl *kuhl* was constructed after sacrificing daughter of *Sparu* clan who was married in an up stream village. As a result, farmers of Kharot village claim to be the owner of the *kuhl*. The farmers of Lahla, an upstream village, believe that *kuhl* passes through their land and therefore, they can claim some extra water rights. However, till date Kharot village has some special rights of water for giving sacrifice of their daughter for *kuhl* construction centuries back. Despite some conflict between upstream-downstream villages, it is one of the largest community managed *kuhl* of the Kangra valley.

Sapruhl *kuhl* put forward a remarkable example of river water linking, made centuries back to provide the regular supply of water. It joins two watersheds of tributaries of Beas river, i.e. Neogle and Baner *khad* (stream). The water of Baner *khad* has been extracted from the left bank by a diversion (previously it was through temporary diversion but after completion of a hydroelectric project the discharged water has been directly merged into the *kuhl*) and merged into Bagar *khad* (stream) from right bank after covering a distance of more than 10 km in pine forest and cultivated land. Further, water from Bagar *khad* is extracted from right bank and merged into parallel flowing Krini *khad* from the left side. Before the merger of Krini *khad* into Neogle near Paror village, *kuhl* has been extracted for Kharot village, last village served by Sapruhl *kuhl*. Both Bagar and Krini *khads* are tributary of Neogle *khad*.

Role of Community Participation: Management, Maintenance and Distribution

Importance of community participation for water management is well accepted in the Water Policy of India. The farmers participation in irrigation management leads to, firstly, relief to the government in terms of the cost and burden of system management; secondly, improvement of system performance due to increased co-operation between farmers; thirdly, improvement of micro-network systems maintenance; and lastly, improvement equity of water distribution (Manzardo, 2000: 184). Traditional community based *kuhl* irrigation systems are based on an elaborate and well-defined system of rules, rights, and responsibilities of water allocation between various upstream and downstream villages. Many of these so-called community-managed *kuhls*, popularly known as "private" *kuhls*, have been taken over by the Irrigation and Public Health Department of the Himachal Pradesh Government as a result of decreasing participation of farmers in maintenance and management. It is evident that the progress of irrigation has been dependent mostly on private organizations as the number of *kuhls* developed by farmers at their own level are more in number than those provided by government agencies (Planning Commission, 2004: 215). It is commonly perceived among the local people that community-based "private" *kuhls* are far more effective than those *kuhls* that have been taken over by the government in the past few decades (Sengupta, S. and others, 2003: 3).

In community managed *kuhls* all tasks related to maintenance of *kuhl*s, distribution of water and water conflicts are managed by farmers headed by a *Kohli* (manager for *kuhls*). The village 'engineer' or '*Kohli*' repairs the temporary bund of boulders and the channel (*kuhl*) to the fields before the beginning of the sowing season and also manages and ensures water supply to individual fields (Joshi, 2006).

As mentioned earlier Sapruhl *kuhl* is a community managed *kuhl* where *kohli* enjoys prime position in its management. *Kuhl*-committee was formed in 1965 to increase the legitimacy of the *Kohli*, to facilitate acquisition of government funds for *kuhl* repair and to defend against external threats to a *kuhl's* water supply (Baker, 2002: 155-56). However, despite the fact that *kuhls* committee is functioning for more than four decades, the role of *kohli* has not lessened. Previously elder son of the *kohli* automatically inherited the right to be a next *kohli* after his father, but after the formation of the kuhl-committee, *kohli* can be elected by voting of committee members if appointed one is not performing better. *Kohli* organizes as well as supervises all tasks related to the *kuhl* maintenance, repair and distribution. In return for his services, he receives a fix share of grain at the time of harvest of *rabi* and *kharif* crops. *Kohli* of Sapruhl *kuhl* receives five *thimbi* (approximately two kilogram) of un-husked rice and two *thimbi* (approximately three kilogram) of wheat at the harvest of *kharif* (monsoon) and *rabi* (winter) crops.

Kohli is responsible for all task related to maintenance of *kuhl* and distribution of water, for which he takes help of all farmers as community participation.

Maintenance of *Kuhls*: Sense of Community Participation

Other than domestic uses of *kuhl's* water, its main significance is for irrigation. *Kuhls* are equally important for both *kharif* (monsoon) as well as *Rabi* (winter) crops but *kharif* crop (Paddy farming) requires large quantity of water for sowing. To meet the needs of large quantity of water and constant flow of water, maintenance work starts with *Khanna* and *Chhang* processes in March-April (before sowing). *Khanna* is a process of annual cleaning and repair of *kuhl* channels, involving removing of sediments. *Chhang* is simultaneous method of removing vegetation from the sides of *kuhl*.

Khanna is performed once in March-April whereas *Chhang* is made twice in March-April as well as in October-November. *Chhang* of October-November is made by individual farmers for small *kuhl* channel adjoining to their farms and in March-April it is collective effort for large channels of *kuhls*. Sometimes both activities, *khanna* and *chhang*, are made collectively by farmers in large sized *kuhl*s and individually in small *kuhl*s near to their farms.

After completion of *khanna* process as mentioned above, construction of *Dunga* (structure for water diversion) is a major task in most of *kuhls*. *Dunga* is a barrier built across the river (*khad*) collectively by pebble stones, mud, pine branches and bamboo sticks. The quality of material used for making diversion may vary along the complete network of a *kuhl*. As per local rules, *dunga* of upstream *kuhl*s must be more permeable than those of downstream *kuhl* (Baker, 2005: 77). Upstream *dunga* constructed only by large pebbles so that water can pass through downstream. Further in downstream *dungas* mixture of stones, mud, pine branches and bamboo sticks may be added. Presently most of down stream *dungas* of Sapruhl *kuhl* has been constructed by the Irrigation Department according to required flow of water. The main diversion is no more requirement as the discharge of hydroelectric project has been merged at the former place of diversion structure (*dunga*). However, at present the main task is only to perform *khanna* and repair if any landslide happens at any stretch of the *kuhl*.

Each cultivator household has to send at least one male person for the maintenance of *kuhl* and related tasks. *Kohli* use to keep daily record during maintenance period of all present one. In case of absence in duties, *kohli* can levy appropriate penalty in terms of money or farmer has to be satisfied with less water, both in timing and quantity. However, households without any male person, ill person, old aged person, landless, shopkeepers are exempted from paying such penalties.

Along with *kuhl* maintenance, farmers start field preparation for paddy cultivation in the last week of April, immediately after harvesting *Rabi* crop. Distribution of water starts as soon as the maintenance work of kuhls and field preparation is completed for the sowing of paddy.

Water Distribution: Task for Present with Shadow of Past

Water allocation to each field is a matter of great skill entirely taken care by the *kohli*, keeping in view special rights of water for some villages. The water distribution system varies from one to another *kuhl* and season to season. Water requirements are less for the sowing of *rabi* crop as compared to *kharif* crops, subsequently water distribution rules are also more authoritarian for the latter. *Kohli* plays a major role in the water distribution during the *kharif* season.

Timely requirement of water for kharif crop, particularly for rice sowing is very important because water is required at different stages in each farm. To avoid conflicts among upstream and downstream farmers, water distribution is made on rotational pattern in many *kuhls*, both community as well as in government owned *kuhls*.

In sapruhl *kuhl*, water distribution starts with first eight days and night regular supply known as *Dol* to Paror and Kharoth villages. *Dol* is a special right for water allocation, for which most of water of *kuhl* is allocated to one village for limited days and nights. Kharoth and Paror villages have the privilege of *dol*, as their daughter was sacrificed for the cause of *kuhl* construction. After eight days, water is distributed on rotational basis, either from up-stream to down-stream or from down-stream to up-stream. Water stealing is common during night times in *kharif* season. The most happening point for water stealing is *Tup* (point where *kuhl* water divided further into two or more smaller *kuhls*). To stop water stealing practices *kohli* appoint *Handa* (guard) within farmers. Normally particular farmer getting water for his field has responsibility to perform as a *handa* at *tup*. According to *kohli* of the Sapruhl *kuhl* water stealing is increasing vary rapidly as community participation is decreasing. *Kohli* himself keeps on makes trips to the diversion (*dunga*) with an assistant or sometimes more. If someone is caught stealing water, he will be penalised with less or no water.

Water distribution management is effective till the advent of monsoon. After the arrival of monsoon and regular precipitation, dependency on *kuhl* water decreases, however, farmer can use it at any time if required.

In rabi crop season, *kuhl* management and water distribution system is not as rigid as compare to *kharif* season. The moisture is retained till October and for sowing of wheat only small quantity of water is required. After sowing even from December to March end winter rain by western disturbances preserve significant moisture for the growth of crops. As per *kohli* of the present *kuhl*, *rabi* crop is a peaceful period but it does not help in keeping the momentum of management which is one of the causes for decreasing community participation for management of the *kuhl*.

Despite best community participation, regular water supply, large cohesive network, and above all, support from government and non-government agencies the importance of *kuhls* water for irrigation and other domestic uses is decreasing very fast. Sapruhl *kuhl* not only supplies water for irrigation but it also caters clean water for other domestic uses.

Kuhl Water Uses: Past, Present and Future

Sapruhl *kuhl* was constructed mainly for irrigation purpose but along with irrigation it also serves for different uses. In the past (up to beginning of 70s of 20th century) water uses of *kuhl* was mainly for irrigation, large domestic uses, and for drinking purposes (particularly in winters when silt contents are very less). In down-stream *kuhls* however it was not used for drinking and spring water used there for the purposes. Water mills (*gharat*) were also largely depended upon gravity of *kuhl* water. After electrification *gharat* were replaced by the electrified mills and many *kuhl* channels leading for water mills also vanished with time.

Presently, Sapruhl *kuhl* is experiencing transformation both at the level of community participation as well as in water uses. In upper parts of the *kuhl* the water utility is, however, same but in lower parts, it is mainly for irrigation. Introduction of widespread tap water access almost in each household facilitated easy drinking water. Though, tap water culture has facilitated safe drinking water but its over-utilization for large domestic uses has decreased use of *kuhl* water. Such conditions can lead to problems in future as dependency on tap water and increasing demand for water. At some particular places it has been noticed that sewerage outlet have been merged into the *kuhl* and down stream settlements do not use polluted water other than the irrigation purposes.

According to *Kohli*, area under cultivation is also decreasing in command areas of Sapruhl *kuhl* which has resulted into less community participation. Increased non-farm employment, increase in inequity and conflict between head-enders and tail-enders in the consumption of water and contributions for maintenance, and a decline in the authority of *kohli* has resulted into a decrease in participation in maintenance of the *kuhl* work (Baker, 2005). Main factor for non-farm employment is decreasing land holding size which cannot sustain the family needs. Secondly, young generation has no interest in subsistence rice-wheat cultivation and is opting employments in government and largely in private sectors. It is noticed that in such conditions it is difficult for young generation to spare time for the maintenance of *kuhl*.

Only few *gharats* are functioning at present, many among existing one are suffering from lesser water in *kuhls* and rest due to less number of customers. There were around 20 water mills along one of stretch of Sapruhl *kuhl* at present only 4 are surviving out of these. Rapidly decreasing number of *gharats* has affected *kuhl* maintenance because in the past owners of *gharats* had large participation in *kuhl* maintenance for the regular supply of water required throughout year.

Government and non-government agencies are making all efforts to save this indigenous system by reducing the problem of maintenance by making *kuhl*s channels paved. Despite large funding from National Bank for Agricultural and Rural Development (NABARD), reconstruction is not up to mark to sustain it for long time. The future of the *kuhl*s depends upon the intensity of community participation. In future, it seems that other than irrigation there might be only small prospectus for domestic and water mills.

One of the main problems in most of *kuhl*s is increasing depth of river bed due to extraction of sand and stones. Increased depth requires more elevated diversion or extended *kuhl*'s point where it can meet river bed. Both techniques are relatively difficult when community participation is decreasing. In Sapruhl *kuhl* this problem has vanished after merging water of hydroelectric project. Some of the *kuhls* have become seasonal giving water during rainy season or little after because the forest cover has ceased to accumulate water for long (HP HDR, 2004: 215)

Sustainability of Kuhls*: A Task to Save Indigenous System*

Decline cannot be taken as the end of indigenous system of *kuhl*s. The indigenous system has to be revived by taking proper steps in this direction. Few suggestions in this direction that can be opted or can further be refined for the cause of *kuhl's* survival are as follows:

- Keeping in mind the importance of *kuhl's* water for agriculture and decline of traditional subsistence rice-wheat cultivation, the need of the hour is to diversify the agriculture system by introducing commercial agriculture. By introducing floriculture and horticulture, two promising fields of commercialized agriculture for which Kangra valley is already recognised, traditional rice-wheat farming can be replaced.
- Palampur tea, renowned brand of the valley, is facing decline due to high production cost due to small size of the tea gardens and frequent drought in the months of April-May, which is the main season for the production of best quality tea. On other hand, as a result of increasing non-farm employment, traditional wheat-rice fields have been converted into fallow lands. Both problems could be overcome by converting fallow lands into

tea gardens. By converting these areas into tea gardens, production cost for tea can be decreased and *kuhls* water can be used for irrigation for tea gardens.

- State Department of Fisheries is evolving package of practices and also initiating a Scheme on 'Running Water Fish Culture' in order to exploit fast flowing channels, *kuhl* and tributaries of major rivers. By making small ponds close to the *kuhl* channels, its water can be used for fish production. Fish can be reared in small as well as in big ponds for which water from a *kuhl* is sufficient. In rural areas, it can help in reducing rural unemployment by introduction of fish farms.
- As many small *kuhls* were serving water mills and these *kuhls* were also functioning as irrigation channel and were maintained mainly by the mills owner. After the collapse of many water mills such small channels left with low or no maintenance and water supply. Some *kuhl* channels can be rejuvenated by indirect approach of reviving of water mills.
- In absence of community participation, paved *kuhls* remains single alternative for the longevity of *kuhl* and to spare regular maintenance work. Leakage in the money invested in *kuhl* constructions is an alarm for the resultant leakage of *kuhl* channels, which could be a serious problem in the future. Proper checks on such constructions are required from government, *kuhls* committee and farmer's side for the durability of the channel.
- To create an awareness *kuhl* system should be introduced in text books of Himachal Pradesh School Education Board. It must be considered as heritage of the state so that awareness can be created among people regarding the cultural and scientific heritage of their land.

Conclusion

The intrinsic technological simplicity of local engineering and community managed irrigation systems makes Kangra *kuhls* important option for water needs of different purposes. But mountain societies are changing due to rapidly altering socio-economic and administrative system. These changes have made an impact on reducing traditional management and participation rate which has consequently hampered centuries old irrigation system of the *kuhls*. Though, the uses of *kuhl's* water has decreased from past to present, but, keeping in mind the future aspect of increasing water demands, sustainability of both *kuhls* and role of community becomes important.

REFERENCES

Emmanuel, B. (2000) *Common Pool Resources and Communal Control: Two Case Studies in Himachal Pradesh*, India 8th IASCP Conference Bloomington, Indiana, USA May 31–June 4, 2000.

Baker, J. M. (2005) *The Kuhls of Kangra Community Managed Irrigation in Western Himalaya*, University of Washington Press Seattle and London.

Fourniau, V., (2000), Some Notes on the Study of Irrigation to the History of Central Asia, in *Sharing Water: Irrigation and Water Management in the Hindkush-Karakoram-Himalaya,* edited. Kreutzmann, H. Oxford University Press, Karachi, Pakistan, p. 36.

Joshi, V.K., (2006), *Catching the Water*, accessed from www.boloji.com/environment on February 12, 2008.

Kayastha, S.L., (1964), *The Himalayan Beas Basin: A Study in Habitat, Economy and Society,* Banaras Hindu University Press, Baranas, India, pp. 80-88.

Manzardo, A.E., (2000), Farmer Participation in Irrigation Management in State-sponsored Minor Irrigation Systems in the Indian Himalyas, in *Sharing Water: Irrigation and Water Management in the Hindkush-Karakoram-Himalaya,* edited. Kreutzmann, H., Oxford University Press, Karachi, Pakistan, p. 184.

Planning Commission (2004), *Himachal Pradesh Development Report, 2004,* Planning Commission, Government of India, New Delhi, pp.215-16.

Planning Commission, (1966), *All India Review of Minor Irrigation Works Based on State-wise Field Studies*, Committee on Plan Projects (Planning Commission) Irrigation Team, New Delhi, June 1966, p.25.

Sengupta, S. and others, (2003). *Developing Markets for Watershed Protection Services and Improved Livelihoods in India,* Winrock International India, New Delhi and International Institute for Environment and Development, London, (*www.winrockindia.org*).

The Government of India, (1991), Ministry of Water Resources-CAD Division, *Farmers Participation in Irrigation Management*, R.S. Pathak, New Delhi.

Chapter 25

Globalization: The Imperatives of Energy Law for Sustainable Development

Sukhwinder Virk and *Ivneet Walia*

Globalization: The Imperatives of Energy Law for Sustainable Development

Among our society's many pressing challenges at the start of the twenty-first century, how society responds to the human induced alter nation of Earth's natural systems surely ranks as the most profound in terms of its implication for the future of all life as we understand it. One cannot at once melt the glaciers and polar icecaps, alter the climate, raise the relative levels of the seas, cause extinction of a wide range of species, and watch the rapid growth of the human population in crowded human settlements around the globe, without asking some fundamental questions: How shall we cope? Our past accomplishments are no sure guide for this future, are they?

During the last century, the use of fossil fuel resources—oil, natural gas, and coal—dominated world primary energy. In 2001, fossil energy use made up seventy-nine per cent of world primary energy consumption. In comparison, renewable (including large hydro, traditional biomass, and new renewable like solar, wind, geothermal) made up fourteen per cent and nuclear seven per cent of world primary energy use. Furthermore, demand for energy services continues to increase with growing economies and population size.[1]

Development goals of the international community were identified in 2000 at the meeting of the United Nations General Assembly (the

Millennium Assembly), and are known as the Millennium Development Goals (MDGs). Through these goals, the international community aims to achieve the following:

- Eradicate extreme poverty and hunger;
- Achieve universal primary education;
- Promote gender equality and empower women;
- Reduce child mortality;
- Improve maternal health;
- Combat HIV/AIDS, malaria, and other diseases; and
- Ensure environmental sustainability.

With regard to this last goal, environmental sustainability is to be promoted by integrating the principles of sustainable development into national policies and programmes. Without access to modern forms of energy it will be virtually impossible to reach any of these global development goals. Energy was first acknowledged as a key part of the global political agenda in the process leading up to the World Summit for Sustainable Development (WSSD) held in Johannesburg, South Africa, in 2002. Energy, as outlined in the UN Secretary General Kofi Annan's WEHAB (Water, Energy, Health, Agriculture, and Biodiversity) agenda, was finally recognized as a necessary factor for sustainable development.[2]

An awareness and understanding of the environmental consequences of past and present energy systems is also becoming more relevant and systematic. Energy use contributes to indoor and urban air pollution, acidification, and global warming. It is responsible for eighty-six per cent of global anthropogenic emissions of sulphur dioxide, the main chemical responsible for environmental acidification that damages forests and lakes. As for global warming, the use of fossil fuels leads to major emissions of carbon dioxide and methane, the main greenhouse gases. Fossil fuel use contributes approximately seventy-eight per cent of anthropogenic emissions of carbon dioxide and twenty-three per cent of emissions of methane, as well as a significant fraction of emissions of long-lived small particulate matter, which poses significant risks to human health when inhaled. The consequences of greenhouse gas emissions from fossil fuel use global warming are particularly worrisome, and are of growing international concern. It is estimated that global emissions of GHG will have to be reduced by sixty per cent or more to meet the objectives of the United Nations Framework Convention on Climate Change (UNFCCC). Achieving this while expanding economies now based on the use of fossil fuels is one of the major challenges facing the energy system.[3]

In the pursuit of sustainable energy system pathways, three main strategies are identified. On the energy supply side, these include the exploration and adoption of more renewable energy sources such as biomass, wind, solar, hydro, and geothermal. Renewable energy fiows on Earth are thousands times the current global energy use. The second strategy on the energy supply side involves the exploration and adoption of advanced energy technologies, including advanced fossil fuel technologies, with near zero emissions of greenhouse gases, and nuclear technologies if the issues associated with such technologies can be resolved. On the energy demand side of the equation, strategies for improved energy efficiency at the point of end use in buildings, electric appliances, vehicles, and production processes must also be pursued to tap the very large economic (including an accounting for external health and environmental costs) potential form or efficient use of energy, thereby reducing the need for more supply.[4]

Over the last two decades, China has demonstrated a development strategy that has allowed for a significant decoupling of economic growth from energy use. The energy intensity of the Chinese economy has been reduced by approximately fifty per cent during the last twenty years, thereby significantly reducing costs, imports, and environmental degradation. Large opportunities to continue to improve energy intensity exist. The current development strategy of China is known as the "3 E strategy" and promotes:

- *Economic development*: provide energy services for a fourfold expansion of the economy by 2020;
- *Energy security*: avoid becoming overly dependent on oil and gas imports; and
- *Environmental protection*: protect public health, ecosystems, and limit climate change.

"GHG emissions trading," is emerging in a variety of forms, at a variety of governmental levels, engages both the public and private sectors in innovative partnerships, and will ultimately involve both emissions reductions and the capture and storage of GHGs in so-called carbon sinks. If successful, GHG emissions trading may significantly reduce the cost of emission reductions, encourage new, more efficient technology, and unleash considerable capital for energy investments in the developing and developed world. Derived from the lessons of the very successful sulphur dioxide (SO_2) allowance trading programme created in the United States by the 1990 Clean Air Act Amendments to promote market based trading in SO_2 emission reductions from electric power plants, the concept first appeared in the GHG context in the late 1980s.

The key provisions of the Marrakech Accords concern the establishment of concrete rules and guidelines to support a market-based approach to GHG emission reductions and sink enhancements. To do this, the Accords create a trading vehicle in the form of the emission reduction unit (ERU). Each ERU is equal to one ton of carbon dioxide equivalent (calculated using IPCC global warming potentials), is transferable and bankable (subject to certain banking limitations), and can be used to meet a Kyoto Party's emission reduction targets. A supervisory committee of ten members of the Parties to the Kyoto Protocol or independent entities accredited by the supervisory committee must verify all ERUs generated by GHG reduction projects. To participate in a project and be allowed to earn and trade ERUs, a nation must be a Party to the Kyoto Protocol and have in place a national system of GHG emission measurements that meet IPCC best practice guidelines.[5]

Expressions in National and International Energy Law, New Zealand: Examples for this broader expression can be found in the environmental legislation of New Zealand. *The Resource Management Act, 1991* (RMA) is guided by the principle of "sustainable management," which is not identical with sustainable development, but nevertheless related to it.

Germany: The German Energy Report 2001 states the three objectives (or pillars) of sustainable energy as follows: "Energy is sustainable when it meets the equal goals of supply security, economy and environmental protection."

European Union: At the level of the European Union, the EU Strategy for Sustainable Development contains a number of energy-related measures including a phase out of subsidies for Fossil fuel production and consumption by 2010. There is a plethora of Directives regulating electricity and gas, energy efficiency, renewable energy, and energy taxes. However, the overall approach is based on weak sustainability.[6]

Other Measures: Among the legal measures to promote energy for sustainable development, by far the most significant is legislation to remove fossil fuel and nuclear subsidies. Subsidy removal not only is a costless measure, but by definition, it is certain revenue enhancing one. As market mechanisms increasingly are being used instead of command and control measures to promote sound energy policies, creating a level playing field for resources in the market place is essential. The political difficulties of eliminating subsidies and the transition problems for local economies in fossil producing countries cannot be minimized. Nevertheless, countries such as Brazil, China, the Czech Republic, India, The Netherlands, Poland, the United Kingdom, and Russia have reduced or eliminated fossil subsidies successfully.

Enactment of temporary incentives to introduce new technologies into the market place has been used effectively in many countries. While long-term subsidization of any fuel, technology or product distorts the market and is therefore theoretically undesirable, temporary subsidies to bring new technologies into the market place can be effective, useful, and often essential to accelerate their market acceptance. Also, where fossil fuel subsidies persist, non-fossil fuel subsidies are justifiable to level the playing field for them. A good example of effective use of such temporary incentives is found in Denmark's introduction of wind power. From the start of its wind power programme in 1976 through 1996, the Danish government spent $75 million on wind turbine R&D.

Taxing pollutants or polluting fuels can be an effective way of raising the funding required for clean energy resources while promoting emission reductions in the marketplace. Such taxes make the polluters pay the externality costs of the damages to society from their pollution. They raise the price of emissions intensive goods and lower profits for fossil fuel use, thus allowing market forces to reduce emissions. Taxation of carbon dioxide emissions or polluting fuels is one of the most direct ways of addressing global warming and raising revenues for clean energy. Carbon taxes have been imposed in Brazil, Denmark, Finland, Italy, Latvia/Lithuania, and Sweden.[7]

One of the most effective measures to promote energy for sustainable development is the environmental impact assessment or statement (EIS) such as required for all major "federal actions significantly affecting the quality of the human environment" by the *U.S. National Environmental Policy Act of 1969.* The EISs must detail the environmental impacts of any proposed action, any unavoidable adverse environmental effects, alternatives to the proposed action, mitigation measures that could alleviate impacts, short- *vs.* long-term effects, and any irreversible commitments of resources. Laws requiring environmental disclosure by utilities of their emissions and power generation sources are very helpful in allowing consumers to select clean energy options in deregulated markets. Information required typically includes the reporting of generation sources, fuel mix, fuel emissions, kWh price, price volatility, and contract terms. Standards are a particularly effective and low cost way of promoting use of energy efficient equipment and assuring that emission reductions will be achieved. Standards for minimum efficiency performance of products like appliances, light fixtures, ballasts, motors, and the like, are effective in removing from the market place the least efficient products.[8]

Many countries today have laws providing for the recycling of their waste paper, glass, and metal products. For example, in Denmark, half of all waste is recycled and eighty per cent of new paper is made from used paper. Almost every city in the United States has legislated are cycling programme for paper, glass, plastic, and metal wastes, with either curb side pickup or establishment of a central recycling municipal facility. Education of the public is vital to let the people know the importance to them of taking the measures necessary to increase energy efficiency, to build the political support necessary for enactment of appropriate legislative measures, and to inform them of the options available to them.[9]

Effective enforcement is critical to the success of any standards programme. In practice, governments and regulatory agencies often come to identify with the industries or companies that they regulate. Also, political pressures often prevent effective government enforcement. Citizen enforcement, adopted in the United States in the Clean Air Act and other environmental statutes, has been found to be a most effective enforcement mechanism. Non-governmental organizations (NGOs) in the United States are able to hold regulators' feet to the fire very effectively by filing suit to enforce standards, with the award of attorney's fees for such litigation; the very presence of citizen suit provisions enables the NGOs to influence government enforcement policies.[10]

Conclusion

Lastly, based on our past experience, the road to sustainable development will be both difficult and by no means assured. It will require firm resolve, political will, technological innovation, and above all the education necessary to achieve what has been clearly articulated by the international community of the past thirty years as necessary for our survival in the decades ahead. There are abundant examples in both developed and developing countries of the successful adoption of cost-effective measures to reduce energy consumption, lower energy costs and reduce emissions. A wide variety of legislative and regulatory programmes have been undertaken and the legal and financial mechanisms for doing so are also many and varied. These measures can be advanced on a basis of long-term profitability; indeed, many energy efficiency savings are so compelling that they should be undertaken just to save money. But achieving these goals will take determined action and political will among all the governments and international institutions of the world.

NOTES

1. Philippe Sands, (2003), *Principles of International Environmental Law*, Cambridge University Press, Cambridge.
2. Alexandre Charles Kiss, (1975), *The Protection of the Environment and International Law*, Hague Academy of International Law, Sijthoff, Leiden.
3. D.C. Esty and M.H. Ivanova, (2000), *Global Environmental Governance*, Yale School of Environmental Studies.
4. A.J. Bradbrook, (1996), "Eco-Labeling: Lessons from the Energy Sector", *Adelaide L. Rev.*, p. 35.
5. A.J. Bradbrook, (2000), "The Development of a Regulatory Framework on Consumer Protection and Consumer Information for Sustainable Energy Use", *Asia Pacific Journal of Environmental Law*, p. 239.
6. C. Redgwell, (1997), "Privatization and Environmental Regulation: Some General Observations", *Journal of Energy & Natural Resources Law*, p. 36.
7. T. Walde, (1996), *The Energy Charter Treaty: An East-West Gateway for Investment and Trade*, Kluwer Publishers, London.
8. A. Bradbrook and R. Ottinger, "Energy Law and Sustainable Development", *IUCN Environmental Policy & Law Paper* No. 47 pp. 115-137.
9. A. Ogus, (1994), *Regulation, Legal Form and Economic Theory*, Oxford University Press, Oxford.
10. UNEP, (2000), "World Summit Highlights Role of Energy in Sustainable Development," Energy + Sustainable Development: A Newsletter of UCCEE and UNEP, December.

Chapter 26

Impacts of Globalization and Tourism on People of Himachal State

Arun Sharma and *Madhuri Aggarwal*

Introduction

Globalization, as a concept, refers both to the "shrinking" of the world and the increased consciousness of the world as a whole. It is a term used to describe the changes in societies and the world economy that are the result of dramatically increased cross-border trade, investment, and cultural exchange. "Globalization" carries multiple meanings, nuances, and applications. Few of these can be understood as the formation of a global village through closer contact between different parts of the world, with increasing possibilities of personal exchange, mutual understanding, and friendship between "world citizens," and creation of a global civilization. The World Bank defines globalization as the "Freedom and ability of individuals and firms to initiate voluntary economic transactions with residents of other countries." Marshall McLuhan's idea of "the global village," was introduced in his book *Explorations in Communication* (1960). The United Nations has coined the term "Our Global Neighbourhood" to describe an emerging world-political context. Globalization theory aims to understand complex connectivity proliferating at the global level considering both its sources and its implications across the various spheres of social existence. Globalization has brought forth supranational organizations and international regimes, that is, commonly accepted laws and commonly accepted practices. The loss of sovereignty by the nation state to transnational and supranational organizations is of greatest concern. A world system perspective is a world with a common political system (with a common social and cultural system), linked by a common language, cultural practices and institutions. In sociology and communications, globalization is understood as global mass culture dominated by the modern means of cultural production (movies, television, the Internet, mass advertising and so on). Mass communication produces images that cross and re-cross linguistic frontiers more rapidly and easily than goods and services and speaks across languages in an immediate way. Global mass culture is dominated by the ways in which the visual and graphic arts have entered directly into the reconstitution of popular life of entertainment and of leisure with the image, imagery, and styles of mass advertising. This is dominated by Western cultural values and techniques. This process is homogenizing but also enormously absorptive of techniques and practices. Economic globalization refers to free trade and increasing relations among members of an industry in different parts of the world (globalization of an industry), with a corresponding erosion of national sovereignty in the economic sphere (IMF, *World Economic Outlook,* May 1997). The spread of capitalism from developed to developing nations. "The concept of Globalization refers both to the compression of the world and the intensification of consciousness of the world as a whole" (Roland Robertson, 1992). "The process by which the world becomes a single place" (Anthony King, 1997).

Culture

Culture is a modern concept based on a term first used in classical antiquity by the Roman orator, Cicero: *"cultura animi"*. The term *"culture"* appeared first in its current sense in Europe in the 18th and 19th centuries, to connote a process of cultivation or improvement, as in agriculture or horticulture. In the 19th century, the term developed to refer first to the betterment or refinement of the individual, especially through education, and then to the fulfilment of national aspirations or ideals. In the mid-19th century, some scientists used the term "culture" to refer to a universal human capacity. For the German non-positivist sociologist Georg Simmel, culture referred to "the cultivation of individuals through the agency of external forms which have been objectified in the course of history". In the 20th century, "culture" emerged as a central concept in anthropology, encompassing the range of human phenomena that cannot be attributed to genetic inheritance. Specifically, the term "culture" in American anthropology had two meanings: (1) the evolved human capacity to classify and represent experiences with symbols, and to act imaginatively and creatively; and (2) the distinct ways that people living in different parts of the world classified and represented their experiences, and acted creatively. The term "culture," which originally meant the cultivation of the soul or mind, acquires most of its later modern meanings in the writings of the 18th-century German thinkers, who on various levels developing Rousseau's criticism of modern liberalism and Enlightenment. Two primary meanings of culture emerge from this period: culture as the folk-spirit having a unique identity, and culture as cultivation of inwardness or free individuality. The first meaning is predominant in our current use of the term "culture," although the second still plays a large role in what we think culture should achieve, namely the full "expression" of the unique of "authentic" self.

Background

Tourism is arguably the world's largest industry and continues at tremendous annual growth rates. A traveller can decide today to go to the North Pole and be there by tomorrow. Global infrastructures such as transportation and communications and global policies for free trade have created a situation where people and businesses in the global North can easily access natural resources and cultures in the global South. Until 1999, when thousands of people around the world began organizing against it (e.g. the Battle in Seattle), globalization was not regarded as a danger to local economies and cultural diversity. In fact, politicians and the media tout globalization as the path to greater wealth and success. Although globalization may be the most primary transformation of the world's political and economic structures. Since the industrial revolution, its implications have yet to be fully understood and debated. Most of the economic restructuring is in the interest of big business, not in the interest of the public. Under the banner of free trade, corporations have come to shape our lives through the consumer products we buy (including technology), the media that feed us information, even the educational system that trains us. Politicians chant the mantra of privatization and globalization. Globalization is a leading threat to local communities, particularly in the India: "Before British rule and the infusion of Western systems, people in the country lived in relatively self-sufficient communities. The modes of production and style of life were largely in harmony with the natural environment. British rule changed the social and economic structures of modern societies. The new structures, consumption styles, and technological systems became so ingrained in modern economies that even after the attainment of political independence, the importation of Western values, products, technologies and capital continued and expanded." The development of vast infrastructures such as roads and other transportation routes goes hand in hand with tourism development. As more tourists seek out hard-to-reach "frontier" destinations, those areas become popularized, and soon private industry takes over. Once an area is targeted for tourism development, the process begins with road building and displacement of the local population. Communication systems go in, as do energy-intensive and pollutive accommodations for visitors. The roads and communications in turn provide other industries with easy access to cheap labour and natural resources. This cycle of development is occurring at alarming rates in small communities and villages throughout the world; many of these areas are considered the most important biologically diverse regions of the planet. At the same time, roads built into places to serve primarily as transportation routes for extractive industries such as oil, logging, and mining inevitably become new corridors for colonists, including tourists. Tourism increases local reliance upon a global economy, leaking many economic benefits outside of the community back to the companies and countries that control most of the travel infrastructure. At the same time, tourism decreases dependence on local resources, as technologies, food, and health services are imported. Local people may also be pushed out or sell out, and local prices for commodities and services rise, as do taxes.

Literature Review

Globalization involves the movement of people, goods, ideas and information across national boundaries. It has been defined as 'the intensification of worldwide social relations which link distant localities in such a way that local happenings are shaped by events occurring many miles away and vice versa' (Giddens,1990: 64). In many respects globalization and industrialiization overlap, the one projecting on to the increasingly fast development of the other. What is new and important about contemporary globalization is the speed, extent and the impact of the changes that flow from it. The effects of globalization currently emanate most strongly from two main centres of Asia on India and China. Ripples of change from these centres are beginning to affect even the smallest and most remote communities worldwide. Industrialization in the state of Himachal Pradesh has resulted in massively increased exportation of a whole range of commodities that have strongly affected established producers in other parts of country: as we shall see, economic changes invariably underpin changes in relationships. In parallel with the rapid advancement of information and transportation technology, major global occurrences are currently transforming societies around the globe. Modern globalization, a concept associated with late capitalism and built on a hegemony promoting neo-liberalism policies, is radically altering world economies and societies. Globalization is a social construct (Rees, 2000) that is shifting the way we view the world—from one with multiple economies and diverse societies to a 'one-world' economy and homogenized society. Tourism, a phenomenon based on travel patterns of people, technology and cultural values, is a major vehicle, or operative, in effecting the globalization process. Tourism, now a universal practice, is flourishing rapidly to become one of the leading industries in the world today. World Travel and Tourism Council and others have referred to tourism, indeed, as the world's largest industry (Cooper and Wanhill, 1998; WTTC, 1996). In 1980, the WTO Conference in Manila declared that "world tourism can be a vital force for world peace and the role of tourism as a vehicle of international understanding and peace derives from the notion that interaction between hosts and guests makes understanding possible among peoples and cultures" (Var and Ap, 1998: 45-57). International tourism is regarded as a catalytic force for tension reduction and peace-building (Yu and Chung, 2001). Mohammed Hosni Mubarak, President of Egypt (2000) states, "Tourism and peace are intertwined. Tourism fosters understanding and peace, which support one another and enable continuity. It also broadens opportunities for cultural exchange and encompasses nations from all parts of the World."

Research Objectives

Globalization and sustainable development are unfolding simultaneously. It appears that tourism fits or may not fit well with the notion of sustainability. In most cases, when globalization and tourism intersect with sustainable development, there appears to be a less than compatible or desirable relationship. Differing values, goals and objectives tend to clash and appear contradictory. Tourism in this context can wield the power of a double-edged sword. With its swipe, it advances the goals of globalization. At the same time, it has potential negative implications, which can hinder sustainability. The purpose of this paper is:

1. To highlight outcomes resulting from the interrelationships between tourism and globalization as expressed through culture.
2. To understand the impacts of globalization on the culture and living standard of the local people of Himachal Pradesh.
3. To know the perception of individuals towards globalization and tourism.

Research Methodology

This paper highlights the impacts of globalization on culture of Himachal Pradesh by considering the tourism industry as a catalyst for the same. This research is a qualitative study. Data collection is conducted through in depth interviews among long and short term travellers as well as among local people of the state. Research questions centre on the process of globalization, the role travellers play in the creation of modified culture and diffusion of existing ones and community perception towards the same. A hermeneutical approach to data analysis was chosen. After qualitative analysis paper concludes both positive as well as negative impacts of globalization on culture with suggestions.

Analysis of Data

This research leans heavily on what the informants had to say on the topics, while the structure of the quotes lead the reader to understand why the researcher has chosen to interpret the final conclusions in a certain way. H. Russell Bernard states that: "Qualitative analysis is the search for patterns in data and for ideas that help explain the existence of those patterns" (Bernard, 1989: 319). He goes on to say that "Qualitative data analysis depends heavily on the presentation of selected anecdotes and comments from informants that lead the reader to understand what took (the researcher) months to figure out" (Bernard, 1989: 322). "Hermeneutic" is developed from the Greek word "hermêneuô", to interpret or translate. Originally it was connected to the interpretation of religious texts, but developed into the meaning of the practice and process of interpretation. The hermeneutic cycle refers to the process of returning to the source of study to understand and interpret meaning and reality in new ways. "Hermeneutics represents not so much a highly honed, well-established theory of understanding or a long-standing, well-defined tradition of philosophy as it does a family of concerns and critical perspectives that is just beginning to emerge as a programme of thought and research. Hermeneutical theories of understanding argue that all human understanding is never 'without words' and never 'outside time'" (Wachterhauser, 1986). As the research progressed into written form, the discourse between the interviewer and interviewee became a text through transcription, a written work. Both speech and writing are "alternative and legitimate of discourse", but writing involves characteristics that distance the text from the discourse (Ricoeur, 1982: 13). Although in a discourse situation the interviewee's intention and meaning often overlap, in the written text this possibility is absent and there is no way to return to the situation to verify the meaning that the interviewer has given in the transcription. The approach to the analysis and interpretation of the research material was to return to the original material as often as possible, while bearing in mind that there are certain fundamental truths to each subject matter inspite of the challenges posed by discourse and text interpretation. The aim has been to balance between an interpretive approach and the truth of reality. Just as physical laws of nature govern the material world, so also do certain laws of reality govern the more contingent world of human science and action.

Tourism *versus* Culture

Tourism can contribute to cultural revitalization, drawing from authentic sources and stimulated by an increasing market of postmodern tourists who are searching for 'meaning and truth' (UNESCO, 1996) in culture. Tourism, as a mechanism in the globalizing process, creates new spaces for new cultural encounters and alliances. When a 'tourist' and 'host meet', each carries within them a meaning of their own identity and each gets something new from the experience (UNESCO, 1996). Cultural diversity provides a wide range of unique tourism products that are authentic and original. One of the main attributes of tourism is to provide diverse experiences through contact with new cultures and cultural expression. As demand for cultural tourism products and new spaces increases, promising opportunities present themselves for economic revitalization, particularly in economically depressed areas. Potential opportunities for local entrepreneurship and empowerment are created. As heritage and cultural attractions become high demand commodities, the focus of political and economic agendas is shifted towards their revival, preservation and maintenance. One main tenet of globalization is an economic development agenda where goals and objectives are aimed at producing a 'one homogenized global' society, with common standards and economic uniformity that will improve the well-being of all society.

Acculturation

However, Hughes (1989) states that tourism and culture are seen to have a potentially destructive relationship (Macintosh, Hinch, & Ingram, 2002). Johnson (2000) argues that tourism is the prime threat to indigenous homelands and cultures through its exploitation, dislocation and desecration. Tourism can contribute to acculturation and cultural erosion. An even larger contradiction and potential threat, the demise of cultural diversity on a global scale due to acculturation, is emanating from global tourism and other global economic activity. On the one hand, tourism thrives on its ability to offer diverse and unique attractions and experiences, but on the other, it contributes to acculturation of host cultures. Acculturation, according to Kroeber (1948) comprises those changes in a culture brought about by another culture and will result in an increased similarity between the two cultures. Although this type of change may be reciprocal, it is more often an asymmetrical process resulting in the absorption of one culture into the powerful other. Through globalizing processes, languages and ethnic dialects have succumbed to the English language, and many have or are in danger of becoming extinct (BBC, 2001). Arguably, a primary goal of globalization may be acculturation on a global scale, where diverse cultures will be absorbed by Western cultures into one homogenized world and 'global market.' There is widespread evidence of acculturation processes taking place around the globe as Western influences infiltrate foreign countries, transforming their cultures and languages. As acculturation advances, cultural diversity is disappearing Cultural appreciation/Peace Tourism plays a major role in international relations and world peace (Matthews, 1975; Var and Ap, 1998).

Cultural Conflict

However, predominant notions that tourism generates cultural harmony, and is a vital force for peace have been exaggerated (Robinson, 1999). According to Robinson, there has been little evidence that tourism brings the world together. Further, he states, "tourism is one globalization influence that can initiate dramatic and irreversible changes within the cultures of host communities" (Robinson, 1999: 22). The idea that we should sustain and protect cultures is not yet fully developed. Robinson (1999) notes that the most obvious conflict is between tourist and host, engendered in part by the fundamental difference in goals—the tourist is engaged in leisure, the host is engaged in work. Another source of conflict, he states, is between the often persuasive and economically powerful developers and operators of the international, mainly first world countries, the tourism industry and the host country. He contends that tourism turns local cultures into commodities where religious rituals, ethic rites and festivals continue to be reduced and sanitized to conform to tourist expectations, resulting in 'reconstructed ethnicity.' Part of the problem stems from the packaging of culture away from the cultural site, which is another typical feature of globalization—businesses residing outside a country where the activity occurs (Robinson, 1999). The result is that host communities find culture and traditions under threat from the purchasing power of the tourism industry. Neither are tourists better off from a cultural viewpoint. Instead of getting rich and authentic cultural insights and experience, tourists get staged authenticity (Robinson, 1999). Cultural disharmonies within local communities often emerge as a result of a lack of understanding of tourism.

Tourism Myths and Realities

The tendency of large-scale tourism to dominate a whole regional economic base can be observed in many areas throughout the world. Tourism threatens and often destroys locals' traditional means of livelihood, or local self-reliance, and can ruin local industries with its build-up of transportation, communications, and economic infrastructure. Liberalization in economic sectors such as agriculture, or expansion of other industries such as logging or mining, also create conditions ripe for tourism development since they help to erode a community's self-sufficiency and create dependency upon a market over which locals have no control. It is no coincidence that those who have lost their lands or have no market for their crops are forced into service-sector employment in the tourism industry and are increasingly dependent on the whims of the global market and the corporations which run it. Tourism is the world's largest employer according to estimates of the World Travel and Tourism Council. It is often touted as a creator of employment and a mechanism of development for the communities where it imposes itself. Often, however, the jobs that tourism creates are not adequate living-wage, secure jobs with benefits, jobs where people can develop skills, and they usually do not comply with labour standards. Another serious threat to sustainable tourism projects is the WTO's prioritization of global commerce over everything: self-reliance of communities, environment, human rights, health and safety. New issues such as investment, government procurement, and competition policy will severely limit the opportunities for communities to create sustainable, tourism alternatives. The WTO's goal for a "harmonization" of standards around the world will facilitate the growth of a consumer culture in addition to the erosion of self-reliance of communities and regions. According to Wallach and Sforza in their book Whose Trade Organization? "Differences in standards, even if they express differences in cultures and values, are deemed inherently undesirable because they fragment the global market." There will be no way to enforce standards for the tourism industry such as prior-informed consent, support for local initiatives, or environmental regulations, within these uniform global standards designed by corporations.

Culture of Himachal Pradesh

Himachal Pradesh was one of the few states that had remained largely untouched by external customs, largely due to its difficult terrain. With the technological advancements the state has changed very rapidly. Himachal Pradesh is a multireligion, multicultural as well as multilingual state like other Indian states. Some of the most commonly spoken languages include Hindi, Punjabi, Pahari, Dogri, Mandeali, Kangri and Kinnauri. The Hindu communities residing in Himachal include the Brahmins, Rajputs, Kannets, Rathis and Kolis. There are also tribal population in the state which mainly comprise Gaddis, Kinnars, Gujjars, Pangawals, Bhots and Lahaulis. Himachal is well known for its handicrafts. The carpets, leather works, shawls, paintings, metalware, woodwork and paintings are worth appreciating. Pashmina shawl is one of the product which is highly in demand not only in Himachal Pradesh but all over the country. Himachali caps are also famous for art work of the people. Local music and dance reflect the cultural identity of the state. Through their dance and music, they entreat their gods during local festivals and other special occasions. Apart from the fairs and festivals that are celebrated all over India, there are number of other fairs and festivals, including the temple fairs in nearly every region that are of great significance to Himachal Pradesh. The day-to-day food of Himachal is very similar to the rest of the north India. They too have lentil, broth, rice, vegetables and bread. As compared to other states in north India non-vegetarian cuisine is more preferred. Some of the specialities of Himachal include Manee, Madeera, Pateer, Chouck, Bhagjery and chutney of Til. Around 96 per cent of the population of the state is of Hindus. The major communities includes Brahmins, Rajputs, Ghirath, Kannets, Rathis and Kolis. The tribal population comprises the Gaddis, Kinnars, gadoun (jadoun), Tanolis, Gujjars, Pangawals and Lahaulis. The Gaddis are the shepherds who transhumance from the alpine pasture regions to the lower regions during the cold winter season are mainly Hindus. The Kinnars are the inhabitants of Kinnaur and they generally practice polyandry and polygamy. The Gujjars are nomadic people who rear buffalo herds and are mainly Muslim. The Lahaulis of Lahaul and Spiti and native of Spiti and Kinnaur region mainly comprises Buddhists. Here are also tribal population in the state which mainly comprise Gaddis, Kinnars, Gujjars, Pangawals and Lahaulis. Though Hindi is the state language, many people speak Pahari also. Pahari itself has many dialects and all of them trace their origin to the Sanskrit language, also known as origin of all languages. A majority of the population is engaged in agricultural practices, however, the more educated of them are now moving towards tertiary sectors. As per the traditional dressing norms the dress of the Brahmin male includes *dhoti*, *kurta*, coat, waistcoat, turban and a hand towel while that of the Rajput male consists of tight fitting *churidar pyjamas*, a long coat and a starched turban. With the changing time the dress up of the people has now become a mixed one. Though the above mentioned style is now hardly followed, people have started wearing western style of clothes. The typical house is constructed of clay bricks and the roofs are of slate. In some areas the slate roof is also replaced by timber. The handicraft that comes out of this state and is worth appreciating are the carpets, leather works, shawls, paintings, metalware, woodwork and paintings. Pashmina shawl is the product which is highly in demand not only in Himachal but all over the country. Colourful Himachali caps are also famous art work of the people. A tribe, namely Dom is expert in manufacturing bamboo items like boxes, sofas, chairs, baskets and rack. Metalware of the state include utensils, ritualistic vessels, idols, gold and silver jewelleries. Weaving, carving, painting, or chiselling is considered to be the part of the life of Himachalis. Himachal is well known for designing shawls especially in Kullu. The architecture, objects, shops, museums, galleries and craftsmen charm with the variety perfected through time. Women take an active part in pottery and men in carpentry. For ages, wood is used in Himachal in the construction of temples, homes, idols etc. Music and dance of Himachal Pradesh reflects its cultural identity. Through their dance and music, they entreat their gods during local festivals and other special occasions. There are also dances that are specific to certain regions of the state. Some of the dance forms of Himachal are Losar Shona Chuksam (Kinnaur), Dangi (Chamba), Gee Dance and Burah dance (Sirmour), Naati, Kharait, Ujagjama and Chadhgebrikar (Kullu) and Shunto (Lahaul & Spiti). People of the state generally prefer folk music. There is no classical form of music, as for the Himachal Pradesh is concerned. Himachali dance forms are highly varied and quite complicated. These dances are very vital part of the tribal life. It reflects the culture and the tradition of Himachal Pradesh. Hardly any festivity here is celebrated without dancing. Some of the dance forms like Dulshol, Dharveshi, Drodi, Dev Naritya, Rakshas Nritya, Dangi, Lasa, Nati and Nagas are danced all over the region. Apart from the fairs and festivals that are celebrated all over India, there are number of other fairs and festivals also that are at the high point of Himachal Pradesh. These festivals are the time for the Himachalis to adorn colourful dress and accessories and get mixed up with the rest of their kins. Some of these fairs and festivals in the upper regions are the Kullu Dussehra, Shivratri Fair (Mandi), Shoolini Mela (Solan), Minjar Fair (Chamba), Mani Mahesh Chhari Yatra (Chamba), Renuka fair (Sirmaur), Lavi Trade Fair (Rampur), Vrajeshwari fair (Kangra), Jwalamukhi Fair (Jwalamukhi), Holi Fair (Sujanpur), and Naina Devi Fair (Bilaspur), Fulaich (Kinnaur valley). In the lower regions of Himachal are temple Fairs in Una District such as the Peeplo Fair, the 'Mairi' Guruduwara Fair, the 'Chintpurni' temple Fair, the 'Kamakhya temple" Fair, including the annual Himachal Hill Festival in the village Polian Purohitan during the fourth week of October.

Impacts of Globalization on the State

Globalization is not easily defined. For some, it is a positive process leading to shared social values worldwide. For others, the term has a negative meaning, and critics see it as marginalizing less dominant cultures, particularly those in the developing world. Globalization have both positive as well as negative effects.

Positive Effects

1. Increased Competition: One of the most visible effects is the improved quality of products due to global competition. Customer service and the 'customer is the king' approaches to production have led to improved quality of products and services. As the domestic companies have to fight out foreign competition, they are compelled to raise their standards and customer satisfaction levels in order to survive in the market. Besides, when a global brand enters a new country, it comes in riding on some goodwill, which it has to live up to. This creates competition in the market and a 'survival of the fittest' situation.

2. Employment: With globalization, companies have forayed into the developing destinations and hence generated employment for them. It has given an opportunity to invest in the emerging markets and tap up the talent which is available there. In developing destinations, there is often a lack of capital which hinders the growth of domestic companies and hence, employment. In such cases, due to global nature of the businesses, people of developing countries too can obtain gainful employment opportunities.

3. Investment and Capital Flows: A lot of companies have directly invested in developing destinations like Baddi Barotiwala of Solan district and Una by starting production units, but what we also need to see is the amount of Foreign Direct Investment (FDI) that flows into the developing countries. Companies which perform well attract a lot of foreign investment and thus push up the reserve of foreign exchange.

4. Foreign Trade: While trade originated in the times of early kingdoms, it has been institutionalized due to globalization. Previously, people had to resort to unfair means and destruction of kingdoms and countries to get what they wanted. Today, it is done in a more humane way, with mutual understanding. People who operate in uncivilized way have to face the WTO and other world organizations that have been established with a view to control and regulate the trade activities of the countries.

5. Spread of Technical Advancements: While it is generally assumed that all the innovations happen in the Western world, the know-how also comes into developing countries due to globalization. Without it, the knowledge of new inventions, medicines would remain cooped up in the countries that came up with them and no one else would benefit. The spread of know-how can also be expanded to include economic and political knowledge, which too has spread far and wide. The most obvious example of the spread of knowledge is that the Western world today are waking up to the benefits of Ayurveda and Yoga—traditional Indian practices, while the Western antibiotics and flooding the Indian markets improving the quality of life (and the longevity too) of people in India.

6. Spread of Culture: Not all good practices were born in one civilization. The world that we live in today is a result of several cross-cultural movements coming together due to phenomenon of tourism. People of one culture, if receptive, tend to see the flaws in their culture and pick up the culture which is more correct or in tune with the times. Societies have become larger as they have welcomed people of other civilizations and backgrounds and created a whole new culture of their own. Cooking styles, languages and customs have spread all over world due to globalization. The same can be said about movies, musical styles and other art forms. They too have moved from one country to another, leaving an impression on a culture which has adopted them.

7. Spread of Education: One of the most powerful effects of globalization is the spread of education. Today, we can move in the search of the best educational facilities in the world, without any hindrance. A person living in Himachal Pradesh or India can go to another continent for a new experience which he may not find in the home state or country. If one is interested, one can even get a specialization in subjects indigenous to a country and spread that knowledge to the home country. A good example of that is how the American managers went to Japan to learn the best practices in the field of mass production and incorporated that knowledge in their own production units.

8. Legal and Ethical Effects: Gone are the days where the limited jurisdiction became a hindrance in the prosecution of criminals. These days, due to international courts of justice, criminals can no longer seek asylum in a foreign country and are brought to justice. Due to globalization, there is also an understanding between the security agencies and the police of two or more different countries who will come together to curb global terrorism. Hence, it is now possible to catch the perpetrators of crime irrespective of which country they choose to hide in.

Negative Effects

1. Consumerism: Large multinational companies promote their products globally, and there are few countries where the logos for Coca-Cola and Nike haven't appeared. The negative effect of global marketing is that local companies are edged out of the market and the multinational companies impose American or European consumer trends on other cultures. Similarly, the fast food industry promotes values of production efficiency. As a result, traditional cuisine appears less cost-effective and profitable than fast food, causing traditional food outlets to lose business.

2. Western ideals: Another criticism is that Western nations, particularly the United States, impose cultural values on others through media and popular culture. Critics of globalization call this "cultural imperialism," because the West promotes its culture as having more worth, or being more correct, than other regions' cultural values. The domination of news media and Internet services by Western companies, helps maintain this influence over local views, according to critics.

3. Language: Language is a key expression of cultural diversity. Critics of globalization claim it marginalizes some languages and may even cause some languages to die out. Others say this is a myth. Because the world's dominant economies speak English, it is often seen as the main culprit in making other languages less important. Certainly, English is widely used as a second or third language, and this helps the globalization of business trade; however, if business communities see more benefits in speaking Spanish or Chinese, they learn those instead. The best example in the Himachal Pradesh is a Tibetan community spreading the Lama Culture in the state.

4. Poverty: Some United Nations members, including the Vatican City, claim that globalization increases poverty amongst young people, the old, women, indigenous peoples and migrants, which has a cultural impact. A representative from Cuba said one result of globalization was that 20 per cent of the world population consumed 80 per cent of global production, leaving 80 per cent of the population in increased poverty. One way to reduce poverty in these groups is for wealthy nations to accept more imports from developing countries.

5. Social exploitation: In order to cut down costs, many firms in developed nations have outsourced their manufacturing and white-collar jobs to Third-World countries like India and China, where the cost of labour is low. The most prominent among these have been jobs in the customer service field as many developing nations have a large English-speaking population—ready to work at one-fifth of what someone in developed world may call 'low-pay'. This has caused a lot of resentment among the people of developed countries, and companies have been accused of taking their jobs away. The best example in this regard is jobs of BPO (business process outsourcing)/ITES (information technology enabled services).

6. Changing food habits: Fast food chains like McDonalds and KFC are spreading fast in the State. People are consuming more junk food which has an adverse impact on their health. Apart from the health concerns, there is something else that globalization has been criticized for, and it is the accuzation that it has opened floodgates for restaurants and eateries which are insensitive to the religious beliefs of the host nation.

For example, a lawsuit had to be filed against McDonalds in India, after it was accused of serving beef in their burgers.

7. Transferring diseases: When the first-known case of AIDS came up in America, only few would have traced its origin to Sub-Saharan Africa. Globalization bought people from various countries together, and this is perhaps the reason that a virus from a jungle was transported to almost every country in the world.

8. Environmental degradation: It is an issue which has been debated ferociously in various international meetings, and it has to be accepted that globalization is one of the most important factors that has aggravated the situation. The amount of raw materials needed to run industries and factories is taking a toll on the natural reserves of planet earth, and pollution has severely impacted the quality of air that we need so very much for our survival. The best examples are cement factories and hydropower projects in the state.

Recommendations

On the basis of above study following points are recommended:

1. The products offered by foreign companies should be accepted only after testing and retesting time to time, there should be cross quality check on the same.
2. There should be very strict clear-cut guidelines to the tourists regarding do's and dont's at a destination right from the beginning of there journey in the itinerary itself.
3. There should be ban on the short dress wearing at social locations as well as social occasions.
4. Visa facilitation should be strictly on norms without compromising any point.
5. There should be equal pay policy by the multinational companies as they pay in their country in order to protect employees exploitation.
6. There should be proper medical check on arrival of the tourists in order to protect the local from the viral diseases.
7. Government must be strict against seasonal short term employment offered by various companies.
8. The local people must be trained on technical skills in order to understand the pros and cons of the globalization.

9. There should be no compromise against cultural and environmental pollution either by companies or by tourists.
10. Authorities should cross check the activities of the groups or organizations with a clearly mentioned Standards of operations.

Conclusions

Globalization is the buzzword of today. Economies of the world are being increasingly integrated as new technology and communication has brought people together. We often hear the phrase that the 'world has become a global village'—which itself signifies how much has changed in the world in the past few decades. American businessmen are investing their time in studying the culture of the Middle East, so that they can negotiate with their counterparts in a better way. Young graduates in India are being taught how the Americans roll their R's, so as to make a seamless conversation with their clients in many of the call-centres! The phenomenon that is globalization, has brought new dimensions to this world, and people are mingling with each other like never before. The social, economic, and political changes that globalization has brought have been accompanied by some challenges. Much research on the preceding issues has tended to stem from developing countries and regions, which have undertaken tourism as a development strategy. As the dynamics of tourism and globalization extend to local rural areas, communities and different levels of governments are increasingly recognizing culture as an important asset in formulating new tourism development strategies. The discussion above suggests that tourism, globalization and sustainability are contravening concepts. This can become a dilemma that will produce major challenges to Indian rural communities striving for sustainability. The debate on uniformity *versus* diversity will also become more profound where tourism and culture are perceived as a means to achieve goals of both globalization and sustainability. To address pending challenges, researchers and planners for community tourism development need to build new theoretical frameworks and proactive planning approaches that can mitigate the negative consequences while, at the same time, optimize the benefits that can result from the interrelationships between this triad of concepts. A primary prerequisite to this is that understanding culture is essential to understanding tourism (Robinson, 1999). Globalization definitely has brought the world a lot closer in terms of economic cooperation and trade. However, there is an urgent need to address all those concerns which can make globalization a tool for developed countries to gain an upper hand over developing countries. The world leaders need to give every country, irrespective of its economic and military status its due right in the comity of nations. People in developed countries who have lost their livelihood because of outsourcing, and people in developing countries who face poor working conditions and low compensation, are a harsh reality of globalization. Corporations who have made hefty profits on the cost of these two marginalized groups of people need to find a way out so that globalization becomes a phenomenon that encompasses every life and not a tyranny that masquerades itself as a revolution.

REFERENCES

David, Korten, 'When Corporations Rule the World' (West Hartford, Conn.: Kumarian Press, 1996), 54.

http://www.buzzle.com/articles/globalization.html

http://www.newworldencyclopedia.org/entry/Globalization

Masson, P.R. (2001), *Globalization facts and figures* (Vol. 1). International Monetary Fund.

Mitlin, D.(1992), A guide to the literature, environment and urbanization. *Sustainable Development*, 4, pp. 111-124.

Moscardo, G. (1999), Making visitors mindful: principles for creating quality sustainable visitor experiences through effective communication. *Champaign*, IL: Sagamore.

Mowforth, M. (2008), *Tourism and sustainability: Development, globalization and new tourism in the third world.* Routledge.

Murdock, J. (1993), Sustainable rural development, towards a research agenda. *Geoforum*, 24, pp. 225-241.

Rees, William (2000), The dark side of the force (of globalization). Parklands Institute Conference Paper.

Richards, G. (1996), Production and consumption of European cultural tourism. *Annals of tourism research*, (2), 261-283.

Smeral, E. (1998), The impact of globalization on small and medium enterprises: new challenges for tourism policies in European countries. *Tourism management*, 19(4), 371-380.

Suarez-Orozco, M. (2001). Globalization, immigration, and education: The research agenda. *Harvard Educational Review*, 71(3), 345-366.

Var, T. and Ap, J. (1998), Tourism and world peace. In William F. Theobald (ed.), *Global Tourism*, 2, pp. 45-47.

Woodward, D., Drager, N., Beaglehole, R. and Lipson, D. (2001), Globalization and health: a framework for analysis and action. *Bulletin-World Health Organization*, 79(9), 875-881.

World Commission on Environmental and Development. (1987), *Our Common Future*. Oxford: Oxford University.

Yeniyurt, S., and Townsend, J.D. (2003), Does culture explain acceptance of new products in a country?: An empirical investigation. *International Marketing Review*, 20(4), 377-396.

Index